Newport Jazz Festival

Newport Jazz Festival

The Illustrated History

Pictures and Text by **Burt Goldblatt**

THE DIAL PRESS NEW YORK

Published by

The Dial Press
1 Dag Hammarskjold Plaza
New York, N. Y. 10017

Copyright © 1977 by Burt Goldblatt
Designed by Burt Goldblatt

Manufactured in the United States of America

First printing

Library of Congress Cataloging in Publication Data

Goldblatt, Burt.
    Newport Jazz Festival.

    1. Newport Jazz Festival.   I. Title
ML38.N4N44   785.4′2′0797457   77-2747
ISBN   0-8037-6440-5

Opposite title page. 1958. Onstage, Big
Maybelle backed by members of the
Newport Blues Band. The raised plat-
form on the left holds the camera crew
shooting a segment of the film *Jazz on
a Summer's Day.* Clustered in the press
pit in front of the stage, photographers
take pictures against the glaring stage
and motion picture lights.

In memory of Pete Brown, Big Sid Catlett,
Bill Harris, Billie Holiday and Johnny Richards,
whose friendship and music
still enrich my life immeasurably.

ACKNOWLEDGMENTS

Many people have generously contributed their time, and opened up their files to me in the preparation of this book. Friends and aquaintances helped me to reconstruct this history, and were extremely helpful with suggestions and contributions. Those who could have contributed and didn't, I understand. Unauthorized books provide their own problems and this book was no exception to that rule.

This preparation has from the beginning been a one-man job and I fully take responsibility for lopsided opinions, mistakes in judgment and factual errors. But I was there, and my eyes and ears were my primary sources for information. I gratefully acknowledge the help given by the staffs of the New York City, Newport and Providence, Rhode Island, public libraries. Their staffs were most generous with their time and patience in my research.

Many people made contributions and allowed themselves to be questioned and interviewed but asked not to be acknowledged. I honored their request.

I worked with two editors on this project. The first was Pat Meehan, who gave me encouragement and a sense of direction before she moved on to another publisher.

My second editor, Nancy van Itallie, followed the manuscript with me to its fruition with well-considered memoranda from which I learned points to be retained or eliminated entirely. For this I am extremely grateful to both of them.

Some of my contributors were as follows:

George and Aram Avakian, Jean Bach, Joe Benjamin, Eddie Bert, Eubie Blake, Ruby Braff, Michael Brooks, Columbia Records, Buster Brown, Marshall Brown, Pete Brown, Ray Bryant, Ron Carter, Judge Arthur A. Carrellas (Newport County Superior Court, Newport, Rhode Island), Emile Charlap, Joe Cinderella, Al Cobbs, Willis and Shirley Conover, Stanley Cow-ell, Eddie Daniels, Johnny Dankworth, Richard Davis, Hermie Dressel, Linda C. Dugan, Roy Eldridge, Duke Ellington, Nesuhi Ertegun of Atlantic Records, Peter Fay and John Newsom of the Music Division of the Library of Congress, John F. Fitzgerald (Town Administrator, Middleton, Rhode Island), Panama Francis, Jimmy Garrison, Stan Getz, Jimmy Giuffre, Mort Goldsen, Paul Gonsalves, Charlie Graham, Norman Granz, Charles E. Hambley (former Mayor, Newport, Rhode Island), Bobby Hackett, John Hammond of Columbia Records, Roland Hanna, Bill Harris, Coleman Hawkins, Roy Haynes, Margo Hazel, Woody Herman, Helen Humes, Oliver Jackson, Quentin Jackson, Budd Johnson, Elvin and Keiko Jones, Hank Jones, Jo Jones, Thad and Elaine Jones, James Jordan, Louis Jordan, Dick Katz, Stan Kenton, Lee Konitz, Gene Krupa, Cleo Laine, Ellis Larkins, Baby Laurence, Florence Lewis, Mel Lewis, Sherrie Levy of Buddah-Cobblestone Records, Eddie Locke, Elaine Lorillard, Don Madison, Jeremiah P. Maloney, Herbie Mann, Sam Margolis, John Maxon, Jimmy Maxwell, Martine McCarthy of Columbia Records, Lou McGarity, Howard McGhee, Ilhan Mimaroglu of Atlantic Records, Bernadette Moore, Chauncy Morehouse, Ray Nance, Charles Nanry (Co-Editor, Journal of Jazz Studies, Rutgers University), Harry Newmark, Chester A. Oakley, Jr. (Clerk, Superior Court, Newport, Rhode Island), and his assistant Rydia Almay, Patrick O'Higgins, Jimmy Owens, Cecil Payne, Bucky Pizzarelli, Russell Procope, Bobby Rosengarden, Jimmy Rushing, Shirley Selzer, Richard Sheffield, Bobby Short, Horace Silver, Maxwell Silverman, Zoot Sims, Willie "The Lion" Smith, Lewis Soloff, Gordon Sweeney, Clark Terry, McCoy Tyner, Burt Westridge, Martin Williams (Director, Jazz Division, Smithsonian Institution, Washington, D.C.), Bob Wilbur, Ernie Wilkins, Spiegle Willcox.

PREFACE

I began to think about writing this book a long time ago. Having attended all the festivals since their inception in 1954, and having known many of the people and understood the principles involved in its creation and production, I decided under the gentle and insistent prodding of Pat Meehan, my first book editor, to make the attempt. "You were there," she would tell me. "Who else saw it all happen?"

I had been photographing the Festival and had kept notes on the performers and the whys and wherefores of many of the images I had put on film. But much work remained to be done besides reaching into my crowded negative file drawers.

I did a great deal of homework before I left for Newport and Providence, Rhode Island, to seek out the newspaper files in the libraries there. Notebooks were filled to capacity with interviews, and my tape recorder had to be overhauled before I was through transcribing interviews.

I spoke to and interviewed 142 musicians plus former audience members and townspeople. I questioned sources that ranged from actual performers, a superior-court judge, the attorney general's office of Rhode Island, and former board members of the Festival to taxi drivers of Newport. Friends passed me on to other friends, who in turn gave me leads, some of which were useful. Everywhere I went I asked for opinions about the location, the economy, the music itself.

So many thousands of performers appeared on the Festival stage that I can only discuss, with the exception of the first year, highlights of each Festival. Much of what I talk about relies on primary sources, i.e., my eyes and ears. Much was constructed from interviews, one source being checked against a number of others. I make no pretense about being a historian. But wherever I could, I tried to supply some background. I always wanted to tell the whole story if possible. Most important of all was the music that I was privileged to hear and see performed. Much of it was preserved on tape and records, and I welcomed the opportunity to listen again to some beautiful and well-remembered moments, often while I was interviewing participants, transcribing notes, or writing the text. I screened motion-picture footage I had taken myself, and viewed the film *Jazz on a Summer's Day* and the New York Jazz Repertory Company's concert inclusion of 1970 Festival movie footage that was shown at Carnegie Hall.

INTRODUCTION

Newport, November 1974

I walked past the twisted chain-link fence and squeezed through the gate that led to Festival Field. Rearing up through the tall weeds like the massive skeleton of some prehistoric monster was the rusting, gutted steel framework of the stage. It was lonely and silent. This stage and all those that had preceded it had been built on high hopes and the sounds of wild cheering and applause. Now only the rustling of grass could be heard in the cold November air. The emptiness was broken only by a housing project in the distance. A few dirty papers blew across the stage, their flight stopped by an abandoned van parked crookedly where the press pit used to be. I stood in the wings for a few moments, then turned and went back to my car, not caring to look back.

Newport, Rhode Island, one of many quiet, pretty New England resort towns, had a population of thirty-five thousand in 1954. However, unlike the other resort communities, Newport has been the summer playground of America's aristocracy for over eighty years. Newport has always been extremely difficult to get to because it is located on an island, Aquidneck. Before the Newport Bridge was completed in 1969, you had to take a train, plane, or bus to Providence and then catch a small plane, bus, or taxi from there. If you drove, you could either come in over the Mount Hope Bridge or ride the Jamestown ferry. It was expensive any way you did it.

But Newport has much to offer. It was once a Navy town, and as you come in on the ferry, you can see old Fort Adams on one side and the War College and Naval Training Station on the other. The ferry docks at Long Wharf, and from there you can see seventeenth-century houses, many of which are being restored. The streets are as narrow as they were when Newport was a colonial town; many are still cobbled. The closest that Newport comes to a main street is Thames Street, on the waterfront. The side streets are dotted with flowers, fences, artists' workshops, galleries, and antique shops.

The wharf area is dominated by one of the town's few tall structures, the steeple of Trinity Church, built in 1726. George Washington worshiped there.

The town also has the oldest synagogue in this country, Touro Synagogue, now a national historic site. The origin of the Old Stone Mill, located in Touro Park, still baffles historians and scholars.

Muggsy Spanier, a great jazz cornetist, appeared at the Festival in 1964. Until he came to Newport, he had never realized that Touro Infirmary in New Orleans, where he had recovered from a physical collapse and bout with tuberculosis, had been named after Judah Touro, a philanthropist whose name crops up throughout Newport's early history. After his recovery Spanier had organized a new group called Muggsy Spanier and His Ragtime Band, which recorded a number of sides for RCA Victor's Bluebird label in 1939. In deference to Dr. Alton Oschner, who had saved his life, Spanier entitled one of the recordings "Relaxin' at the Touro." It became the band's theme song, and a copy of the record is embedded in the wall in the sanitorium lobby. Muggsy's ensemble lead and growly attack still sounded pungent and crisp when he played it again at his Festival appearance.

Most of the homes of the wealthy, their "summer cottages," are located on Ocean Drive. Today these homes, replete with turrets and architectural gingerbread, are mostly museums. In houses such as Château-sur-Mer, Belcourt Castle, The Elms, and The Breakers, the rich tried to outdo each other in grandeur and in furnishings. Marble House, completed in 1892 for William K. Vanderbilt, was reputedly built at a cost of two million dollars; supposedly the cost of its furnishings totaled nine million dollars. Today anyone can view the fads and follies, the marble balustrades and Tiffany windows, the site of much of the snobbery and bad manners of the rich and nouveau riche of an era that ended with the First World War.

All that remains of the last stage erected at Newport as seen through the battered chain-link fence in 1974. On the right, part of the housing project that now occupies the site.

Above. Elaine Lorillard. *Right.* Louis Lorillard.

The Casino Theater, site of the first Philharmonic concerts at Newport and later the stage on which numerous panels and festival programs were presented.

During the summer of 1953 retired philanthropist George Henry Warren, a New Yorker whose family had been summer residents of Newport for many years, and his wife hosted a garden luncheon at their home near the Old Stone Mill. Among the dozen guests was the director of the Rhode Island School of Design, John Maxon, who remembers the occasion quite vividly: "It was a thoroughly proper Newport summer lunch, with the least likely people ever to be involved in jazz. George Warren would have had his back north. It was a curving table, arranged so that the sun would not be in the guests' eyes." The Louis P. Lorillards were among the guests. Louis was tall, round-faced, and balding. "Always impeccably dressed, but a bland and colorless guy."

In a Festival board meeting report of December 5, 1955, Lorillard made this evaluation of his position: "I am President for some reason. Probably because of being called a producer. If anything goes wrong, I have to produce out of my own pocket to make up the difference. But I am not a technician in jazz. Basically my job is to pull things together. I don't intend to keep this job forever. I am sure that if it be deemed necessary, a professional musician or technician in jazz will gladly take my job over. Then I can go back to the travel business where I belong."

During the summer of 1953 the Lorillards had helped in the presentation of two concerts by the New York Philharmonic Orchestra, trying to bring some life into the community. The concerts, planned to be held out of doors at the Newport Casino, were forced by inclement weather to be held in the casino theater, which had poor acoustics. Elaine Lorillard later commented, "Hardly anyone came." The concerts were a financial flop. In addition, as Maxon said, "While it was not a pickup orchestra, I don't think the concerts could have been held any other place that would have made it sound any better.

"At the luncheon, Mrs. Lorillard, sitting on my right, was complaining over the way the concerts were going. Brahms was being discussed, and I remember saying, 'Well, why do you put on a music festival for which there is no particular desire or reason, which are the standard things you hear anyhow? Do you really think people want to hear what they undoubtedly hear in the wintertime? They would like to hear something different. If you want to do something, why don't you put on a jazz festival? It would be a wild success. You can't fail.' The great virtue of the Jazz Festival in its early days was putting on material that hadn't been heard too often. I think there was a great deal of naïveté on the part of Mr. Wein, and that primordial innocence on the part of the city fathers of Newport. The thing which I think is particularly important is that Newport is a very strange place. They really are terribly unimpressed. They're bored and worldly, but they are nice people, and they're terribly grateful for something new. The colonists' reaction to the jazz festival, not the city fathers', is rather like their reaction to the annual hurricane; it was something over which they had very little control, and you went on with what you had to do. I never knew whether Louis or Elaine were remotely interested in it or whether it was a permutation of their relationship. Elaine had her motivations, and I'm sure that Louis had his."

(John Hammond, jazz critic and confidant of many well-known musicians, said later, "Louis couldn't carry a tune, except for a couple of things played by Count Basie.")

"The Festival was a peculiar phenomenon of the fifties. It could never have happened in the sixties, and it happened at a particular point in the evolution of popular music. It happened in Newport, and that was the only place it could have happened."

xii

Opposite. Producer George Wein, 1954. He asked to be photographed with the poster of Aristide Bruant behind him. *Above.* The Emily Post of men's fashions, George Frazier, sits backstage in a scruffy sports jacket with rolled-up cuffs.

Patrick O'Higgins, author of the best seller *Madame* (about Helena Rubinstein, whose advisor he was), also handled publicity for the Festival for three years. In a recent interview he stated, "The Lorillards were eminently respectable in every way, but Elaine wasn't liked by most of the ladies because they feared her, or they feared that she was cleverer or more amusing or whatever. I think what happened was, they said we'll all go to this bloody Festival because it's going to be a terrible flop. Mrs. Lorillard was going to be chased out of town, and much to their surprise it had the exact opposite effect."

George Frazier (former entertainment editor of *Life* and columnist on the entertainment world), in *Esquire*, August 1955, quoted George Wein, the Festival's director, on the Newport old guard: "They resented jazz musicians coming into Newport, but they'll never be able to do anything about it, because the Festival is backed by one of their most respected members, Louis Lorillard, who will fight for his convictions even at the expense of being branded a traitor to his own class."

"Elaine Lorillard," Patrick O'Higgins said, "has always remained a marvelous friend to me and I love her dearly, but in a way I think that it was Elaine's revenge on Newport. In a strange way she just wanted to let Mrs. Van Alen [society matron from one of Newport's first families] know, 'Look what I can do.' I've been on Bailey's Beach [the strip of sand and rocks reserved only for the wealthy] and seen ladies suddenly disappear into a cabana so they wouldn't have to say hello to her."

John Maxon laughed. "It always amused me that innocent chitchat had more effect on more people than anything else I've ever done. The truth of the matter is, I did give Elaine the idea, and from then on it went." When I asked John Maxon why he never attended a Festival, he replied, "The idea simply never occurred to me."

Elaine thought about Maxon's suggestion, discussing

it with her husband over the rest of the summer. In the fall she made periodic trips to Boston. "Eddie Condon was the only jazz person I knew socially," she said. "I was trying to put the idea into a more concrete form and Eddie suggested Ernie Anderson [producer of jazz concerts and friend to many musicians]. He sent a wire off to Ernie, but he was off in Europe, so I got in touch with a very good friend of mine, Sylvia Marlowe, a harpsichordist. I knew that at one time she had played some boogie-woogie, so that she was sympatico with jazz. I came to New York to see her, and she arranged a meeting with John Hammond. When we discussed the project, he was very enthusiastic."

Hammond made a number of suggestions about who could pull it all together, and among the names was George Wein's. An interesting combination, Mrs. Lorillard and Wein were polar opposites in almost everything except their interest in jazz. She is pretty, lively, and full of life. Patrick O'Higgins described Wein as "shrewd, tough, but there is a great deal of sweetness in him, and he does know his business. He's a jazz impresario the way Mr. Zeigfeld was a Broadway impresario. I've seen George Wein at work, and I've always admired the way he conducted himself. I think he always treated everyone fairly."

For years Wein has been a source of controversy in the music community. He has a saving sense of humor and a guttural, choppy laugh, but his earthiness rubs many people the wrong way. His organizational ability and shrewdness are as undeniable as his lack of sensitivity in his dealings in the music business.

Willis Conover's may be the voice more people hear around the world than any other. Five nights a week, in every part of the world except the United States, he is the jazz voice of the Voice of America. Willis also was the master of ceremonies of the Newport Jazz Festival from 1955 to 1962. In 1957, he was elected to its board of directors. He also supervised the recording and

Record executive John Hammond
(right) jokes with former Basieite Buddy
Tate. *Opposite.* Voice of America
broadcaster Willis Conover.

broadcasting of the Festival for overseas transmission. Conover offered this analysis: "George, after all, has proved that he knew what he was doing because he's now running the Newport Jazz Festival. I think there's no question that from the beginning George felt that the Newport Festival was George Wein's festival; at least he always said, 'my festival,' 'my musicians,' my this, and my that. Occasionally my jesting with people takes a cruel turn, and I'm afraid I did it with him when I said, 'Please don't say "my master of ceremonies" to me.'

"My objection to George as a programer has been that he makes decisions that to me seem influenced by questions of publicity rather than of good programing. George is a sucker for a celebrity, particularly a celebrity outside of jazz. He doesn't need to be. He's a celebrity. He has a lot on the ball. Just as he didn't have to in the old days try so hard to prove that he wasn't cultured, by talking and acting like one of us low-class jazz types. This to me was a kind of insult to the musicians, to say I'm just as bad as you are, in effect. It seems to me, and I exaggerate the point, that if Jesus came back to earth, he would try to get him to get up and MC one night, even if he knew nothing about jazz."

John Hammond said in a later interview: "I have never known George to retain animosity. I can cite case after case where people have screamed at George and written horrible things about him and said worse things, and it rolls off George's back. Frankly, I think George is one hell of a guy. George is a man of tremendous integrity. He has taken some of the most terrible financial beatings I've ever seen and bounced right back. When they closed up the Festival that last year at Newport, he was a broken-hearted man, but he bounced right back. You've got to be tough to run a festival."

George Wein ran a jazz club called Storyville, located in the Hotel Copley Square in Boston. He had been playing piano in a group led by the brilliant jazz drummer Jo Jones, who had sparked Count Basie's great orchestra during the thirties and forties. A few days after they had played together Jo put his arm around his employer's shoulder in a fatherly gesture and declared, "George, you have to make up your mind whether you want to run a nightclub or play the piano. I'm sorry, but I just can't use you." Wein later laughed about the incident, agreeing wholeheartedly that he had played badly.

On the other hand, Budd Johnson, the fine tenor sax man and fatherly figure in the jazz world, told me, "George is all right as long as he's doing his own thing. He plays very good in his bag. I've never seen him force himself on anybody."

"I met George on one of my Boston trips, two weeks before the George Henry Warren party," Elaine Lorillard said. "After dinner with my brother [Tom Guthrie], we went at his suggestion to Storyville to hear some jazz."

At that meeting also was Donald Born, professor of English and the humanities at Boston University. Tom Guthrie had been a student of Born's, and he introduced Elaine to the professor. When Born commiserated with her about the failure of her Philharmonic concerts, Elaine replied that she would be much more interested in putting on a jazz festival. Born knew George Wein and brought him over to the bar to meet them.

Wein acted with complete indifference to the suggestion that a jazz festival be organized. In the August 18, 1967, issue of *Holiday* magazine Wein described that meeting: "There was this society woman at the club that night talking to me about jazz concerts and Newport. I'd never thought about Newport before then, but I figured it might work, and I knew I wanted to do more in life than own a jazz club, and so I kept saying, 'Sure, sure, but call me in a couple of days if you're really interested,' half knowing that these people wander into the club and unburden themselves of some great project and never call you back, and half hoping that she would."

Elaine Lorillard received a note about a week later from Terri Turner, George's girl Friday. "Evidently George had mentioned it to her, and Terri, a jazz enthusiast, had talked George into getting in touch with Louis and me. She said, 'Why don't we come down and talk to you about it, because I think it's a great idea!' Charlie Bourgeois, Terri Turner, George Wein, my husband, Louis, and I were present at that meeting. Meanwhile, Louis had talked to the people at the Newport Casino because we were going to do it whether we got George or whoever. I'm not trying to downgrade George, but it's about time that my husband, Terri, and I got credit for having been the forerunners of the Festival."

James A. Van Alen, president of the Newport Casino and himself a member of one of the socially prominent Newport families, was eventually convinced that the casino could function as a concert site without harm coming to the tennis facilities.

The casino's board of governors voted unanimously to allow its use for the Festival for the nominal sum of $350. Louis P. Lorillard's grandfather had been one of the casino's founders; Louis P. Lorillard was a director of a prominent Newport bank and a board member of the casino. The Newport Casino was having financial difficulties; it wasn't as heavily endowed then as it is today. Somehow, all these factors helped to smooth the way.

In late fall of 1953 George Wein was selected to organize the Festival. The Lorillards deposited twenty thousand dollars in an account to defray expenses for the talent to be booked. They helped find sponsors among some of the country's leading scholars and musicians, including Cleveland Amory, author of *The Last Resorts;* Marshall Stearns, associate professor of English at Hunter College in New York City; Father Norman O'Connor, chaplain of the Newman Club at Boston University, sometimes referred to as "the jazz priest"; John Hammond; and Leonard Bernstein, composer and conductor of the New York Philharmonic.

The Lorillards, leaving Wein in charge, then took off in April of 1954 for a vacation in Capri.

To Wein's everlasting credit, with the Festival barely three months away, he was able to line up talent and make arrangements for it. The man he could not have functioned without was Charlie Bourgeois. Charlie, once a bartender at the Boston Health Club, had presented a series of piano jazz concerts at John Hancock Hall. One musician described him to me as "the man who knew where everything was at and how to get it."

In the August 1955 *Esquire* article Wein described his problems in organizing the Festival: "My biggest aggravation was talent. Everybody apparently decided to ask way above what they usually got. They didn't seem to realize that the Festival was a nonprofit project and that if I made any money the surplus went to assist musicians and jazz in general. The prices I had to pay were absurd. I almost lost my mind because last year the bookers held us up. The bookers never thought it was an authentic thing, a nonprofit thing. They just thought it was a George Wein promotion to make a dollar. Stan Kenton asked for two thousand dollars for two nights just to narrate the thing, plus transportation from the coast. But I needed him because Duke couldn't make it."

Then there were the Newport residents. Invitations were sent to sixty-five Newport families to help sponsor the Festival. There were two acceptances, and only one came from a socialite member of the community: George Henry Warren. (The other acceptance came from Edward Capuano, a businessman from Providence and a comparative newcomer to Newport.)

So in 1954, with the arrival of the first Festival, the massive casino building on Bellevue Avenue, almost strangling in the luxurious vines that covered it, was about to be refurbished with some original American culture. But first there were the social preliminaries.

The Warrens invited a large gathering of the prominent to a garden party at their home in Newport. Henry Warren had long been a fan of pianist Teddy Wilson's,

so Wilson played for the occasion. "He even paid his salary for the evening," Elaine Lorillard said. "Lee Wiley was one of Charlie Bourgeois's favorites, and I'm sure that she appeared at his suggestion." In any event the choices seemed to be just right for the occasion.

During the evening Lee Wiley, blond and lovely in a pink gown, encircled by a crowd of well-wishers, sang music by the Gershwins, Cole Porter, and Rodgers and Hart. Teddy Wilson complemented her soft voice with a gentle touch, accenting in all the right places as her voice floated through the cool night air. The appreciative audience applauded loudly, with shouts of "Bravo!" It seemed a portent of things to come. The crowd mixed happily with the musicians, and everyone seemed to enjoy themselves enormously. At the party, Mrs. Lorillard was heard remarking that "the old-line set will probably come around, but it's the members of the younger set that seem most cautious."

The charter was drawn up and filed with the secretary of state of Rhode Island on April 29, 1954. The fee was five dollars. It was called The Jazz Festival of Newport, R.I., Inc. The five names that appear on the document are those of Louis and Elaine Lorillard and three attorneys. The purpose of the corporation, according to the charter, was to promote an interest in music; hold music festivals, jazz bands festivals and other entertainments for the public; conduct musical competitions; raise funds for the establishment of scholarships for the assistance of talented persons interested in music; and generally conduct and promote various functions, without profit, for charitable purposes.

On April 1, 1958, the name was changed to the American Jazz Festival Inc., and under that name the corporation was forfeited on August 1, 1962. Newport Jazz Festival was incorporated on April 1, 1964. It too was forfeited on August 30, 1968.

The first program book, published in 1954, outlined the Festival's purpose more specifically: "to encourage America's enjoyment of Jazz, and to sponsor the study of our country's only original art form."

John Hammond was introduced by George Wein at the 1975 festival as "the man who has done more for jazz than anyone else I might name." Hammond stated recently, "As far as I'm concerned, Elaine Lorillard should have the whole credit for the concept of the Newport Festival. I think it was the most important social concept of the fifties as far as jazz is concerned and I bless her for it. I only wish she were back on the board of the New York Festival, but I don't think she'd want to be on anything so commercial."

In the beginning there was a feeling of purpose, high hopes, and determination. Beneath those blue-and-white-striped tents was a lot of good feeling and camaraderie.

Memories

The first festivals created an opportunity for many to get away from the hot, humid city every July. For me it was a time to check equipment and figure out how much film I would need to fill my assignments plus whatever I might want to photograph for myself. Reporters, qualified and unqualified, readied their favorite phrases. Festival goers begged rides from friends and overpaid for accommodations, and editors of New York jazz magazines closed their offices for the week. Jazz disc jockeys either taped a week's show in advance or entrusted their shows to associates not so good that their shows would be in other hands by the time they returned, but not so bad that their shows might be off the air when they arrived home. It was a time to renew old friendships with musicians and people in the music industry.

There was something special in that press pit in front of the stage. Of course there was always the smell of sweat-stained clothes; the clouds of dust kicked up; the litter of lens caps, film wrappers, and camera bags; the banter and snide jokes; the elbowing aside to get the best angle for a shot at the stage.

Each year the photographers had a guessing game beforehand about how high the stage would be. In 1954 it was barely a foot off the grass. A few years later it was close to five feet, and later it went even higher. There were also problems about the exterior decoration of the stage. Some years evergreens graced the front of it, making it extremely difficult for a photographer to keep the performers from looking as if they were in Sherwood Forest. In later years the stage lighting became very arty. It was not easy to record something on relatively slow film with such obstacle courses in front of us. We coped as best we could under the circumstances.

There was an awareness among the press that most of the artists appearing onstage would be seen and heard just once by the majority of the audience, while the photographers would see and hear the performers many times during the year. Still, when the press showed little interest, wandering away for a Coke or a beer, there probably wasn't much of interest going on onstage, although it was difficult to be objective, engulfed as we were in a tidal wave of music for so many hours and days.

When I felt nothing worth recording was onstage, I would wheedle my way backstage, mix with the Festival staff, listen to the latest gossip, perhaps catch Sonny Rollins using his exercise equipment, and remind him of the several pounds of popcorn he had consumed one afternoon at my apartment. I might collect a warm bear hug from the likes of Cecil Payne, the fine baritone sax man, or sometimes I would just introduce myself to whoever was available, making friends and renewing old aquaintances.

Working conditions in the crowded press pit in front of the stage, 1967. Onstage (left to right): vibists Gary Burton, Red Norvo, Lionel Hampton, Milt Jackson, and Bobby Hutcherson.

I remember Milt Hinton carefully pulling his bass fiddle from its case, remarking, "It's a contemporary of the Stradivarius violin." I looked on in wonder. Passing from one tent to another, I might see Dizzy Gillespie playing chess with one of the critics, with other musicians looking on and kibitzing. I remember Clark Terry, former Duke Ellington trumpeter for many years, standing backstage in powder-blue shorts, waiting to go on. Or there was Zoot Sims, a fine tenor sax man and sports fan, glove in hand, throwing a baseball around with members of his group at Freebody Park. Lester "Pres" Young, father of the Cool School of tenor sax, in a rare mood, laughing unrestrainedly at trumpeter Roy Eldridge's reminiscences of their days on the road with the Basie Band: fast, loose, funny talk about the women they used to see and their lost youth. Billie Holiday, talking quietly, almost reverentially, to great jazz pianist Mary Lou Williams backstage. Billie's wrist being kissed by her onetime accompanist and fine trumpet player, Buck Clayton. Pianist George Shearing, sitting directly behind the stage, hands folded, waiting to go on, listening intently to the sound and movement all around him. Duke Ellington's band bus pulling into the field, disgorging the fine musicians whose names are legend in the history of jazz. But everyone who was there has memories.

Patrick O'Higgins remembers that after a night spent at the Lorillard home at Newport, Quartrel (named after the four l's in Louis Lorillard), he "woke up, got out of bed, and there rolled up in a rug at the foot of my bed was [clarinetist] Peewee Russell."

Elaine Lorillard remembers an amusing story from the early years. The Lorillard house was filled as it usually was during Festival time, so they "put [Eddie Condon] and some of the other musicians and newspaper people out in Paradise Farm, on the other side of Newport in a section called Middletown. It was a seventeenth-century

Pipe clamped in his mouth, glove at the ready, trumpeter Clark Terry (left) braces for tenor man Zoot Sims' slider at Freebody Park, Newport.

house where Edith Wharton and Henry James had stayed. Eddie was in one of the back servant's rooms, which were like little cubicles. They were all painted white with a little white cot and white bureau. Eddie slept very late. Everybody else went off to the afternoon session. When Eddie woke up, he was sure that he was in a sanitarium, that they'd put him away. He yoo-hooed around the house and there was nobody there, so he wandered outside. You see, Louis's aunt left all the land, about two hundred and fifty acres of it, for a bird sanctuary, so in the barns were ornithologists and people who worked with the birds. As Eddie came out of the house, he saw a man walking down the driveway with a little black kit. He assumed this was one of the doctors. He rushed over to him and said, 'Listen, doc, you got to give me a vitamin or a shot or something; I'm in very bad shape,' because he usually was. Evidently the man was a bird doctor, because he did give him something. The two of them spent the rest of the weekend together at the Festival.''

Trumpeter Ruby Braff remembered standing in the far reaches of Festival Field during an afternoon program of avant-garde music. ''The group onstage had been playing one tune for about twenty minutes, and they sounded horrible,'' he said. ''Standing a few feet away from me was Thelonious Monk, who kept pacing back and forth, back and forth, like a caged lion. Some fans around us, bored with what they were hearing, started to make some unkind remarks about the music. Thelonious came to a halt finally and said, 'They're all needed.' It was a beautiful thing to say.''

It was the love all around, the lack of cynicism and the consideration the artists expressed for each other, their warmth and unpretentiousness—that was the most unique quality in those early years. Newport was a good feeling.

Sometimes it led to more than a memorable photograph. I felt privileged at Newport just to watch Billie Holiday as her dresser put the finishing touches on her hair and gown before she made her appearance onstage.

Mostly I tried to capture something of what was going on around me at Newport. Many shots had to be grabbed in a moment, blurs and all. I loved it; my hope was that a small part of what I was participating in would be caught on film so that it might be shared.

The press gave a great deal of coverage to the first Festival. The local press was amazed: "It seemed impossible that the city could hold such hordes." This was in 1954, when the total paid attendance was a little over 13,000. Other headlines screamed, "Hardy jazz fans brave downpour to hear their favorites go, go, go!" *Down Beat* magazine exulted, "13,000 fans show jazz has come of age." The *Providence Bulletin* said in a front-page headline, "Bop, not rain, 'sends' jazz lovers at Newport." The article went on to describe Stan Kenton, the master of ceremonies for the Festival, as "master of the revels." After the Festival had ended, the *Providence Journal* described some of the proceedings: "Dowagers and debutantes, sailors and their gals and couples from many places mingled with thousands of hepcats under a starlit sky with a full moon at their backs and leading artists of jazz at their front. Never before has there been such an assemblage at Newport, not even for the America's Cup races of two decades ago."

Whitney Balliet reported in *Saturday Review,* "It will be good to see a second festival next year, for jazz goes well, as it should, with sea, air, trees, history, and the *haut monde.*"

Tenor giant Sonny Rollins pumping iron backstage. Health-minded Rollins carries his exercise equipment wherever he travels.

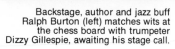

Backstage, author and jazz buff
Ralph Burton (left) matches wits at
the chess board with trumpeter
Dizzy Gillespie, awaiting his stage call.

The terminology used to describe what went on was mostly a juxtaposition of square superlatives. Very few reporters were qualified for the task. Even the trade papers hardly identified the music played and sung. It was a new problem for the press. Jazz had never been given such extensive publicity or coverage. Even in recent years newspapers, like the *New York Times,* lacking qualified writers have sent their classical-music reporters to Newport for the occasion.

All the ills and problems that the Festival would be forced to face in later years were already in view that first year, albeit in microcosm.

Commercialism had been there from the start. *A Weekend with Jazz,* a circular from 1954, offered among other things transportation to and from New York City, accommodations, a tour of the Vanderbilt mansion, The Breakers, and tickets to all concerts for thirty-seven dollars, tax included. The flyer went on to list on their program many big-name artists who never appeared—Duke Ellington, Sarah Vaughan, Charlie Parker, and Art Tatum, to name a few. That practice was carried over into later years by the Festival itself. Before the 1975 Festival one of the artists advertised had not at that point even been consulted about her schedule. The artist did make an appearance, but the premature announcement was indicative of the inner workings of the Festival.

The 1954 flyer was mild commercialism and offered a bargain to be sure, but it was commercialism nevertheless. The travel agency sponsoring the tour was owned by Louis P. Lorillard, president of the Newport Jazz Festival.

From the beginning the Festival Corporation and the business leaders of the town didn't much concern themselves with the feeding, housing, and sanitary conditions necessary for the massive crowds that were attracted. In a town that boasted only four hotels, six

Above. Bassist Steve Swallow and pianist Toshiko Mariano try to figure out the order of tunes they will play on the program. *Opposite.* It's not clear at whom this royal razz is being directed. (Left to right) Miles Davis, his manager, Harold Lovett, and Festival producer George Wein.

motels, and less than a dozen restaurants, the fifty rooms at The Elms, for instance—if they had been available—could have provided welcome accommodations for Festival-goers.

The chamber of commerce and local police force did as well as they could under the circumstances, but the limited housing available in motels and hotels was booked weeks and sometimes months in advance. Some photographers booked rooms by putting down a deposit at the end of one Festival so that they would be assured sleeping space for the following year. Townspeople opened their homes by renting rooms, often at exorbitant rates, but unfortunately they never really wanted the "outsiders."

An article in the *Providence Journal* of July 17, 1954, said, "Newport jazz fans jammed hotels, cleaned out kitchens, slept on beaches." Hotels and motels were jammed with people who had made reservations well in advance. However, many came to Newport with no idea where they would stay. Hotel clerks and police tried to keep track of what small tourist homes still had openings but finally had to wish the visitors good luck in their search. Many fans were forced to sleep in cars and trucks and sleeping bags. Some slept on beaches, including several who bedded down on Third Beach in poison ivy. Some had to walk the streets all night. Black people, especially, found few places to stay.

In 1956 I slept on a cot at the casino in a barrackslike room over the tennis courts with the Duke Ellington orchestra. I remember the embarrassment and humiliation I felt around me as the musicians, hungry and tired from their trip, and despite the wildly enthusiastic reception they had received at the Festival, learned that they would have to sleep in a musty room that apparently hadn't been cleaned or dusted in twenty years. I slept next to Harry Carney, Duke Ellington's great baritone sax player. Harry, a quiet, self-effacing person, glanced my way and in a light but stinging aside said, "Whew, Burt. Some shit, huh?" It seemed to say it all.

In 1959 a photographer friend of mine, black, had reservations long in advance to stay with another woman, a white reporter, at a private home. When they inquired about their lodging, one of the owners dashed inside and disappeared. A moment later she reappeared and told the photographer that the Festival office was on the telephone. The voice at the other end of the line announced to the photographer that she couldn't stay there and asked why she hadn't told the Festival ahead of time, when they had arranged her reservations, that she was black. A few moments later, outside, the owners of the home told the two visitors that the white woman could stay but otherwise they were "full up." Both left. The scene was to be repeated many times.

The Festival had other problems. Each year it led the life of a fly-by-night carnival. The *Providence Sunday Journal* reported in 1966, "Like a carney operator, impresario George Wein must apply for new licenses. And each year there are petitions, zoning battles, litigation, political wrangles, angry letters to newspapers, petty haggling over police protection, hours and seating, and choleric speeches in the State House. Not everyone disliked the festivals. Their biggest booster, The Newport Chamber of Commerce, is gleeful over the estimated one to two million dollars they pump into the local economy annually."

George Wein was quoted in the same article: "Opposition stems from several types of people. If you examine the politics of the people who are against the festivals, you will find many reactionary. Others may not be reactionary, but want to preserve the status quo. They like the town the way it is and want to keep it that way. Another thing that is involved is a fear of strange people, of different people, because they do not dress

Buddy Rich and Jo Jones wait for the other drummers to set up during the preparations for the drum program at the 1965 Festival. Bassist Ben Tucker observes the scene patiently as Jo talks on.

alike, look alike, are not the same color. The festivals bring in a great diversity of people. To call it a heterogeneous audience is putting it mildly." George Wein's concern with people coming to the Festival from different backgrounds and colors was commented on very succinctly by Nat Hentoff, former coeditor of *Jazz Review* magazine. Writing in *Commonweal* in 1960, in an article that was later expanded in his book *The Jazz Life*, he stated, "Despite exposure of the situation, the N.J.F. had never publicly demanded that the town not discriminate. The lame response by Festival officials to criticism of Jim Crow in Newport was, 'Well, there'd be Jim Crow anywhere we went. Besides our musical director is married to a Negro.'"

A Festival board meeting was held on December 9, 1955, at the home of Marshall W. Stearns. George Wein said during a discussion about moving the site of the Festival, "If we decide to hold it in Newport, I believe there is something we should do and something that could be done to solve the question of racial prejudice. We can do it a little bit more quickly than it could be done in the entire country. Nobody has ever taken a stand editorially in the newspaper in Newport on the color question. Nobody has ever been made to feel ashamed of those different innkeepers and these housekeepers that are being un-American by not having Negroes. This has never been done, and I feel that this can be done. The first year the Viking Hotel showed prejudice. In the second year the Viking Hotel did not show prejudice. It is just a matter of hitting them over the head with it."

John Hammond agreed, but Allan Morrison of *Ebony* magazine said, "I don't think that should be the function of the Festival."

"I think that should be the function of life," George Wein interjected.

"The Festival," Morrison continued, "should be moved. Prejudice is an important reason . . . not the only reason. There have been arguments raised here against moving because of the universality of the prejudice. We know there is prejudice everywhere in the United States to a lesser or greater degree. But in a city like New York a Negro has greater leeway in which to move and operate. There is more freedom; there are fewer restrictions. It is a larger city. There are more hotels; there is a greater social life. Newport is restricted; Newport is small, and the prejudice there is more keenly felt than it would be in a large community where there is a liberal tradition and stronger state laws.'' No official pronouncement was ever issued by the Festival on the question of racial prejudice in Newport.

Over the years, with expansion of the programs and the number of listeners, the Festival became big business. Some of it was inescapable, but a great deal of the shift could have been avoided.

In the rush to attract people to the concerts and defray the rapidly rising costs and overhead, pop artists were brought in to supplement the jazz. But the pop artists diluted the importance and purpose of the jazz. The Kingston Trio, Pat Suzuki, Eartha Kitt, Diana Ross, Gladys Knight and the Pips, Johnny Mathis, and later the rock groups—while paying some of the bills—inadvertently attracted the wrong type of listener, sometimes creating a circus atmosphere with people who didn't listen to the music at all.

M. J. Arlen in a July 1966 article in *Holiday* magazine remarked, ''He [Wein] also had Frank Sinatra, paying him some $35,000 for one night's appearance with the Basie Band, and this was thought by a number of critics to be definitely not O.K. Sinatra is a great pop singer, they observed, but he doesn't belong in a jazz festival. Wein objects to this sort of criticism. 'What do they mean, he doesn't belong?' Wein bellows in the classic manner of the wounded impresario. 'Sinatra made the Festival exciting and drew enough people so that I could afford musicians like Shepp and Taylor [referring

to two avant-garde musicians of the period], and so what's wrong with that?' "

One who supports this view is Elvin Jones, one of the finest of today's drummers, who said, "George's and Newport's contribution to jazz has been the bringing of jazz to a mass audience. I see nothing strange about pop being played at a jazz festival; after all, I've played at rock festivals."

For a while the press theorized that musicians should have more say in the selection of the artists who appeared at the Festival. John Hammond, when asked about the subject, said, "It's awfully dangerous to leave it entirely up to musicians, because a lot of musicians can't be completely trusted to be unbiased. No, I think you have to have people who are genuinely enthusiastic."

A jazz fan wrote to *Down Beat* magazine, October 2, 1958, concerning the overall programing of the Festival: "What disturbs me most about Newport is the emphasis on financial gain at the expense of artistic worth. I am dismissing as pure fabrication the remark from a disgruntled customer that Newport is dickering with Clyde Beatty to book the famous Seven Musical Seals for next summer's event. The overall intonation of the group leaves much to be desired."

That same year the *Providence Journal* commented: "The grounds at the Jazz Festival . . . have taken on the appearance of a carnival midway this year and you can buy about anything. You can purchase everything from programs to pizza, rent out cameras or buy souvenir big band plates." All for the love of jazz.

The atmosphere of the Festival is an important question, since the manner of presentation of the music at Newport is the first introduction for many to the world of jazz. For too many years the media had the public believing that jazz was born in a New Orleans brothel. Newport was supposed to debunk, not confirm, this stereotype.

That the Festival has survived at all is nothing short of miraculous. Many concerts have been presented not so much for the paying audience as for the convenience of the record companies. In buying recording rights for the Festival these companies gained influence over which artists would be presented there. *New York Times* jazz critic John S. Wilson commented, "There is nothing inherently disadvantageous in having a jazz festival recorded, but unlike the paying customers, the paying record company is rarely content to take what comes." He went on to reveal that programing was frequently planned around recording new material. Sometimes the orchestras or artists being recorded had not had sufficient time to rehearse their material. Microphone cables and microphones were placed onstage so as to maintain the best sound level in the recording machines. Unfortunately, this did not necessarily mean that the audience out front heard the music the way it should have been presented, since sound recording out of doors is at best difficult to arrange.

Equally annoying was that the Festival also accommodated radio network broadcasts for a number of years. They wished to present the program at a given hour. Consequently, concerts were presented a half hour early, and ticket buyers were not informed of program changes. Since the press were also not informed of these scheduling changes, some of us simply began to stay on after the afternoon concert, spending the evening there with a beer and hot dog for dinner. It didn't help a reviewer to be receptive to what he heard.

Nevertheless, the outdoor setting, with the sounds of the ocean and the sunlight, was a refreshing change from jazz's traditional gloomy nightclub image. Despite the conflicts among the Festival's creators, the inconveniences of the town, the inexperience of reviewers, the demands of record companies, and the tendency toward commercialism, the Festival has for more than twenty years provided a unique forum for jazz musicians. That is what is important and what this book is about.

Sporting the latest in "Mustang" wear, Charlie Bourgeois, left, chief aide to the producer, talks with Dave Brubeck and Sonny Stitt.

The first shell erected at Newport. On the left side of the shell the small black hole was the author's vantage point for photographing the festivities. The door-way on the right led to the refreshment area and tennis courts.

1954 Saturday, July 17, 1954

The first sound heard at the Newport Jazz Festival was the wail of a siren. It belonged to the police escort of the Greyhound bus carrying the first evening's performers, which had left New York City an hour late, since it had waited for three musicians who had stepped around the corner for a short beer. Finally the bus took off without the missing musicians, who turned up later at Newport.

On board was an evenly divided group of traditional and contemporary musicians. Eddie Condon, musician, nightclub owner, raconteur, and drinking companion of the noted and notorious, sat on one side with the gentle-faced, burry-toned clarinetist, Peewee Russell. Sitting nearby was cornetist Wild Bill Davison. The other side of the bus held segments of Dizzy Gillespie's band and the Modern Jazz Quartet: Horace Silver (piano), Kenny Clarke (drums), Percy Heath (bass), and Milt Jackson (vibes). The ride was uneventful until the bus reached the Jamestown ferry, just across Narragansett Bay from Newport. There an officious and recalcitrant ferry attendant refused Condon's request that the bus be allowed to board the ferry ahead of the long line of waiting cars. The attendant had said they'd have to wait their turn. "Shit! Don't you know all those cats in front are waiting to hear us? We go on first, man!" replied a voice from the bus. The attendant turned away. "We missed two ferries that way," record producer and artists and repertoire man George Avakian said. Finally Avakian told the people in charge, "Look, this is ridiculous! You're not going to have a festival without musicians." He got some bureaucratic reply and went back

on the bus and told Condon what the situation was. Condon shouted, "Well, this is real bullshit!" They got off the bus and decided to call Louis Lorillard and tell him there wasn't going to be any Festival. When Condon hung up the phone, he said, "Well, it looks like there's going to be some new attendants on the ferry." The phone rang back immediately, and they were put on the next ferry first. Louis Lorillard had phoned the city manager, who had obviously turned the heat on the ferry management. A police escort was waiting for them at the Newport dock. The bus pulled up with a screech outside the Newport Casino grounds, and the musicians tumbled out amid muttered imprecations, lugging their battered instrument cases through the temporary stage entrance. The crowd made way for them and quickly closed ranks.

The temporary music shell that was to serve as the stage for the concerts was a contemporary-style structure covered in heavy cardboard. It had been designed by Hsio Wen Shih, architect, acoustic expert, and jazz buff. Wen Shih, a short, thin, ascetic-looking individual with glasses, had designed a stage that stood barely a foot off the grass and held only half a dozen musicians comfortably. Erected on a terraced bank, its back was to the championship tennis courts and their grandstands.

Most of the audience sat on folding chairs on the side courts. It was standing room only on the sides and the veranda that overlooked the concert area. The weight of so many people must have put quite a strain on those venerable timbers, which dated back to the 1880s.

1

During the first concert some young fans scrambled to the roof of the casino and merrily did a Charleston on its slanted sides until the police intervened. In Freebody Park, which overlooked the courts, some fans sat on the upper seats of the concrete bleachers to get a free view of the festivities.

The cardboard shell was unusually thick. I particularly remember it because during the first evening's concert I had surreptitiously cut a small hole through it with nail clippers in order to accommodate my camera lens. That evening a number of photographers demanded use of my vantage point; one from *Life* magazine told me in no uncertain terms that he had made the opening. Needless to say, I photographed through "my" hole the rest of the evening.

The first evening's concert was scheduled to get off the grass at eight P.M. A little after nine, the mayor of Newport, John J. Sullivan, rambled on to a restless audience, recalling that Newport had recognized jazz a long time ago, when Henri Conrad's orchestra [*sic*] had introduced "Alexander's Ragtime Band" at the Newport Casino. The mayor's speech was constantly interrupted with catcalls. Nevertheless, as the *Providence Bulletin* reported, "He stuck to his guns and finished his prepared speech." John McClellan, knowledgeable Boston disc jockey, then introduced the master of ceremonies, Stan Kenton. In the temporary stage lighting, Kenton looked tall and distinguished. In from the West Coast, he was without his orchestra. Reading a script prepared by Nat Hentoff, then a Boston disc jockey and contributor to *Down Beat* magazine, Kenton improvised here and there. He described the evolution of jazz from field hollers and spirituals to New Orleans-style jazz, and from that to what grew up in St. Louis and Chicago. He continued: "This country has taken jazz for granted. Europe has recently held several jazz festivals, for abroad they recognize jazz as a distinct form of music.

Wen Shih (*right*) was admirably suited to design the first two shells for the Festival. An architect and acoustic engineer, he was also an erudite jazz buff and publisher of one of the finest of jazz magazines, *Jazz Review*. *Opposite, top.* One of the MCs at the first Newport Jazz Festival, orchestra leader Stan Kenton. It was to be the first of many appearances for him. *Opposite, bottom.* The extroverted, acid-tongued raconteur of the Dixieland jazz set, sometime guitarist and club owner Eddie Condon gave the first Festival a roaring start with his witty observations and introductions.

But only recently has this country accepted it as such. The Newport Festival is the first to be held in this country and tonight makes history." At nine eighteen Eddie Condon stepped to the center of the stage, blinking in the brilliant light of the full moon that shone down. To the strains of a twenty-eight-year-old Dixieland tune, "Muskrat Ramble," the Festival got under way.

Condon conducted his veterans, and as the music swung into the bridge, he picked up his guitar and joined in the fun. Outstanding was the biting sound of Lou McGarity's trombone, lending a freshness to the overall sound. Pianist Ralph Sutton melded well with the group, and his playing drew a couple of encores.

They were followed by a group led by the brilliantly lyrical trumpet of Bobby Hackett, whose playing moved within many styles. Beautifully cohesive and always understated, he was joined by the witty trombone of mainstreamer Vic Dickinson; the youthful, wry Peewee Russell on clarinet; and the throaty voice of Lee Wiley singing "If I Had You." Her phrasing was perfection as she moved from "Soft Lights and Sweet Music" to "I've Got a Crush on You." Her voice radiated a warmth that kept the audience hushed until she had finished. Hackett accented her every turn of phrase.

The first half of the evening ended with the two groups jamming together on a rousing "Bugle Call Rag" and "Ole Miss."

Intermission was skipped, and the history of jazz was upped a few decades when the Modern Jazz Quartet appeared onstage. The press paid scant attention to their music. The subtleties of the group also seemed lost on many of the boxholders. Whitney Balliet in *Saturday Review* magazine described it this way: "The front row members of the audience, many of whom were be-minked, be-jeweled, and white haired, got to their feet in polite confusion and left."

Dizzy Gillespie appeared, a slightly comic figure with a tufted goatee, in a rumpled brown suit; he was accompanied by his plaid-coated group. He provided a

3

touch of humor by introducing the members of his group to each other. The bell of Dizzy's trumpet was bent at a forty-five-degree angle; "so I can hear myself play," he explained. For the first time that evening the crowd erupted into applause.

Dizzy's rendition of "My Man" was clean and uncluttered, and it came alive. Charlie Persip, his drummer, gave just the right accenting and intensity in his accompaniment.

Meanwhile, backstage, George Wein, the producer-director, was running around frantically complaining, "I lost my speech." He scurried away, looking for Nat Hentoff to write him another one.

The Lee Konitz Quartet followed with an intricate set, but the audience didn't seem to be on their wavelength. Oscar Peterson's trio, with Ray Brown on bass and Herb Ellis on guitar, provided enough warmth to ward off the dampness and chill that was now blowing in from the bay. Gerry Mulligan's quartet followed; their counterpoint, with floating and extended lines, had the audience swaying in its seats and humming along with the melody.

Backstage, Ella Fitzgerald sat talking quietly to her accompanist, John Lewis, a stoic figure in jazz. Ella, who had made her first recording in 1935 at the tender age of seventeen, with the great Chick Webb, exclaimed, "With all these musicians back here, I'm real nervous."

Ella's rhythm section was rounded perfection, with Jimmy Woode on bass and the late Shadow Wilson on drums. Wilson was a quiet, gentle man. A drummer for all seasons, he had been honed with the best in jazz. His drumming and brushwork were reminiscent of Big Sid Catlett. Nervous or not, Ella Fitzgerald had the crowd in a frenzy. At the end of her performance the roar was deafening.

The final number of the evening was a jamming of "I've Got Rhythm," performed by one of the most mixed bags of musicians ever assembled on a stage. Tearing into it was a rhythm section made up of Stan Kenton on piano, Milt Hinton on bass, and Jo Jones on drums, with the ebullient Eddie Condon conducting. The front line had Wild Bill Davison, Bobby Hackett, and the ever-surprising Dizzy Gillespie featured on both trumpet and camera.

When Dizzy wasn't soloing or playing ensemble, he walked around the stage photographing the other performers. Clowning or not, his biting, driving horn sparked the other musicians and gave a cohesiveness to a rather disjointed assemblage.

The small stage was soon overflowing as Peewee Russell, Lee Konitz, Milt Jackson, and Gerry Mulligan joined the crew.

The problem with these all-star gatherings is that they have no place to go. Gerry and Dizzy were able to cut through the top-heaviness of so many star performers with slashing solos, goading all the others on. At twelve fifty-five the final notes and the wild cheering crowd could be heard at the Jamestown ferry and beyond.

Sunday, July 18, 1954

Sunday afternoon there was a panel discussion entitled "The Place of Jazz in American Culture." The *Providence Bulletin* called the assembled panelists "the tories of the trade." The distinguished group was composed of Dr. Alan Merriam, instructor of anthropology at Northwestern University; Willis James, professor of music at Spellman College; Henry Cowell, composer and professor of music at the Peabody Institute; and Marshall Stearns, associate professor of English at Hunter College and director of the Institute of Jazz Studies. Father Norman O'Connor, C.S.P. chaplain of the Newman Club of Boston University, acted as moderator. Before the panel assembled, Father O'Connor suggested that the audience wouldn't want to hear a lot of "long hair" talk. Although the panel agreed to keep it

The comparatively small refreshment area at the first festival, when Narragansett Beer was still king. The stairway (far left) leads to the stage. On the right, the championship grass courts. Jazz, anyone?

light, Dr. Merriam theorized that "in the relationship of African music to jazz, there is no direct connection but there has been a certain blending." Professor James livened up the pedantry by demonstrating a series of field hollers and street cries that he said had become a part of the language and voicing of the blues. Professor Stearns defined jazz as "a blending of European and African music over a period of three hundred years which lead from rigidity to mobility." Henry Cowell was the most direct of the panelists: "As a classical composer, I envy jazz musicians who can't read music. Jazz musicians are free; they have it all over us."

In an article that appeared in the 1959 program Marshall Stearns allowed, "About the only thing interesting that can come out of panel discussions is a good fight."

The skies had been threatening all day. Shortly after, the rains came pelting down. Rumors of the evening's performance being canceled filtered down the lines standing on Bellevue Avenue waiting to enter Sunday's concert. Some fans, discouraged by the downpour, sold their tickets at bargain rates. Others jammed their cars down Third Street, through the gates of the Naval Station, which had been selected as a contingency site in case of bad weather. However, the decision was finally made to continue the Festival at the casino. Backstage, madness reigned. There was concern about the piano getting wet. The waterlogged cardboard panels that enclosed the shell started to sag inward from the weight of the moisture. Instruments were wiped off, reeds were sharpened and fitted into place. There was a general cacophony of warming-up exercises. Vic Dickinson sat to one side in a dark raincoat, tuning up. Off to another side sat Bill Harris, tall and distinguished, the antithesis of the popular image of a jazz musician: His unopened trombone case beside him, he unconcernedly read a book.

The rains slowed, and at eight thirty-five a bedraggled crowd of seven thousand fans, wrapped in everything from shower curtains to blankets, settled down for the

Trombonist Bill Harris stretches out (center), in his only Newport appearance, accompanied by bassist Milt Hinton and pianist Teddy Wilson. *Right.* Multi-reedman Gil Mellé and trio. The following day one of his instruments was stolen.

opening set. A tribute to Count Basie was led by Oscar Peterson. Buck Clayton, Vic Dickinson, Jo Jones, and Lester "Pres" Young were all alumni of the Basie Band. Only Ray Brown on bass and Oscar Peterson had not played with the Count. The jazz motif moved back in time to Kansas City. The group worked beautifully; it was an exhilarating experience.

They played music associated with the Count: Lester Young and Buck Clayton moved effortlessly through the familiar changes of Count's most swinging period. While Pres didn't hold his tenor sax at the stratospheric tilt of his Basie days, the clean, uncluttered lines of his playing were emphasized by the slight shrug of his shoulders and the arching of his back as he swung effortlessly.

Peterson stayed onstage with Ray Brown and Herb Ellis. Later, joined by the guitarist Johnny Smith, the group rambled through Johnny's version of "Moonlight in Vermont," one of the first hit recordings in jazz. Smith would win the *Down Beat* poll later that year.

Dizzy Gillespie's quintet followed, lively as ever. James A. Van Alen, president of the Newport Casino, standing in the wings, gazed out at the vast throng and then at Dizzy's group onstage. Perplexed, he turned to Eddie Condon, who was standing beside him. "Mr. Condon, what do you think of all this?" Eddie glanced his way, paused and quipped, "Looks like the end of tennis."

"Tenderly" was raked over for a second time that evening by George Shearing's quintet. It didn't have the bluesy quality Peterson had brought to it, but his bassist, Al McKibbon, fired the drab proceedings with his lovely tone. Gil Mellé, a twenty-three-year-old arranger and tenor sax man, appeared as a surprise addition to the program. He sounded promising, making intriguing sounds. Later that day his sax was stolen; the Festival gave him $150 toward its replacement. Mellé has since moved on to the world of composing for television, and his name often appears on screen credits.

8

The first of numerous appearances of baritone star Gerry Mulligan. Aside from his own scheduled performances, Mulligan loves to walk on unannounced and jam with other groups.
Opposite: A rare public appearance of pianist, teacher and diverse experimenter Lennie Tristano, here with some of his students and followers, among them altoist Lee Konitz (center).

Pianist Teddy Wilson opened with a swinging set, playing clean, flowing chords. His confrere, Jo Jones, with some dazzling brushwork on his drums, left nothing unsaid. Milt Hinton was the bassist with the group; he had been terrified flying to the Festival in a small private plane with Teddy Wilson, the only way they could make it on schedule. The group was augmented by the punchy trumpet of Ruby Braff, a Bostonian I used to see around the neighborhood when we were growing up, and Gerry Mulligan on baritone sax. Bill Harris on trombone, with his staccato, choppy phrases, was letting out an explosion in little controlled bursts. Both Harris and Mulligan, who sounded much looser than in the confines of his own quartet, were particularly potent.

Lennie Tristano, the influential contemporary pianist, appeared next with Lee Konitz on alto sax, Wayne Marsh on tenor, Billy Bauer on guitar, Peter Ind on bass, and Jeff Morton on drums. Tristano was an original in jazz. Most of the musicians who have played and studied with him have been profoundly influenced by his compositional and melodic ideas. The musicians who appeared with him onstage were all pupils of his at one time.

Konitz was the one who had broken through with his own recordings. There was a general curiosity about Tristano's appearance, since he had been away from the music scene for two years. The audience had doubts as to what exactly they were listening to. "His playing was as brilliant and as conscientiously obscure as ever," reported Saturday Review.

For the final set the rhythm section grew muted as a vocalist stepped in front of the microphone. With a roar of recognition from the audience, Billie Holiday sang "Billie's Blues." Moments before, backstage, she had been sick and had emptied her guts. Now Lady Day, standing near the piano, was emptying her soul. Soon she was joined by the musician most identified with her,

Lester "Pres" Young. Though they had not spoken to each other in several years, there was passionate communication between them on that stage. It was to be her last appearance with him in front of a live audience. She was also beautifully reunited with the musical conductor of some of her best recordings, pianist Teddy Wilson. Milt Hinton was on bass, Vic Dickinson on trombone, and Buck Clayton on trumpet. They had been her sidemen on many of her recording dates. Later in her program Gerry Mulligan sat in with the group, which melded beautifully. When Billie's set ended, the audience and all the press burst into a sustained standing ovation. We were paying our dues. Miles away at Sachuset Point, at the Clambake Club, because of the way sound travels over water, people had heard Billie singing. A jam session was to have ended the first part of the program, but overenthusiastic fans advanced on the stage from the sides and the rear, blocking both aisles and the view of those in front. Although Festival officials switched off the lights and the sound system, some musicians on the stage continued to play even after the blackout. After some semblance of order was restored and the aisles were partially cleared, the final segment was presented. The Gene Krupa Trio, focused in a double spotlight on an otherwise darkened stage, was an audience pleaser. The crowd was familiar with Krupa's name, and he performed with a precision and mastery that had the fans jumping up and down. In the final part of his last number he thundered out with a blistering solo, ending with a series of rolls and explosions that pounded the perimeter of the casino. His bass drum stopped reverberating at twelve thirty-five. The audience loved it all.

"Successful beyond the expectations of the committee," George Wein told a press conference. "This is just the beginning; these two nights were only a part of my dream."

He later added: "Now that we've proved this can be done, we can go on to do what we want to do, and that includes a summer center for jazz studies here in Newport. In time I hope the center will prove to be the most important aspect of the whole undertaking, and that the concerts, though they will occur, will be secondary to the school. We want to build something permanent with these festivals."

Press coverage for the Festival was unparalleled. Reporters were on hand from *Time, Life,* the *New Yorker, Newsweek, Seventeen,* and *Esquire.* Most major newspapers and wire services covered it. A correspondent was there from *Figaro* of Paris and at least one newspaperman from Mexico City. ABC Radio broadcast a section of Saturday's concert from eleven fifteen to eleven forty-five.

Part of the folklore of the first Festival is the story that the total profit was only $142.50. It has been repeated endlessly by the press, although Festival financial statements show a profit of $4,106.96 after all expenses, which included the payment to producer Wein of $1,276.00 for expenses plus $1,000.00 for his services, plus a bonus of $600.00 paid to his aides, Charles Bourgeois and Terri Turner.

The following day the local fire company had their fog sprinkler on the casino grounds to water the grass. The championship tennis matches were only three weeks away. The head greenskeeper, Tony Corey, mused, "Got to keep the alcohol from eating away at it. I'll take it slow, and bring it back gradually. We've done a lot of suffering, but I guess it was worth it."

Three days later they were still trying to pry Eddie Condon away from Redney Burke's bar on Williams Street.

The peak of the first festival: Lady stepping out onstage with the crowd roaring approval. It was a deeply moving experience. Her accompanists were pianist Teddy Wilson and bassist Milt Hinton.

1955

In 1955 the casino board of directors voted against holding the Jazz Festival there in the future. Although the president of the casino gave no reason, Elaine Lorillard was told later that "the decision was based on stuffed-up toilets." The toilets in question had been plugged up long before the Festival.

As George Wein told George Frazier in the August 1955 *Esquire* interview, "There was a definite element against us. They resented jazz musicians coming into Newport."

Mrs. Van Alen was quoted as saying, "I don't mind the music too much, but the people are so vulgar."

One society dowager took out special Festival insurance each year to cover any damage that might result from the crowds. Mrs. Louis Brugière, the reigning queen of Newport society, said she would spend ten million dollars if necessary to keep the Festival out of Newport.

The Festival moved to a municipally owned sports field, Freebody Park, normally used for baseball and track meets. A new and larger shell was designed and built. The architect again was Hsio Wen Shih.

Geared up with a glowing press and high hopes, the Festival began anew, to remain at the park until 1965.

The Festival spread out to three days in 1955. The sound system, hailed in press releases as "high fidelity outdoors," ranged from bad to miserable. Microphones either had feedback or conked out altogether.

Friday, July 15, 1955

Although vocalist Teddi King sang well, unfortunately few heard her aside from those in the press pit. The sound system began rebelling early. Despite the mike problems, Erroll Garner, pianist, brought the fans to their feet with "Lullaby of Birdland," "Laura," and a swinging, strident "Lover." Woody Herman led the first of the big bands to be heard at the Festival. Starting slowly with his signature, "Blue Flame," the band finally caught fire in a muscle-filled "Four Brothers." Drummer Chuck Flores fanned the orchestra with a punching, driving solo. Erroll joined Woody in a duet from their recent album, *Music for Tired Lovers,* but the sound system prevented them from making it to bed. After intermission Coleman Hawkins on tenor sax reunited with Roy Eldridge, the key transitional trumpet figure in jazz. Although there were few sparks, Roy took a lovely solo on "I Surrender, Dear." Jo Jones was on drums and Joe Turner, "the Kansas City blues shouter," joined them in a rousing "Wee Baby Blues." It was all laughter and smiles.

Louis Armstrong and his All-Stars played his standard set. His vocalist, Velma Middleton, tested the construction of the stage with her three-hundred-pounds. Her energetic gyrations proved the soundness of the architect's design. Louis ended the set with the national anthem and walked off the stage with a smile. Someone

Woody Herman and his Herd, the first big band to appear at the Festival. The sax section, with baritonist Jack Nimitz (center), ignites in a searing chorus from Four Brothers.

13

in the front boxes was apparently offended by his rendition and was heard muttering, "Sacrilege, sacrilege." Louis had made a simple statement of love.

Saturday, July 16, 1955

Dinah Washington broke it up the second evening with a moving group of ballads including "Pennies from Heaven," "Teach Me Tonight," and "A Foggy Day." She came back for two encores, but could have stayed on all night. During the evening Gerry Mulligan came on unannounced on a number of occasions; his infectious exuberance booted the other musicians along.

Al Cohn on tenor sax and Bobby Brookmeyer on valve trombone played too brief a set. Bobby, with his eclectic knowledge of jazz and wry sense of humor, was outstanding.

Two trumpets dominated the Festival for me. The first was that of Clifford Brown, a gentle, introverted human being. Elvin Jones thought Clifford's articulation came directly from Fats Navarro. "Only Fats gave it a warmer, bluesier feeling."

Clifford played a brilliant set with Max Roach on Saturday night. Bud Powell's brother Richie was on piano, Harold Land on tenor, George Morrow on bass. Max goaded them from the beginning, lashing out with "Jordu." Then Clifford came on with a lush, warmly woven solo on "I Don't Stand a Ghost of a Chance."

The final number of Dave Brubeck's set that same evening was "Tea for Two." Dave's regulars were augmented by Chet Baker on trumpet, Gerry Mulligan on baritone, and Max and Clifford. They crackled! Max attacked the standard savagely. While the group pounded away to the closing moments of the evening, the most telling statements were made by Max and Clifford. The crowded audience left their seats to encircle the stage,

14

and George Wein came out waving his arms like a wind-mill to halt the festivities. Clifford ignored the producer, digging his head deeper into his shoulders, scrunching his face up even more than it had been, and blasting out a gorgeous, fire-breathing final chorus.

At that moment the rain, which had been threatening all day, started to spatter down against his horn.

It was Clifford's only Festival appearance; the follow-ing June he and Richie Powell and Richie's wife, Nancy, were killed in an accident on the Pennsylvania Turnpike. Both musicians were twenty-five years old.

Sunday, July 17, 1955

A joyous reunion of Count Basie, Lester Young on tenor, Ruby Braff substituting for the ailing Buck Clay-ton, and Ed Jones on bass with drummer Jo Jones fol-lowed. Before the group started, Jo had seated himself at his drums looking disturbed that someone had fouled up his drum setup in some way. The cymbals were not set up correctly or his bass foot pedal was not in place. Whatever it was, it bothered him for a few numbers and Jo vented his annoyance by playing so loudly that he drowned out the soloists. They finally settled into a good groove, and Pres, with his masterly sense of tim-ing, accented by Count Basie, had a natural brilliance and spontaneity. Later, Jimmy Rushing joined them as a surprise guest, adding an emotional depth both moving and beautiful on ''I Want a Little Girl,'' with ''Bye, Bye, Blues'' as an encore.

After the set ended to tumultuous applause, Pres wandered backstage to the large blue-and-white-striped musicians' tent to relax. Jo Jones entered the tent and Pres, looking bemused, gently chided him: "You're no trouper."

Jo looked at Pres, his longtime buddy and companion

Right. Dinah Washing-ton, queen of the eve-ning, with two encores. *Opposite.* A walk-on per-formance by Gerry Mul-ligan as he joins Chet Baker's quartet.

16

of countless days and years on the road with the Basie band, and replied, "You couldn't play if your mouthpiece was over there," glancing to one side of the tent, ". . . and your horn was over there," indicating the opposite side.

"You're no trouper," Pres repeated gently.

In desperation Jo knelt and picked up a bass drum, slung it over his back, hunching over like Quasimodo in *The Hunchback of Notre Dame,* and started striding around thumping out intricate rhythms with his hand on the edge of the drum head. "You know I can play anything I want to on these things," he pleaded.

Ignoring the display of virtuosity, Pres rose abruptly and started to dance toward the tent door, scat singing, "Ju jah juboo wah baba jabadoobadoo joobah joobah . . ." past the tent flap and into the sunlight.

Jo turned to musicians Ruby Braff and Sam Margolis, who were sitting nearby, and shouted, "There goes the greatest drummer in the world!"

The second trumpet star of that festival was Miles Davis, who stepped on the stage with an ironic eloquence. It was a completely unscheduled appearance. Miles, in a white jacket and black bow tie, looked the antithesis of what the critics had intimated he had been going through for the past couple of years. He had shaken off the junk and personal problems that had led the jazz establishment to write him off.

Accompanied by Gerry Mulligan on baritone, Zoot Sims on tenor, Thelonious Monk on piano, Percy Heath on bass, and Connie Kay on drums, Miles opened with a driving, emotional assault, "Hackensack." The tempo and smoldering intensity of Miles's solo was like spontaneous combustion, which spread to the rest of the sextet. For about ten minutes they held that audience by the throat.

Members of the press were uneasy. After all, this was someone they had written off. George Avakian remembers, ''Miles came out on that stage like a walk-on. He blew *so* beautifully!''

Miles and the sextet continued the set with '' 'Round About Midnight.'' Miles played with great emotion. His solo, particularly after the bridge, had a clarity and austerity that were to mark much of his later work. He got at something more than the truth. The audience sat spellbound. He concluded with ''Now's the Time,'' which he had first recorded with Bird in 1945. The audience gave the group a standing ovation. Miles left the stage as quietly as he had come on. Later, in response to the critical acclaim for his Newport performance, he was quoted as saying, ''I don't know what all those cats were talking about. I played the way I always play.'' Despite his disclaimers, Newport was a turning point in his career.

Dave Brubeck was the man the fans were waiting for, and his group did not disappoint them. Plagued with sound problems the evening before, he had cut his set short. That last evening, though, he rocked the audience with ''The Trolley Song,'' swung into ''Crazy Chris,'' and climaxed with a lilting ''Don't Worry About Me.''

Tenor man Ben Webster joined Bobby Hackett and trombonist Kai Winding for ''Royal Garden Blues.'' Kai was joined by J.J. Johnson on trombone and Dick Katz on piano, playing ''It's All Right with Me.'' Katz moved

through the changes as if he were talking about his inner smiling thoughts.

A romantic and too brief medley followed, leading off with Bobby Hackett's lush tones on "Someone to Watch Over Me." Altoist Bud Shank played a moving solo on "Lover Man," and ballad master Ben Webster created a solo of quiet beauty on "Someone to Watch Over Me."

The Festival closed with Count Basie and his orchestra romping through a set that exploded with vocalist Joe Williams shouting out the jazz anthem of the band, "April in Paris," and "Every Day" and "The Comeback." The band started to move off the stage at midnight as someone in the trumpet section softly blew "Be It Ever So Humble, There's No Place Like Home."

It was the first festival to be entirely recorded by the Voice of America; NBC Monitor had their program "Bandstand USA" broadcast some segments.

Belcourt, the former Belmont estate that had been purchased by the Lorillards, was used during the afternoons for two panel discussions, which were accompanied in part by live music. On Saturday the discussion was entitled "Jazz from the Outside Looking In." The crowd, composed of children, schoolteachers, and jazz buffs, listened quietly in the sunny, grass-filled courtyard to an eminent group of scholars. The high point of the discussion was the heat generated by one of the participants, Dr. Norman Margolies, a psychiatrist, who stated that "jazz was originally protest music, originating from and attracting devotion from three groups: Negroes, intellectuals, and adolescents—who use it to express their resentments." His opinion was vigorously disputed by Father Norman O'Connor.

The afternoon was enlivened by The Six, a Bob Wilber–led aggregation that played pleasantly if innocuously.

The Sunday afternoon forum, entitled "Jazz from the

Opposite. A nervous Miles Davis, thrust into the spotlight of the Newport stage as a last-minute addition to the evening's program, rises from obscurity to the overwhelming acclaim of the critics. *Top.* His sidemen Gerry Mulligan and Zoot Sims. *Bottom.* Miles's masterly solos brought a hush to the audience.

19

Below. At the panel table in the courtyard at Belcourt mansion (left to right) anthropologist Richard A. Waterman; Professor Marshall Stearns making notes; Father Norman O'Connor; Dr. Norman Margolies, a psychiatrist; Eric Larrabee, editor of *Harper's* magazine, and Henry Cowell, composer and musicologist, engage in a semantic free-for-all. In the balcony above them (front row, left to right) the former jazz dentist Dr. Stanley Schwartz, who used to treat his patients, musicians and buffs alike, to the sounds of jazz piped into his office. Beside him are *Metronome* editor Bill Coss and his wife.

Left. The Six with reed-man Bob Wilbur (center) and beside him, handling the remote radio broadcast, announcer Al Jazzbo Collins of radio's Purple Grotto Fame.

The world of fashion was starting to notice jazz, naming brands of lipstick "Red, Hot and Cool." *Above.* A model poses prettily behind the bandstand while the performers are onstage.

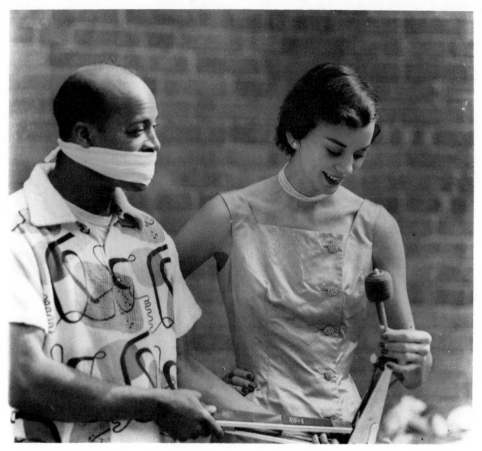

Opposite. Overflow crowds forced the Festival to move out of the courtyard and relocate at the front entrance of the former Belmont mansion. Onstage (left to right), vibist Teddy Charles, pianist Mal Waldron, bassist Charlie Mingus, reedman Teo Macero, trombonist Eddie Bert and trumpeter Art Farmer. *Above.* Fashion shooting extended to the rhythm section, here in the person of a giant of jazz percussion, drummer Jo Jones.

Inside Out,'' included on the panel musicians Dave Brubeck, Gerry Mulligan, and Gunther Schuller, composer, musician, jazz scholar, conductor.

Gerry said that ''the jazz musician, like the traditional musician, is faced with the problem of getting tired of what he is doing even before the audience does.'' Picking up his baritone from its stand, he then joined Dave Brubeck in a duet that brought cheers from the audience.

Gunther Schuller stated, ''It's on-the-spot composing that gives jazz its spontaneity, which is much greater than eighty musicians playing together from a score can achieve.''

Bassist Charlie Mingus had a contemporary group of musicians, which included Art Farmer on flugelhorn, Eddie Bert on trombone, Teddy Charles on vibes, John LaPorta on reeds, Teo Macero on sax, Britt Woodman on trombone, and Elvin Jones on drums. They played a stimulating group of originals after the discussion ended.

One of the participants, checking his date book for the occasion, reminisced, ''We got paid five dollars for driving up from New York City and back. Unbelievable! And thirty-five dollars for the gig. We rehearsed quite a bit, three days rehearsing, six thirty to eleven.'' When I inquired if he had been paid for rehearsing, he said disgustedly, ''No, we never got paid for that stuff.''

The local papers called the Festival a smash success. The *Newport Daily News* headline ran: ''Satchmo the most.'' *Metronome* magazine, after taking the Festival to task for its faults, concluded: ''The Festival was not one to miss, if only in the immense amount of talent spread out before the audience.'' *Saturday Review* said, ''Like the army of Darius the Persian, an elephantine and onsweeping thing. It lit the air with music. . . . As a celebration of American Jazz, the second Newport Festival was a happy successful occasion.''

1956

The Guinness Book of World Records might well have listed the opening concert, Thursday evening, July 5, 1956, as the only one ever held underwater. George Wein spent the daylight hours looking out at the rain from his hotel window repeating, "You know, I think it's getting lighter." Wind-whipped rain came down without letup all day and continued into the evening. The seating area on the field was a muddy swamp, and the tent area backstage was not much better. Nevertheless, twenty-five hundred or so fans sat shivering, huddling under beach unbrellas, slickers, blankets, and shower curtains, braving out the storm.

Willis Conover, the MC, set the tone for the evening, saying to Eddie Condon, "We mix it with water for you tonight, Eddie." Count Basie's band, in mud-spattered uniforms, rushed up the stairs that led to the stage, looked out at the storm-drenched sky, and muttered, "What the hell, let's blow." They opened with the "Star Spangled Banner."

One of the most distinctive features of the 1956 Festival was that much of the music presented either had been commissioned for it or was original compositions. George Wein had asked Duke Ellington for a new composition, and the Duke and his alter ego Billy Strayhorn complied with "The Newport Jazz Festival Suite." J.J. Johnson contributed a still-untitled piece. His music copyist stamped it "NPT" for identifying purposes, and when J.J. saw it on the charts, he decided that was the title. Charlie Mingus presented two originals, "Tonight at Noon" and "Tourist in Manhattan." Saturday afternoon, after a panel discussion, Teddy Charles's Tentet played no less than four originals during an afternoon set: "Show Time," "Green Blues," "The Emperor" and "Word From Bird." A gust of wind blew some of the charts off the stand during the performance. Teddy, unflustered, leaned toward Charlie Mingus, his bassist, shouting, "You got the right idea, man, forget the charts and blow."

Other originals presented that year were Dave Brubeck's "Two-Part Contention" plus a piece dedicated to Duke Ellington, "Duke." Metronome magazine hinted that both had been around for some time.

The Modern Jazz Quartet, surmounting the weather, played an evocative new blues composition by John Lewis, "Two Degrees East, Three Degrees West." A cascade of water trapped in the peak of the overhead part of the stage greeted Sarah Vaughan, dousing her. In defiance she shouted, "Shit!" to the amusement of the audience, and when she completed her rendition of "Over the Rainbow," she announced, "That's what we need now, a rainbow!"

When Dave Brubeck came onstage with his group, calling themselves the First Camera Quartet, the group walked to the edge of the stage, while two of the group, cameras at the ready, photographed the people in the press pit.

Tenor man Paul Gonsalves in the midst of his twenty-seven choruses. They must have heard him and the roar of the fans at his former stomping grounds in Pawtucket, Rhode Island. During the performance teenagers and adults sat on the backs of their chairs while dancers gyrated wildly in the press pit. It was a bewildering sight.

25

Altoist Bud Shank gave a
moving and sensitive
performance, but his set
was too brief.

Count Basie returned to finish the evening. The band crackled with marvelous soloing by trumpeter Thad Jones. Vocalist Joe Williams walloped the audience with "Every Day," "All Right, Okay, You Win," and the first evening ended with a roaring ovation from the audience.

Down Beat magazine summed up the second evening very succinctly. "Too much Louis, not enough Ella. He demonstrated with finality that it takes more than rolling eyes, handkerchief on head and chops, and the same old Paramount Theater act, to warrant an hour's time at an American festival of jazz." *Saturday Review* reported, "It was like an old beer, flat."

Two early standouts on the final Saturday evening program were the Bud Shank and Jimmy Giuffre groups, both showing what could be accomplished with a simple rhythm section. Bud created a bluesy up-tempo feeling on Miles Davis's "Walkin'" and played a sensuous, moving flute solo on "Nature Boy."

Jimmy Giuffre played one number on tenor, "East of the Sun," and then used an extremely low-register clarinet on "Down-Home" and "My *Funky* Valentine."

On July 7, 1956, Duke Ellington lit the fuse that would explode into a new musical life for his then-fading band. George Avakian explained how it all happened: "My crew came to Newport to set up our equipment. It was raining and windy. The engineers were getting this real continuous howl of wind at quite a scale of intensity on the two microphones that were on the stage. You didn't need more than two mikes: You need a piano-bass mike and then a horn mike, and you can do the job. Today that number would be considered impossible. The recording engineers were muttering under their breath about not having brought some cheesecloth. Apparently that works in situations like that. One of the engineers said, 'Hey! Nylon stockings!' Debby Ishlon, Columbia Records publicity director, was standing right there. I told her to take off her nylons. They put one stocking around each mike, and it cut the wind down within

Backstage, Duke's men, just in from the road, relax and prepare to go on. *Above left*. Russell Procope adjusts his tie while Sam Woodyard (*below left*) tunes up his drums. *Above*. Johnny Hodges assembles his alto.

limits. We recorded on three different nights at that Festival. Every night the atmosphere was different. That plus the number of people sitting on the concrete bleachers at the end of the field made the sound different. It bounced differently. The echo and amount of moisture in the air all had an effect on the sound. We had to make sure it sounded like the same Festival when we got through.

"Shortly before the band went onstage, Duke Ellington got them together. It was the only time I ever heard him do this. He said something like: 'Well, you know, guys, I know we've worked on this new piece for this Festival, and George is sticking his neck way out, making this recording. I know we're going to give a good performance. I want you to know that it means quite a bit to just everybody, George, us . . . and I'm going to try something a little bit different and just see if it works. Let's play "Diminuendo and Crescendo in Blue." ' I didn't realize it at the time, but the band just looked at each other, and Paul Gonsalves said, 'That's the one where I blow?' Duke said, 'Yes . . . and keep on blowing. We'll tell you when to stop. That's all you've got to do.' "

The excitement built slowly. After playing "Diminuendo in Blue," Paul started to dig in with his tenor, and along about his fourth chorus, a woman with platinum blond hair and a black dress started dancing wildly in the aisle. "The audience started to really feel the electricity the band was creating," continued Avakian. "Duke kept shouting encouragement to the sections of the band. The audience started to ease out of their chairs to get a better view.

The Duke pauses momentarily to make a notation on a chart in front of him. The swirl of activity around him seldom seemed to interfere with his concentration.

"Jo Jones, the drummer, was in a cubbyhole beside me. I was crouching down near him, being careful not to get in the way of that rolled-up *Christian Science Monitor* he kept swatting the stage with, beating out the rhythm. Jo kept swatting that stage, yelling out encouraging words. The sax section were the only ones able to see Jo. They started to shout back at him. The rhythm section, Sam Woodyard on drums and Jimmy Woode on bass, started to play to Jo, as much as to anyone else. More people began to dance in the aisles."

The press pit, where I stood, was completely filled. Photographers, part of the audience, and some of the dancers were wildly gyrating. "Paul played a fantastic twenty-seven choruses," Avakian recounted. "Duke himself was swinging pretty hard on piano. The clarinets came in when Paul finished his last chorus.

"There was supposed to be a four-bar break after they finished. It was extended to seven, heightening the tension even more. It was excruciating. The final choruses finished with Cat Anderson on trumpet, wailing out those screaming high notes." Pandemonium broke out after that.

The Festival staff had been cautioned backstage that it was long past midnight and a local ordinance forbade the music to go beyond that hour. Sensing a potentially riotous situation, Duke decided to continue. The band swung into "I've Got It Bad and That Ain't Good." Johnny Hodges's solo spread out like oil on troubled waters. They followed it with "Jeep's Blues." As the band swung into the coda of "Tulip or Turnip," George Wein came out in an attempt to end the performance, announcing, "Duke Ellington, ladies and gentlemen! Duke Ellington!" But the crowd shouted, "No! No!" Duke continued with "Skin Deep," featuring a thunderous solo by Duke's drummer Sam Woodyard. The band finally signed off with "Mood Indigo," ending the evening with a standing ovation.

"Funny thing," Avakian recalled. "All during Paul's solo he was blowing into the wrong microphone. We had marked the correct one with a piece of white tape. I had told the band before they went on to stand so that you will be heard equally between these two mikes, because we're recording you. Paul simply forgot. Here are these two mikes, side by side, no more than a foot apart. I saw that he was blowing straight into the PA mike. Long as it is, his whole solo is slightly off-mike. We were able to correct it slightly. Marvelous as its impact is and all that, it still is slightly under what it ought to be in places.

"It's a fantastic tribute to Gonsalves, who was never a soloist like Coleman Hawkins, Chu Berry, or later, John Coltrane. He was tremendously impressive, but he built the chorus of a lifetime there, and not necessarily because we were recording.

"So Gonsalves really meant it when he said, 'Is that the one I blow on?' Duke had read correctly that there might be a tremendously electric performance if he pulled a surprise like that. It was the infectious rhythm of the band plus Paul that made it great. What really happened there was a fantastic combination of the rhythm section and all the horns, just being right in there and swinging away like the Ellington band had seldom swung. It was one hell of a swinging record. It just goes on and builds. It's simply something that could not be duplicated."

Ever after when Duke was asked his date of birth, he would say, "I was born at the Newport Jazz Festival, July 7, 1956."

In many ways he was. Willis Conover said, "That night at Newport was like a rebirth of the Ellington band. Duke had been going through a very lean period in the preceding decade."

1957

There was quite a Fourth of July fireworks display at Newport in 1957. The small explosions came from juveniles heaving fireworks over the stone wall at the fans sitting in Freebody Park. But there was one big explosion, according to *Down Beat* magazine: "There are many stories about the backstage scene following the concert. Some say that Wein and Armstrong engaged in a heated argument. Others say that Louis chewed out Velma Middleton and his group for being late coming onstage."

Willis Conover, the master of ceremonies that evening, said, "From what I heard, George Wein went to Joe Glaser, Louis's manager-booker, and told him, 'I know Louis likes to do his set program, "Sleepy Time Down South," "Indiana," et cetera, and wind up with a current hit, but we want this program to be a little different. It's his birthday. Make sure he knows about the birthday arrangements. Wouldn't it be wonderful if Kid Ory and the others who played with him on the Hot Fives and Sevens could join him?' That was what George Wein wanted. It was not what Louis Armstrong wanted. He was going to do his same program. They were both somewhat upset about it." Wein denied having an argument with him.

Down Beat magazine quoted Wein as saying, "I didn't even speak to Armstrong after the concert. We had to bring the cake on during a number. Maybe that got him mad, but he would have stopped the show before we could have done it any other time. Johnny Mercer waited around two hours, and Ella kept her gown on.

Teagarden and Kid Ory were waiting backstage with their horns. I don't know what happened. Joe Glaser agreed to come up here so the program would be new . . ."

Willis Conover described what happened then: "Right in the middle of Louis's program—not while he was playing, but during an announcement—they wheeled on an enormous birthday cake, with the appropriate number of candles. I announced the fact that it was his birthday and the audience joined in singing 'Happy Birthday' to him. I've seen pictures of Louis at that moment published in the trade magazines. Obviously they didn't notice what I'd noticed. Louis is boiling with anger. He's not making faces, he just has this real stony look. He said, 'You know, folks, it's time to play the "Star Spangled Banner." ' He played it and walked off the stage. Backstage he started screaming, 'That goddamn motherfucker, I'll kill that son of a bitch!' You could hear him all over the park. I never heard Louis talk that way in my life. The Lorillards told me to get George somewhere else because he might kill him. That's how angry he was about messing with his program."

George Wein stated in his Boston newspaper column the following year, "When I arranged for Louis Armstrong to come back to Newport this year, my enemies laughed and my friends were afraid. A repetition of Louis's 1957 performance would have been disastrous for both him and me."

Some of the best music heard at the 1957 Festival was

31

The only man to hold the office of President on a permanent basis— Pres Lester Young—shares the piano stool with his former boss, Count Basie.

played at a private press party given at the Viking Hotel by concert and jazz record producer Norman Granz. The people most noticeably not invited were the Lorillards.

When I questioned Norman Granz about his failure to invite the Lorillards, he bluntly said, "I just didn't care for society people and didn't want them there for just that reason." Norman, feeling in an expansive mood, having concluded a deal to record the entire Festival, threw the party to celebrate. "In exchange for paying for the talent that appeared, I was given the recording rights," Norman said. It was quite a party. "A spread of food to warm the cockles of the most ravenous guest was laid out with a goodly supply of spirits to accompany them"—that was the way the press described the event. The jamming of the jazz musicians that night provided the perfect finishing touch to the party. Gerry Mulligan on baritone, Roy Eldridge on trumpet, Pete Brown on alto, Coleman Hawkins on tenor, Specs Wright on drums, Nat Pierce on piano, Walter Page on bass, Cannonball Adderley on alto—the list went on and on. The trade papers reported it as being more swinging than any of the other Festival events.

Willis Conover looked out at the vast audience the first night and announced, "Lulu White [the New Orleans madame at whose house of easy virtue many of the early jazz greats had entertained] would never have believed it."

In 1957, according to official Festival figures, more money was spent—$40,113.75—than had been spent for talent in the three previous years combined. The producer, George Wein, more than tripled his annual fee for the three previous years, receiving $13,000. Many of the same artists appeared, and in a number of cases they provided little new material.

Bobby Henderson's solo piano work sparkled in a set devoted to the music of Fats Waller. Clarinetist George Lewis had preceded him with some New Orleans stalwarts, playing traditional New Orleans music. Later Jack Teagarden joined an entourage from New York City's

Above. Lyricist and singer Johnny Mercer biding his time, waiting to honor Louis Armstrong by wheeling the cake onstage in celebration of his birthday. *Opposite.* The cake in question rests forlornly backstage while Satchmo quizzically reads a letter. His vocalist Velma Middleton looks on.

Metropole (a midtown jazz bar) with Red Allen on trumpet and Buster Bailey on clarinet. Jack's trombone and vocals always impressed me. He played "China Boy" and "Basin Street Blues," singing the lyrics in that tongue-slurring way of his. Jack always seemed to play without the slightest feeling of condescension and always seemed to be enjoying himself.

Ella Fitzgerald made a repeat appearance that year. She ran into a rhythm snag on a couple of numbers and expressed her temper by shaking her head and glaring at her accompaniment. It was all smoothed over by the time they reached "Air Mail Special," which she took at breakneck speed, ending in a note so high one felt like wincing. She dedicated her final number to Louis Armstrong, imitating his growly rasp on "I Can't Give You Anything but Love." The crowd loved it and gave her a tremendous ovation.

Friday afternoon some of the happiest moments occurred with Ruby Braff's octet, featuring clarinetist Peewee Russell. Ruby had said in his opening remarks, "No psychological or psychotic music . . . no fugues . . ." Peewee, looking frail and sensitive, played with a completely blues-rooted sound. The feeling that he projected when he soloed on "Nobody Else but You," playing in a low register, had a freshness and directness that touched the audience deeply.

Gigi Gryce's Jazz Laboratory, with Gigi on alto sax and Donald Byrd on trumpet, highlighted the afternoon. Donald moved easily, propelled by the hard-swinging Hank Jones on piano and the heavily charged drums of Osie Johnson, whose natural brilliance and spontaneity were as easygoing as the sound of his laughter. Osie and I used to talk at length about Big Sid Catlett, to me the epitome of all jazz drummers. Sid was also one of Osie's favorites.

I enjoyed the two accordion groups that performed.

Above. In a huddle beneath the stage, producer-entrepreneur Norman Granz (right) discusses some of the finer points of the music with Erroll Garner (center) and bandleader Stan Kenton. *Opposite: Top.* Waiting to join Armstrong in the festivities, trombonists (left to right) J. C. Higginbotham, Jack Teagarden, and Armstrong's trombonist Trummy Young. *Bottom.* Trumpeter Donald Byrd checks over the charts with Jazz Lab co-leader, altoist Gigi Gryce.

Both Leon Sash, a blind musician, and Mat Mathews, who played an Italian button instrument, provided an exciting change of pace, their instruments rarely being heard in a jazz context.

Friday evening opened with a six-piece group led by Bobby Hackett. The arrangements were quite different from Hackett's usual charts. Hackett did a stunning solo on "My Funny Valentine." The group played a mixed bag of styles and music, running the gamut from Ellington to Dixieland to Monk to an original written by pianist Dick Cary called "Handle with Cary." They played well. Unfortunately, the sound system amplified them as soloists and not in ensemble, leaving the audience to assemble the sounds in their heads. Not a very satisfying way to listen to music.

Carmen McCrae opened with the Festival theme song, "I'll Remember April." It had been played on five separate occasions during the Festival. Her rhythm section had arrived late, and subbing for them was the piano of Junior Mance with Jimmy Cobb on drums. Later she swung into a pulsating "Skyliner." Ray Bryant, her regular pianist, finally arrived with Specs Wright, her drummer, and with her husband, Ike Isaacs, on bass, she finished her set with a swinging "Perdido."

George Shearing sounded best when he linked up with the Adderley brothers, Cannonball and Nat, on "Nothing but D. Best," a piece named after his former drummer, Denzil De Costa Best.

Roy Eldridge on trumpet, Coleman Hawkins on tenor, and Pete Brown on alto played an interesting set. The Hawk was outstanding. But the topper, "Sweet Georgia Brown," was filled with a humorous exchange between Roy and drummer Jo Jones that reflected their exuberance, and encouraged by the audience, they moved into a series of flamboyant byplays that had everyone smiling.

Stan Kenton played an hour-long set that was enough to satiate the hunger for his music in the most ravenous adherent. It was a good chance to hear his new soloists,

Billie Holiday sometimes showed a tough exterior, but it seemed to be just a protective shell she had built up over the years to cover her own insecurities. *Left.* Lady prepares for her performance aided by her dresser. Later she lights a cigarette (*above*) and, with a uniquely feminine touch, adjusts her earring (*opposite*).

Lennie Niehaus on alto, Bill Perkins on tenor, Kent Larsen on trombone, and Sam Noto on trumpet. Stan mamboed up his theme, "Artistry in Rhythm," shifted gears on "23N,86W," and went on through the biting buildup of "Peanut Vendor."

Pianist Cecil Taylor's first appearance at the Festival was impressive. His group—Steve Lacey on soprano sax, Dennis Charles on drums, and Buell Neidlinger on bass—was one of the few that played contemporary sounds at the Festival. Taylor played a brief but exhilarating set and crowded into three numbers savage barbs and sharp bursts of energy that somehow seemed inappropriate, compared to all the mainstream music that dominated the Festival. I enjoyed the seldom-heard "Johnny Come Lately," written by Billy Strayhorn.

Most of the audience and critics were overwhelming in their praise for the Farmingdale (High School) Band of Long Island. The orchestra's director, Marshall Brown, had been hired to teach instrumental music. He persuaded the school to let him select the best musicians and form a jazz band. "I felt the standard band repertory was too limited and that we were ignoring the most important native music we Americans have," he said. Deriving arrangements from Basie and Woody Herman patterns, he gave the students a grounding in jazz history and the styles used by the jazz greats. The eighteen-piece orchestra, with members an average age of fourteen, played eight tunes. Nothing comparable had ever been heard in jazz. The complex big-band arrangements plus the age bracket of the individual soloists seemed to leave the audience in awe. The star of the orchestra was fourteen-year-old Andy Marsala on

Above. Backstage, like a monk in repose and prayer, Paul Desmond escapes the outside heat and glare of the sun.
Right. Andy Marsala (center), star altoist with the Farmingdale High School Orchestra, rehearses with other band members in the shade of the tent.

alto sax. John S. Wilson in the *New York Times* commented that Marsala "has already assimilated the style of Charlie Parker, and gave evidence in a well constructed solo on 'Ghost of a Chance' that he is beginning to create in terms that are no longer derivative."

The band was interrupted with frequent bursts of applause. "They obviously were the hit of the afternoon," said one of the trade papers.

Saturday night's two standouts were Billie Holiday and Mary Lou Williams. Billie Holiday made her final appearance at the Festival that year, and despite the desperate strained sound that was beginning to creep into her voice, I still couldn't hear her without getting a lump in my throat. Whenever she sang, I anticipated a sweet taste on my tongue. It never turned bitter. Billie could sing with richness of soul that surmounted whatever vocal quality was lacking.

Later in the program Mary Lou Williams, the legendary jazz pianist, appeared briefly with Dizzy's big band, playing several parts of her "Zodiac Suite," which she had introduced at Town Hall in the late forties.

The next day Mahalia Jackson stood on the stage, gazing thoughtfully at the audience, the bright Sunday afternoon sunlight reflecting off the warm browns of her skin. Her strong hands were pressed tightly together, fingertips touching. She momentarily closed her eyes. Everything around her seemed to be unimportant. And like the gulls circling the blue sky above, she too started to soar. Her presence and her voice produced an extraordinary afternoon of gospel music.

John Hammond, who had arranged for the gospel program to be held at the Festival, remembering Mahalia's appearance, said: "The Lorillards had arranged for Mahalia to sing at the Trinity Episcopal Church that

39

morning. It was the last bastion of Newport's high society. The concert was a sensation. It was the only time that the [Clara] Ward Singers sang on the same program with Mahalia. The Ward Singers were so great that Mahalia had to give her all. I never heard Mahalia sing better in my life. One year we had this religious afternoon at Freebody Park. Backstage Mahalia was storming at me, 'How dare you put me on the bill with Mama Ward, Gertrude Ward! I can't stand the woman [she used much more colorful language, I can assure you]. John, you've really put me into a terrible position.'

"I told Mahalia, 'You're so great that nothing can faze you.' I did as much soft-soaping as I could."

The Clara Ward Singers' guiding hand was Mrs. Gertrude Ward, mother of the group's leader. Clara (on piano and organ) provided the accompaniment for the group, which also included Mrs. Willa Ward Moultrie; Marion Williams, later to gain fame on her own, singing in a gospel musical based on Langston Hughes's verse, "Black Nativity"; Kathleen Parham; and Frances Steadman.

Starting with their theme song, "Meeting Tonight," they romped, kicked, clapped, and helped lay down some of the foundation stones of the movement—theatricality, twisting, turning steps—later adopted by rhythm and blues and rock music in the following decade. They continued with a solemn "The Lord's Prayer," sung by Mrs. Moultrie. Marion Williams followed with the spiritual "Swing Low, Sweet Chariot," climaxing with a swooping, shattering cry.

Reminiscing about their days on the road and the bandstands they once shared, two close friends, trumpeter Roy Eldridge and Lester Young, enjoy a few quiet moments away from the preparations around them. Roy warms up and enlivens the occasion with a well-remembered moment from the past. The sound of their laughter was beautiful to hear.

40

The Back Home Choir, with fifty members, sang en masse except for one solo number, "Let Me Touch the Hem of His Garment," by Charles Banks.

The Drinkard Singers from Newark, New Jersey, five girls and a boy, made a triumphant blending on "Everybody's Talkin' About Heaven" and had the audience in their palms with "That's Enough."

But it was Mahalia who dominated the afternoon. Her strong, vibrant voice surged out, and she sang every lyric as if she had written it herself. She gave it all depth and meaning and joy. She effortlessly moved with ecstasy and power from one song to another. Here and there she embellished and improvised. Sermonizing between numbers, she said, "Even rock and roll gets its spirit, power, and bounce from the church." The audience clapped, laughed, and sang along with her on numbers like "When the Saints Go Marching In" and sat hushed on "Never Walk Alone." During the afternoon she showed the similarity between "Sometimes I Feel Like a Motherless Child" and Gershwin's "Summertime." Mahalia summed it up in a *New York Post* interview:

"Why 'Summertime' is nothing but 'Sometimes I Feel Like a Motherless Child.' I'm taking nothing from Mr. Gershwin in saying that. Anybody with common sense over 40 years old knows what that came from."

Mahalia had sung thirteen songs that afternoon. The enraptured audience gave her a standing ovation. A blond woman standing in a box near me turned her smiling, rain-spattered face to her friend and said, "Tears of joy."

What the audience hadn't seen were the tears streaming down Mahalia's face as she hurried offstage.

Elaine Lorillard described Mahalia coming off the stage in tears after her performance. "Mahalia had seen the people drinking beer out in the park." It was obvious, Elaine said: "Beer cans everywhere and people drinking and sitting around those beer cans.

"I tried to approach her, and I asked her to come to my house after the concert. Mahalia just looked me straight in the eyes (she had the most beautiful eyes I'd ever seen—they were lavender) and said, 'Where is the ladies' room?'

"She was also angry that we were selling beer. She absolutely refused to sing anyplace where liquor was sold."

Mahalia had once turned down a ten-thousand-dollar offer to sing in a nightclub. "I can't be bothered with folks talking and drinking and listening only to themselves," she said solemnly.

Sunday evening opened with Jimmy Giuffre's group, but the late-arriving audience muffled the group's efforts. In the press pit we were able to hear the nuances of their music. Jim Hall on guitar was particularly impressive, and Jimmy on baritone, clarinet, and tenor melded with a beautifully integrated rhythm section that included Ralph Pena on bass. The group moved as one on the lovely "Train and the River" and projected a fresh, enthusiastic intensity on "Four Brothers."

The rest of the evening was all Basie's, particularly when he was joined by Lester Young and the buoyant vocalist Jimmy Rushing and Jo Jones on drums. On "Sent for You Yesterday" Jimmy and Pres exploded with a roar and spontaneity that kept pounding away, joyfully intense. Jimmy's enthusiasm drew a roar from the fans, and he came back for a brief encore.

"Louis was the source and the river," venerated trumpet star Rex Stuart once told me; "we [other jazz trumpeters] were just the tributaries and streams." Armstrong in a familiar pose shouts, *"Oh, yeah!"* Behind him clarinetist Edmond Hall smiles in assent.

43

Many of the musicians liked to be paid in cash at the end of the evening's performance. Here blues shouter Joe Turner counts his money as his accompanist, pianist Pete Johnson, looks on.

1958

The fanfare that preceded the 1958 Festival sounded like a continuous clap of thunder.

In typical ragtag fashion, the Festival catered to the radio, television, and film-production interests before considering the needs of the cash-paying jazz fans.

Each evening started at least half an hour before the originally scheduled time of eight thirty P.M., without previous announcement of time changes. People would walk into the grounds and find a concert in progress, with Ellington or Brubeck giving a brief rundown of what was being played at the Festival that evening for a radio broadcast. As one critic told me afterward, one wondered "what the hell was going on, and who was minding the store?"

The newspapers and wire services gave extensive coverage to the July Festival well in advance. In the middle of March there were pictures of George Wein at an airport, smiling ear to ear, with Marshall Brown, director of the Farmingdale High School Band, which had played at the 1957 Festival. They were off on a quest for the Holy Grail—the International Youth Band. "It's one of the most exciting jazz projects of all time," said Wein. "We thought this was one excellent way to spend some of our surplus." In May 1958 *Metronome* said of the forthcoming events: "The American Jazz Festival is beating the bushes of Europe, Asia, Africa, South America, and Australia for its musical jamboree over the July 4th weekend." The article described the activities in eighteen countries in the search for talent, noting that two of them were behind the Iron Curtain.

In response to the project Vice President Nixon stated in a letter to the Festival that it was "an outstanding example of what can be done by private citizens and groups in furtherance of the concept of 'people to people.' . . . I am sure that this will not only be a meaningful experience for the musicians involved but it will also symbolize the great interest in this form of artistic expression . . . shared . . . in all areas of the world."

One of the Festival press releases called for uniforms for the International Youth Band, including jackets of light blue, the color of the United Nations, with the flag of each musician's nation sewed on the breast pocket—presumably another way to spend surplus funds.

Efforts were also made to relieve some of the Festival's housing problems by bringing up a giant Mississippi River boat, the *Delta Queen.* Unfortunately, it was not available. "Person to Person" was also interested in doing a show from the Lorillard home in May, but technical problems prevented it.

New Yorker magazine compared the Festival to "a contented city dog grown sleeker and rounder."

No less than four record companies taped segments of the Festival. The welter of microphones, cables, tracking facilities for motion-picture cameras and dollies around the front of the stage, plus platforms with cameramen affixed on top of either end of the stage gave the Festival the look of the stage set for *Ben Hur.* Innumerable award ceremonies and presentations of plaques by trade magazines to musicians prolonged the discomfort of the audience, tightly packed on wooden folding chairs for hours on end.

The filming had been arranged by Elaine Lorillard. Jean Stein, daughter of Jules Stein, president of M.C.A., the giant booking corporation for musicians and entertainers, had suggested the film idea to photographer Bert Stern. Aram Avakian, George Avakian's brother, was brought in because he knew about jazz; Bert's agent came up with the money. Ansco had promised an experimental, fast positive-reversal 35-mm color stock. Later Ansco dropped out, and Bert's agent kept hustling up money as the bills came in. Aram Avakian told me in an interview: "We went up to Newport with ten thousand dollars to make a film short on the Festival. We ended up with a subjective documentary-feature of a public event, a new concept in the U.S. at the time.

"We went up with some free-lance documentary guys. Bert had shot some motion-picture footage. I had directed some documentary things before but had never handled a 35-mm camera. There were two other peripheral nonunion documentary workers. There were no full-fledged special cameramen around. Neither Bert nor I had ever done anything like this before."

George Avakian, music director for the film, told of the problems of filming: "The first night's filming turned out to be a fiasco. No one seemed to know what to do. Bert had never made a film before, and my brother got so upset that he ended up getting violently ill during the filming. Fortunately we were able to locate a doctor to take care of him. The morning of the second day Bert simply turned the filming over to Aram. Aram, as a film editor, decided what he wanted to get and moved on from there. He had two cameras on each end of the stage set on platforms, one camera on a dolly moving on a track in front of the stage, one camera out in the audience with a zoom lens, and two guys with hand-held cameras. It's an absolutely classic job of film cutting; Aram did the film cutting in his head as he shot it. There was only one chance to get the shots he wanted, since it was a live show. He had worked out a complicated method of communicating with the wing cameras

46

Three jazz figures who each made only one appearance at the festival. *Opposite, above.* Duke Ellington's alter ego, the late composer-arranger Billy Strayhorn. *Opposite, below.* Trumpeter Rex Stuart jots down some notes backstage. *Above.* Vibist Lem Winchester, a Wilmington, Delaware, policeman who moonlighted as a jazzman, finally left the police force and died playing Russian roulette.

with a mike, and runners to the other cameras when they weren't nearby."

One sidelight of the filming was clarinetist Tony Scott's Sunday afternoon performance with a quintet. As the act was not going to appear on film, the cameramen were relaxing around the stage with their cameras set up; they were going to be shooting someone else later on. After Tony had played briefly, he started a tirade, saying, "You guys with those cameras. You're interfering with us and you're interfering with the audience. You should realize that people are here to hear music, not to have you get in our way." Tony kept up his tirade between a couple of numbers, growing progressively more antagonistic. At first some of the audience was on Tony's side. Eventually they began to realize Tony's anger was a totally phony thing. After a while Tony said, "All right, all right. I'll leave it up to Father O'Connor. Father O'Connor, what should I do? Should I keep on playing?" Father O'Connor finally yelled, "Play." When the set finally ended and Tony climbed down the stairs, Miles Davis, standing in the wings, said, "What's the matter, Tony? They call you a nigger?"

Aram described putting the film together: "I came into New York City with over one hundred thousand feet of exposed negative color stock. We took it to a major lab in town. The lab wanted the business; things were slow. They assumed we had the money to pay for processing. They went ahead and processed it, and we got the work prints and started to cut them. We continued to shoot inserts at Bert's studio. It took several months for them to realize that we didn't have the money. We started to raise money based on the work print that we were cutting. We must have had about forty screenings to raise the money needed to get distribution. I used to cut specifically for screenings, staying up one time for seventy-two continuous hours in order to get it ready in time to show it to a particular distributor. What I objected to

47

mostly was the fact that Bert was saying that he had
directed it all by himself when in reality I directed at
least half of it. Bert took some of the performance close-
ups, but there was another cameraman taking them
also.''

Aram explained about getting releases from the musicians: ''We shot strictly on what I thought would pay off
as a sequence. We didn't try to get clearances in advance or try to concern ourselves with the clearances on
music. The basic premise was, if we get a terrific
sequence, then we'll go for the rights. No one refused
clearance. The only problem was the fee Louis
Armstrong received, twenty-five thousand dollars, and
the rights to ''Sweet Georgia Brown'' were also quite expensive. Obviously we couldn't have a film without
Louis. Louis and Mahalia in my mind were the climax of
the film.''

When the film *Jazz on a Summer's Day* was released
in 1960, among the worldwide comments was Kenneth
Tynan's in the *London Observer*—''The color photog-
raphy is breathtaking. The jazz itself is, to say the least,
eclectic.'' The *Boston Phoenix* called it ''an entertaining
film, but today it strikes a chord of melancholy nostalgia
for an era when Louis Armstrong was America's International Ambassador of Good Will, not an Uncle Tom. . . .''
Judith Crist, in *New York* magazine, called the film a
''perceptive document of a time and place, a vivid ad-
venture in sight and sound, a dazzling delight in
glorious color.'' The more sedate, music-hating *Illustrated London News* said, ''What I do actively dislike
about jazz and about jazz-films of this sort is the obliga-
tion to gaze upon the faces of the noticeably unlovely
people who seem to respond to it most—especially
those who take the stuff with alarming seriousness and
without a smile or a laugh. Jazz taken seriously is a
menace and a bore.''

48

Opposite, above. Jazz singer Anita O'Day checks some notes on her program. *Opposite, below.* A last glance in the mirror before going out to greet her sidemen (*above*), pianist Jimmy Jones and bassist Whitey Mitchell.

Dick Katz, a fine jazz pianist, reviewing it for *Jazz Review* magazine said: "A requisite for enjoying this film is that one not be a jazz devotee. Although it is a semi-documentary of the 1958 Newport Festival, the music in it, what little quality there was, functions mainly as a prop for spectacular visual effects. . . . I came away from the theatre feeling that jazz was once again the butt of a bad joke, and as a jazz musician, I felt I indirectly had been had."

One of the comments in the trade was, "You know, the picture was so good I'd rather go to the movie than go to the Festival."

The first evening of the Festival was devoted ostensibly to the music of Duke Ellington. A group of Duke's alumni played a set of standards associated with themselves as sidemen with Ellington. *Down Beat* described the performance as of "more historical than musical significance."

They played "Concerto for Cootie," "C Jam Blues," "Boy Meets Horn," "Chelsea Bridge," "Le Grand Romp," and "Perdido." Bassist Oscar Pettiford played beautifully, but *Down Beat* remarked, "Sonny Greer's inconsistency [on drums] marred the performance."

Later on, Miles Davis made an appearance with a remarkable group composed of John Coltrane on tenor, Cannonball Adderley on alto, Bill Evans on piano, Paul Chambers on bass, and Jimmy Cobb on drums. The group played no Ellington tunes. Asked backstage why he had not played some Ellington music, Miles replied that he thought that performing familiar material effectively would be the best tribute.

Joe Morello, Dave Brubeck's smashing drummer, was the standout with that group. One critic facetiously called the group the Joe Morello Quartet. Both Brubeck and his altoist, Paul Desmond, seemed subdued, and as a trade paper stated later, "Paul occasionally reached the heights to which he can go. Brubeck is obviously being brought into line by Morello's drumming, although it would be wrong to say that Dave swings more now than he used to."

Duke Ellington took over the rest of the evening, introducing two new numbers, "El Gato" ("The Cat"), suggested by his high-note specialist on trumpet, Cat Anderson, and "Multi-Color Blue," written by Duke and Billy Strayhorn. Duke, having just arrived in the U.S. after an extended world tour, looked tired. Shortly before the concert started, he walked onstage and improvised a few bars on the piano, ostensibly to find out what the damp weather had done to it. Duke had started the evening earlier with a pickup group for the CBS radio broadcast, playing "Princess Blue," a number he had dedicated to Princess Margaret. Duke said, "I won't take the time to describe it, but I hope you'll enjoy it."

Quincy Jones, later reviewing the recorded results of the evening for *Jazz Review* magazine, remarked, " 'Jazz Festival Jazz' sounds like something Tom Whaley [Duke's copyist] whipped up when he was asleep on the bus on the way to Newport. I don't think this kind of program as a whole, by the way, indicates that Duke is putting on Newport. If he had the time, he'd do it well. . . . but musically, this is the outside of the band. They didn't let the people all the way in. And yet it is a fantastic band."

Mahalia Jackson appeared at the end of Duke's set to sing the "Come Sunday" segment of "Black, Brown, and Beige." It took a few minutes for Duke to find the right introductory music suitable for her appearance. Mahalia was introduced by pop singer Frankie Laine. Despite the uncertain start Mahalia and Duke blended beautifully together. The *New York Times* reported that they "poured out a rousing version of 'Keep Your Hand on the Plow' with Mr. Ellington's brass section crying exultantly through dry mutes behind her."

Duke's band demonstrated succinctly the roots of jazz in gospel music. At one twenty-five A.M. Duke Ellington announced, "Nothing follows Mahalia Jackson." The tired audience seemed relieved.

50

Newport ambience had a way of throwing old friends and acquaintances together. Miles Davis greets Dinah Washington warmly while her husband, former football star Night Train Lane, stands in the background. Whatever Dinah said broke Miles up completely.

Backstage, Mahalia said after the concert, "I had been worried all day about my appearance with a jazz band. If the Duke wasn't so great, I never would have done it."

The next evening opened with a CBS radio broadcast that necessitated some tiring stage waits. During the time allotted for commercials there was absolutely nothing going on onstage. The poor fans sitting in the concrete reaches of the park had suffered quite enough through the years from bad sound. This time they understandably expressed anger at the delays and started to boo and shout. The master of ceremonies told them, "You have to sit in the five-dollar seats in order to boo."

The second evening had been planned as a Benny Goodman night. The musicians in his band were not thrilled with playing the old arrangements. One told me, "You always played the same things with him. We wanted to play something different, but it didn't work out that way. It wasn't really a set band. We weren't working for him every week, you know. Who cared? We rehearsed from five fifteen to six and then from eight thirty to eleven. That's probably what put the crimp in it. We had rehearsed for three days prior to going up to Newport. The band was well juiced by the time they got on the stand. It was mostly the fact that the band didn't want to play the same old things."

"It was a good band," another sideman told me, "but it was like you were chained to the same old arrangements."

"During the radio-broadcast portion of the program," one of the sidemen told me, "one of the trombonists kept making a razzing noise every time Goodman counted off the tempo."

The *Providence Journal* said, "Last night Benny Goodman rolled his hips in a fashion which might have made Elvis Presley jealous and seemed to get a genuine boot out of the music of his band. That is until one of

51

his bandsmen had the misfortune to blow a couple of notes off-key—then the old Benny Goodman returned. Even though his back was to the audience you could feel the glare."

Metronome magazine said of the evening, "It was tedious in the extreme. . . . It took a mighty strong need to reminisce to accept dance band sets and early-1940 dance band arrangements so written that seven brass and five reeds sounded like five brass and four reeds."

Down Beat said, "The Benny Goodman Band made mincemeat of Benny Goodman night. His playing was quite erratic in sound."

The *New Yorker* called the band "ragged and dispirited . . . he played nervously and off pitch."

Surmounting the rest of the evening's raggedness was the Teddy Wilson Trio, which played a finely balanced set. Martha Tilton later joined the Goodman band to sing "And the Angels Sing," but some clinkers from the trumpet section marred her performance. Jimmy Rushing sang "I'm Coming Virginia" and George Fraser's witty "Harvard Blues," and he did a duet with Martha Tilton on "A Fine Romance."

Goodman returned with his quartet to play a good Gershwin set, with pianist Roland Hanna outstanding on "Lady Be Good." The group rocketed through "I've Got Rhythm." Some of the audience started to dance in the aisles, à la the Paramount days, on "Sing, Sing, Sing," and the evening ended early at eleven thirty P.M. An unscheduled event during the evening was the birth of a baby in the far reaches of the audience, while the Goodman band performed.

"Rock and Roll came to Newport at Saturday evening's concert, and fared a bit better than some of the more legitimate presentations," was the way *Down Beat* described the next evening. The *New Yorker* chose to ignore the blues evening entirely in their review.

John Hammond talked about the presentation at length in a recent interview: "The Newport police were

Opposite, above. There was a tenseness backstage in the musicians' tent before the Goodman band went on. Benny sat by himself, warming up, until he asked trumpeter Bernie Glow (rear) to join him.
Opposite, below. Bandleader Benny Goodman smiles as his former vocalist Martha Tilton joins the band onstage.
Above. Outstanding that evening was the beautifully balanced set of pianist Teddy Wilson.

particularly terrified about crowds on Saturday night. I had insisted that we have my two favorite R.B. singers, Chuck Berry and Big Maybelle. I also liked Dinah [Washington], but Dinah was still more commercial than that. I knew that this might be a little rougher than anything that Newport had previously encountered. And so Chuck arrived in town with sort of a purple Cadillac with a couple of white chicks. This was quite a thing to start with. And Big Maybelle, who was monstrous-looking but absolutely the best. Just the best blues singer around. Chuck was asked—not by me, but specifically by George Wein—not to gyrate. They didn't want to have any bumps and grinds. That's a bit like asking Tempest Storm not to wiggle. This was a different kind of band than Chuck had worked with in the past. I thought that might calm him down, but it didn't. They started dancing in the aisles, and the police were frantic. Big Maybelle was pretty raunchy, but the best! As a matter of fact, she cut Dinah to shreds that night. We really had a blues night. It was the first time Newport recognized rough vocal blues. I was not terribly popular with the board. Two of those sequences are the highlights of *Jazz on a Summer's Day.* I think that night made history and also got us ejected from Freebody Park."

The Newport Blues Band accompanied Chuck Berry and Big Maybelle. They included Jack Teagarden on trombone, Lennie Johnson and Buck Clayton on trumpets, Georgie Auld and Buddy Tate on tenors, Rudy Rutherford on clarinet, Tom Bryant on bass, Pete Johnson on piano, and Jo Jones on drums. Chuck at one moment, singing "School Days," started to skip across the stage with his guitar in hand. He was jerked to an abrupt halt when he ran out of guitar cord.

Joe Turner, better known in jazz circles, sang opposite the blues band. He swung out with "Let the Good Times Roll," "Corina, Corina," "Honey Hush," and "Shake, Rattle and Roll." The crowd loved his last number, which was more rhythm-and-blues oriented, and gave him an ovation.

53

Above. French pianist Bernard Peiffer introduces his daughter to the world of jazz at Newport. *Opposite.* Duke watches his orchestra closely center stage as great gospel singer Mahalia Jackson steps to the microphone uneasily aware that beer was being sold in the park around her.

Elaine Lorillard said later that some of the audience were appalled that rock and roll was to be part of the program. They had demanded their money back and they received it. "My husband, Louis, and I thought it only fair that they do."

Bassist Bill Crow reviewed the recorded performance of Ray Charles at the Festival that evening for *Jazz Review* magazine: "Here is another performance of Ray Charles doing what he does best: singing the blues. . . . Without the restriction of juke box length, and with a fascinated audience to draw him out, Ray . . . builds up a cumulative message in the best tradition of southern Negro preaching."

"Mahalia Jackson was genuinely religious," said MC Willis Conover. "She felt that there should not be a mixing of secular and jazz music. Her problem was solved when the evening's [jazz] concert ended at fifteen minutes to midnight on a Saturday night. I announced at one minute past midnight, 'Ladies and gentlemen, the world's greatest gospel singer, Miss Mahalia Jackson.' "

Mahalia started her concert with "Dear Lord, Forgive." She held that audience through the intermittent rain that fell, had them handclapping on "Didn't It Rain," and won them. They clapped, sang along, cheered, and solemnized with her on "The Lord's Prayer." The audience pressed against the barrier fence near the box seats, and she brought the crowd to a cheering, foot-stamping ovation. When Mahalia came back, responding to her audience, she said humbly, "You make me feel like a star." "I'm just getting warmed up," she said then, following with three more selections. They didn't want to let her go, despite the torrent of rain falling on them when the concert ended at one thirty A.M.

"An interracial crowd took advantage of the invitation given at the concert to hear Miss Jackson Sunday morning," said the local paper. The next morning crowds were at the Mount Zion AME Church, located behind the old Jewish Cemetery off Bellevue Avenue, where Judah

Touro lies buried. They arrived an hour early to hear her sing a program of gospel music. The Reverend Alvin J. Simmons opened the morning service but omitted his sermon to give her more time to sing. The congregation was completely enthralled.

Some of the afternoon concerts had much more content than the evening affairs. Outstanding were John LaPorta's group. His bassist, Dick Carter, had trouble with a broken string, and his bass fell over and was damaged. A replacement was brought up, and they swung through four originals. Reedman LaPorta seemed to swing from an inner necessity, and although under Bird's influence, he spoke fluently. His solos moved with fervor. The group played with a freshness and directness that was lacking in more widely known ensembles.

Pianist Thelonious Monk's afternoon set was urbane and witty. He played only a brief four numbers but made telling statements in each of them. The beautifully swinging Roy Haynes on drums with Henry Grimes on bass made intricate statements and were continually compelling. There was always something going on. Monk left the stage with the audience crying for more, more!

Anita O'Day had told Elaine Lorillard backstage, "This Festival is better than Jesus Christ." She appeared in a wide-brimmed black and white hat, a chic black dress, and white gloves. She sang "Boogie Blues," "S'Wonderful," a roaring, witty "Sweet Georgia Brown," and Miles Davis's "Four." Her set was full of laughs and hard-driving accompaniment with the ornamental structure of Jimmy Jones's piano doing more than keeping up with her changes. Jimmy compressed, heightened, and wove a tapestry of sounds behind her, nicely accented by Whitey Mitchell on bass.

The International Youth Band played a mixed bag of arrangements by Adolphe Sandole, John LaPorta, Jimmy Giuffre, Bill Russo, and Marshall Brown, its director. Opening with Brown's "Don't Wait for Henry," they

seemed to lack a cohesiveness, although there was some good solo work by Bernt Rosengren of Sweden on tenor, Hans Salomon from Austria on alto, and Roger Guerin of France and Dusko Gojkovic from Yugoslavia on trumpets. Hidden away in the band with nary a comment from a reviewer was the guitar of the most famous musician to finally emerge from that band, Gabor Szabo, a Hungarian expatriate. John Mehegen, in the *New York Herald Tribune,* suggested that ''perhaps Mr. Brown could have strived for a broader emotional spectrum of collective expression which could have compensated for the lack of individual virtuosity in the band.''

John S. Wilson, in the *New York Times,* also observed that ''solo improvisation did not appear to be one of their strong points.''

William Russo, who worked with the band and arranged for them, wrote angrily to *Jazz Review* magazine: ''The band was a good band. Whatever problems it had were connected with the nature of the project and particularly with the limitations of the players themselves, who had difficulty in ensemble playing (no European band player gets our jazz band background) and in their improvising.''

John Hammond commented on the International Youth Band: ''The only problem was that Marshall Brown was not the most inspiring leader in the world. The International Youth Band was a problem because they were mostly professional musicians. It wasn't a youth band. It was an international band of all-stars.

''They didn't like to be treated like high school students by Marshall Brown and there was fantastic resentment from the Yugoslav, and from the British, and from the other people who were in this band. All of them could outblow Marshall. He may have been fine in Farmingdale, but he was a disaster as a leader of both of those bands. That's my frank opinion. Marshall's heart

Left. Pres casts a long shadow in the direction of Miles Davis. Two giants of jazz who never played together, coming from different generations in jazz, they nevertheless have great respect for each other's virtuosity. Here they share a musical thought.

Opposite, left. Jimmy Giuffre waits nervously on the steps leading to the stage. *Opposite, above.* A warm afternoon rehearsal onstage with altoist John La Porta (center) and his rhythm section. *Opposite, below.* Members of the International Jazz Band wait to mount the stage with MC Willis Conover. *Above.* The second Newport stage bedecked with banners, and the press and fans waiting for this widely publicized event.

was very much in the right place, but he was no inspiration to any real improvising jazzmen.''

The final total cost for the band was fifty thousand dollars.

Max Roach became the house drummer of the evening, first playing a long, extended set with his own group, then mixing it up with Dinah Washington, Urbie Green (trombone), and Terry Gibbs (vibes). His appearance with his own group was marked by the mastery he'd been displaying since the middle forties, when he became the drummer most in demand by the bop groups then recording. During the evening he played tight incandescent patterns and seemed to get to the core of what great jazz drumming is all about.

Backstage I had watched Max set up his drums and, like sharpening a finely honed blade, tune himself up for a couple of hours before his actual appearance. The crowd of observers around me backstage was composed of all the drummers playing the Festival that evening. It was a tribute to the mastery he had long displayed. Max has the ability to make every beat an important assertion without overpowering or overdramatizing. However, when he played an extended solo with his group, patrons in one of the higher-priced boxes out front did not receive or appreciate his message; they raised sticks with white handkerchiefs in the air and waved them feebly as a gesture of surrender.

Dinah sang well in a set that included "Lover Come Back to Me" and three blues songs of Bessie Smith's— among them "Backwater Blues." She later joined Terry Gibbs on vibes, plunking away with a pair of mallets beside him.

Louis Armstrong, aside from his "Tom" jokes and bad-taste announcements, played superbly.

Sunday evening's was the longest of all the Festival concerts. Starting at eight P.M. for radio broadcast, it ended at two A.M., six hours later.

59

1959

The 1959 Festival opened with three full-fledged lawsuits. The first suit maintained that Elaine Lorillard had conceived the idea of presenting the Festival in Newport "late in 1953 and that her estranged husband, Louis Lorillard, agreed to compensate her for conceiving, promoting and working for the Festival, at such time as the defendant showed a profit in its operations. She declared that she was ousted as a director of the corporation and from the duties she performed for the defendant at a board meeting December 5, 1958, which she contends was illegal in that proper five days' notice of the meeting was not given to board members." The second suit involved the publicity director, Russell Jalbert, regarding payment for his work on publicity.

The third suit involved payment for a fashion show presented the year before.

The four weather-perfect days attracted more than jazz listeners to the Festival. An article in the *Providence Journal* mentioned two hearses on the scene. One, from Connecticut, was loaded with teen-agers and college kids. The police halted it and confiscated five cases of beer and a life preserver from the Jamestown ferry. When the police finally released them, the group proceeded to speed up and down the streets of Newport, blowing their horn and shouting, "Have respect for the dead!" (The other hearse belonged to Jimmy Smith, the jazz organist. It carried his trio, electric organ, electric guitar, amplifiers, assorted speakers, and wiring equipment. After Jimmy did his afternoon set, he left for another engagement as soon as he had carefully packed it all back into the plush-lined interior of the vehicle.)

Thursday evening the usual mike trouble developed, but the sound problems did not seem to bother clarinetist Peewee Russell as he took a long solo and a few choruses on "Wrap Your Trouble in Dreams," accompanied by Buck Clayton on trumpet, Bud Freeman on tenor, and Vic Dickinson on trombone. Peewee always played with a simple eloquence that heightened the emotions of his listeners. Ruby Braff on trumpet and Jimmy Rushing, the great blues singer, joined the group for "St. Louis Blues," and they carried the drive over to "I'm Gonna Sit Right Down and Write Myself a Letter." Ruby seemed to goad Buck, and the final choruses filled the stage with driving power and warmth. Ray Bryant on piano played exuberantly and added a vitality and blues-rooted feeling that complemented the rest of the group beautifully.

The Four Freshmen followed. They seemed quite out of place at the Festival, and the fans didn't give them much response.

Down Beat summed up the evening: "And what could be crueler than putting the brilliant Lambert-Hendricks-Ross singers on the same program with the Four Freshmen?"

George Shearing with his new fifteen-piece band didn't come off much better when comparisons were made with the other band scheduled for the evening, Count Basie. The Shearing band was put together with New York studio musicians. A trade paper called the band and its arrangements "warmed-over Claude Thornhill."

Vibist Milt Jackson, with borrowed guitar, tries his hand at strings instead of mallets accompanied by bassist Percy Heath. There were looks of delight and surprise all around the tent as Milt picked away.

"Aside from the bass work of Israel Crosby, the Ahmad Jamal trio sounded like good cocktail music," said the trade papers. What the press seemed not to notice was the difficulty of a group playing the type of music Jamal created, the little figures and nuances that get lost in the context of an outdoor setting.

At twelve fifteen A.M., when Count Basie played his first four bars, the audience suddenly came alive. They rose and pressed toward the snow-fence barrier until the cracking of wood was heard, but the police were able to settle them down. Vocalist Joe Williams joined the band with a rousing welcome from the fans. He warmed the cool night air with his popular versions of "Shake, Rattle and Roll" and "All Right, Okay, You Win." Joe was followed by Lambert, Hendricks and Ross, singing with the Basie Band. Following Joe must have been difficult, but the trio pulled it off successfully in their first appearance at the Festival. They opened with "It's Sand, Man," and by the time they got to Horace Silver's "Doodling," the crowd refused to let them go; they were dancing in the aisles when Joe Williams joined them for his hit, "Every Day." Basie finally swung into a few bars of "One O'clock Jump," and the evening ended.

As the members of England's Johnny Dankworth Orchestra pulled into the backstage area and as the band members descended from their bus in the backstage area, the manager clapped his hands together briskly, calling out like a schoolmaster, "Chaps! Chaps! Don't separate!"

Friday evening the Johnny Dankworth Orchestra from England swung and played cohesively, sparked by some good solos by Johnny on alto sax. The band played well because of its leader, who also was its chief writer and arranger. "The ensemble work was excellent," the newspapers reported.

The other outstanding group, and the peak performance of the evening, was Thelonious Monk's. Arriving at Newport late, he had not had time to get his press

Opposite. A tired-looking Gene Krupa dresses for his appearance. *Above.* Ramsey Lewis's rhythm section, drummer Marcel Fournier and Israel Crosby, pause for the press.

badge at Festival headquarters. He was prevented from entering. Monk paced up and down by the gate, trying to convince the guards to let him in. "Man, I've got to play!" He was finally identified by someone at the gate and admitted.

Pianist Erroll Garner opened Saturday evening to a pretty bare press section. A report in the *Newport Daily News* explained later that Garner had become shy about flashbulbs after he had been involved in a traffic accident a few years earlier in which blinding lights were a factor. "For the first time in Festival history photographers will be banned from the forestage area, at Garner's request. They may presumably shoot from afar with telephoto lenses." Backstage there were irritated complaints from the press. Later the Festival issued a letter to the press explaining Garner's request and apologizing for the confusion that resulted from the Festival's overzealous interpretation of the request.

Duke Ellington was the Festival peak in 1959. The critics kept saying that this was a comeback for him. (Every year seemed to be reported as a comeback.) In any case Duke's band was continually compelling. From "Idiom '59," a new composition, the band swung into his newly created score for the film *Anatomy of a Murder.* One of the numbers from the film score was "Flirty Bird." Altoist Johnny Hodges played magnificently. His solo was a gorgeous assault on the senses, reaching both the heart and the mind. Duke also made interesting use of two drummers in tandem, Sam Woodyard and Jimmy Johnson, and they rocked the field with "Skin Deep." Jimmy Rushing joined them to sing some blues that energized even the press section to "finger popping and head rolling,'' as one of the trade papers described it. People started to dance in the aisles as the evening closed.

Among afternoon highlights was the jazz ballet performed at the Rogers High School auditorium. It was described in the program as a reinterpretation of the Harlequin, Pantaloon, Pierrot, and Columbine story in the manner of the Renaissance commedia dell'arte. It featured Leon James and Albert Minns, who had provided one of the best afternoon events the year before, a demonstration of jazz dance with a lecture by Dr. Marshall Stearns. They worked within the confines of a five-hundred-dollar budget and used the recorded sounds of the Modern Jazz Quartet playing ''Fontessa'' and ''Rose Truck.'' Utilizing American jazz and Latin steps in their roles, they moved from cakewalk through Charleston, lindy hop, into mambo, cha-cha, and rock and roll.

On Sunday afternoon the Charlie Mingus Quintet was changed to a quartet. Vibist Teddy Charles had decided to take his boat from City Island, New York, in order to avoid the traffic; he had to wire from Guilford, Connecticut, that he had been becalmed there.

A good gospel program was presented that afternoon. It did not include Mahalia Jackson. She had to cancel out because of adverse criticism about playing a jazz festival. Sitting in the audience was a teen-ager, Dionne Warwicke. Her mother was performing with one of the

Opposite. Behind the stage George Shearing sits and listens to the sounds all around him with wife Trixie and blues singer Jimmy Rushing in the background. *Above.* Old friends from their days with Count Basie greet each other warmly: (left to right) Jimmy Rushing, trumpeter Buck Clayton, a beaming Helen Humes, guitarist Freddie Green and his wife.

gospel groups. She would be performing there as a star in a few years herself.

Sunday evening the only fire, quickly extinguished, came from a flag at the top of the shell that had wrapped itself around a floodlight.

MC Willis Conover read a telegram from Louis Armstrong, who had fallen ill in Rome. His doctor had told him not to attend "because I'm unable to blow up a storm."

Willis's second special duty that evening was to request everyone in the audience to light a match and hold it aloft in honor of two great jazzmen who had died that year, Sidney Bechet and Lester Young.

Monk had further tribulations on his ferry ride home. Monk's car was the last to board the Jamestown ferry. One of his group said, "I hope we don't have any trouble reaching the other side." Monk assured him, "Nothing ever happens on these trips." Moments later the ferry stopped while the crew hurried around checking the problem. It turned out to be Monk's car, parked on a pin that controlled the steering.

In August 1959 headlines announced that the Festival was considering plans to move. The city council was dunning the Festival for payment for police and other services.

Local papers reported: "Lorillard said he was appalled that a discussion on immediate payment came before the council. He recalled that the council had praised the jazz festival in the past for bringing in so much new business to Newport. One estimate of this financial influx was $1,000,000."

1960

Success of a sort had come to Newport and the Jazz Festival. For a number of years now, the college crowd had made Newport the "in" place to be for the July Fourth weekend. The kids had planned all year for the big weekend at Newport. They came to drink, raise hell, and release their inhibitions. It was a substitute for panty raids and had replaced the Ft. Lauderdale beach scene in spring.

They started drinking as soon as they got into "Dad's car," and they supplemented their cases of beer and bottles of booze with new supplies from the liquor stores in town. The greedy town merchants didn't care how old they were as long as they had the money to pay.

Item: July 6, 1959 (Providence Journal)

"Sunday morning at 1:00 A.M. one liquor store was open and selling beer and liquor to what appeared to be college age boys. An attendant was asked, 'What time do you close?' He replied, 'When they stop buying.'

"Asked when that would be he answered, 'It was 2 o'clock last night and I hear it's 5 o'clock this morning.' "

Obviously there seemed to be little policing of packaged-goods stores in town. It was nothing new. It had been happening for years.

In mid-June 1960 Governor Christopher Del Sesto of Rhode Island warned that the state would insist on compliance with liquor laws during the Festival, especially in regard to closing hours. The city manager, George E.

Bisson, retorted, "Of course the laws will be enforced. Who said they wouldn't? The answer is quite obvious."

Underage drinking was not a new problem to Newport. One of the local newspapers had published a five-column headline on the front page on July 17, 1954: "Tavern Loses License for Serving Teenagers." Drinking was only part of the problem. The town had very few hotels and only a couple of motels.

Item: July 17, 1954 (Providence Bulletin)

"Newport Jazz Fans Jammed Hotels, Cleaned Out Kitchens, Slept on Beach."

The Festival itself didn't help the situation. The Kiwanis organization handled the refreshment stands inside the park. They sold beer to one and all.

Item: July 6, 1959 (Providence Bulletin)

"The wild drinking, brawling, and 24-hour reveling was done mainly by college age and high school age youths who plainly paid no attention to the music at Freebody Park and never appeared at any session not held under cover of darkness. The beer stands in the park on busy nights sold approximately one bottle of beer per person at the Festival—about 2,000 bottles an hour at 50 cents each—but most of the buying was done by the few thousand young people who paid little attention to the music."

Producer George Wein's right-hand man, Charlie Bourgeois, greets Dave Brubeck and part of his quartet as they arrive at Freebody Park: (left to right) Drummer Joe Morello, Charlie Bourgeois, Dave Brubeck, and altoist Paul Desmond.

Item: July 6, 1959 (Newport Daily News)

"But the problems of handling thousands of young people roaming the streets, many with no intention of going to the Festival, were greater than ever before and an entirely new phase in this sixth annual event. Many were rude, raucous and aggressive, although in general they were only seeking an exuberant outlet for youthful energies.

"The worst jam developed Saturday night on Middleton Avenue outside the gates, when a mob estimated at more than 3,000 surged back and forth before the ticket windows. Police finally massed their cruiser cars and motorcycles in a flying wedge, pushing the crowd back into Memorial Boulevard amid a shower of beer cans.

"At no time during the weekend did the situation get entirely out of hand, thanks to a splendid display of patience and cool-headedness by police, whose nerves were worn ragged. Only a spark would have been needed to reverse the general good humor of the drunken youngsters, but police prevented the spark from igniting."

Through the years the Festival programs were growing to be gargantuan. One critic told me, "George Wein thinks that he's the only one who knows what's right for the Festival. He won't listen to anyone!" The many hours of music included artists with no relationship to jazz. "People like Eartha Kitt, the Kingston Trio, Pat Suzuki, just don't belong here," one of the sidemen at the Festival told me. And this lowering of critical standards in the selection of artists appearing there attracted the wrong kind of listener. It gave the Festival a carnival atmosphere.

I queried one prominent board member, John Hammond, about the feasibility of including jazz musicians on the advisory panel. He said, "It's awfully dangerous to leave it entirely to musicians. A lot of these musicians work as sidemen on dates and so on. They can't be entirely trusted to be unbiased in the situation. I think you have to have people who are genuinely enthusiastic."

But the suggestion was noted in George Wein's column in one of the Boston newspapers: "Two weeks ago I asked for helpful suggestions from the critics and musicians alike concerning the possibility of having an auxiliary board of musicians who would have a voice on the board of directors of the Newport Jazz Festival. The idea was to create a board of seven or nine musicians which would meet two or three times a year and discuss the wants or needs of the musicians at Newport. The board would consist of many varied types of musicians and would have a non-musician, non-voting chairman." Needless to say, nothing ever came of it. Nat Hentoff asked in his *Jazz Review* column later, "So when is the first meeting, George?"

The Festival was cramming too many big-name artists onto the programs, ostensibly to attract people to the concerts. It gave little help to musicians who did not have high-powered booking agents with publicity organizations and large influential record companies behind them. Newer and lesser-known musicians were relegated to the morning or afternoon programs, which usually produced the best music but which were also the most poorly attended. Some of the board members were used strictly for name value, having little or no interest at all in jazz. Many never attended the Festival or a board meeting.

One of the former directors said of his connection with the Festival: "I had taken some out-of-town friends to the Festival to show them what it was all about. When we had sat through one of the evening's first performances, we wandered over to get a beer and hot dog. In order to arrive at the refreshment-stand area, we were forced to walk through ankle-deep muck from the previous night's rainfall, and as we passed the outdoor sanitary outhouses, a trough leading from them was

Poet Langston Hughes relaxes backstage, warming himself from the cool night air amid a clutter of instruments.

dumping right into the walking area. We got soaked in filth to our ankles."

"Did you ever do anything about it?" I inquired.

"Well," he replied lackadaisically, "I rarely went to board meetings or concerts."

The idea seemed to be to get as many people as possible to come to the Festivals. It didn't matter much that some major artists appeared five years in a row. It didn't seem to matter much if those attending the Festival had to sit on wooden chairs for six hours at a stretch.

In 1958 the Festival's public-relations firms noted: "We are planning to issue specially designed nontransferrable press passes to the people from the press attending the Festival. This coverage will be limited, if possible, to only 150 people from all media, with strict controls on attendance." The Newport papers that year noted that 700 press people were in attendance.

As the Festival stretched out in attendance, commercialism, and programing, the crowd seemed to burgeon forth too, with more raucous, destructive behavior. The eighty-man Newport police force coped as best they could but were entirely ineffective when it came to controlling a doubling of the population of Newport at Festival time.

Over the years incidents occurred in greater and greater number and seriousness:

Item: July 6, 1957 (*Providence Bulletin*)

"A few battle casualties resulted from last night's hullabaloo. Police and ushers again rode herd on fence jumpers, confiscating numerous bottles and cartons of beer being lugged in the gate, and broke up several packs of revelers who were bent on getting their jazz kicks in a physical way."

Dusk, and a final re-
hearsal of the Newport
Youth Band. Sitting
stage front, the band
director Marshall Brown.
Beside him, leaning on
the piano, trumpeter
Louis Mucci.

Item: July 7, 1958 (Newport Daily News)

"During the Saturday afternoon concert . . . a few college boys gathered on the dividing grass strip opposite Middletown Avenue. . . . The young men were soon joined by male and female chums. . . . Cases of beer, cans and bottles, materialized and were put to efficient use. . . . The merrymakers festooned trees with the empty tins and stuck bottles into the parkway flowerbeds. . . . As the afternoon concert broke up, the crowd on the grass plot swelled to several hundred. . . . The affair was all in the spirit of fun and the participants were not acting maliciously.

"However, it became obvious that matters had gone a bit too far. Police moved in en masse and broke up the shindig. . . . On orders of Acting Police Chief Radice, no more partying in the streets was allowed."

And so with all of these forces developing over the years, a number of new problems arose in 1960.

The Lorillards had been involved in a divorce action in 1959. Elaine Lorillard was suing the Festival for $100,000. "I didn't sue the Festival in the beginning," she explained in an interview. "I had no intention of it. A lawyer friend of mine told me [the meeting in which she was ousted as a director] was illegal. I was not officially notified of the meeting. A couple of other board members were not officially notified. Marshall Brown called me and said, 'You better get down there because they're having a secret meeting and you will be ousted.' I showed up and upset everybody because they thought they had it all beautifully planned. My lawyer said to them, 'All Elaine is asking for now is for you to acknowledge her place in the Festival and keep her on as an honorary person.' I did not ask for money at that time and did not threaten to sue. That was refused. Marshall Brown was the only member of the board who tried to prevent this. He tried to help me, and he did let me know about the meeting, which could have jeopardized his position with the Festival."

A former board member who attended the meeting told me later that Elaine's husband, Louis, had stood up and said that he could not serve on the board if his wife continued on it as a member. There was a heated debate, much recrimination, and finally Elaine tearfully rushed upstairs to seek refuge. The meeting broke up hurriedly after a vote was taken to disfranchise Elaine. It was a foregone conclusion; all the money guarantees for the Festival came from Louis Lorillard.

Elaine Lorillard told me that she ended up with about seven thousand dollars, barely enough to take care of the legal fees for her suit. The newspapers erroneously reported later a figure of forty thousand dollars made in settlement. Mrs. Lorillard stated that figure was her share in the sale of their jointly owned New York apartment. The seven thousand dollars came from her husband, she told me, not from the Festival.

"Elaine is bitter at me," John Hammond told me later. "I didn't care about either of the egos of the Lorillards. I cared about the future of jazz. Therefore, I voted in the best interests of the music. Elaine has suffered terribly not being connected with the Festival. I only wish she were back on the advisory board of the New York Festival, not that she would want to be on anything as commercial as the New York Festival."

Two jazz festivals opened on the night of June 30, 1960. (Some joker at police headquarters opened a third as well. There was a sign on the wall that said Jazz Festival, with an arrow pointing in the direction of the cell block.) The rebel festival, as the newspapers referred to it, was reported in the local papers as "the sound heard round the block." Freebody Park, site of the main event, was only a few blocks away.

71

Mrs. Lorillard described how the second festival came about: "In 1960 Nat Hentoff called me from New York and said that Charlie Mingus and Max Roach were fed up with the Festival. They said they didn't believe in the idea of it. I went to Cliff Walk Manor and spoke to the owner, Nicholas Cannarozzi [about having an independent festival there with Mingus and Roach]. He was delighted with the idea and very cooperative. It was a lovely setting, right beside the ocean. We were going to have this marvelous publicity. All these musicians sleeping in tents, the way it really should be, except Charlie Mingus and Max Roach slept in the hotel. They were photographed putting their own stakes in for the tents. It was beautiful. There was a lot of intrigue, and they were suspicious that I was really only crossing them and going back and forth to George. It was ridiculous. I was suing George and the Festival. I wasn't about to jeopardize that."

The *Providence Evening Bulletin* gave the story a four-column headline across its front page: "Jazzmen in Revolt." The article described the background to the opening performance to an audience of fifty. "The revolt got in motion two months ago when the Newport Festival in a New York advertisement listed Mingus as a 1960 performer at Freebody Park. Festival officials say Mingus had agreed, over the telephone, to appear for $700, but later insisted on $5,000, mentioning the Goodman fee. Wein says Goodman received $7,500 for an entire evening's program and out of this paid his 17-man band, plus singer Jimmy Rushing."

On Wednesday, July 29, 1960, the Newport City Council rescinded a prior license it had issued for the Cliff Walk Festival. The waiting for the town council's decision on a new license became interminable. Charlie Mingus, one of the star attractions of the rebel Festival, impulsively decided to quit but was coaxed into staying on. At four P.M. he went over to the Hotel Viking and accused the regular Festival's producer, George Wein, and its president, Louis P. Lorillard, who was not present, of

Opposite. Receiving final instructions from producer Wein, trumpeter Ruby Braff, looking adamant in some bit of show biz tomfoolery, holds Pee Wee Russell's clarinet as Pee Wee stands by with Ruby's trumpet. *Above.* Gillespie altoist Leo Wright caught in a thoughtful moment.

pressuring the town council to obstruct their obtaining of a license.

Wein tried to calm Mingus down but only seemed to antagonize him more. Amid the verbal scuffling, Louis Lorillard's name echoed throughout the argument with accusations that with all of his money he could run the town.

The *Newport Daily News* reported on July 1 that Mingus walked into the adjacent lounge and shouted, "Acid, George! Not a gun, acid in his face." With that Mingus left the hotel. The remark was taken to apply to Lorillard.

The town issued a new license that restricted the use of loudspeaker amplification of the music at the maverick concert. The musicians had worked furiously to set up a stage, which they had decorated with red bunting. They also had erected tents on the grounds for their sleeping quarters. Seats were set up on the broad lawn for five hundred people.

Thursday evening, June 30, 1960, the Newport Festival opened with a relatively small audience of five thousand. The Newport Youth Band, under the guidance of Marshall Brown, was making its third appearance there. They played well on the originals written by Ernie Wilkins ("Bluer Than Blue" and "Bronxville Express") and were better sounding in ensemble and solos by Ronnie Cuber on baritone and the band's chief soloist, Andy Marsala on clarinet. Jazz critic-musician Leonard Feather contributed an aimless tune with an 'original' title, "Lullaby of Newport." The band sounded better than on their recent recordings. They had been rehearsing more. In fact, the preceding evening the police had answered a complaint made by neighborhood residents that the music was keeping them awake.

Altoist Cannonball Adderley joined Andy Marsala in a duet that had been worked out on "Party Line." Some-

73

one shouted up from the audience during the duet, "Sic 'em, Cannon!" They sounded good together, and Cannonball told the audience after the set, "Why, he's only sixteen. I was playing two years before he was born." The audience smiled and applauded.

Cannon took over the stage with his brother Nat, swinging "Del Sasser" with an emotional concentrated solo that had the audience shouting, "Yeah, Cannon!" Nat played trumpet incisively, with a skillful and reflective wit, on his composition, "Worksong."

Nina Simone, appearing for the first time at Newport, sang an impressive set. Her own piano work helped emphasize the warmth of her message. I enjoyed her tambourine banging on "Little Liza Jane." It gave it a mocking quality and turned it into a shout. John Hammond told me about his meeting with Nina backstage: "When Nina got through singing, she sort of stormed off the stage. Jane Pickens, former member of the singing Pickens sisters, was sitting beside me. Jane said to me in her big southern drawl, 'John, I just think this woman is so wonderful. I just want to go backstage and hug her.' I said to her, 'Jane, I'm afraid that's very, very risky.' I took Jane backstage, and Nina's husband said, 'Stay away! She's in a rage!' Jane said, 'What do you mean, stay away?' She barged right in, and there was Nina, eyes, you know, slashing. Jane comes in, throws her arms around her, and says, 'Honey, you're the most wonderful singer in the world. This was the greatest experience of my life.' In two minutes Nina melted. She loved it. Only a white southerner could do a thing like this, and do it so that it means something."

The Art Farmer–Benny Golson Jazztet made their first appearance at the Festival with their recently organized group. Art Farmer told architect Hsio Wen Shih, designer of the Festival stage, in *Jazz Review* magazine,

74

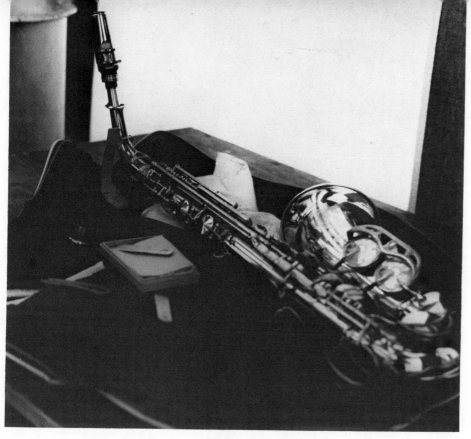

Opposite. Framed by smoke and darkness, alto star Cannonball Adderley warms the air with some fast runs. *Above.* Adderley's horn, case, and spread of reeds.

"Everyone in the group is still developing. And all of us agree that we have to satisfy our own needs as musicians. We have to satisfy the public too, but our own needs come first. We'd like to play anywhere we can get the public to really listen, but we don't ever want to feel that we have to lighten up on what we're doing. We believe that what we're doing has musical merit, that it's right for us, and we believe that we can reach a sizeable audience by doing just what we want to do." The group obviously shared Art's feelings. They melded well, opening with "It Ain't Necessarily So," a song Benny said he had always liked. Benny said of his arrangement, "I tried to make it as loose as possible. The bridge is the only time we're playing complete ensemble."

The Jazztet then played Benny's "Killer Joe," which he had written sitting down one day at the piano. "I started messing around on two chord progressions—I had about three or four different melodies—and I eliminated the others and decided to use the one I have now. As I was doing it, it made me think of one of those hip cats—standing on the corner." They finished the set with Art's "Mox Nix," named after an expression Art picked up from a Brooklyn woman. "It's a German expression," he said. "It means 'never mind, that's all right.'"

Brubeck's group followed and played a good swinging set with Paul Desmond on alto breaking out occasionally, obviously feeling good.

Maynard Ferguson ended the evening with some exciting arrangements that moved from the shouting of Stan Kenton's sound to the beauty of Maynard's ballad treatment of "Lamp Is Low." There was good solo work by trumpeters Rick Kiefer and Jerry Tyree. The most impressive sound was Rufus Jones's drum work. He kicked the band with moving solos and masterly booting during the ensembles, giving them a charge that everyone seemed to feed on. Trombonist Slide Hampton's "Newport Suite" added to the growing list of originals written with the Festival in mind.

In Newport town itself people poured off the ferries as they docked. Cars loaded with teen-agers and college students started to arrive in droves. It was what the Rhode Island public safety commissioner had warned about on June 16: "It's a tough situation down there, and they're asking for trouble if they close their eyes to it." The cars, many of them convertibles, came loaded with trouble. The early part of the evening a few teen-agers were arrested outside the park for drinking and reveling. The following morning the traffic on the streets started to back up for miles. The cars just inched forward, making no progress. It didn't seem to bother the occupants very much. As the day warmed, the kids peeled off their shirts and opened cans of beer stashed under seats and floorboards. They were having fun. Fights started to break out around the town. Usually over nothing at all. It didn't take much. They weren't going anywhere. As we walked to Freebody Park, moving at a much faster rate than the cars, I kept hearing singing and shouting and cursing at passers-by at peak voice from both the guys and their girl friends sitting on the ends of overloaded convertibles. The few police directing traffic seemed to look the other way, not noticing all the violations around them. They hadn't cracked down other years, so why start now? But the Festival had lit a long slow-burning fuse years ago, and it was still smoldering.

Friday afternoon the streets began to be littered everywhere with beer cans. Drinking was going on openly on all the streets. The police again let the college kids sleep on the beaches, and the liquor stores were doing an avalanche kind of business. One liquor store on Bellevue Avenue decorated the store windows with pictures of jazz artists and musical instruments and posters saying Welcome Jazz Fans, Official Jazz Festival Liquor Headquarters. They had reportedly sold over thirty-six

Opposite. Willie The Lion relaxes between sets, enjoying his cigar. *Above.* Ragtimers Eubie Blake (front) and friend Don Lambert rehearse onstage.

hundred dollars' worth of beer and liquor the previous day. Only the rain seemed to hold violence in check.

As at most afternoon programs, the audience on Friday was sparse but attentive, and like most afternoon programs, it produced some of the best music. Pianist Willie "The Lion" Smith described it for the audience, "The Lord gave you two hands, and you've got to use them." The ebullient Willie had a cigar propped in one corner of his mouth, derby hat tilted at a jaunty angle. Willie had given lessons to the great Fats Waller, and Duke Ellington acknowledged his debt to the Lion on many occasions. Eubie Blake, at seventy-seven, the dean of the school of stride piano, spunky and thin with parchmentlike skin stretched over his wiry frame, occasionally moved into a rolling gait as he settled down at the piano with another anecdote. The third pianist in the stride triumvirate was Don Lambert, who had dropped out of sight a number of years earlier after recording some superb sides for Bluebird. Don was found playing in a West Orange, New Jersey, bar.

The program was narrated by Rudi Blesh, lecturer and author of *They All Played Ragtime* and *Shining Trumpets.* Rudi told the audience; "Ragtime was an essentially happy music. It wasn't worried about atom bombs—it was perhaps worried about where the rent was coming from—and it wasn't ashamed to let you know what tune was being played." The pianists played tributes to two of the masters of the music, James P. Johnson and Fats Waller. Willie kept pounding away in his flamboyantly visual style, romping through "Carolina Shout" and "Ain't Misbehavin'." Eubie's tribute to James P. Johnson swung through his composition that had become the theme song of the twenties, "Charleston." His hands moved gracefully, with a freshness and vigor that seemed to roll the years back from his face. Don Lambert, playing in a less formalized manner, relentlessly explored with a beautiful light touch "I Know That You Know." They played singly and also in some duets that brought smiles and cheers from the audience. They all seemed to play without the slightest trace of condescension. A trio, made up of Danny Barker on banjo, Bernard Addison on mandolin, and Al Hall on bass joined them in what appeared to be a revival of "house-rent party" music. One of the local newspapers said about the afternoon, "The Newport Jazz Festival would hardly be dedicated to jazz if it didn't do wonderful things like this—even if they don't make money."

While the second evening's program was getting under way, some playful college types turned on the fire hoses on the second floor of the Viking Hotel and flooded a number of rooms.

Hardy fans got a good evening of music along with the rain that drenched everyone sitting in the audience. Pith helmets, baseball caps, hoods and parkas, inverted cardboard boxes, parasols, and folded newspapers did little to protect them.

That evening everyone on the program had room to stretch out their performances. The Festival had also stretched out the seating capacity of Freebody Park from a crowded 13,000 to 16,500. But the enlarged seating capacity didn't matter much on Friday; there were only 7,200 fans inside the park. A number of them sought shelter in the Kiwanis refreshment area where bare light bulbs festooned the tents so that you could almost read the No Minors Served signs at the beer stands. A reporter told me he saw underage kids being sold cups of beer again and again. After all, the organization used the money derived from the sales for worthy projects.

Meanwhile the rival camp at Cliff Walk drew an audience of one hundred patrons to their afternoon session. The sets played during the afternoon were augmented by other musicians joining the rebel camp. Coleman Hawkins came over and seemed quite at home with Max Roach and Charlie Mingus. The afternoon sets were usually limited to three or four numbers, but the setting, with the ocean making lovely sounds a few hundred yards away at the bottom of the cliffs, melded beautifully

with whatever combination was onstage. Some of the musicians took up the hat for contributions from the hangers-on outside the snow fence that had been erected.

Back at Freebody Park the main event swung out with the Dizzy Gillespie quintet, The Gerry Mulligan Concert Jazz Band, and the Louis Armstrong All-Stars. Dizzy's group played well, with good rhythm backing by Junior Mance on piano, Art Davis on bass, and some sparkling alto and flute work by Leo Wright. Diz played a lovely muted solo and in duet with his flutist on the tune named after Dizzy's wife, "Lorraine." Dizzy also sang a humorous, salty-flavored "I'm Gonna Go Fishin," ending his set with his African-inspired "Kush." Diz had recently come back from a State Department tour of Africa and had added a new group of hats to his colorful wardrobe. Backstage I went to the press tent to get out of the rain momentarily. I introduced myself to Langston Hughes, drying himself off from the downpour; a gentle man, he graciously allowed me to photograph him.

Mulligan's orchestra gave immediate gratification, both to the press section and the audience, bearing up soggily under the downpour. Mulligan played with intensity and imperative insistence, making both his solos and band come vividly to life. They played with a suppleness and grace on some of the older things associated with him, "Walkin' Shoes" and his score for the film I Want to Live. The ensemble work crackled on "Blueport" and the lovely "Sweet and Slow," with a stately and measured arrangement by Al Cohn. I wished that his brilliant valve trombonist had had a chance to solo more; the lanky Bobby Brookmeyer had to bank his fires for the night under the impact of the close-packed arrangements. Gerry and his altoist, Gene Quill, made the most pointed statements in that set.

Armstrong came on with his crew of All-Stars, and I had the feeling that I was watching and listening to an old television commercial for a product no longer manufactured. He played his usual program almost in the

Brubeck bassist Gene Wright (*left*) and Tommy Potter (*above*), one of the finest bassists to come out of the Bop era, rehearse in the musicians' tent.

same order he had performed it during his other appearances. Louis ignored the driving rain. Looking up at him from the press pit, I noticed the steam emanating from the bell of his horn, silhouetted against the lights as his music met the chill night air. Barney Bigard on clarinet and Trummy Young on trombone booted the group along, but Louis's unvaried program seemed to pall on even his most devoted admirers.

The people who slept on the beach Friday night must have had a few lessons in underwater swimming. It came down in a torrent throughout the night.

During the afternoon Mingus rode up and down the main thoroughfares of town standing on the seat of a convertible, his bass in hand, appealing to one and all: "Come to my festival!" All day long the crowded streets simmered and echoed with the clatter of beer cans being discarded everywhere.

On Saturday at noon the clogged streets and prevalent drinking and fights made the townspeople nervous. When the Newport city manager was asked if it might be wise to get more police help, he said, "The city of Newport is perfectly capable of maintaining its own law and order. We certainly need no assistance from Governor Del Sesto or from any of the governor's state troopers."

About four thirty P.M. there was a big melee on Memorial Boulevard as two rival fraternity groups battled each other. Police finally broke it up. At seven thirty there was another battle on the other side of the boulevard. Fights were breaking out all over town. The *Providence Journal* reported: "There was one clear, foreboding incident on Saturday afternoon. A lone Newport policeman marched out on Easton's Beach in Newport to break up some over enthusiastic revelry.

"He was quickly surrounded by young people and pelted with beer cans. He retreated and left the beach to the youngsters."

Above. Onstage with the Armstrong Band including clarinetist Barney Bigard, trombonist Trummy Young, Armstrong, and bassist Arvell Shaw. *Opposite.* Art Farmer in an introspective moment backstage.

80

"I asked one of the policemen how things were going," one reporter stated. " 'It's the beer again,' he said. As I moved on, the two policemen were making youths drop their open cans of beer before they went further toward the park. It was a futile gesture, like trying to stop a herring run with your hands."

The final evening of music for 1960 opened with the Newport Youth Band going through their now-familiar paces, having opened the festival and played an afternoon performance on Saturday. They were followed by a somewhat uninspired group led by trombonist Tyree Glenn but the sparkling touch of pianist Tommy Flanagan on "How Could You Do That to Me" booted the group until they were joined by veterans, tenorist Georgie Auld and trumpeter Harry Sweets Edison. The group suddenly became alive. Auld in particular played beautifully, rushing in with warm, breath-catching, Pres-inspired phrases on "Lester Leaps in," while the one-note accents of Sweets Edison were like punctuation marks, always in the right place. The final number, "Without a Song," had the group really together with everyone obviously feeling good. Dakota Staton followed with a dozen numbers but her set was routine, uninspired and had little to do with jazz.

Backstage the Festival staff had their hands full with kids climbing over the wall. "They kept coming over like flies," one staff member said. "We catch three and heave them out, and six more would be there. Christ! What an evening!"

The main riot started outside the gates at Freebody Park. Acting Chief of Police Joseph Radice had taken a second swing around the city about three P.M., and Festival officials had told him that the Festival was sold out. About four P.M. he telephoned the city manager, George E. Bisson, and told him to be prepared for trouble. Bisson took a look for himself and agreed. At about four thirty he asked the state police for help. The *Providence Journal* reported, "At 7 P.M., Bisson said, there were pockets of trouble. At 7:30 there were seething masses."

A siren wailed outside the gate of Freebody Park. A member of the audience had been hit over the head by a bottle thrown over the wall into the park. The reporter stated in his article, "I walked across Middleton Avenue toward a house I thought might have a telephone that I could use. I walked up the steps of the porch looking from one sober face to another for the owner. A grim young man stretched his arm across the stairs in front of me. A small club was in his hand. I showed him my identification and asked if I could use the phone. For a moment he considered. Then he shook his head. 'No, I've got children trying to sleep in there.' "

Back at Freebody Park Lambert, Hendricks and Ross came on for a long set with several new Ellington numbers in their repertory.

Oscar Peterson's car had been trapped in the crowd that evening. A fan at one of the houses along the way recognized him, saw the trouble he was having, and allowed him to park in his yard. Oscar continued on foot the rest of the way and finally got to Freebody Park unscathed.

Reports said there were about twelve thousand kids outside the gates of Freebody Park. The police moved in to clear the area, and the beer cans started to fly. The cops began to use their clubs, meanwhile trying to protect themselves from getting hit by the barrage of cans. "Kill the bastards! Kill the cops! Get the stinkin' bastards!" was the battle cry of the teen-agers as they heaved their cans of beer. Someone rang in for the fire department, and as firemen strung hoses to turn on the water to control the crowd, they were bombarded with missiles of all sorts.

Onstage, pianist Horace Silver opened his set with his own composition, "Señor Blues." The group kept up the pace until you felt you had been on a roller coaster ride, constantly repeating that first big plunge. Horace played with a fierce determination, head beaded in sweat, chin dug into his neck and shoulders, feet rising and falling, as he relentlessly exploited every stop and turn along

82

the way. The veins in his neck bulged out anew as he threw himself into "Sister Sadie." "You scarcely had time to catch your breath," one critic stated. But the audience loved it, and their applause seemed to egg him on to even more passionate statements. You felt like stopping for a moment and taking a deep breath when his set finally ended.

Ray Charles followed with a slow start but soon caught up to Silver's pace with "Let the Good Times Roll." The people in the audience started to move in their seats, and a few started to dance. From the press pit it looked a little like the audience might get out of hand, but the Pinkerton guards calmed down the more active participants. That and a romantic ballad by Ray seemed to soothe them. Bassist Ray Brown, standing in the wings, told a friend, "Who wants to follow that?" At ten thirty the area outside the park was filled with detachments of military police. The governor had summoned the Air and National Guard. There were also Marine and Navy shore patrolmen fighting the surging, battering crowd. The crowd heaved itself at one of the wooden gates and partially forced it open. But quick-thinking attendants forced it shut by backing a truck up against it. At about eleven P.M. the governor ordered more state troopers in, and the decision was made to use tear gas. They started firing the canisters at about eleven thirty. Police were coming into the area from all the surrounding communities. Bloody heads seemed to be everywhere. "Kill the cops! Get the bastards!" mixed with the sounds of broken glass as the bloodied police and troopers started to drive back the crowd. The mob smashed in store windows along the way.

One reporter for the *Providence Journal* said, "I have experienced genuine fear twice in my life. Once was in combat in Europe during World War II; the other was Saturday night in Newport during the riot by drunken, wild-eyed young people." He had arrived in Newport with his wife to attend the concert at Freebody Park. They ended up in the middle of a swirling mob that was making repeated attacks on the police and troopers and guardsmen. Most were in their teens, all carrying cans of beer or bottles of liquor. The reporter and his wife were able to make their way back to the ferry, and they talked a couple of women in a waiting car into taking them on board.

The police, aided by the other law-enforcement officers and tear gas, were finally able to push the mob back toward the central part of the city, and from there they broke it up into smaller groups, arresting youths along the way. Battery A, 243rd Automatic Weapons Battalion joined the 118th Engineers of the National Guard, and they arrived about two A.M.

Oscar Peterson ended the concert with "Blues for Big Scotia" and at two fifteen the last notes faded away. The people at Freebody Park had been held longer to avoid getting them into the battle outside and they walked home quietly. As I swung toward Bellevue Avenue, I saw signs of destruction. There was a Volkswagen completely tipped over, and in the rear window were cases of beer that had been somehow overlooked by the mob. The riot had been broken by then, and by five A.M. city crews started to clean the streets and repair the damage.

Early the next morning kids of ten and eleven were seen on the streets, salvaging deposit bottles. One of them even found a six-pack of beer. He said he would bring it to his father. The jail cells in the police station were crowded with 170 prisoners. They were arraigned before Judge Arthur J. Sullivan in district court on charges ranging from assault to idling. The police decided to release most of those picked up during the night, only holding those charged with the more serious offenses. The town clerk was nearly overwhelmed with the job of processing all the complaints. The captain of detectives ordered the defendants' names taken, and he told them, "You participated in a riot. We have technical charges against each one of you. You are to leave the city at once. If any of you are found congregating in the

The sweat-beaded face of pianist Oscar Peterson, just after he leaves the stage. Peterson had a harrowing experience getting to the field through the riot-torn streets.

city, you will be subject to a sentence of five years in prison and a one-thousand-dollar fine.''

The rebel festival meanwhile had continued all during the riot without any trouble. Other musicians swelled the group and produced some good music. Working with Charlie Mingus and Max Roach were Teddy Charles on vibes, Wilbur Ware on bass, Arthur Taylor on drums, Kenny Drew on piano, Kenny Dorham on trumpet, Coleman Hawkins on sax (later joined by his sidekick, Roy Eldridge, on trumpet), and many others.

At nine twenty Sunday morning the Newport City Council met with Governor Del Sesto at the Middletown home of his military aide, Commander William Gosling, USN (ret.). The governor had slept there for a few hours. He met the city council dressed in a blue bathrobe and told them the decision to close down the Festival was theirs alone.

The council met at City Hall an hour later and had a heated debate on the relative merits of the Festival. Acting Police Chief Radice, red eyed and weary looking, told the council members: ''My men have short tempers now. They've had damn little sleep since five A.M. With or without the Festival we've got to have more men. I don't want to go through it again. It's asking too much of my men.''

The city mayor, James L. Maher, had to lash out occasionally to halt interruptions as one of the councilmen spoke. Councilman Erich Taylor criticized the state police for their handling of the crowds. ''Very poor police work,'' he vehemently stated, discussing the effort to clear out the rioting fans on Middleton Avenue.

Left. An overturned Volkswagen, empty beer cartons jammed against the back window and its motor fluids staining the pavement, as neighborhood youngsters reconnoiter the morning after the riot at Newport. *Right*. Fiddler Butch Cage (left) and guitarist Willie Thomas shade themselves from the strong afternoon sun while waiting to make their appearance with the rest of the musicians on the sad afternoon finale of the Festival.

While the debate was raging, the Festival producer, George Wein, sat dismally backstage at Freebody Park at a makeshift table, a telephone beside him his only companion, waiting for the council decision.

The vote was 4 to 3 against the Festival, with the mayor voting to continue it. In the meeting room to one side sat Festival President Louis P. Lorillard. He had remained there without saying anything or taking any position. The Festival's attorney, Richard B. Sheffield, said he would abide by the council's decision.

The city council allowed the afternoon program to take place at Freebody Park. It was a program of the blues narrated by Langston Hughes. Some of the musicians were late arriving because of the roadblocks, but Hughes occupied the time of the small audience of two thousand by recounting some blues history. The three-hour program included performances by Muddy Waters, Otis Spann, and Jimmy Rushing. It was probably the only wake held in Freebody Park. It was fine music, beautiful music, sad music. When it was over, MC Willis Conover sadly told the fans about the town council's decision: "Instead of treating the sickness, they shot the patient. But the germs are still there." Langston Hughes had written a blues for the occasion about an hour before the concert on a Western Union blank. He handed it to Otis Spann, who slowly sang it.

It's a gloomy day at Newport,
It's a gloomy, gloomy day,
It's a gloomy day at Newport,
It's a gloomy, gloomy day,
It's a gloomy day at Newport,
The music's going away.
What's gonna happen to my music?
What's going to happen to my song?

At five forty-five P.M. the people filed slowly out of the park. When the musicians at the rebel festival heard the news, Max Roach said, "It's a tragedy. It's the worst thing that could have happened to the jazz world." Coleman Hawkins said, "It's terrible. Nothing worse could have happened."

The *Providence Journal* reported: "Only Charlie Mingus showed joy: 'That's the way it should be. They did it themselves. They deserve it because they confused rock 'n roll with jazz. They lost their identity with jazz.'"

"I feel terrible about it because the original idea was such a wonderful one," Elaine Lorillard said. "I extend my sympathies to the Festival board, but I knew three years ago that this would happen. I wasn't surprised."

Elaine told me in a later interview about that riotous night and its aftermath. "That night I wanted to go early to the Festival at Cliff Walk Manor. When I started driving down Bellevue Avenue, it was the most frightening sight. I had heard through people in the town that they were advertising tickets, although they knew that they were sold out days before at the main Festival. This was something I tried to prevent when I was with it. . . . [Because of this the young people] were drinking beer and getting angrier. And I don't blame them. They were hoodwinked into coming to something where they could not be supplied with the proper facilities or tickets to even get in. It was greed, absolute greed on the part of the people who put on the Newport Jazz Festival. We got some of the overflow, and they were grateful."

The press had a field day with the riot. It was picked up by all the wire services, and for the first time jazz was front-page news across the world. The *Providence Journal* headlined, "Jazz Festival in Newport dead." "Era of big jazz buried." The *New York Herald Tribune* said, "The disgraceful Battle of Newport. . . . Perhaps the most discouraging aspect of the whole sorry mess was the emptiness and futility of it all. American youth hit some sort of a new low at Newport this weekend."

Life magazine covered it with pictures under the headline, "The wild Newport stomp." The British trade papers called it "the blues for a doomed Festival." Even

Backstage in the press tent, producer George Wein sits forlornly at a makeshift table, as he waits for the City Council's decision on whether the Festival can go on.

Izvestia, the Russian newspaper, got into the act with a tirade about our decadent youth.

The *Newport Daily News* editorialized under the headline, "Newport's darkest hour." "A major factor in the debacle was greed—of those who wanted a complete free hand to pour beer into the visitors, of those who upset police traffic plans with moans that their business was being cut off. . . ."

On July 7 the Newport County Restaurant Association (a notable group of jazz lovers) stated, "Many of our members were compelled by circumstances to lay in heavy inventories of food and other merchandise and to engage extra personnel to cope with the heavy business of the Festival. From the proceeds of this business many other merchants and segments of the economy would benefit directly or indirectly. The cancellation of the Festival was the easy way out."

I boarded the train at Providence for New York City. Sitting nearby was the veteran trombonist, Miff Mole. In the twenties he had been a major figure in jazz. Unknown to this generation of fans, he had come up to Newport, sick as he was, to participate in the Festival. Having been cancelled out, he headed home. Sitting in the rear of the car were a few of the college "heroes" of the riot. They started to mock him as a broken-down jazz musician. I changed my seat and sat with him for the rest of the trip home.

Item: July 5, 1960 (Washington Post)

"Hyannis, Massachusetts. Fast-moving police seized seventy-two of a delegation of self styled 'refugees from Newport' who turned from the Rhode Island city's short-lived jazz Festival late yesterday, ostensibly to 'conquer' Hyannis. . . . Rain showers and the word 'these cops aren't folling' brought the situation to all quiet at two A.M."

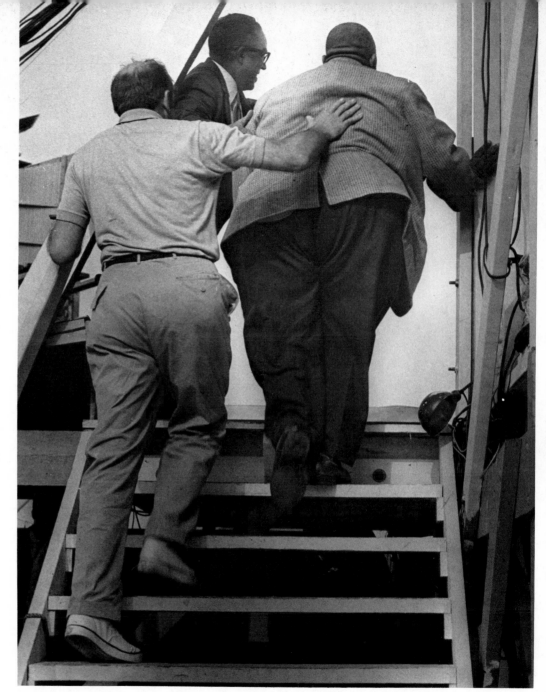

Opposite. Blues singer Jimmy Rushing, one of the last performers to make an appearance that afternoon, gets an encouraging pat on the back as he mounts the steps to the stage to be greeted at the top by Langston Hughes. *Above.* Surrounded by Butch Cage and Muddy Waters and his Blues Band, MC Willis Conover announces the City Council decision to end the festival: "Instead of treating the sickness, they shot the patient. But the germs are still there."

After the final bars are played, Jimmy
Rushing wipes the tears from his eyes.

While the embattled city still echoed with anguished
cries of the city fathers and the protestations of the Festival, the press published reports of a suit to be insti-
tuted by the Festival against the city of Newport for four
million dollars. Announcements were made after a Festival board meeting.

One would have thought that such a suit would have
been implemented immediately, but the court record of
the suit was not filed at superior court, Newport County,
Newport, Rhode Island, until March 10, 1961, nine
months later.

One of Louis Lorillard's last memoranda issued by
the Festival might shed some light on the intervening
period:

> "July 14, 1961
> "Memorandum to the Board of Directors of The
> Newport Jazz Festival, Inc. From L. P. Lorillard,
> President
> "Since my last memorandum to you on February
> 7th, the following sequence of events has taken
> place.
> "After our application for a license was turned
> down by the City Council, another party applied and
> was also denied. The Mayor then appointed a com-
> mittee to investigate the possibilities of interesting
> some producers in the re-establishment of the Fes-
> tival and as a result a new corporation was formed
> called Music at Newport, Inc., produced by Sid
> Bernstein and John Drew with the help of various
> local people, and primarily financed by a Mr. Margo-
> lis. At no time was the Newport Jazz Festival directly
> approached other than the fact that Music at New-
> port was willing to accept a list of our clients whose
> refunds had not been made good promising them a
> free ticket to an afternoon concert. This offer was
> rejected on the basis that it would endanger our suit
> still pending against the City of Newport. The new

corporation then advanced $10,000 to the City to defray the cost of additional police protection and promised that should more be needed, they would be glad to pay them from the profits of the Festival. . . .

"The local and state publicity given to the Festival was great. However, there were a very few jazz critics present. . . . The estimated figure for attendance at the four evenings and two afternoons was some 55,000. However . . . a more accurate account would drop that to around 30,000. A later acknowledgment from the group stated that they were spending some $200,000 on talent. From what I gather . . . the programing was very poor. . . . The City of Newport was . . . under martial law with some 135 policemen augmenting the present 78 man force. . . . There was no trouble either within the Park or in the surrounding area. In my estimation, this so-called eighth Newport Jazz Festival lost between $50,000 and $75,000 and the citizens of Newport are now wondering where the cost of the additional police protection is coming from other than their own pockets.

". . . Those city officials who were finagling in the negotiations with the new group have been overwhelmingly defeated in the polls. Therefore the political situation is far better than it has been for many a year, and it appears that a group more favorable to us will be in office at such time as we decide to again hold a Festival. . . ."

The suit asked for $750,000 for damages suffered by cancellation of the Festival by the city despite the Festival's payment of $4,800 to license the Festival. Although a number of motions were filed by the attorneys representing the Festival, the suit finally was allowed to lapse and nothing ever came of it, whether by intent or supposed jockeying to obtain a new license is not known. The last memorandum on the suit was filed December 11, 1961.

At a board meeting held early in 1961, one of the members made some notations about how the Jazz Festival could proceed in Newport in the future. Some of the suggestions made seemed intended to turn the Festival and Newport into an armed camp.

—Tickets to be sold by subscription. No tickets sold at the gate.

—Whether or not beer will be sold on the grounds to be considered.

—The Festival to split the cost of 500 extra policemen.

—The police to strictly enforce no drinking in public, anywhere, anytime.

—The police to be stationed in every package store.

—Cars to be inspected as they enter Newport. No spirits to be brought into the city.

—Every bottle of liquor to have a special stamp identifying the fact that it was bought in Newport. Any bottle without stamp to be impounded.

—Streets surrounding the park to be open only to the press.

—No loitering to be allowed near entrances.

—Jeeps with loudspeakers to clear the streets—in case of trouble.

—Hotel bars to be closed at 8:00 P.M. except to press, radio, TV, etc.

A final note questioned the constitutionality of these restrictions. It all sounded like the Newport Martial Law Jazz Festival.

1962

The Festival was billed "Newport '62" with a subhead that read, "The Meaning of Jazz." The Festival was no longer a nonprofit corporation. Changes had been made. Gone were the board members and the advisory panel. Gone was the socialite backer, Louis P. Lorillard. George Wein was now completely in command, listing himself as producer-director in the program for that year. The Festival was back at the old stand in Newport, two years after the riotous debacle. There had been something called "Music at Newport" in 1961, but George Wein was not in attendance, nor did he have anything to do with the Festival that year.

Comparatively, 1962 was a good Festival musically.

George Wein played piano at an engagement at the former site of the rebel festival, Cliff Walk Manor, a week before the Festival officially opened. Coincident with that was his reconciliation with the directors of the rebel festival, Charlie Mingus and Max Roach. It was implemented with their presentation at the 1962 Newport Jazz Festival. All had been forgiven, it seemed.

The chill air was also warmed opening night that year by the heat generated in Roy Eldridge's trumpet as he goaded his group with his lusty power, without the strident tenor of Coleman Hawkins. Hawk had been caught in a traffic jam and did not arrive until the end of the set. But the urgency in the group's playing, whether on a ballad like "Autumn Leaves" or breaking out with an audience-shaking sizzler on "Undecided," was magnificent. The quartet played with a vigor and self-assurance that made them move as one. The salty sparring of Jo Jones on drums and Jim Neves on bass with Bill Rubenstein on piano was a joy. Backstage Hawk and Roy joked with each other about Hawk's tardy arrival. Standing there watching the festive punches, I had to laugh along with them as Hawk said, "You know I wanted to be on time." Roy solemnly said, "No, I don't." Hawkins described the road tie-up but was interrupted by Harry Edison, the fine trumpet player formerly with Count Basie's best band. "I've been to carnivals and tent shows," he said. "People come in on wheelchairs asking for Coleman Hawkins. Why, they used to listen to you when they were on two wheels," he said emphatically. Hawk smiled and responded with, "Why, you're the only trumpet man I know who still carries the number-one trumpet method book in his case." Uproarious laughter all around.

The rest of the evening's program was highlighted by Dave Brubeck's quartet punctuated with the exuberant drumming of Joe Morello. The group was later joined by vocalist Carmen McCrae, but it couldn't equal the pace of Roy's quartet. Gerry Mulligan and his quartet opened with some new material, "Love in New Orleans." When Mulligan's group started to play, the Redmen, a benevolent organization on the other side of Aquidneck Island, started celebrating the holiday by firing off a barrage of fireworks. Gerry told the audience, "It's part of our rhythm section." Gerry was later joined by Coleman Hawkins, who proceeded to show his preeminence on tenor saxophone. The group's backing was gently sympathetic, and Hawk warmed to the occasion by playing a

Bassist Charlie Mingus always plays at peak capacity and expects no less from the musicians who serve as his sidemen. Mingus goads, cajoles, and brings out sounds from his group that are always exciting.

masterly solo on "Body and Soul" without ever once referring back to the now-classic recording that he had
made of the tune in 1939. Hawk never seemed to want to
look back. Hawkins later joined Harry Edison's quintet
with vocalist Joe Williams. Joe sounded great, and the
backing of Harry on trumpet and Jimmy Forrest on tenor
was augmented by the baritone of Gerry Mulligan, who
got so excited with the sounds he was hearing that he
grabbed his horn, ran out on the stage, and started to
wail. It was the climax of the evening and left the crowd
limp.

Jazz has been called America's only indigenous art
form. I would like to nominate tap dancing as another.
Marshall Stearns did a marvelous job in his presentation
of the program of tap dancing the following afternoon.
Aside from an occasional background remark from one
side of the stage, where his podium stood, he seemed
just as spellbound as the audience with the dancing.
The musical backing was just right. I was fascinated
with all the dancers, but I especially enjoyed Baby
Laurence for the effortlessness of his movements.

The program was called "Tap Dancing and Its Relationship to Jazz." It was one of the most memorable
Newport events I had witnessed.

Honi Cole's routines turned me on also. Honi was supplementing his income by stage-managing the Apollo
Theatre in New York City. "I used to keep a book on
various stages throughout the country," he said, "and if
the stage was good, I was willing to work for a little less
money." A good stage in most tap dancers' estimation
was one made from maple. The Newport stage was covered for the occasion with temporary maple flooring.

Marshall Stearns said in his introduction, "These are
the last of the breed, the last of the great tap dancers."
The pathos and humor of the dance entranced the audience. They applauded with gusto, appreciating the foot-
tripping parodies, the fragments of vaudeville trappings,

Above. Two generations of Count Basie
vocalists, Jimmy Rushing and Joe Williams. Rushing has had a primary influence on post-war rhythm and blues
shouting. Joe Williams sang with the
Count Basie Orchestra for seven years.
A powerful, romping, earthy singer who
imbues everything he does with a feeling for the blues. *Opposite.* Dave Lambert (right), gets his charts together
backstage.

and the sliding, turnabout quicksteps that alternately brought joy and laughter as they moved through dusted-off routines and demonstrations of superb artistry.

Saturday evening opened with the Gene Hull Band from Bridgeport, Connecticut, made up of local musicians that seemed to have "go" power in whatever they played. Well rehearsed, they ranged through a series of Kenton-Herman-like arrangements that whizzed by the ears, punctuating the air with an eager, gutsy fullness of sound.

Carol Sloane used to attend the Festival in its early years. A Rhode Island woman, she was making her second appearance with the Festival. She had formerly sung with Les Elgart's orchestra and had recorded an album the previous year that was selling well. Coleman Hawkins joined her with a beautiful backing on "Willow Weep for Me." Carol sang well throughout her set, closing with a personally intense rendition of "Will You Still Be Mine?"

Charlie Mingus followed with a set of originals that showed anger and humor, sometimes at the same moment. His pianist, Toshiko Mariano, seemed unequal to the task of keeping up with his bass. Whatever Mingus played had validity and spontaneity. Mingus was incapable of boring anyone. His music dug too deep, throwing his critics off-balance on many occasions.

Max Roach with a large vocal group met resistance from the sound system, which had been functioning well throughout the Festival. The voices came through in muddled form, killing the presentation of his quartet with eight voices.

But the standout on Saturday evening was the surprise appearance of Duke Ellington's orchestra supplying background music for two superb dancers, Bunny

Briggs and Baby Laurence. They had agreed beforehand not to try to outdo each other. How well they stuck to the bargain was difficult to decide. It amused me to see the band smiling widely and chuckling as the two dancers tried to "cut" each other with a dazzling display of virtuosity that left everyone breathless. Duke's band was known to hardly ever lift their eyelids for anything at all; so to see such stalwarts as altoist Johnny Hodges, eyes wide open, sitting upright, fully awake and smiling, and other members of the band laughing and nodding at the excitement those feet generated, almost making that wood on the stage smolder as they moved through their cutting steps, was truly amazing. Briggs was the better showman of the two. He had told Marshall Stearns, "Working with Duke is an inspiration. You have to create, and sometimes I feel like I'm dancing on a cloud." When Bunny first saw Baby dance, he told Stearns, "When Baby was through, there wasn't anything left to do." He went home that evening and told his mother that he had seen someone dance and his feet had never touched the floor. They later became good friends and learned a great deal from each other. It was the peak of the evening and the Festival.

Sunday afternoon the audience heard Clara Ward and her gospel singers. Clara Ward described her music as "music with the old Baptist beat," and she infectiously made the audience clap time with her program. Closing with a rollicking "Joy in the Room," her group set the tone of the rest of the afternoon program. Her gospel group was lovingly booted to glory by the surprise accompaniment of Jo Jones on drums.

Oscar Peterson's group swung mightily. With Ray Brown on bass and Ed Thigpen on drums Oscar demonstrated that he could play with his trio as if they were one. Master of Ceremonies Duke Ellington said at the end of the set, "I've a confession to make. That was a fraud. That was not Oscar Peterson. That was four of his imitators all playing at once."

96

Right. A raucous savagery of sounds assaults the ear when blind, multi-talented Roland Kirk takes the stage. *Left.* Harry Sweets Edison.

Sonny Rollins's tenor sax, flashing the sun's rays brilliantly as he tilted it to one side, seemed to be on fire, and his solos had the same blinding effect. They were well constructed, moving chunks of sound with a clarity and vividness that grabbed the audience. He played with an inexhaustible energy that got to you. "Complete command," was the way one critic described his afternoon set.

In a switch from the usual Festival presentations Count Basie played the afternoon's closing set. Roaring from the band's opening theme, they shouted down to the closing moments of the afternoon, juxtaposing his former great blues vocalist of the thirties and forties, Jimmy Rushing, and his present vocalist, Joe Williams, into a group of duets that left the crowd clamoring and shouting, "More, More!" There was no time for anything else but to get scrambling through the crowd for a quick shower and a bite to eat before the evening performance in two short hours.

Sunday night Thelonious Monk joined Duke's band, playing Billy Strayhorn's arrangement of his composition, "Monk's Dream." Monk melded beautifully with them. It was the kind of programing that showed another dimension of both Monk and Duke.

After intermission Monk came on with his own quartet playing a moving set followed by singing group Lambert, Hendricks, and their replacement for Annie Ross, Yolande Bavan.

Roland Kirk closed out the evening with his multi-instrumented mouth. Playing two, sometimes three, instruments at once, he was the "discovery" of the Festival that year. Many ears opened up that afternoon, but few of them belonged to the reviewers present. They hardly mentioned his performance.

Unmindful of the preparations and movement around them, two jazz giants, Coleman Hawkins (left) and Thelonious Monk, relax and talk about one of Hawkins' other talents—cooking soul food.

1963

Peewee Russell, the gentle, modest, and self-deprecating clarinetist, had arrived a week early at Newport in 1963. He and his wife, Mary, were the houseguests of producer George Wein. "I was here at the beginning," he reminisced, "when we didn't know if people would go for a Festival or not. Money was no problem, but we didn't know if jazz would draw enough people to make the effort worthwhile."

"I don't ever want to go home again," Mary exclaimed. She described the courtesies of the people in the town. "Cars stopped for us when we crossed the streets," she said, looking amazed. "In New York they would have run you over. I can't wait to visit the mansions tomorrow," she said excitedly.

Amid all the courtesies extended were the restrictions being posted on large signs as you entered Newport. Security seemed to be number one on the minds of the city council and the safety department. Precautions and safety factors that should have been observed years before were now the norm.

Barriers had been erected on side streets; snow fencing protected planted areas. At a meeting shortly before the Festival opened, Police Chief Radice had instructed his seventy regular members of the police department to be courteous to the visitors, but if any rowdiness developed, they were to take the offenders into custody at once.

A police car with dogs patrolled the streets, and the Navy's shore patrol had seven wagons in the area, while some state-prison guards on their days off as well as the

one hundred extra policemen brought in from outlying communities were supplementing the regular police. As usual, accommodations were hard to find and expensive, the papers reported, but certain beaches were again being allowed for sleeping.

The Festival was a four-day affair again, and squeezed into the programing were juxtapositions of different styles and artists, allowing comparisons and contrasts in performance. And it worked. Peewee Russell was one of the contrasts on Thursday night, with pianist Thelonius Monk. George Wein is to be congratulated for the success of the pairing. Peewee played two numbers with Monk's group, "Nutty" and "Blue Monk," and his clarinet melded interestingly with the group.

The fusions were extended to musicians of more common roots and persuasions. A reunion of Dizzy Gillespie on trumpet with Milt Jackson on vibes on Friday evening proved equally stimulating. Dizzy had an excellent sextet that year, and Kenny Baron on piano, Chris White on bass, and Rudy Collins on drums provided a vital, though relaxed, set with just the right impetus. Dizzy played a hauntingly lovely solo on "Stardust," and James Moody on alto sparkled when he soloed on Monk's "Round About Midnight."

Thursday evening the Newport Jazz Festival house band opened with a driving, exuberant set that contrasted veteran saxmen Coleman Hawkins and Zoot Sims in a spark-flying duet on "What Is This Thing Called Love?" What a lovely interplay between the two horns! At times it was almost wittily barbed as they threw fours at each other, at the same time maintaining a sense of humor. The contrast was heightened by the interplay of the two trumpets of Clark Terry and Howard McGhee. They played against each other with something unexpected always going on. Clark on flugelhorn drew on his vast repertoire, skillfully and imaginatively lighting the stage. Terry played a lyrical "Stardust," while drummer Roy Haynes provided the right dash of pepper to the stew. Joe Zawinul on piano played with a nervous energy that seemed to evolve from a necessity born of always saying the right thing at the right moment. What a sizzling group!

Cannonball Adderley's group followed, keeping up the jet thrust. Playing three numbers, Nat Adderley's trumpet wailed out some unearthly screams when he heightened their "Brother John" rendition by removing his mouthpiece and playing his trumpet "raw" while Yusef Lateef blew oboe in oriental-sounding screams. The crowd cried for more when they had finished the short set.

Nina Simone captured the crowd with a beautiful medley from *Porgy and Bess,* but her set was too long. The audience got restless as she moved from one solemn mood to another, and her critiques from the stage between numbers didn't endear her to the press section, which soon emptied, filling the refreshment area. "The audience didn't know whether they were being entertained or lectured," said one of the trade papers.

At the end she complained, "I still have so far to go—after all of these festivals—all this proving—they tell me I still got so terribly far to go."

Blasting out the final set of the evening, Stan Kenton appeared with one of the best-sounding bands he had ever put together. It featured a fine new alto sax, Gabriel Baltazar, blowing with a relentless compelling quality on "Turtle Talk." Altoist Charlie Mariano had a reunion with his former boss, flying in from Japan for the occasion.

The evening ended with a blues interplay of three altos. Cannonball joined Baltazar and Mariano, and the

Above. Nina Simone's style is a unique mixture of folk, gospel and jazz. *Left.* Martial Solal has a delicate, sometimes poetic touch. *Opposite.* McCoy Tyner backstage.

three locked horns in an extended vehemence, with each expressing their own unique vision and personal intensity of feeling.

Friday afternoon was billed as "New Faces in Jazz." The faces that held your attention were in pianist McCoy Tyner's trio, with Mickey Roker on drums and Bob Cranshaw on bass. McCoy crackled with eagerness. It was such a pleasure to hear a group playing with one mind. His solos in "All of You" were marked by moments of tenderness and fire and seemed to evolve from an inner necessity.

The afternoon ended with altoist Paul Winter's sextet playing a group of originals. The group melded well, but Jay Cameron's baritone seemed to carry the group. Jay had been rehearsing in his automobile in the parking lot that evening when Nesuhi Ertegun, an executive with Atlantic Records, had almost caused him to swallow his reed by creeping up on him unawares and shouting out, "You're under arrest."

Among the many problems Friday evening were the constrictions placed on some of the artists by RCA Victor and Columbia Records. Part of the program was being recorded on stereo equipment, and the recording companies demanded new material. Lambert, Hendricks and Bavan, for example, introduced a number of new tunes with complicated arrangements. It didn't make it easy on the band accompanying them. There had been little time allotted for rehearsal, and with the intricate lyrics it was disastrous. The musicians in the band were all sight-reading, and it was difficult to hang loose under those circumstances. One of the musicians in the band told me later, "We just couldn't get moving on those charts. Remember, we had only one crack at them, since we were being recorded live. It just was too difficult."

101

It didn't make it easy on the audience either. The special mikes and mass of cables had been placed so as to record with optimum sound. That placement did not allow the people in the audience to hear the musicians the way they should have been heard.

Vocalist Joe Williams ran into similar problems. Part of the first half of his program contained a number of new tunes and arrangements. The musicians backing him were all of high caliber, but the sparks couldn't fly under those circumstances. It was a long closing set, eleven numbers long, and although there were some fine moments—pianist Junior Mance backing with his trio on "Without a Song," and Clark Terry on flugelhorn on "April in Paris"—much of the program lacked the proper fire.

But when Zoot Sims on tenor started to dig relentlessly on "Some of This and Some of That," the crowd started to feel the message and clamored for more. They were clapping with the music, and when he shouted, "Come on, everybody, dance," a number of them took his suggestion and started to dance in the aisles. Three policemen saw the movement in the audience and almost leaped over the snow fence to break it up. They relaxed when they realized what was actually happening. "Roll 'Em, Pete," the finale of the evening, had some brilliant byplay between Terry and Howard McGhee, and with Joe Williams trading scat singing with drummer Mickey Roker, who answered his gibes with intricate rolls and cymbal work, the audience was completely caught up in the spontaneity of the moment and let out a roar of such dimensions that the whole shell seemed to rock.

Earlier that evening the Maynard Ferguson Band had turned the audience on with a swinging program that included some brilliant solo work by Lannie Morgan on alto, searing through "Cherokee"; tenorist Willie Maiden with a lush, compassionate solo on "Getting Sentimental over You", and the spirited trumpet work of the former International Youth Band member from

102

Coleman Hawkins (left) is badgered but polite backstage to admirer Bud Freeman who reflects on another period in time, plays a few riffs for him to jog his memory, and finally breaks up when Bean answers with a wry comment.

Yugoslavia, Dusko Gojkovic, in an interplay with trumpeter Maynard and the former Farmingdale High School Band member pianist Mike Abene on "Fox Hunt." Sonny Stitt joined them for the final numbers, playing alto with their rhythm section on "The Gypsy" and ending with a gutsy, concentrated blues that showcased his formidable talent for finding roots and nurturing them.

Gerry Mulligan's sextet, expanded from his former quartet, crackled with enthusiasm. Art Farmer in particular settled into an emotional groove with a style on flugelhorn that was more blues rooted than cerebral, and Jim Hall on guitar swung with a cool, perceptible undercurrent of humor. In the too brief set, Bobby Brookmeyer on valve trombone showed how empathy could be directed to produce a warm, raging excitement without the need to feed the young audience's paranoia.

The small crowd in attendance at the Saturday afternoon presentation of "An Afternoon at the Hoofers' Club" proved once more the narrowness of management thinking in presenting an outstanding event such as this during the afternoon. Only big-name artists were presented during the evening presentations, ostensibly to attract larger crowds. I had fortunately taken along my movie camera that year to record some of the more interesting moments. I remember climbing up the girders of one of the lighting supports, twisting my legs around so that I was on a level with the stage. I sat there transfixed through the rest of the afternoon and filmed the performance. In screening those films recently I could almost hear the feet tapping and sliding on the stage.

It was a marvelous afternoon. Dancers Cholly Atkins, Ernest Brown, Honi Cole, Charlie Cook, Chuck Green, and Pete Nugent delighted the audience. Gildo Mahones, piano and bass, Sam Woodyard, Duke Ellington's drummer, and the lyrical trumpet of Clark Terry provided a beautiful backdrop for the array of talented feet that moved across that stage. Chuck Green explained and demonstrated different steps and rhythms,

The 8 mm motion picture footage above was taken during the performance. It was an outstanding event. (Left) The dancers perform in unison. (Center) Charlie Cook stands over Ernest Brown as he does the split. (Right) Chuck Green's easygoing, graceful movements. *Opposite.* The dancers onstage (left to right): The late Pete Nugent, Cholly Atkins, Chuck Green, Honi Coles, Ernest Brown, Charlie Cook, and, at the podium, Professor Marshall Stearns.

moving from waltzes to rock and roll. The showmanship was dazzling. Marshall Stearns had captivated Freebody Park once again with another great dance program.

The good weather continued for another evening. Saturday highlights included Ruby Braff on cornet, with a compulsively lyrical tone, as he and the Newport Jazz Festival All-Stars moved through "Just You, Just Me," segueing into an outstanding solo again by Braff on "When Your Lover Has Gone." Al Grey joined them for the last two numbers and, working with his trombone plunger mute, gave a gutsy, full-of-feeling treatment to "You Can Depend on Me."

Ramsey Lewis, working with a tightly disciplined crew, moved with a great deal of melodic invention and virtuosity through three extended numbers. The group's versatility opened up when his bassist, El Dee Young, played a sinuous, graceful, and elegant solo on "Hello Cello." His group really pleased the crowd and was a tough act to follow. Nancy Wilson only provided more fodder to the "what-does-this-voice-have-to-do-with-jazz" school. Her performance might have worked in a small, chic supper club, but despite a favorable audience reaction, the consensus among true jazz aficionados was thumbs down.

Tenorist Sonny Rollins blazed out after intermission with a tooth-jarring version of "Remember." His random-seeming sounds rejuvenated with imaginative skill a sentimental melody into a vigorous assertion. His guest was Coleman Hawkins on "All the Things You Are," and the two tenors established a spontaneous intensity. Unfortunately, Hawk's mike conked out occasionally, making Sonny seem overpowering, but the recording of the mating was able to put them in proper balance when it was re-created later that year in a recording studio.

Duke Ellington brought the evening to a climax, playing a mixture of standard fare with some surprises. His program put his soloists on display with good effect. Jimmy Hamilton on clarinet played "Silk Lace."

Left. Tenor master Coleman Hawkins (seated) relaxes backstage and gives his nod of approval as Zoot Sims warms up. *Opposite.* Ramsey Lewis can achieve with block chords, accents, arpeggios and trills the immediacy other instrumentalists get with volume.

Clarinetist Pee Wee Russell performing
with the Thelonious Monk Quartet. *Opposite*. Howard McGhee wearing his
eyepatch, his signature for a number of
years. It was to come off later that year.

Tenorist Paul Gonsalves, back with the band, having recovered from a bout of pneumonia contracted while on tour in Sweden, repeated his now-famous solo from "Diminuendo and Crescendo in Blue." Paul played well but didn't match his 1956 triumph.

The Duke's war-horses were put on display to good effect—"I Got It Bad," his medley of "Black and Tan Fantasy," and "Creole Love Call." The parade of soloists to center stage included Lawrence Brown on trombone, Russell Procope on alto and clarinet, and Ray Nance on trumpet. The band was in a good groove. As Duke later explained backstage: "Maybe it was because we've been laying off for almost two weeks."

A prime highlight was the appearance of Cootie Williams growling on trumpet, after a twenty-year hiatus away from the band. Duke announced his number as a "new tootie for Cootie, based on the old tootie." Dancer Baby Laurence joined the band as they played "Take the A Train" and turned the band and the audience on with a series of brilliant turns, breathtaking patterns, and slides that took on a dreamy quality as he spun through the night air.

Duke ended the set with a half-sung, half-spoken recitation honoring Martin Luther King, Jr., to the music of "Joshua Fit the Battle of Jericho":

> King fit the battle of Alabam, Alabam, Alabam,
> King fit the battle of Alabam, and the bull got nasty, ghastly, nasty.
> The bull turned hoses on children and people and the water came splashing, dashing, crashing.

And a few stanzas later:

> Little babies fit the battle of police dogs, police dogs, police dogs,
> Little babies fit the battle of police dogs, and the dogs came growling, howling, growling. . . .

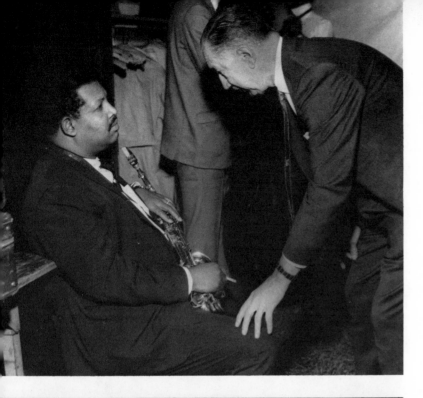

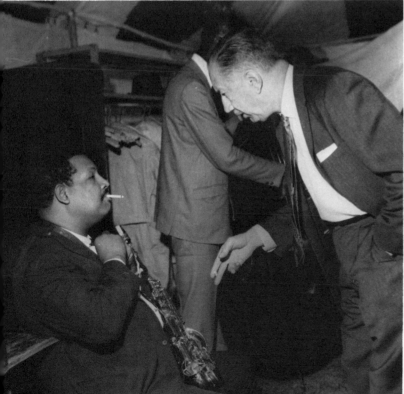

Left. Ignoring the swirl of activity around them, Cannonball Adderley (seated) converses quietly with clarinetist Pee Wee Russell. *Opposite.* An early morning rehearsal of the group backing singer Joe Williams (left) are (right to left) trumpeters Howard McGhee and Clark Terry, tenor men Zoot Sims and Coleman Hawkins and pianist Junior Mance.

One of the local papers said his militancy was "entirely out of place and uncalled for and a poor way to end a performance."

Dave Brubeck made a hit the final evening with some new material. Earlier in the evening flutist Herbie Mann played a seemingly interminable hour-long set of Afro-Cuban music. Martial Solal, the French-Algerian pianist, played some interesting music backed by a fine rhythm section that included Teddy Kotick, bass, and Paul Motian on drums.

Jimmy Smith on organ stirred things up with a direct appeal to what one of the papers called "the baser teenage emotion." He played four extended blues numbers, exciting the young audience to such a pitch that many of them started to stand on chairs and dance. It was a nervous time for the helmeted police, who tried to prevent some of the fans from climbing over the snow fence in front of the box seats. The press started pulling their equipment together, having visions of another breakout like the one that had occurred outside the field area in 1960. George Wein finally came out on stage and tugged at Jimmy's shirt in an effort to stop his incendiary playing. MC Willis Conover finally quieted them down with a promise of more if the kids returned to their seats. It was touch and go, but order was finally restored.

Encores were provided by John Coltrane, who followed with his quartet. McCoy Tyner, his pianist, had told me, "John always stressed the fact that the music doesn't play itself; you've got to play it." And the quartet meshed beautifully with Jimmy Garrison's bass moving with tight nervous energy, McCoy intense and imperative, Roy Haynes on drums. It produced some exciting, searching music. Coltrane led the group with tense transitions from tenor to soprano, weaving, turning, restlessly exploring with a fierce drive.

111

1964

Thursday evening got off to a rousing start with a program entitled "Great Moments in Jazz." A group of veteran jazzmen provided some fine moments. During the afternoon rehearsal scheduled pianist Joe Sullivan had collapsed from exhaustion. A fire rescue truck was summoned, and Joe was taken to the Newport Hospital. Later that evening hospital authorities reported his condition as satisfactory. Another less serious crisis arose when the local beer-truck drivers went on strike. Unfortunately, it had no effect on beer supplies in the area. The liquor stores in town posted large signs in their windows citing how many cases were on hand for the Festival fans, and the Kiwanis organization that handled refreshment and food concessions in Freebody Park said that they would be unaffected, being well supplied with beer.

The opening-night musicians started with a bright, swinging "Sweet Georgia Brown," on which Edmund Hall on clarinet stood out with a punching solo filled with sharp edges accenting a sinuously weaving intensity. The tall, distinguished-looking Hall was ably supported by the tasty trumpet of Joe Thomas, trombonist J. C. Higginbotham, and bassist Slam Stewart, with Jo Jones giving crackling support on drums. George Wein filled in for the ailing Sullivan.

The second set of the night featured some wailing, stomping solos by trombonist Lou McGarity, on a leave of absence from his regular New York studio job. McGarity played with a melodic inventiveness and compulsive drive that seemed to be a release from his more

stilted studio requirements. Particularly on "I Found a New Baby," he achieved a fluency that galvanized the rest of the group. And clarinetist Peanuts Hucko, too long buried under other group soloists, later asserted a startling new personality with a richly played solo on "Stealing Apples."

The second half of the evening was all Louis Armstrong. It did get a little wearing when he played "Hello Dolly" six times at the request of fans. His new vocalist, Jewel Brown, poured into her black satin gown with a white collar, did some good vocalizing on "Lover Come Back to Me" and "I Left my Heart in San Francisco."

Alternating on cornet were Muggsy Spanier, with his piercing power still intact; Wingy Manone, clowning around with bumps and grinds; and the still agile George Brunis, at sixty-seven years of age playing well but performing with kindergarten-type humor.

The breeze gave a great deal of trouble to the Rod Levitt Octet performing that afternoon. During their performance it upset some of the arrangements, causing Levitt to start again on "Vera Cruz." His performance was again disrupted when Jayne Mansfield, clad in a tiny bikini covered with a short jacket and carrying a Chihuahua dog with painted red toenails, strode by munching a slice of pizza, followed by the press and a crush of photographers. She later said in an interview, "I think jazz is more exciting than topless bathing suits." The Levitt Octet produced in their brief program some fine solo work by Gene Allen on baritone and Cy

113

Stan Getz and Astrud Gilberto.

Johnson on piano. Their final piece, "Down Memory Lane," was a capsule history of jazz from Dixieland through swing, bop, and finally to the new free-form music. Collectively, the band swung beautifully. At one point the flutist, George Marge, had to turn his back on the audience in order to overcome the wind, which was distorting the notes he was blowing.

Ethel Ennis followed them with a fine set of vocals. Her warm voice got through to the sun-drenched audience, especially her ballad treatment on "But Beautiful" and her low-key rendition of "Yesterdays."

Pianist George Russell's sextet was outstanding, particularly in the work of trumpeter Thad Jones and bassist Steve Swallow. Swallow accented and moved fluently between Russell's piano figures. It didn't seem to matter what turn of phrase Russell moved into; Swallow, like someone on a surfboard, anticipated every current and wave coming by, never faltering for an instant. They moved from "Outer View" through "Stratusfunk," "D.C.," and "Divertimento," and they were finally joined by singer Sheila Jordan on the old country-music standard written by the former governor of Texas, Jimmie Davis, "You are My Sunshine." Her singing was brilliant and vital.

Tenorist Stan Getz's quartet played the second evening with a penetrating quality that showed precisely that Stan knew what he wanted to get from his group and got it. The quartet made intricate statements, flourishing within the confines of the melodic quality of Stan's solos. Garry Burton, his vibist, seemed to have expanded during the year, moving with apparent ease, exuberant, countering Stan's sax with intense moments of lushly sensitive sound.

Stan was later joined by Astrud Gilberto, the Brazilian vocalist, in a recap of their bossa nova hits, "Girl from Ipanema" and another bossa nova melody. The little-girl quality in her voice, along with the freshness and popularity of their recent albums, captured the audience.

Above. Trumpeter Wingy Manone regales pianist Billy Kyle (center) and trombonist George Brunis with some funny stories. *Opposite.* Muggsy Spanier warms up for his performance and reminisces with old friend, bassist Bobby Haggart.

Trumpeter Chet Baker, back from an expatriate life of problems, joined them later, playing with the old lyrical omniscience he had projected with Gerry Mulligan's group in the fifties. Dressed in red pants and blue jacket, his high cheekbones and angular chin jutting out, he swung on flugelhorn and propelled the whole group in an interplay with Stan that delighted the audience and press alike.

Pianist Thelonious Monk followed with a group that was in rare playing form despite the fact that Monk was breaking in a new bassist, Bob Cranshaw, and Ben Riley on drums. Tenorist Charlie Rouse soloed with wit and imagination, fitting in with Monk's thinking. The group shone on "Rhythm-a-ning." And Monk and Rouse had a compelling, buoyant quality that brought smiles all around the press pit, a sure sign that something of value was happening onstage.

The Saturday afternoon program, despite the rain that finally fell during Dave Brubeck's solo piano performance, produced some memorable moments that year. "The Piano Workshop," as it was called, provided an outlet for a myriad of styles on the keyboard. The performers ranged down in age from seventy-year-old Willie "The Lion" Smith. Willie, a legendary figure in jazz, lip-crunching a black cigar and wearing a Panama hat, helped to synthesize his life in music with a series of old tunes, narrating as he played "Tea for Two," "Love Remembers," and the brisk, punchy "Fingerbusters." Willie played with wit, precision, and the proper blues background that was infectious in the warmth that he projected. Monk provided a contrast in style with his witty rendition of "Tea for Two" later in the day. He had obviously meant it as a tribute for the Lion, and as one of the critics succinctly put it later, "Monk's stride effect was dues paying to the whole school of Harlem pianists." Later Joe Sullivan jumped into the piano circle, despite his doctor's orders, and livened the scene with "Little Rock Getaway" and "Gin Mill Blues." An eight-handed jam session wound up the afternoon with To-

116

Above. A relaxed and happy ambience filled the backstage grounds when this gathering took place. Old friends (left to right) Ben Riley, Sonny Stitt, Howard McGhee, Thelonious Monk and Max Roach. *Opposite.* Singer Abbey Lincoln making her first appearance at Newport.

shiko Mariano, Dave Brubeck, Billy Taylor, and George Wein combining forces.

Saturday evening trombonist J.J. Johnson came on board with an eager, intense group propelled by a supple rhythm section that breathed fire into every note. Drummer Louis Hayes played with ferocity and determination, while pianist Harold Mabern projected just the right feeling and drive to balance J.J.'s insatiably imaginative trombone solo. Moving from John Coltrane's ''Impressions'' through a tender ''My Funny Valentine,'' the group transformed the Dixieland anthem ''When the Saints Go Marching In'' into a fiercely individualistic concept. J.J. was a perfect fusion of inner tranquility and controlled rage. Relentlessly shifting gears, exploiting every stop and position along the way, his solo left you gasping for air. His rhythm section, while lighting some of their own fires, kept pace and accented beautifully.

Johnson joined tenorist Sonny Stitt, trumpeter Howard McGhee, and drummer Max Roach in a tribute to the late Charlie Parker. Before their last number, MC Father Norman O'Connor called for a moment's silence in tribute to Parker. A hush fell over the fourteen thousand people in the park.

Highlighting the final part of the evening was the performance of drummer Max Roach and his wife, Abbey Lincoln, in their ''Freedom Suite.'' While a commentary would have helped the audience to keep up with the sharp changeovers from primitive African rhythms to contemporary jazz, Abbey was superb in creating and maintaining the proper balance between narrative and drama—no mean feat in an outdoor stadium. But despite the fine presentation, some fans, uninterested or bored with the set, made rude remarks during intense sections of the suite.

The final Festival evening didn't reach the previous peaks, but there were some good moments in Dizzy Gillespie's group. James Moody on alto and flute was su-

perb throughout, bassist Chris White gave strong support, and drummer Rudy Collins played with brilliance and taste. But Dizzy gave everything his spur-of-the-moment intensity, whether vocalizing on "Gee, Baby, Ain't I Good to You" or attacking the breathtakingly uptempoed "Dizzy Atmosphere."

By the time vocalist Sarah Vaughan appeared, the crowd had thinned out, as fans tried to beat the crush going home. Nevertheless, Sarah was in a fine groove and was greeted with enthusiasm.

Organist Jimmy Smith's program was exciting only for the length of time he held notes. He hit his peak with one that extended for four minutes thirty seconds. It was as if he were taking out his aggressions on the crowd, and his program did little to enhance the evening.

The Festival presented some down-to-earth programming in Moms Mabley, the first comedienne to grace that stage at Newport. Dressed in a bright-flowered wrapper, with an orange floppy hat to top it off, she proceeded to convulse the audience with her wry humor. I laughed along with the rest of the audience, but it's extremely debatable whether she belonged at a jazz festival.

The liberal Newport policy of allowing fans to camp on local beaches was jeopardized early Sunday morning when a giant bonfire was started near some bathhouses and other public buildings. A small group of youths resisted police efforts to reduce the fire and move them away from public property. About one hundred police were finally required to quell the disturbance, and seventy teen-agers were carted off to be arraigned in court. Most were fined an average of seven dollars plus court costs and released. George Wein, the Festival producer, said that the disturbance affected the Sunday night attendance, but that he thought "the beach incident was played up far beyond its importance."

Opposite. J. J. Johnson. *Above.* Comedienne Jackie Moms Mabley emphasizes a point.

119

1965

Toward the end of July 1964 the Newport City Council, because of the complaints of city residents about the noise the Festival generated in the residential area surrounding Freebody Park, and those of the town merchants about the hardships caused by the rerouting of traffic away from their businesses, plus the unprecedented crowds pushed off their beach sleeping area by damp weather, barred any further music at Freebody Park.

In December the newspapers announced the lease by George Wein of thirty-five acres in the northern section of the city, on vacant land adjacent to the town dump and sewage plant. Wein announced plans to erect a shell facing north, which would project sound only toward the naval base and not toward any residential area. The city had already granted Wein his license for 1965.

The temporary stage erected at newly named Festival Field was well constructed of precast aluminum sections bolted together. The seating arrangement was laid out as it had been in previous years, in an oblong shape. Preparations even included spraying the area with insect repellent. But the last row of the twelve thousand seats abutted the rear fence, and I didn't envy the people that would be sitting back there, almost a fifth of a mile away from the stage. The blue-and-white striped tents backstage and the canvas around the temporary snow fencing gave it a festive atmosphere. Outside the field an area had been reserved for parking twenty-five hundred cars.

The Newport area awaited the Jazz Festival this year.

Along with releases outlining safety commission reports, directional regulations, and police schedules for vandalism prevention, reports had been filtering into the newspapers over the past week that the citizen-band radio club was to be on hand again with walkie-talkies in case of any emergency, that a judge had offered his services if needed in any arraignments of troublemakers, and that state police and national guardsmen were on the alert. With new traffic regulations and roadblocks set up all over town the usual rumors flew: fifteen hundred cars were headed toward Newport, coming up the New Jersey Turnpike; five hundred kids were trying to storm the park; Frank Sinatra, who was scheduled to appear, was ill or the National Guard had been called out to protect him on his way from Providence—all were rumors and all were dreamt up by bored people looking for excitement. It all sounded like the invasion of France was about to begin.

But everything was normal for a Festival at Newport. The lesson had come hard in 1960. The only major change in the city in 1965 was the ban on beach sleeping, something that everyone now agreed should have been imposed years before.

The Festival was close to a sellout. Advance sales

Some of the finest drummers in jazz getting set up for an afternoon of drumming on the new stage at Newport. On the left, Buddy Rich converses with Jo Jones as they make minor adjustments in their setups. At the far reaches of Festival Field some fans sit almost a fifth of a mile away from the stage.

121

were so large for the Sinatra concert that George Wein adopted a policy of requiring those purchasing tickets for his appearance to also buy them for at least one other concert. While the stage was being readied for a performance, the producer was quoted as saying, "This is the year of truth for the Festival. If we can get through this Festival, I think we'll be here many, many years."

Thursday evening did not have too many auspicious moments. The music of Pete Seeger, a folk artist who knows where he's at in the folk idiom, did not work well in contrast with jazzmen. Seeger always seemed to be feeling more than he could express. And contrasting his style with Memphis Slim on piano and Willie Dixon on bass made for unevenness. Seeger was fine, however, reminiscing about Huddie Ledbetter.
    Muddy Waters's band was less susceptible to generalization, and the earthy quality of the group was heightened when trumpeter Dizzy Gillespie and saxophonist James Moody joined them. The combination of pianist Otis Spann, Dizzy's horn, and the harmonica of James Cotton crackled with a bluesy humor. The grouping seemed to bring out the best from everyone, as if it had always been there waiting for this moment to surface.
    Later Diz joined the Les McCann Trio, and with an abrasive, compulsively swinging Moody on tenor, joined by Milt Jackson on vibes, he brought some exuberant moments to an otherwise dull evening. Vocalist Joe Williams followed, but his set did not catch fire with the audience the way it had the previous year.

Friday afternoon, entitled "New Things in Jazz," brought in few fans to listen. MC Leonard Feather warned that "listening to this new music is not easy but involves real effort, not mere receptiveness." There didn't seem to be much rehearsal or cohesiveness to the two meandering compositions, Mike Mantler's "Communications" and Carla Bley's "Start." Neither piece did more than perplex an audience trying to understand,

122

Cecil Taylor plays at fever pitch, scarcely giving you time to catch your breath. *Opposite.* Carmen McRae.

and the Jazz Composers Orchestra failed to either excite or intimidate. The only sound faintly resembling a reminiscence of where jazz had once been was that of trombonist Roswell Rudd as he used his plunger to gain a momentum in his solo. Archie Shepp's group was well rehearsed, and the prepared contrasts reinforced the solos, making them sound more complex than they were. His vibist, Bobby Hutcherson, complemented Shepp nicely with an easy expressiveness and with considerable vitality. Their rendition, ''Le Matin des Noirs,'' brought moments of tenderness with an evocative interplay between Shepp's sax and Hutcherson's vibes.

Paul Bley's trio followed with a set of pieces composed by his wife, Carla. The easy expressiveness of his bassist, Steve Swallow, did not have too much space to surface within the confines of Carla's music, although Paul played well and kept the group tightly knit.

Cecil Taylor's group was a complete turnaround in pace. He didn't allow you to catch your breath. After a while his intensity of feeling wore you down until you felt like wincing. The breathtaking pace on three successively up-tempo numbers, mixed with Taylor's intensity, was a jarring, teeth-rattling experience. In retrospect, the things Cecil played don't seem so radical anymore. Taylor was very impressive that afternoon, but his sustained energy gave one the feeling that he had just discovered free verse.

Friday evening late arrivals forced some switching on the programing. Miles Davis had not fully recovered from his recent hip operation and had canceled out.

Monk was not too inspired that evening. Carmen Mc-Crae sang a smashing ''Sweet Georgia Brown,'' and her voicing was sinuous and graceful with phrasing coming from deep inside, broad and deep and dynamic.

Diz replaced Miles for the evening, playing a scorching set. Pianist Kenny Baron energized and returned in kind the impetus given by Dizzy. He moved with an instinctive, fluid quality through ''Chega De Saudade,'' with his conga drummer, Big Black, playing with sparks

123

Drummer Louis Belson demonstrates a series of beautiful drum rolls for the fans at Festival Field. *Opposite.* Two participants in the drum afternoon pause briefly to greet each other: Art Blakey and Elvin Jones.

flying from his hands, punctuated with musical tones that gave the whole thing an acrid quality. Baron swung quietly through "Morning of the Carnival," letting it come out easily and naturally.

The afternoon of the drum workshop, Saturday, was a model of what the Festival could and should achieve. It began with a call by MC Billy Taylor to Buddy Rich to "kick off the tempo." Rich, white teeth flashing in a tanned face, grinned and got himself and three other drummers—Art Blakey, Elvin Jones, and Jo Jones—off with an ensemble number, each man doing his thing but not trying to cut the others. They passed beats and riffs along the line of drum setups strung out across the stage. Blakey was smiling; there was a broad grin on Elvin Jones's face. Jo Jones was riding lighter than air on his brushes. Using a minimum of words to have the drummers explain different phases and styles, Billy Taylor was outstanding. The spontaneous intensity of each soloist without any striving for superiority was beautiful to watch. Each man in turn made his work more complex and less susceptible to generalization. It was a memorable afternoon of jazz.

Jo Jones, hanging loose, feet enclosed in his twenty-year-old shoes, played with a grin, sun glinting off his bald pate. First on brushes, showing infinite variety, he moved on to sticks, mallets, and then fingers, paying his dues to great drummer Big Sid Catlett, demonstrating how Sid moved with his large arms over his cymbals. Jo radiated a special eloquence.

Louis Belson followed with a demonstration of rolls and how they developed, going into his foot-pedal work, then gradually building up to a highly innovative solo that showed an outwardly complex structure with a subtle incessant roar intensifying each moment to a climax of masterly and penetrating power.

Elvin followed, demonstrating the polyrhythmic dialogue he would use in a small combo. Elvin had George Coleman on tenor, Johnny Coles on trumpet,

125

and George Tucker on bass playing behind him, and he moved gracefully, with a passionate expressiveness, sometimes with fierce determination.

Roy Haynes was next; he built up gradually, using a complexity of rhythms. Then he zoomed upward, alternating on tom-toms, high hat, and cymbals, pacing down to his snare with intricate statements overlapping one another. He then worked into a polyrhythmic duet with tenorist Coleman to break open the afternoon with bursts of applause from the audience.

Blakey, playing with an expressive nervous energy, was completely in control. Called upon to demonstrate the talking-drum element in jazz, he imposed his implacable will with crisp, jarring switches from snare to tom-tom, crashing cymbals with an anticipatory delight and ending with a brutal amalgamation of his accumulated understanding.

The *pièce de résistance* was Buddy Rich. Rich's left hand was fantastic. He started with rolls, driving with his pedal work, only occasionally moving to a cymbal. He kept his roll going with one stick; the infinite variety made those drums an extension of himself. Relentlessly shooting up fresh and vigorously whenever he slackened his pace, he suddenly exploded with a roar and crash of cymbals, adding further emotional dimension, superimposing his will at the climactic moment. He was unrelenting in his driving force, sweat streaking down his face and soaking his collar. Rich took a short bow amid the roar of the audience, gracefully announcing how proud he and Louis Belson were to be among such drumming greats. They played a short ensemble piece, ending the afternoon with a grin from ear to assaulted ear as Elvin lifted Buddy into the air for the sheer joy of it.

Saturday night opened with a roaring jam session with Howard McGhee on trumpet; Illinois Jacquet on tenor; Tony Scott, back home after five years, on clarinet; and Buddy Rich on drums. In the nondescript blues

A relaxed Duke Ellington greets tenor man Illinois Jacquet warmly, joshes him about a half-remembered experience, and ends with a bearhug.

and ballad medley they played, Jacquet was lyrically eloquent, and Buddy soloed under umbrellas held by Howard McGhee and Tony Scott as a downpour soaked the audience. The rain came so suddenly that there was little time to take cover, and people in the boxes ran to the canvasing along the fence, pulling it over themselves without any room to spare.

The program suffered from the scheduling of Herbie Mann, always a crowd pleaser, ahead of Earl Hines, the fine pianist. Mann played a roaring set with his octet. They swung through "Comin' Home," and there was some fine vibe work by Dave Pike on "Stolen Moments." But it was, as they say, a hard act to follow. The crowd kept demanding more from Mann, but MC Mort Fega cooled the audience down. Hines played a brilliant set. His "Man with the Horn" was a lovely demonstration of his piano mastery.

Duke Ellington closed the evening with a good grouping from an obviously tired band. His recent original, "Nippon Ad Lib," had good clarinet work from Jimmy Hamilton with a fine interplay of piano from Duke. Altoist Johnny Hodges swung nicely on "Passion Flower," and there was some good solo work from trumpeter Cootie Williams, tenorist Paul Gonsalves on "Chelsea Bridge," and a new vocalist sitting in with the band, pianist Dollar Brand's wife, Bea Benjamin, on "Solitude."

Sunday afternoon ran so long that Lee Konitz on alto had nothing left to do but dismiss his group, play a note on stage, and ask the crowd to join him in singing along with him. Smiling, the audience complied with his request.

A broiling sun beat down on the spectators, and helicopters passed overhead for test landings behind the tent area in preparation for Sinatra's arrival for the evening program.

Despite all the excitement and interruptions, there was too much good music on the program. Highlights

127

were pianist Wynton Kelly playing Ferde Grofé's "On the Trail" from *Grand Canyon Suite;* Albert Mangelsdorf's burnished trombone work; pianist Don Friedman dueting with Hungarian guitarist Atilla Zoller on a sparkling "Spring Signs"; Dollar Brand, the South African pianist, showing some individuality on the keyboard; and pianist Denny Zeitlin, a medical student finishing his internship at Johns Hopkins in psychiatry, sounding fresh and cogent on one of his own pieces, "Quiet Now."

The most extended set of the afternoon belonged to Stan Getz. Stan propelled his group with a set from "Chego De Saudade." Vibist Garry Burton filled that vast stage with passion. In the romantic "My Funny Valentine" Steve Swallow on bass moved gracefully with drummer Joe Hunt, providing a quiet scintillation to the group, always tasteful and moving. Wes Montgomery made a brief appearance with Wynton Kelly on piano, and the fine bassist Paul Chambers mixed it up with drummer Jimmy Cobb.

The final evening belonged to Frank Sinatra. The skies were clear, and every seat had been filled early. Fifteen thousand people were on hand to see Frank's helicopter descend at seven forty-five P.M., followed by another chopper carrying Quincy Jones, his conductor for the evening. After the landing Sinatra and party stayed in a house trailer backstage until nine thirty, when he went on. A cordon of thirty policemen had surrounded the landing area immediately after landing. Out front 280 seats usually reserved for press people were reserved exclusively for Sinatra's friends. And we in the press had problems. An edict had come down from Sinatra that five minutes would be allotted to picture taking during the first few minutes of the program, and that was it. There was a mad scramble to shoot fast and furious.

You could see the excitement and tension building up in the audience from the moment the helicopter appeared in the dusk sky with its flashing red and green

128

Chairman of the Board Count Basie, whose orchestra was Conducted by Quincy Jones for the occasion. *Opposite.* Sinatra in action.

lights. When he came onstage, Frank appeared relaxed. His crew of sound engineers were off to one side of the stage, moving their dials and adjusting their equipment. It was all unnecessary. The sound balance was fine to begin with. They should have left it alone. They had distorted the balance of the speakers for the people in the audience.

Oscar Peterson had appeared briefly before Sinatra, and Basie had played a couple of numbers—both to no avail. The people wanted Sinatra, and Sinatra only. They got him. From the moment he stepped onstage with a short monologue—"With all those beards in the audience it looks like a state home for the hip"—to his roaring off into high gear with "Get Me to the Church on Time"—he had them in the palm of his hand. Looking around me I saw hardened booking agents, artists and repertoire men, record-company presidents, musicians, and people who had been there alongside me for years, listening quietly in awe. He sounded great. As good as he ever sounded on record. Better, as a matter of fact. All the magic was still there, and he glided through his program of twenty songs. "Street of Dreams" had an intense and imperative message, and his "Where or When" was a beautiful projection of warmth. Whatever he sang had substance. The audience responded with a genuine outpouring of warmth in return. His impeccable phrasing, his way with a lyric—that night he had it all— and if he had had the greatest public-relations firm working out a dramatic departure, they couldn't have come up with a more effective answer than that slowly ascending helicopter blinking its lights good-bye. When the crowd finally drifted off, something seemed to be missing that night. I think it was the opportunity to tell him in person how great he had sounded to us all.

129

1966

The Festival was finally ensconced in its new $200,000 complex off Connell Highway. An air of permanence pervaded the sloping grounds that had been expanded to eighteen thousand seats. The shell and complex had been designed by Russell Brown. The stage swung around for 60 feet, with a width of 55 feet, and flared out to the rear stage area for 120 feet. The enormous stage had been designed to provide space for a one-hundred-piece orchestra, a seventy-voice choir, and some of the stars of the New York Metropolitan Opera Company. Through a previous arrangement they would be presenting their first concerts on the new stage shortly after the Festival ended.

The complex out back had a contemporary Japanese look and a number of refinements for the comfort of the musicians.

The two-story structure had a fifty-foot bridge ramp that led directly from the stage to the dressing rooms, which included showers, lounges, and permanent lavatories, the lack of which had always been a sore spot with the Festival's critics. Other facilities included a central control room that overlooked the stage and could also be used for recording facilities. A new press room had been promised for later in the season. Drummer Buddy Rich summed it all up backstage: "This is first class here; this is the first time anyone has treated the performers like human beings." The programing was speeded up by such refinements as having drum setups all prepared on dollies which could be swiftly wheeled out onstage without the interminable waiting periods.

Buddy Rich booted the Newport All-Stars for a comparatively large opening-night audience of eight thousand. Bud Freeman was on tenor, Ruby Braff on cornet, Gerry Mulligan on baritone, and producer Wein held down the piano chores. Rich swung the group from the opening notes. Ruby played beautiful choruses with an eagerness and just the right flow to provide a relaxed happy-with-what-I'm-doing feeling on "Rose Room" and the lovely "Sometimes I'm Happy." Mulligan surprised everyone by using an alto sax on his decade-old chestnut, "Bernie's Tune." He played with a penetrating, Bird-like intensity, with delicate spacing, sweeping and soaring in with a sinuously crisp solo that took everyone unawares, and gave fellow musicians and audience alike immediate gratification.

The Archie Shepp Quartet also shook up Festival Field that evening. It was a shocker to begin with to find Shepp, an avant-gardist of jazz, featured on opening night. With a tongue-in-cheek ambience he assaulted the fans with an irritating march; a raucous, blaring segment of Billy Strayhorn's "Prelude to a Kiss"; and a caricature of his own cerebral style of playing, intermixing it with a poetry reading entitled "Malcolm, a poem based on Malcolm X." "Take this cannibal's kiss and turn it into revolution . . ." he said. Part of the audience interrupted his reading and jeered him. "I know you racists don't like jazz," he shouted into the mike. "If you think I'll go on under these conditions, I won't." However, he did finish the poem and played another number to a cheering audience.

131

Ella Fitzgerald sings with the Duke Ellington Orchestra.

Saturday afternoon provided heat from two directions. One was the torrid 102-degree temperature. The other was an afternoon of avant-garde music by the field's chief protagonists.

Most of the tenor work that afternoon seemed like an affectation of John Coltrane, who closed out the afternoon. The Jazz Crusaders made an unscheduled appearance, providing some good trombone work by Wayne Henderson, and the group melded well.

Trumpeter Bill Dixon followed with one very extended number called "Pomegranate." Aside from Ken McIntyre on bass clarinet and alto sax nothing much seemed to happen. Judith Dunn danced in time to a recording of the traffic noise in Times Square at rush hour. Pianist Horace Silver cleared the air with his quintet, swinging all the way.

Tenorist Charles Lloyd's quartet followed strongly with the supple pianism of Keith Jarrett, who also beat a tin cup while Lloyd shook the maracas on one of their numbers. Jarrett, a flamboyant visual performer, took a stunning solo, intense and imperative all the way.

John Coltrane's quintet featured a gutsy bass by Jimmy Garrison, filled with masterly plucking, switching to a series of bow-tip pulls, followed by broad stroking, and ending with a beautiful run of chords. Coltrane played uncompromisingly, never accommodating, letting his feelings come out of his horn. His expressive playing came out with bursts and clusters of eloquent statements.

Nina Simone was the standout on Saturday night. She sang a compelling mixed bag that included everything from blues and work songs to ballads. She didn't have to shout to get her message across, nor did she depend on vocal nuances to express herself. Accompanying herself on the piano, playing with a fine, modulated, expressive quality, she reached out to that audience, and she fearlessly told them, "Shut up!" in order to quiet them down when they had brought her back for an en-

132

A few years before his performance at this festival, John Coltrane said, "In music it's the little things that count. Like the way you build a house. You get all the little important things together and the whole thing will stand up. You goof them and you got nothing."
Here he relaxes and warms up backstage.

core. She broke up the evening with a huge ovation from the crowd.

Monk played more lyrically that night than he had in a long while.

Topping off the evening was the newly organized big band of Thad Jones (formerly in the trumpet section of Count Basie's band) and Mel Lewis (former drummer with Stan Kenton). It was originally put together as a rehearsal band, to give good free-lance musicians an opportunity to blow for the sheer joy of it on big-band jazz arrangements.

It took a few numbers for the band to find its groove. But "Willow Weep for Me" was a stunning arrangement by trombonist Bobby Brookmeyer. He played a delicately shaded solo backed by Thad with lightness and grace. Thad's "Pixie" started the band roaring, with trumpeters Richard Williams and Bill Berry trading pungent fours. Plunging into "The Big Dipper," the arrangements seemed fresh and had that quality Thad was later to describe as "the same type of feeling you get in a small combo. My arrangements are like a thread that ties the music together." In a big-band milieu dominated by the sounds and arrangements of Basie, Ellington, and Herman, "the band was like a breath of fresh, gusty air, I inhaled deeply and felt light-headed."

The band backed vocalist Joe Williams for two Ellington numbers that kept one on the edge of his seat, tense and joyous at the same moment—a reverent and penetrating "Come Sunday" and "Jump for Joy." They finished the evening with a loose, swinging "Roll 'Em, Pete."

It was a scorching Sunday afternoon. The seating area had been hosed down by a fire truck earlier, but it soon dried up and the dust started blowing skyward again. The men in Woddy Herman's band had peeled off their jackets. Woody came out front in a short-sleeved shirt, open at the neck, and a few moments later stomped off his theme, "Woodchoppers Ball," which he described as "the one that's kept me eating over a long period of lean years."

"The Preacher" raised the temperature on the stage to the boiling point.

The surprisingly small audience of twenty-five hundred fans were with the band all the way. There was some good solo work from Dick Rudabusch and Bill Chase on trumpet. Then followed a sizzling "Sadie" and a funky "Hallelujah Time," with tenor star Sal Nistico blazing out, building up into bursts of choruses and byplay with tenorist Bob Pearson. Some driving ensemble work by his young group of crew-cut kids freshened up Woody's old war-horse, "Apple Honey." The nostalgia fermented more strongly with the addition of three of Woody's former Four Brothers—tenorists Al Cohn, Zoot Sims, and Stan Getz. A ringer, Gerry Mulligan, took the late Serge Chaloff's place on baritone. Starting with Jimmy Giuffre's "Four Brothers," the ensemble playing had some ragged edges. You just can't thrust stars onstage and expect them to pick up where they had left off twenty years before, when they had been sidemen with Woody's orchestra. But to see and hear the four of them together was a distinct pleasure. When Stan Getz stepped forward to play "Early Autumn," one of the pieces that had pushed him into the limelight at the start of his career, Zoot quipped, "Why does he always get to be soloist?" Stan shaped it into a new framework with warm, flowing chords, playing with an intense, romantically lush feeling. The "brothers" seemed to be enjoying themselves. Zoot reduced every note to an assertion, swinging out with a bluesy feel, and Gerry ran all over the field like a halfback, carrying the ball with an exuberance, bobbing and weaving, making the whole a vital evocation of joy.

The Thad Jones-Mel Lewis Orchestra making its first appearance at Newport. Alto soloist is reedman Jerome Richardson. This was the first edition of the band, and nearly every member of the organization was a soloist.

A surprise guest on the afternoon program, Tony Bennett felt uneasy with the setting and the sharp-shooting jazz critics in the audience, but he projected warmly and received an ovation from the relaxed crowd of festival-goers.

When the former Herdsmen had left the stage, Woody invited drummer Buddy Rich to join him. They engaged in some genial horseplay and kept up a running conversation. Rich at one moment said, "Look, no hands," while he kept the pot boiling with his agile foot-pedal work, pausing later in their duet to ask Woody, "How do you like it so far?" Woody finally leaned over facetiously to kiss Rich. They climaxed their set with a torrid "Golden Wedding," with Rich shattering the tepid air with an aggressive intensity that brought the audience to their feet in a standing ovation as he heaved his sticks into the air.

The surprise of the afternoon was the appearance of vocalist Tony Bennett, backed by Woody's band. Tony sounded relaxed and swinging on a wistful "Shadow of Your Smile" and a sparkling "Keep Smiling at Trouble." His taste was questionable in his selection of "Georgia Rose," a twenties tune written when Tin Pan Alley had already started to have guilt feelings about its abuse of blacks in other songs of the period. But he meant well. The orchestra gave him good support, and the fans behaved as if they were at a sneak preview. George Wein asked the audience if they would like to have him back next year, and the fans heartily concurred with shouts of "yeah!"

Sunday evening opened with some lovely Gershwin tunes played by Teddy Wilson on piano and bassist Gene Taylor. Drummer Buddy Rich, the hero of this year's Festival, complemented the trio with clarity and vividness. Teddy sounded ageless, making everything flow easily, fresh and direct. Rich broke up the evening early, soloing on "Somebody Loves Me." Slowly building, his solo moved with a light but fierce determination, musically pushing and driving on a level few drummers reach and building to the climactic moment ten minutes later, which had the crowd roaring. He was joined later by Clark Terry, who sang and romped his way through "Bye Bye Blackbird" and "I Want a Little Girl." His closer was his "mumbling" style of vocalizing, which brought chuckles and laughs.

Duke Ellington was feeling good, and his band sounded relaxed. As his tenorist, Paul Gonsalves, told me later, "We were just in a good groove tonight, with everybody feeling good, relaxed and hanging loose." There are very few musicians who can step out on a stage and articulate well enough, as Duke did that night, in telling an audience how to respond to jazz coolly. "One never snaps one's fingers on the beat. That's considered aggressive. Only on the afterbeat. And to be cool, while snapping one's fingers on the afterbeat, one tilts his left earlobe slightly." And Duke very nearly had about fifteen thousand people snapping their fingers on the afterbeat and tilting their earlobes properly.

The band wheeled out the old standards one never tires of hearing, especially when they're played with the mellow verve and passionate feeling of Johnny Hodges on "I Got It Bad" and, later, "Things Ain't What They Used to Be." They did some newer and tastier morsels, such as "West Indian Pancake," with Paul Gonsalves moving with catlike grace, each phrase illuminating the other, making it hard not to get caught up in his uninhibited energy and style. The band moved into the stunning arrangement of "La Plus Belle Africaine," which also featured some screams in the night by trumpeter Cat Anderson and a lilting, tasteful solo by Harry Carney on baritone.

There was a flurry of excitement and laughter earlier when Sam Woodyard's drums had been shifted around onstage and he had made a hasty stage entrance, with Duke facetiously announcing to the audience, "He hasn't always been a jazz drummer, he used to be in vaudeville."

Pianist Jimmy Jones took over Duke's chair during the final segment of the evening. Ella Fitzgerald sounded fine belting out "Thou Swell," shifting into a more romantic and lush "Satin Doll," and singing her version of

Seated on a high stool, the Rev. Malcolm Boyd reads from his book of hip prayers, *Are You Running with me Jesus?*, accompanied by guitarist Charlie Byrd.

"Mack the Knife." Duke, standing in the shadows on-stage, shifted to the piano spot, and Ella announced, "You were a long time coming." Dueting with Paul Gonsalves on her final number, Ella closed the evening with a romantic encore and a satisfied audience.

There was a guitar and a trumpet workshop Monday afternoon. George Wein took the stage to say, "The term *workshop* may be wrong here, since our aim is not to teach but to show different impressions of how instruments are used."

Outstanding in the guitar workshop was George Benson, playing "C. C. Rider." His organist, Lonnie Smith, didn't have need for volume in order to express some soulful moments.

The second half of the afternoon was the trumpet workshop, which featured Kenny Dorham, Thad Jones and Howard McGhee together and solo, Red Allen, Ruby Braff and Clark Terry together and solo, and Jimmy Owens on flugelhorn. When Bobby Hackett and Dizzy Gillespie joined horns, Wein announced, "A historic moment in jazz." There were some fine moments: a delightful "S'Wonderful," and despite their disparate styles, a relaxed "Green Dolphin Street." Hackett finally dedicated "Struttin' with Some Barbecue" to Louis Armstrong on his birthday.

The afternoon ended with a jam session, and Dizzy joined all the crew onstage with Jimmy Owens on flugelhorn to highlight the afternoon with a series of runs, each more intense than the last. Soaring, he let it all come out naturally, and with a finely modulated shout that came from inside, he jarred all the others off-stage. Backstage, amid all the congratulatory hugging and kissing, a young daughter of one of the performers came over to Diz, smiled, and handed him a dandelion.

138

Miles came on for a brief set Monday evening. He was followed by flutist Herbie Mann, one of the Festival's favorites this year. Playing with more restraint than usual, Mann nevertheless stirred up the audience, embellishing some fine Jimmy Heath arrangements. Conga drummer Patato Valdez left the stage piqued at one point during the playing of "Project S" but came back to finish an exciting "Summertime." Mann brought the crowd to a high pitch of excitement—they yelled and screamed for more—but the schedule was full and Mann left the stage, disappointing a lot of fans.

The end of the evening was all Basie's, part nostalgia and the other half "now." They kicked off the set with his flagwaver, "Singin' the Blues," which had some fine relaxed solo work by Al Aarons on a muted trumpet and Eric Dixon and Eddie "Lockjaw" Davis sizzling on tenors from their first choruses.

The Count announced singer Jimmy Rushing as "a little young cat who was chirpin' the blues with us back in those days." Rushing moved through "Someday Sweetheart," "Sent for You Yesterday," and "Goin' to Chicago." Basie obviously felt like playing piano this evening, giving him strong support. Jimmy was a little hoarse, but he soon had the stage bouncing with his infectious bursts of energy. "Jumpin' at the Woodside" brought the evening to a roaring finale, with Lockjaw talking out loud about how he felt inside and trumpeter Roy Eldridge savagely shouting and relentlessly digging in with a screaming, too short solo. Later Roy came down front to play some muted blues. It was a perfect finale.

Above. The late Harry Carney was the first and for many years the only great soloist on the baritone sax. Harry was only sixteen when he went on the road with the Duke Ellington Orchestra. *Opposite.* Johnny Hodges joined Ellington two years later and stayed with the orchestra for over 25 years. A master of ballads, Johnny was an integral part of every Ellington arrangement.

139

1967

If 1966 had been the hottest Festival to date, with temperatures rising during the afternoon to 104 degrees, 1967 was the wettest and foggiest. For four successive days there was either rain or an intermittent blanket of fog.

On Thursday evening Count Basie sat in his dressing room backstage with a constant stream of musicians paying court. Short and stocky, wearing a colorful sport shirt, he had stood in the wings earlier, during pianist Earl "Fatha" Hines's set, listening quietly. His hands were nestled in his pocket for warmth as he strode across the bridge leading from the stage to his dressing room. After changing into his dark band uniform he went toward the stage, to be greeted on the way by producer George Wein. They paused to discuss his program for the evening. While they were talking, Basie abruptly broke off in order to listen to Willie "The Lion" Smith onstage. "Hah!" He slapped his knee with gusto, laughing loudly, and then just as quickly he resumed his talk with Wein. A short while later flutist Herbie Mann paused momentarily to pay his respects to Basie and said, "I've been waiting nineteen years to ask you, Count. Can I sit in with you in Saint Louis while you're there?" Basie replied, "Sure, sure you can." A smile lit up Mann's face at the answer.

It had rained torrentially all day long until late that afternoon. The Joseph Schlitz Brewing Company was sponsoring the first evening's program, a brief history of jazz. The beer company, the first commercial sponsor for the Festival, had provided twenty-five thousand dollars for the first performance. The backdrop of the stage had an appropriate banner with the name inscribed on it, and it naturally was the only beer sold on the field at the refreshment stands.

From the drums of Africa, interpreted by Michael Olatunji and his colorfully dressed percussion group, the history then abruptly moved to Chicago. The MC of the evening, Father Norman O'Connor, described the Grand Terrace Ballroom and the Elite Club, while Earl Hines settled down to a twenty-five-minute set of brilliant piano. Squaring off with his own composition, "It All Depends on You," he was joined by Ruby Braff on trumpet, replacing Roy Eldridge, who had wired the Festival that he couldn't make the schedule. The sound system gave Ruby a harder tone than he usually had, but they sounded well together. Hines, sitting in the piano chair ramrod style, got the Festival off to a flying start.

Pianists Willie "The Lion" Smith and Don Ewell provided an opportunity for the audience of five thousand sitting in the damp, cold field to warm up with some foot-tapping stride music. Willie egged the crowd on to applause with, "How's that? Now, how's that!" They ended their set with a romping duet on "I Found a New Baby."

Trumpeter Buck Clayton and Buddy Tate on tenor brought back the sound of Kansas City. They swung happily with Count Basie and his rhythm section. Basie smiled all the way, with Buck and Buddy punching out some moving and beautiful solos. The rest of the band took their seats while they were playing. As Buck and

An early morning rehearsal of the Lionel Hampton Orchestra. The revival of a band like Hamp's presents certain problems, but when showtime arrives and a live audience is waiting out front, everything seems to fall into place.

141

Buddy left the stage, tenorist Sal Nistico started digging in with "Swanky," driving hard and aggressively. Harry "Sweets" Edison took a stunning trumpet solo on "Willow Weep for Me." Then came a wild and humorous "Boone's Blues," with Richard Boone, from Basie's trombone section, scatting through with a tongue-in-cheek-scratch-my-back style that seemed all his own. Backstage the musicians were also turned on by Boone. Some had clustered around the wings of the stage to hear him. "Ain't he something else?" a trumpeter remarked.

Vocalist Joe Williams joined the band for a couple of numbers, and with Sweets Edison playing a soft obligato behind him he sang a moving "Nobody Knows the Way I Feel This Morning." The evening closed with an updating of jazz from bop to the New Thing, with trumpeter Dizzy Gillespie, the Modern Jazz Quartet, pianist Thelonious Monk, drummer Max Roach, and saxophonist James Moody.

Multi-reedman Albert Ayler, dressed in a white plantation overseer's suit, brought the cold evening to a close. Some of the fans were impressed with Ayler's group and applauded loudly after each number. But after five successive hours in the cold and damp it was time to go.

Saturday afternoon Acting City Manager John F. Fitzgerald told producer Wein that the city council had voted unanimously to fine the Festival two thousand dollars for going one hour and eleven minutes over the midnight deadline specified in Wein's contract with the city. Wein said, "We shall contest this in court if necessary. We will contest this to the bitter end. It is an insult to the Festival and shows a lack of compassion and understanding for what we have been trying to do here in Newport." Nevertheless, despite all the protestations, nothing ever came of it.

I arrived backstage Saturday afternoon and watched the musicians preparing to go on to a program entitled "The Five Faces of Jazz." The program was intended to show the many ethnic influences on jazz. I was surrounded by a cacophony of sounds as the various musicians warmed up. There were musicians here from Hungary, Germany, Africa, Japan, and Brazil, all playing the international language, music. Some of them openly paid their dues to American jazz. Guitarist Gabor Szabo, for example, who had left Hungary in 1956, said, "The [Voice of America jazz] broadcasts were my only influence during my early years, with the exception of Roy Schmidt of the Hungarian Hot Club, who guided me to an understanding and appreciation of jazz." In 1958 Szabo had played at Newport with the International Youth Band.

Another musician heavily influenced by the Voice of America broadcasts was trombonist Albert Mangelsdorf from Germany. Standing backstage in an impeccable blue plaid suit, he said that he had first heard jazz during the Second World War from records brought over by the GIs and had later listened to the broadcasts. He used to play at the dance halls frequented by the soldiers. He also had been a member of the International Youth Band. The thin, ascetic Mangelsdorf said, "I don't think it is really a national or a racial thing. The ability to swing, to create jazz, and also to receive it, can happen, and is happening, anywhere."

Michael Olatunji from Nigeria stood listening to the discussion from the side. His strong body was encased in a beautiful white robe profusely decorated with blue and gold designs, and a blue and red fez was planted firmly on his brow. He smiled as he set up a small electric heater in front of his two goatskin drumheads to dry off some of the Newport moisture. "Beat is the most important thing in rock and roll and jazz," he remarked. "Everybody experiences a heartbeat, and this is the experience of drums. Africa must get credit for this contribution to jazz. I've learned orchestration and

Milt Jackson on vibes, James Moody, alto, Dizzy Gillespie, trumpet, Max Roach, drums, Thelonious Monk, piano, Percy Heath, bass. With the exception of Moody, all were there in the beginning when Bop music was in its formative stage.

arrangement in this country, but that's all." Olatunji adjusted his loose-flowing trousers and prepared to go on-stage, and as he strode toward the door with his drums, I noticed another American contribution he had acquired—his sockless feet were encased in loafers. Nobuo Hara, leader of the Japanese orchestra the Sharps and Flats, made the parting shot. "Jazz essentials? They have always been the same. Rhythm, melody, and harmonic arrangement," he said smiling, wiping off his tenor sax with a soft cloth.

Some of the same faces that had appeared earlier in the day showed up for the evening concert Saturday. Flutist Herbie Mann had arranged the afternoon program, and he showed up this year with Roy Ayers on vibes and Chick Ganemian playing an electrically amplified oud. The combination of the fiery Ayers with the raspy, grating oud opened up different perspectives, particularly on "In the Medina," which highlighted the oud.

The evening stretched out too long, particularly when Nina Simone came on for an hour. In a white net dress with a satin lining that matched her skin, she held the audience and dramatically dug in deep with one of the late Langston Hughes's last poems set to music, "Backlash Blues," which she transformed into a biting piece of expressive agony. It made you wince and evoked memories of Billie Holiday's "Strange Fruit."

It is hard to understand the thinking that went into placing Earl Hines between Herbie Mann and Nina Simone. Earl, one of the greats of jazz piano, played with a simplicity that was deceptive. He showed exactly what could be done without gimmicks, playing with substance and relevance. And most importantly, he swung all the way, opening with "Second Balcony Jump" and an exhilarating "Bernie's Tune." Tenorist Budd Johnson joined him, playing a lyrical "It's Magic" offstage; then he moved into "Summertime" as a tribute to Sidney Bechet, and in a quiet and almost passive way he projected not only Sidney's style but a pungent sound of

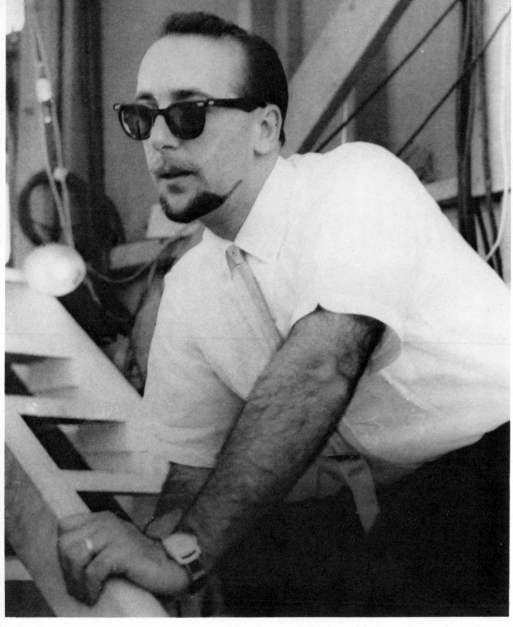

Above. Flutist Herbie Mann plays frantic
surges of notes into a microphone.
Here he relaxes offstage. *Opposite.*
Possessed of a quiet swinging energy,
pianist Earl Hines (left) says something
meaningful every moment he is on.

his own. At the end of his solo Budd stood quietly, calm
as always, and smiled to the audience, which didn't
want them to leave. The group had been on for twenty-
five minutes, but time was a big factor tonight because
of the previous night's fine. Some groups had been
asked to shorten their sets, and they left the stage despite the protests of the audience.

Gary Burton's and John Handy's groups both had
trouble with the sound system, having to fight feedback
and speakers all the way. But Handy in particular came
through with his sax swooping in and out to good effect. They portrayed James Meredith's troubles entering
college on "Tears for Ole Miss."

Dizzy Gillespie's group got into a humorous, self-
deprecating mood with Dizzy's vocalizing, but he as-
tonished everyone with a newly written ballad (so new
that he sang the lyrics from a chart). It was another facet
of his enormous talent he hadn't exhibited before.

Drummer Buddy Rich's band was the brightest moment of the evening. Just hours before the start of the
concert Rich had been summoned to the Newport Police Department to answer a complaint from the federal
government about failure to file income-tax returns from
Nevada for 1961, 1962, and 1963. Rich waived a removal
hearing, and with a one-thousand-dollar bond posted by
the Festival he was able to play. It seems incredible that
with all that must have been on his mind that night he
played a magnificent solo at the close of his *West Side
Story* medley. He was astonishing in his virtuosity. His
solo had a clarity and vividness that projected in sharp
relief and detail his inexhaustible energy as he built up
from bursts of small explosions to a whirlpool frenzy
and passion. As his solo grew quieter toward its close
and his sound grew fainter and fainter until it scarcely
could be heard, a stagehand, thinking the concert had
ended, started to advance onto the stage. He was restrained by George Wein. And the quiet once more grew
into an explosive burst that jolted the audience to their
feet in a standing ovation.

Dizzy had joined Rich in some verbal and musical sparring on a blues and then stayed on for his final number.

The concert ended at twelve thirty-seven, the intermission having been eliminated. The city council took no action this time to penalize the Festival, and Acting City Manager Fitzgerald noted, "Wein got an A for effort."

The Sunday afternoon program opened with the Sharps and Flats. The eighteen-piece band played with precision, highlighted by some good tenor from the band's leader, Nobuo Hara. The band played a program of Japanese music, but the precision of the band's section work lent itself easily to swinging sounds. The outstanding soloist was bamboo flutist Hozan Yamamoto, who improvised with them on some traditional Japanese music. His playing had an intense delicacy and was continually compelling. Asked backstage who it was he listened to in jazz, he replied in halting English, ". . . especially Sun-Ra."

Bobby Hutcherson opened the vibes workshop Sunday afternoon, playing a very moving and beautiful "Softly as in a Morning Sunrise." Garry Burton followed, playing an unaccompanied solo that glowed with little nuances all his own, making a shimmering group of intricate statements.

Billy Taylor broke into the afternoon workshop inexplicably with an hour-long set. Billy played with tremendous drive and captured the small two thousand-plus audience from his opening statements on "I Love You."

Red Norvo continued the workshop with some beautifully tasteful music. The young audience was completely unfamiliar with the short, bearded performer, but they would remember him after his warm, empathetic

set, as he moved with ultimate grace and elegance, improvising, occasionally inserting a small barbed chord, and playing with delightful ease, looking at times as if he were brushing a mosquito off his keys. Going from vibes to the wooden-keyed xylophone, he garnished his set with a stunning resonance on his standby, "I Surrender, Dear." Milt Jackson displayed some old-master virtuosity, gracefully effervescent and with seemingly infinite variety on a smashing "These Foolish Things."

Sitting back in the wings, Lionel Hampton had listened with head-nodding pleasure, a wide grin on his face, occasionally grunting his delighted approval. Hamp then took center stage and smashed out a feverish solo on "How High the Moon," moving his mallets as if they were on fire, playing by sheer compulsion. As his solo unfolded, the audience kept interrupting him with bursts of applause. The other five vibists joined him to end his set on "Hamp's Boogie-Woogie." Hamp turned around during the grouping, facetiously acting startled, and said, "I'm surrounded." He removed his jacket and dug in with the rest. With a flood of perspiration running down their faces, Hamp and his colleagues took a bow to a cheering, smiling audience. It was a Festival peak.

Sunday evening Woody Herman came onstage in hat and raincoat, unperturbed by the heavily falling rain. Woody's band played an exciting "Greasy Sack Blues." Soloists Cecil Payne on baritone, Carl Pruitt on bass, and Steve Marcus on tenor had some especially good moments on the new ballad "Free Again."

The Blues Project was the Festival's introduction to rock music. George Wein's wife, Joyce, speaking for him, since he was out of town, said, "George heard the group perform at the National Academy of Recording Arts and Sciences in New York and liked what he heard. George feels it's good to have young groups like this on. He thinks the best of them will end up in jazz somewhere."

After an interminable waiting while the giant ampli-

146

The Sharps and Flats Orchestra from Japan. Hozan Yamamoto plays a beautiful solo on his bamboo flute. The section work was precise and swung with some excellent tenor by the band's leader Nobuo Hara.

fiers, trailing wires and plugs, were set up, the five musicians came onstage and proceeded to bombard the mist-wrapped audience with waves of sound. Part of their short set was listenable, while some of their playing simply cleared out sections of the jazz-oriented audience, driving them toward the refreshment area or out the gates entirely. I was intrigued by one piece, "The Flute Thing." "We're dedicating it to peace and the end of this dishonorable war," said the group's spokesman, lead guitarist Danny Kalb. The initial theme sounded like a child's game song. It was all improvisation after that, from the flute to the organ and back. Backstage the group's flutist, Andy Kullberg, asserted, "The arrangement was not intended to be political music." Some of them would form the nucleus of the first successful rock-oriented jazz group, Blood, Sweat and Tears.

The high spot of the evening, and probably of the whole Festival, was a superb unaccompanied drum solo by Max Roach entitled "It's in Five." Max produced a highly individualistic clarity of sounds, giving new dimension and sensitivity without ever pounding or generalizing. It all seemed to come from inside, this easy expressiveness always intense and passionate, making those sticks a part of himself. The audience recognized a masterpiece and gave him a tremendous ovation.

Pianist Bill Evans, with drummer Jo Jones behind him, emphasized the contrapuntal. Miles Davis closed the evening with some good moments, as did his tenor, Wayne Shorter. But the Festival's sound system distorted the music, making for uneven listening.

On Monday afternoon, rumors flew that some of the Festival would be canceled. Even the Kiwanis refreshment stands did not start to prepare food for the Festival, thinking it would all go to waste. But producer George Wein came onstage and dispelled the rumors, introducing trumpeter Don Ellis and his orchestra, saluting his courage in coming in from sunny California. Ellis

148

came to the mike and said, "I've heard about New England weather, but this is ridiculous." The damp audience of two thousand, the smallest of the Festival, heard some excellent music. Ellis's seventeen-piece orchestra included four drummers, three string basses, and Ellis playing an electrified trumpet with four valves. Theirs was innovative music all the way; the five reeds, some of them electrified, and electric piano drew on Turkish and Indian music. The complex, multirhythmed sounds were both interesting and disconcerting at times. You had to listen with different ears in order to discern the nuances presented. The band reflected the breakout that was taking place in jazz at that moment, the rock-influenced directions that it was moving into. Ranging from fuguelike sounds to German operatic musical effects, the band stirred up a great deal of discussion after the concert closed with something called "P. T. Barnum's Revenge," which was amusing, sometimes echoing Louis Armstrong, with some far-out effects. It was like moving from realism to abstract art in one sitting. By the time the concert ended, the audience had shrunk to a few hundred people.

It took half an hour to mop the stage dry before the final night's program. It had become a small lake.

The first group on Monday evening was the Milford (Massachusetts) High School Band, led by former tenor sax star Boots Musulli, who had played with the Stan Kenton Orchestra and other big-name organizations. Some of the youngsters played instruments that looked bigger than they were. Much of their music had been

Opposite. Dizzy Gillespie sits in with the Buddy Rich Orchestra. Always relaxed, Birks enlivened the program with humor as well as music. *Left.* The late Wes Montgomery. This was to be his only appearance at the Festival. Completely self taught, his fabulous technique and frantic finger movements sometimes gave the impression that he had eight fingers on each hand.

written by the band members themselves. They played well.

The night air was set in motion by organist Milt Buckner, Illinois Jacquet on tenor, and drummer Alan Dawson wailing and splitting the air with some great and happy sounds. At one point Buckner played organ with his protruding stomach alone, holding his arms in the air to the merriment of the audience.

Vibist Red Norvo came on with the Newport All-Stars, Ruby Braff sliding in nicely with Red, and the fine rhythm section of Jack Lesberg on bass and Don Lamond on drums.

Dave Brubeck played a tribute to Fats Waller, sounding better than he had in years, and Paul Desmond's solos were relaxed and beautiful.

Stokely Carmichael of the Student Nonviolent Coordinating Committee arrived at the Festival gate about eight P.M., in a green sweatshirt emblazoned with Malcolm X's picture. He was followed by a large entourage of reporters, photographers, policemen, and the curious. Fending off questions, he announced that he was there on vacation and would not be interviewed. The year before he had created quite a stir by charging police brutality after a fracas developed near a booth that he had set up inside the grounds of the Newport Folk Festival. At the gate he spotted a familiar face and shouted, "Hey, brother, can you get Wes Montgomery over here?" A Festival official soon arrived at the gate to

150

Right. The Don Ellis Orchestra with leader Ellis playing a four-valve electrified trumpet. The band needed a stage this size to hold the seventeen pieces, including four drummers and three string bassists. The band created something of a sensation. It was the first completely electrified orchestra to appear at Newport. *Left.* Woody Herman wearing his favorite raincoat to ward off the wet night air.

give him entry. Shortly after Stokely was seated, guitarist Wes Montgomery came onstage, and during a break between numbers Stokely shouted to him, "Bumpin', Bumpin', Bumpin'." Wes answered the request, playing the tune that had been a hit a year before.

Lionel Hampton appeared with his Reunion Band, made up of former band members who had played with him through the years. The band had some good soloists in Frank Foster on tenor, Joe Newman on trumpet, and trombonists Al Grey and Benny Powell, and they were well rehearsed. They swung all the way from Al Grey's "Turn Me Loose," featuring Grey's gutsy trombone and the crackling trumpet of Wallace Davenport, through "Thai Silk," a lush-sounding arrangement that Hamp had dedicated to the queen of Thailand. A Quincy Jones arrangement featured trumpeter Jimmy Nottingham in a humorous conversational gambit with Benny Powell, throwing riffs and instrument-formed suggestive words back and forth. Then Milt Buckner on piano and Illinois Jacquet on tenor came out, and the band started wailing on "Flying Home." The music grabbed that audience and held onto it for the rest of the night. They danced in the aisles and stomped on their seats while Hamp and Milt Buckner were hamming it and mugging in a hilarious dance routine onstage and Jacquet kept wailing chorus after chorus. It was Hamp's first appearance at Newport, and the crowd let him know that it was a triumph. George Wein came stage front and announced, "Not even Duke Ellington . . ." as the crowd roared into the night.

1968

By 1968 total Festival attendance since 1954 passed the one-million mark. But this year the dissension between the townspeople of Newport, as represented by the Newport City Council, and the Festival was more persistent than ever. The *Providence Journal* reported in June: "The latest dispute erupted among city councilmen over police costs which the producer George Wein has to pay. One member charged that the figure set this year was a 'gross overcharge.' The council voted 5 to 2 to bill the producer $15,500, or about $2,000 more than he paid last year. The increase was felt necessary by the city's police department, and the council agreed— despite the donation without charge for the first time of 35 state troopers and state police auxiliaries." When producer Wein received his bill in 1967, he blew up and insisted that the city would have to take him to court in order to collect. He later changed his mind and paid up. It was a condition the city council had set before he could receive his 1968 license.

The program opened unannounced far in advance of the scheduled time of eight P.M., a procedure the Festival has steadfastly and inexplicably adhered to through the years.

Mongo Santamaria started the festivities off Thursday evening with Dave Brubeck's "Take Five." It was the Latin end of the Festival, but aside from the fine, liquid tone of Hubert Laws on flute, there didn't seem to be much else happening.

Guitarist Jim Hall, back on the East Coast after five years, had good rhythm backing from bassist Victor Gaskin and Roy McCurdy on drums. Hall explored all the tenderness of "My Funny Valentine" and then moved into "Up, Up, and Away" with a subtle, swinging pace and that way he has of finding melodies within and without a tune's basic structure, always subtle and graceful. Barney Kessell joined him, and the two guitarists did a sizzling version of "Manha de Carnival." Their virtuosity, playing against each other, making intricate statements yet keeping dynamic control, was stunning.

After intermission vibist Garry Burton's quartet ran into amplifier trouble. Drummer Roy Haynes crackled with a solo that had a swinging complexity; he built slowly like a sliding noose, tightening up as he moved from his foot pedal to his high hat. Switching to mallets to get that *chunk-a-chunk* sound, he focused his aggressive energies on his fantastic variety of sounds and complex movements.

Friday afternoon saxophonist Archie Shepp played a wild short set that included a poetry reading by Leroy Bibb, who rarely spoke into the mike.

Thankfully, drummer Elvin Jones appeared, and with Joe Farrell on tenor, soprano, and flute playing with a supple, smoldering intensity, things started to warm up. Jimmy Garrison plucked out a marvelous bass solo on "Jim's Idea," and Elvin was fresh and vigorous and exuberant, making subtle transitions without any grotesque shock effects yet never losing the audience's attention.

Cannonball Adderley's group, dressed in green and

153

A hot and hazy day at Newport. Onstage, altoist Johnny Hodges, Duke Ellington at the piano and (right) altoist Benny Carter.

gold African tunics, played a good crowd-pleasing set. Joe Zawinul, the Viennese-born pianist, moved with cat-like grace, digressing occasionally into what sounded like space music on his composition "Rumpelstiltskin." Nat Adderley impressed most with his scat singing and his trumpet work on a blues with bassist Victor Gaskin, screaming appropriately at the right moments. They ended the set with their enormous hit, "Mercy, Mercy, Mercy."

Dizzy Gillespie highlighted the Friday afternoon performance dressed in gaudy striped shorts with knee socks, clowning his way through his set, keeping the audience rocking with laughter. At one point he introduced female sax player Vi Redd as "a young lady who has been enjoyed many times before . . ." Later while she warmed up with pianist Mike Longo, Dizzy interjected, "That's close enough to jazz," convulsing the audience once again. But despite all the male-chauvinist-inspired humor she encountered, Vi fluffed it off and played a fine, Bird-inspired solo on "Lover Man."

Clark Terry's big band closed the afternoon, with Clark at one point facetiously introducing his tune "Mumbles" as "composed by George Wein and featuring the boy singer." Zoot Sims had been caught in a traffic jam, and Joe Farrell took over his sax chair. The band swung mightily with some fine charts by Phil Woods. The former trumpeter with the Newport Youth Band, Jimmy Owens, sizzled through one of his own compositions, "Complicity." Clark played a stunning solo on Billy Strayhorn's "All Heart," and the rest of the band melded beautifully together. Jimmy Cleveland and Julian Priester in the trombone section made some telling statements along with Frank Wess on flute, and bassist Joe Benjamin did a witty solo on Jimmy Heath's "Serpent's Tooth."

Schlitz Beer was back again this year, sponsoring what was called a salute to big bands. Even the music

154

Two vocalists of the '40's brought back the past. *Right, top.* Bob Eberle who used to sing with the Jimmy Dorsey Orchestra. *Bottom.* Jack Leonard of the old Tommy Dorsey organization. *Opposite, left.* Archie Shepp combining the saxophone sounds of John Coltrane and Ornette Coleman. *Right.* Altoist Vi Redd, probably the best female jazz musician since Mary Lou Williams.

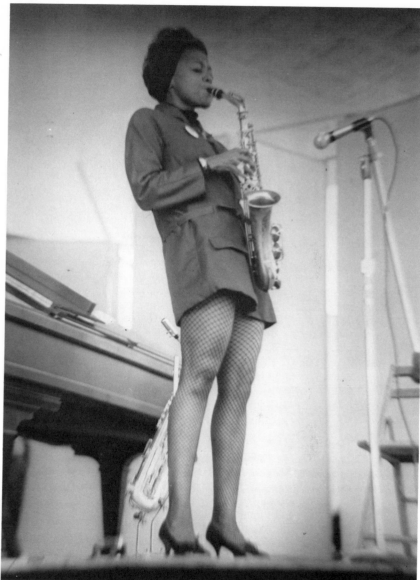

stands had been emblazoned with Schlitz medallions for the occasion. The Basie band sounded better; a driving new drummer from Chicago, Harold Jones, booted Basie's well-oiled machine forward with tenorist Eddie "Lockjaw" Davis bouncing through "I Wished on the Moon" and trombonist Richard Boone singing a tongue-in-cheek version of "Going to Chicago."

The band lingered nostalgically for only two numbers; both featured the tenor sax of former Jimmy Lunceford band-member Joe Thomas. Since retiring from the music business, Joe had become one of Kansas City's leading morticians. Though he had seldom played since his retirement, he performed well, swinging on "Cheatin' on Me," playing with verve and doing a light, pleasant vocal with good backing from the band. He had a warm bluesy sound and played a crisp, expanded solo on the original arrangement of "For Dancers Only."

After intermission former radio-announcer Andre Baruch, with notes prepared in cornball fashion by critic George Simon, "presented" a re-creation of some big-band themes, played by Woody Herman's orchestra with arrangements put together by pianist Nat Pierce. Baruch was, unfortunately, completely ignorant of jazz. The lead-in was "Don't Be That Way," supposedly honoring Benny Goodman. Tommy Dorsey was honored with "I'm Getting Sentimental over You," and Jack Leonard, Dorsey's former vocalist, looking fit and trim, sounded good on "Marie." The whole trumpet section played Bunny Berigan's solo in unison, but MC Baruch didn't recognize it. Jimmy Dorsey was honored by a medley, with Bob Eberly flashing that toothpaste smile and barely a trace of voice. Glenn Miller was saluted with "Moonlight Serenade" and "Tuxedo Junction," trumpeter Erskine Hawkins playing well but without much fire. The band flourished a bit within the confines of nostalgia on "Nightmare" and "Summit Ridge Drive," Artie Shaw's contributions to the evening. But Woody's band made some great sounds of its own on "Free Again," with

156

Opposite, top. Trumpeter Joe Thomas. *Bottom.* Tenor man Joe Thomas. Both musicians were top performers during the Swing era. Tenor man Thomas was a star with the great Lunceford orchestra, while trumpeter Joe Thomas played with both Fletcher Henderson and Benny Carter. *Above.* Former bandleader Charlie Barnett, away from the jazz scene for a very long time, still had that urgent tone in his playing.

former Newport Youth Band baritonist Ronnie Cuber and trombonist Bob Burgess getting a chance to break out a little.

Charlie Barnet was making his first and only appearance that night at the Festival. Backstage it was like old home week. Hermie Dressel, Woody Herman's manager, said, "There was a great deal of warmth and hugs and reminiscing and love pervading the backstage area. Woody hadn't seen Charlie in many years, and Charlie was unhappy with his soprano horn that night. He was having a lot of reed trouble. You know, he hadn't played and hadn't had a band together in a very long time. Charlie was kind of fussing and fuming about that, and Woody stood on the sidelines kidding him. They were warming up together in the big dressing room. The following Christmas Woody had me send Charlie an old, beat-up soprano case. Jesus! It looked like it dated from the Civil War! Woody put about three dozen used old filthy beat-up reeds in it. That was Charlie Barnet's Christmas gift from Woody that year."

Onstage there were some ungracious moments. Duke Ellington had been scheduled to introduce Charlie Barnet to the audience. Charlie had rehearsed with Duke's band for several days, but no Duke appeared for the introduction. Charlie came onstage without any introduction while his extra sidemen shifted music stands in Duke's orchestra, looking for space. When pianist Nat Pierce, trumpeter Clark Terry, and drummer Steve Little finally settled in, Charlie announced, "As you can plainly see, I'm not Duke Ellington." Looking well cared for and trim, the wealthy former band leader put the band through a medley moving from "Cherokee" and "Skyliner" through the Bill Holman original, the fiery "Introduction to an Ending." Barnet played good soprano and alto throughout. Ellington finally appeared, telling Charlie, "Love you madly." With Dick Wilson on drums supplementing Rufus Jones, the rest of the set was standard Ellington, highlighted by Paul Gonsalves on "Up Jump," Johnny Hodge's lyricism on "Passion Flower,"

157

Sonny Criss and friend relax on the porch of the boardinghouse where he was staying. Superstitious friends were concerned that the black cat might bring him bad luck on the day of his appearance. But the afternoon was all Sonny's and he played brilliantly to an enthusiastic crowd.

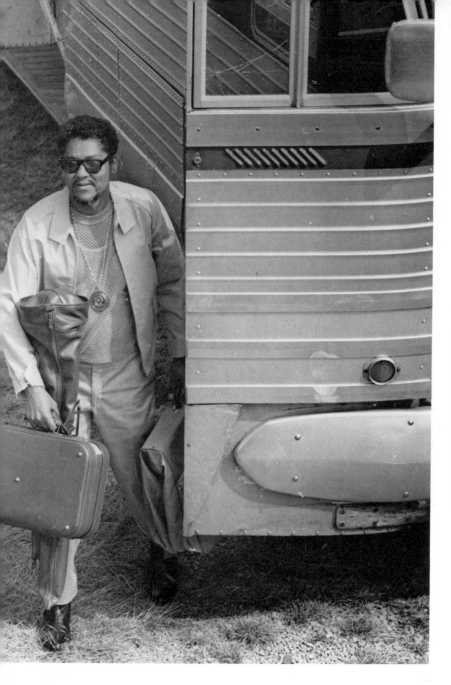

Left. Trombonist Jimmy Cleveland leaves the band bus. *Above.* Family, friends and lovers greet each other amid clutter of baby carriages. That's pianist Billy Taylor (center) and on his left, trumpeter Jimmy Owens.

and something entitled "The Busiest Intersection," which featured a battle between the two drummers onstage.

Dizzy Gillespie closed out the evening with Candy Finch and Art Blakey drumming, Gil Fuller conducting, and some uninspired ensemble work. The band sounded best on a pop tune of the day, "Ding-a-Ling."

The evening ran forty-five minutes over the prescribed midnight deadline, and the city charged Wein four hundred dollars for overtime police salaries. Wein, the newspapers reported, wasn't upset about it. "You can't run a smooth show with four big bands and make the stage changes necessary in four hours," he stated.

One of the smallest Newport audiences ever—seventeen hundred—attended the Saturday afternoon concert. But they heard some of the best jazz played at the 1968 Festival. Tal Farlow on guitar, who had made very few public appearances in the previous few years, being in semiretirement, highlighted the afternoon. Guitarist Bucky Pizzarelli remembered hearing about Farlow's prowess in 1943: "Tal is from Greensboro, North Carolina. My best man, pianist Buddy Neal, was stationed down there and . . . the talk was all about this local guitarist, Tal Farlow. I heard nothing but raves about this man. But I had never heard him. I first heard Tal in 1947 at a small club on Forty-seventh Street. Teddy Napoleon was on piano and bassist Georgie Shaw. Tal sounded incredible. I felt as though I had known the guy for years, from listening to all my friends talk about him. Tal was really the first guy to break the barrier, doing for the guitar what Bird did for all the other instruments. I listened and didn't know what he was doing, but it was so beautiful. It was all wrong, but it came out so right."

Tal Farlow's first appearance at the Festival created a sensation. He had the afternoon audience talking in hushed tones and received a standing ovation.

160

Tal wiped everybody out that warm afternoon, including Jim Hall and Barney Kessel—Barney had delayed his departure home just to hear Tal play. Johnny Knapp was on piano, Junie Booth on bass, and Mousie Alexander on drums. They played an intense "Summertime," a richly woven "My Romance," uncompromising and making every chord meaningful and vivid. The crowd interrupted several times with bursts of applause and finally gave them a standing ovation that brought an encore of "Fascinating Rhythm." Tal's playing was filled with an extraordinarily passionate expressiveness.

That afternoon, shortly before we left for the field from our Newport rooming house, I had photographed altoist Sonny Criss sitting in a rocker on the porch, fondling a black cat. I had heard stories that he had had a lot of bad luck, and I hoped it was not a portent of that afternoon's performance. But sitting on a high stool, Sonny kept Tal's fire burning with another intense set. From "Willow Weep for Me," the uneasiness left him and he drove straight ahead with a bluesy, penetrating quality. Topping off the set with "Yesterdays," he too received a standing ovation.

Altoist Benny Carter appeared with Johnny Hodges, accompanied by Duke Ellington and his band's rhythm section. Duke had been undecided up to the time they went onstage about what they would play. It was still up in the air when Duke opened with "Satin Doll." Then Duke announced, "When a symphony man wants to know about jazz, he goes to Benny Carter, and when a jazzman wants to know about symphony, he goes to Benny Carter. Ladies and gentlemen, Benny Carter." When he heard the announcement that he was to be soloist on "Take the A Train," Benny looked slightly bewildered, but Duke played a refresher chorus in case he didn't remember the melody. Rufus Jones then took a drum solo, covering any hesitation in the following number, "Come off the Veldt and into the Bush." And Johnny Hodges, looking as though he had played enough for the afternoon, bade Duke adieu and started

161

to leave when Duke announced "Passion Flower."
Johnny swung out in an up-beat style that seemed to
unnerve the audience used to his more passionate treatment of the tune. And he swung beautifully, in a way
reminiscent of those recordings he had made in the late
thirties with his own orchestra. Benny joined him on
"Things Ain't What They Used to Be." And then Duke
produced a lead sheet for Carter with some lean jottings
of something they had been playing at the Rainbow Grill
in New York. Carter grabbed onto "A Little Bit of Jive,"
and he intensified it with his lilting lyrical quality, playing eloquently and with deep feeling.

Saturday evening opened with a British import, the
Alex Welsh Band. Trumpeter Welsh started out by remarking that he assumed he had brought the fog rolling
in the field with him. Welsh has a good, crackling tone
and took a good solo on "I Hadn't Anyone 'Til You." The
band played well and sounded even better with the addition of veteran jazzman Bud Freeman on tenor, moving
with a lyrical ease on "Exactly Like You" and a bold,
empathetic version of "I've Got Rhythm."
Clarinetist Peewee Russell held the audience with an
expressive and piquant solo on his "Peewee's Blues."
Joe Venuti, sixty-four years young, swung his violin
through "Body and Soul" with masterly technique; then
he did a zestful fresh-sounding "Sweet Georgia Brown."
In a slightly wrinkled tuxedo, violin cupped under his
chin, his eyes gleaming, he proceeded to amaze and as-
tound an audience that had seemed prepared to offer
him sympathy after the sound system backfired as he
drew his bow across his strings. But Venuti swung with
his foot tapping away, volatile, stern looking yet seeming to derive an enormous amount of pleasure from
being able to play well.

Above. Duke Ellington, the old
charmer, sets everything right after Ms.
Crawford allowed the audience to
shake her up.
Opposite, left. The feral intensity of
Horace Silver surfaces during his solo.
Right. Dionne Warwicke takes the stage
for the first time at Newport.

162

Along with Schlitz beer Pepsi-Cola contributed to the well-being of jazz by underwriting part of Saturday evening's presentation. In fact, the backstage dressing-room area had a Pepsi-Cola machine without any charge or deposit on bottles. For the third time this Festival Duke Ellington was presented onstage.

Joan Crawford, representing the Pepsi-Cola Corporation, had arrived backstage in a Rolls limousine, accompanied by armed escorts. Onstage she was introduced by Festival producer George Wein to the audience. Ms. Crawford proceeded to bore the audience with a long, cliché-ridden speech outlining the contributions of jazz to American culture. A heckler shouted, "Wrap it up, Joan!" Other snide asides followed, intermixed with the general noise from an out-of-doors audience of over twenty-two thousand people. Her voice grew shrill as she spat out, "Ladies and gentlemen, shut up!" As she finished her eulogy for Mr. Ellington in a somewhat shaken voice, Duke the charmer emerged from the wings, guided her to center stage, kissed her twice on each cheek in the prescribed Duke Ellington manner, and announced that she was charming and delightful and that, of course, he loved her madly and he hoped to reflect her grace and beauty in his music that evening. It was a thoroughly professional rescue operation, carried out like clockwork by a master of charm. After guiding her to the wings, he returned to his piano and took his band through a resplendent group of standards and some smash dancing by tenorist Paul Gonsalves, who performed a daring entrechat after his solo on "Body and Soul."

There was more dancing on Duke's final number, "Acht O'clock Rock," by Trish Turner and Tony Watkins, with Woody Herman getting carried away in the wings and dashing out for a few choreographed steps of his own.

Later Dionne Warwicke arrived onstage. She was the reason for the huge audience. The young former gospel singer turned pop singer turned movie star sang a

164

pleasant set with the audience backing her all the way. It wasn't jazz, nor was it expected to be, but she did sound good on "Walk on By" and "San Jose."

The evening drew over twenty-two thousand people, the largest crowd in Festival history. But lessons learned hard in 1960 seemed to have been forgotten. Although it was limited by contractual stipulations to seating no more than eighteen thousand at the Festival Field site, after all the seats had been sold, the management began to sell standing room at $3.50 a person. The *Newport Daily News* reported on July 8—"City Manager Cowles Mallory said 'I think there were more than 18,000 people myself, but it's difficult to estimate something like that and I don't anticipate any action by the city against the festival in this area.' " Thousands of fans sprawled on the grass behind the seats. Many curled up in blankets near the food stands. Other fans unable or unwilling to buy tickets encircled the field. The security seemed nonexistent, and the police did little or nothing to prevent the crowd from sitting immediately behind the main gate and on the hills surrounding Girard Avenue. The laxity extended to a new policy inaugurated by the Festival: Spectators purchased coupons for beer when they bought their tickets, and there was no check on the number of coupons or the age of the purchaser. Police were finally posted at the ticket booths to check identification.

After dancers Trish Turner and Tony Watkins had finished their dance routine with Duke Ellington and his orchestra, Woody Herman, in one of his off-the-wall bits, came snaking out from the wings to greet a smiling and surprised Duke. Multi-talented Woody then choreographed a few steps of his own with Trish.

"An Afternoon with Ray Charles" on Sunday drew one of the largest afternoon crowds in memory at Newport. Supported by good weather and a large orchestra (which included the fine twenty-one-year-old soloist Billy Preston on electric organ and piano), a group of singers and dancers, and the Raelettes, Ray took over the afternoon. Ranging through "Georgia on My Mind," the 1937 hit "Marie," and his own "Premium Stuff," playing excellent jazz piano throughout his set, the exuberant, charming Ray gave the audience seventeen numbers. It was enough to satiate the most ravenous Charles fan, and the audience swayed, rocked, and cheered him on all the way.

Sunday evening featured Roland Kirk and crew. Roland is a direct link to the one-man bands of yesteryear, the difference being the quality and quantity of music that he produces. With his together group—Ron Burton on piano, Vernon Martin on bass, and Jimmy Hopps on drums—Roland must have left scorch marks where he stood. He went from a hot tenor solo on "Alfie" to a fantastically intense stritch solo and a simultaneous-three-instrument solo. His instruments took on the look of an auto dump, with pieces of clarinet missing and other parts taped together. He made swinging sounds on a flute, nose flute, and manzello. When begged by the audience for his encore, he stretched out with the manzello and performed a group of John Coltrane tunes. He finished by sending a large gong flying up in the air. It landed with a gigantic crash as the audience cheered until they were hoarse.

Ray Charles sings a fusion of Gospel, jazz and blues. His ability to reach audiences is due to the sincerity and feeling he projects. And amid all the blues-rooted drive, he maintains a sense of humor.

Don Ellis's orchestra followed, with Ellis in a white satin suit, half the band members wearing red velvet jackets trimmed in gold braid, and the other half wearing black vinyl jackets. The band was almost completely electrified, starting with Ellis's trumpet, and they electrified the audience. Playing numbers with peculiar time signatures—"The Great Divide," thirteen-four; "A New Kind of Country," seven-four—they broke out in lively, imaginative arrangements with brilliant rhythmic support from three drummers and two bassists. They swung mightily. In a Bird-inspired number, "K.C. Blues," four-four, they rocked with a fluid and biting quality. Frank Strozier on alto and tenorist John Klemmer were the free-swinging heroes. Closing with a satirical "Injun Lady," Ellis showed some of his chop prowess to good advantage, leaving the audience in an effervescent glow.

In between, MC Flip Wilson did his best to top the low level in blue humor he had presented at Birdland years before. The fans simply ignored his tastelessness.

Then George Wein announced that due to construction of a connecting road to the new Newport Bridge, the Festival would have to be moved elsewhere. New sites were being sought by Governor John Chafee and his state commission. According to the governor's executive secretary, Donald W. Wyatt, the governor would do anything "within reason" to keep the Festival in Rhode Island. Plans were being made to dismantle the stage, dressing buildings, and the administration office after the Smothers Brothers' concert at the end of August. The owner of the land in question, Anthony Buccola, told an interviewer: "I wouldn't blame George for leaving, though, he gets so much trouble from the people here. Other places would welcome him, and he'd probably get a site for free. I think George is a good fellow, and I hope he stays."

1969

If the access road to the Newport Bridge had gone through the center of the stage as had been planned the previous year, it would have been less hectic than the bad scene that prevailed at Newport in 1969. (The state had run out of funds and had to delay construction for a while.)

Newspapers reported, "This year after what he called a lot a soul-searching, Wein decided to appeal to youth." Another article quoted him as saying, "This is not just another pop festival, of which there have been several. This is a total music Festival including everyone from Miles Davis to James Brown."

The article continued: "Cooperation with the city manager, City Council and Police has been better than ever. He paid special tribute to the police, who probably have had more experience with music Festivals and large crowds than the police of any city of comparable size. 'They know how to respond to youth and have shown good judgement,' he said."

Advance ticket sales totaled seventy-five thousand dollars by noon of the first day. A total attendance of ninety thousand was expected over the four days.

Meanwhile, the congestion of the roads had been building. Cars waited bumper to bumper on the newly opened Newport Bridge in a line that stretched two miles, from the tollgates to Jamestown. When the bridge had opened, residents thought they had seen the last of the long lines waiting for the ferries. But only two lanes had been opened, and Newporters perched themselves on roofs watching the traffic pass.

Tickets were in such short supply that some fans sat in their cars all night waiting for the booths to open, to purchase those few remaining on sale.

The Festival's first program started at six P.M. Thursday. It was an unusual starting time, but it was deemed necessary in order to accommodate the producer's desire to cram together six hours of music. It was to be the only full evening of jazz at the Festival this year. Most of the audience didn't get seated until much later because of the downpour that arrived almost with the opening set.

Guitarist George Benson played while those hardy individuals in slickers and dripping umbrellas filed in and settled down on puddled seats. Playing mostly in the more commercial vein, he did get in some good licks on "Straight No Chaser." The only really adventurous crew that evening was drummer Sonny Murray's. It sounded together, even though its members had been assembled just for this appearance at Newport. But too much of what was performed had been heard before, played by better groups and soloists.

Vocalist Anita O'Day, making her first appearance since 1958, unmindful of the rain pelting down around her, came onstage, tastefully dressed in a bone-colored suit, an orange scarf whipping around her neck. She became a highlight of the evening as she swept through a group of romantic ballads, including "Let's Fall in Love" and "It's Wonderful." She did a warm rendition of the Beatles' "Yesterday" and a skillful and concentrated segue into Jerome Kern's "Yesterday." With a bow to

169

Bassist Slam Stewart has a style all his own. His infectious humor captured the young audience early on and he received a tremendous ovation.

the lowering skies she sang "Here's That Rainy Day." Then she imitated a sax section on Jimmy Giuffre's "Four Brothers," closing her set.

Trumpeter Freddie Hubbard, whose aggressive energy was in complete control, played with a tightly knit group. His tenorist, Junior Cook, played a striding, driving fusion of free-swinging changes, and the fierce, controlled turmoil of the rhythm section buttressed him.

Altoist Phil Woods, freshly in from Paris, moved in with his European Rhythm Machine, composed of Henri Texier on bass and Daniel Humair on drums, both from France, and featuring former International Youth Band pianist George Gruntz from Switzerland. Creating a whirlpool frenzy on "I Remember Bird," Woods played with a new maturity and a creative pugnacity, using techniques he had perfected during his long apprenticeship in Europe.

And Woods, looking like Emiliano Zapata in his long hair and drooping mustache, blazed away on Herbie Hancock's "Riot" and Carla Bley's aurally graceful piece, "Ad Infinitum."

Pianist Bill Evans opened to clearing skies with former Newport Youth Band member Eddie Gomez on bass and Marty Morell on drums. Evans, his face buried in his chest, played a series of stunning choruses with his characteristic catlike grace, uncompromising but always with that loose, seemingly random touch. Joined by flutist Jeremy Steig, they played a penetrating version of "Lover Man" with Steig crackling out a wispy solo, intense yet tender.

Entertainment was provided by Sun-Ra and his Arkestra. The group sounded ragged that evening, but visually they were a delight. They were enhanced further by something called the Joshua Light Show, which consisted of abstract projections of colored light. It amused the audience for a while but soon became a repetitious bore. The long, mostly uninspired evening closed with guitarist Kenny Burrell, whose performance was marred by the defective sound system.

Friday afternoon opened hot and humid with a Canadian group called Lighthouse. They were pleasant but obviously affected by other trends in jazz-rock and didn't seem to have much voice of their own. Despite imperfections, however, and the inevitable nervousness of a first appearance before a large gathering they played well.

George Wein then introduced the group that would provide a jam session for the rest of the afternoon. It was quite an array of talent, with trumpeter Howard McGhee taking a guiding hand in lieu of organist Jimmy Smith, who had gotten stuck in traffic coming up to the Festival. Breaking out with Duke Ellington's "Take the A Train," the unwieldy group of fifteen stars were considerate of one another. Ray Nance on violin took the first solo choruses, and then the line of soloists passed riffs for one another to feed on, each seeming to give the others sustenance, until tenorist Brew Moore, his sax cocked at Lester Young's Basie-period horizontal angle, energized each of the others into doing his own thing.

McGhee turned to trombonist Benny Green, who swung into his "I Wanna Blow Now" routine, scatting between choruses. Green finally started to shake up the crowd, driving forward with gutsy, savage blasts. Then singer Eddie Jefferson paid his dues to Coleman Hawkins, the great tenor star, by expressing a warm, beautifully thought-out lyricism on "Body and Soul," sounding better than he had in years. Then the tenors took over and interpreted their thoughts on Hawk, with Nance's violin sounding as if he was releasing pent-up emotions, without the slightest trace of condescension. Bird received a tribute with McGhee and Charles McPherson on alto backing Jefferson on "Now's the Time." Pianist Hamp Hawes put in a brief appearance, with Larry Ridley on bass and drummer Art Blakey giving him tasteful support on a brief trio set. And with bassist Slam Stewart bowing and singing, tenorist Buddy Tate took the last full choruses, bringing them home with a crisp solo. He finally shifted into a blues, and everyone joined in for the final message of the afternoon.

The bans on sleeping out were rarely enforced during the Festival. Touro Park was crowded with jeans-clad kids, and college students, some carrying grass-stained sleeping bags over their shoulders and little else, were not bothered by the local patrols. Although the city manager had stated that the park would be closed in the interest of public safety and because there were no sanitary facilities in the area, nothing was done about the assorted bands of freaks and gypsies that slept there. "You can't stop someone from sitting on a park bench at two A.M.," the city manager said. Lolling in the sun during the afternoon, entertaining themselves with guitars, reading, and eating seemed to be the youths' main interests.

The Festival security force of 100 was completely inadequate for dealing with the crowd of close to 30,000 both seated in the park and camped around outside the field. And since both the city and the Festival had ignored the expected influx and had not provided enough security, they were largely responsible for the dangerous situation.

The multitudes were attracted to Newport by the rock groups that were featured. Producer George Wein stated, "Rock is what's selling the Festival. Rock groups were so anxious to play here at the Jazz Festival that most of them came at their lowest rate."

"It's all in the name," commented one Newport businessman during the second evening of jazz-rock. "Ask for a license for a rock festival and it is denied. Ask for a jazz-rock festival license and it's granted." The hyphenating seemed to make the difference. Someone had applied for a license the previous year to hold an Indian-music festival and had been turned down. The reason given was the "element" that it might attract. But, for the most part, the people attracted to this Festival were obviously not jazz lovers.

172

Above. Buddy Rich, the yardstick most drummers are measured against, in action.
Opposite. Red Norvo's contribution to the language of the mallet ranks alongside Coleman Hawkins' in the development of the tenor sax as a solo instrument. His use of mallets has had a profound effect on everyone who plays vibes.

During the intermission a presentation was made to the producer. The Canadian jazz magazine *Coda* commented: "George Wein was presented with an award from A.S.C.A.P. for his contributions to jazz in the last 16 years and here he was trying to tear the music down with his mammoth presentation of rock."

With 22,000 people attending the Festival and another 10,000 outside camped around the perimeter of the field one would have to be totally blind not to expect trouble. The police knew it. George Wein had had enough close calls to realize it. And most of all, the city council and the hungry businessmen of Newport knew it. They all ignored it. It was obvious from the streams of cars backed up for miles. Sitting in the glow of bonfires, with the acrid odor of pot drifting over the field, the motley crowd presented an incongruous and frightening sight.

On Friday evening Steve Marcus, a musician camped in both jazz and rock, played both guitar and tenor and received mixed reactions from the audience.

Three blues-oriented English rock groups appeared that evening. Jethro Tull, led by Ian Anderson, an Afro-haired flutist, presented some vaudeville-inspired humor with ordinary drumming and flute work. Jeff Beck, a wild blues guitarist, had a frantic sound. Ten Years After, with what sounded like a boogie-woogie influence, was slightly more jazz inspired than the other two groups. But all during the first half of the program tension had been building. The hordes of youths outside the wooden fences were pressing against them, constantly climbing over, until the pressure broke a large section. Scrambling youths tumbled over security guards and each other in their efforts to get into the park, and fans in the audience cheered them on. George Wein, looking tense and somewhat frightened, rushed onstage and urgently requested that those in the audience stay in their seats. Citing recent disturbances around the country at other festivals and concerts, Wein pleaded, "If something happens here at Newport tonight, it might affect the whole pop scene. We might lose the whole thing if it erupts," he said, sweat beading on his face.

This Festival was one of the few where I wished that I had been outside the gate. No one could possibly appreciate or evaluate anything any of the performers might have been trying to say while listening to them from the press pit or from the first sixty rows of seats. But friends back at the refreshment area told me there was just as much distortion back there.

The enormous crowd had really come out to see Blood, Sweat and Tears, a quasi-jazz, pop, and rock organization featuring two trumpets, a trombone, and an alto saxophone, which immediately differentiated it from other rock organizations of the time. Their importance was also apparent to the National Guard, who flew trumpeter Lew Soloff to Newport straight from summer camp duty. The band played with polish and relentlessly exploited the sounds of blues, erupting into some exciting brass figures. The band's altoist, Fred Lipsius, got into a good groove on both electric piano and alto, playing a crisp and to-the-point solo. David Clayton-Thomas's voice was expressive and punchy; he didn't resort to the screams so common in other groups. They were the best of the rock at the Festival.

Roland Kirk followed, and this blind multi-instrumentalist delivered some fiercely individualistic solos that seemed bred in chaos as he blared out with a jolting, I-can-play-louder-than-you set, obviously trying to garner more attention and applause than the rock groups. He achieved his goal, and the producer finally had to come onstage to end the set, to the dismay of both Roland and the audience.

The Saturday afternoon program opened earlier than the scheduled two P.M., again unannounced. I had been on the field earlier to photograph a rehearsal and re-

174

Above: The late Bobby Hackett played the lush, romantic ballads that made him famous.
Opposite. Miles Davis is one of the few jazz musicians to achieve commercial success and still retain his artistic integrity. Here he electrifies the crowd at Newport.

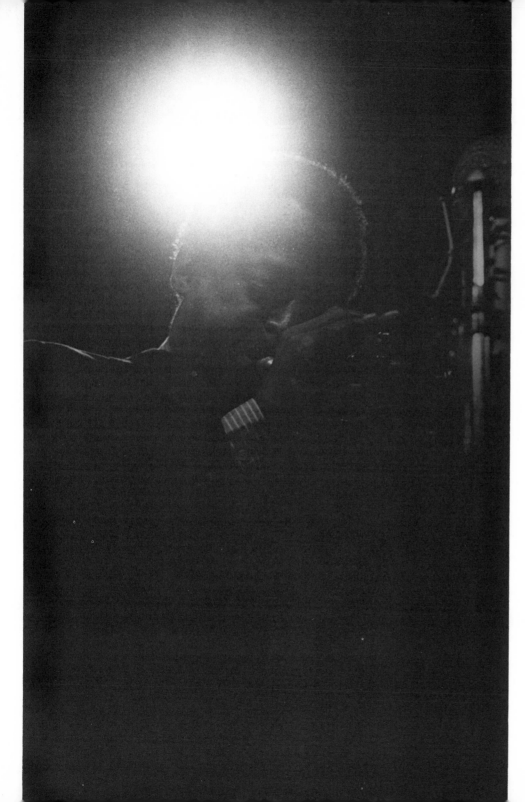

mained for the concert. The Newport All-Stars opened the afternoon, and Ruby Braff played outstandingly. It was a good-sounding group, with Miles Davis's drummer, Jack DeJohnette, filling in for scheduled drummer Don Lamond. Vibist Red Norvo projected nicely—he was witty without being pretentious—and the afternoon gave everyone a chance to spread out. Guitarist Tal Farlow and Larry Ridley on bass backed the crew with melodic imagination.

John Mayall's group was another blues-oriented gathering, John pointing the way vocally and with harmonica. There was nice flute work from Johnny Almond. Most of all there was a relaxed, together quality about the group.

Trumpeter Miles Davis, with Chick Corea on electric piano, Dave Holland on bass, and Jack DeJohnette on drums, went nonstop in what sounded like one continuous piece, with Miles fiercely pugnacious and uncompromising.

As the Mothers of Invention appeared, there was a sudden rush of fans past the youngsters doing men's work as security guards during the afternoon. The rush bowled over a few people as we photographers scrambled to get our camera equipment together and out of the way. Wedged in the way we were, there was absolutely no way to shoot or listen to the music. The group's work, a takeoff on everything and anything, tweaked everything from Vietnam to animal husbandry. Everything about the group seemed to be a put-on; they sported outlandish raggedy clothes and a collection of odd instruments from gongs to electric clavichord. Leader Frank Zappa, a twenty-six-year-old West Coast musician, has said of the Mothers, "Sure, we're satirists, and we're out to satirize everything."

Drummer Art Blakey had the newest edition of his Jazz Messengers on hand, but the tempo on "Night in Tunisia" didn't leave much breathing space for his group. Although trumpeter Woody Shaw exploded with some sizzling choruses, the attack started to take on a desperate, strained sound after a few minutes.

Saturday night the field was packed, and thousands of people milled about the gates and the walls. Wein told the audience in his introductory remarks, "You're all beautiful people." But the tension had been building all evening, and it continued to build through the first part of the evening's program. The huge crowd inside and outside the park became unruly. Kids were constantly trying to sneak over the ten-foot wooden walls, and the security guards and police made only a half-hearted attempt to prevent it, obviously having been cautioned to avoid confrontation at all costs. Their restraint probably did prevent wholesale rioting when the walls were finally breached later in the program for the second evening in a row.

The evening started off pleasantly enough with the winners of the Montreaux Jazz Festival. A Finnish quartet played a short set that was good listening. Pianist Dave Brubeck accompanied by Gerry Mulligan on baritone provided some intense moments. Sly and the Family Stone came onstage with a program that seemed to stir up the feelings of the audience. The leader, Sly, a former disc jockey, organist, drummer, and songwriter, ladled out psychedelic soul with chunks of tunes from other generations flying in and out of "now" songs in rapid-fire succession. They had what looked like fifty speakers and assorted electronic equipment with wires and mikes spread across the huge stage. Sly and company stirred the audience into a furor. A light show flashed on the huge screen behind their gyrations as they produced a bombardment of ear-shattering unmusical explosions; in the press pit we felt assaulted from the stage. And then a twenty-foot section of fence was breached, and in desperation the gates were opened to allow the hordes in to prevent further damage.

When the break occurred, the security guards tried to grab onto some of the people rushing by. "You hold two or three of them," one guard shouted, "and five get by."

Wein rushed onstage, pleading for restraint as the hordes vaulted over snow fences toward the stage. Rain came lashing down from the sky moments later, and the audience scrambled out of their seats to get closer and under cover. "Under here," someone shouted at me, tugging at my sleeve. I hugged my equipment bag and narrowly made it to the stage overhang. In the rush and scramble, camera equipment and bags were kicked over, bodies tumbled over pell-mell, and there were curses, shouts, and screams. Onstage the group went right on playing, unconcerned, even seeming to derive pleasure at all the confusion. Nina Simone shouted them on from the box seats. Security guards pushed and pummeled their way through the mob and spread themselves around the perimeter of the stage to prevent any assaults on the performers. Sly belatedly told the fans to "cool it," and the audience slowly settled down as the peace symbol was projected on the forty-foot light-show screen.

The World's Greatest Jazz Band played a good set with some fine soloing by soprano Bob Wilber and tenorist Bud Freeman, who blended the sounds of their reeds with lovely effect on "Just One of Those Things." Maxine Sullivan was delightful, joining the band with some tender vocals; she was particularly outstanding on "Skylark." Stephane Grapelli, the elder statesman of violin with Django Reinhardt's quintet of the Hot Club of France, brought some needed joy to the evening. The French musician stomped off "On the Sunny Side of the Street," producing bursts of energy and melodic invention that were enough to wipe away the bad vibes left over from some of the preceding cacophony. He was accompanied by producer George Wein on piano; the light, swinging touch of Gus Johnson on drums; bassist Larry Ridley; and the nimble fingers of guitarist Tal Farlow, who gave sympathetic support all the way. They ended the brief set with a concentrated and free-swinging "How High the Moon."

Sunday afternoon belonged to James Brown, with his line of dancers in the background bopping away and a driving rhythm-and-blues band. It was an excellent show; Brown released fiery bursts of energetic dancing, perspiration pouring down his face, his satin shirt a sopping mass clinging to his skin, as he begged, cajoled, and contrasted ballads like "If I Ruled the World" with such scorching up-tempo tunes as "In a Cold Sweat." Comedian Nipsy Russell joined him, telling the audience to stay in college. "If they can make something out of moldy cheese," he said, "they can make something out of you."

The final evening started an hour earlier than originally scheduled with the Illinois State Band. I arrived a few minutes before they ended their set, but what I heard sounded fine, with good section work and a couple of good solos. But the crowd came to hear vocalists B.B. King and Johnny Winter. B.B. King had been playing the rhythm-and-blues circuit for twenty years before most of the younger rock-oriented musicians were born. And it was said that his easygoing style had affected most of the younger English players who invaded America in the late sixties. King mentioned it in an interview at the time: "They imported the blues back to the States. Now there are some very good white kids singing and playing the blues. I'd say some are just as good as me." The forty-three-year-old blues singer was being kind. B.B. played with a passionate expressiveness, and the mostly young audience appreciated his message and shouted for more when his set closed. MC Billy Taylor told the crowd that if they calmed down, King would be back to do a duet with the fair-haired Texan, Johnny Winter. This seemed to calm them down. When the two finally appeared together, there was no contest between the guitar picking of the two. Winter's rhythm section had trouble getting with it, but B.B. gently instructed them on the right path. They played an extended "Every Day" with the audience standing and cheering them on all the way.

Pianist Herbie Hancock, trumpeter Johnny Coles, trombonist Garnet Brown, and tenorist Joe Henderson played some moving and beautiful music—Coles always understating in that bluesy, tender style of his and Brown expressing pain and joy at the same time.

The final blasts of the night came from drummer Buddy Rich and his orchestra. Buddy said at the time: "I tell the guys in the band, 'Your life's your own when you're off the stand, but every night I own you for five hours.' I ask no more than I give myself. I kill myself every night, and I expect them to wipe themselves out too." The band shook up the audience. Gerry Mulligan sat in on "Rotten Kid," playing with a singing quality, moving around the stage with obvious pleasure, and even joining in from the wings for a few choruses.

The aftermath of the Festival was a fifty-thousand-dollar tab for producer Wein, from Newport, half of the sum going for overtime police protection and the other half for a city council–ordered chain-link fence around the park. Also on the bill was a proviso that no further rock acts were to be booked at Newport festivals. Wein said in a *Down Beat* magazine interview, "I've a lot of soul-searching to do. The Festival was sheer hell—the worst four days of my life."

1970

The extra expenses incurred by the previous Festival necessitated cutting the 1970 Festival down to three days. Pressures from the city also delayed it until after the July Fourth weekend.

As Louis Armstrong prepared to celebrate his seventieth birthday, Newport honored him with the proclamation of Louis Armstrong Day. The first evening concert on July tenth was billed by Schlitz beer as "A New Orleans Tribute to Louis Armstrong."

The weather had been threatening all day, and the first night's attendance only filled a third of the eighteen thousand seats in Festival Field. It was a beautiful, heartfelt honor to Armstrong and an excellent tribute to early jazz and the music of New Orleans. The eleven-piece Eureka Brass Band, led by Percy Humphrey on trumpet, opened by marching around the stage, playing and strutting around the piano the way the New Orleans bands used to swing back from the cemetery after a funeral. The marching was quite animated, considering the ages of some of the participants. There were eighty-five-year-old drummer Cie Frazier, bass drum strung around his waist on a strap; Percy Humphrey, a young sixty-five; and trombonist Jim Robinson, blaring out broad and deep at seventy-eight. The band presented a living tribute, opening with "Bourbon Street Parade" and adding Captain John Handy on alto. It was happy music, and the audience moved with the band, rising from their seats to get a better look as applause broke into every solo.

Bobby Hackett's quintet continued the tribute. After a fast-paced "Undecided," Hackett moved into a tasty trumpet solo on the lovely "Some Day." Trombonist Benny Morton, the gentle and witty former Basie sideman, made an eloquent statement of love on "Swing That Music."

A Danish group, the New Orleans Classic Ragtime Band, continued the historical portrait of early jazz with a medley of rags from "St. Louis Pickle" to Scott Joplin's lilting "Ragtime Waltz." Graceful and witty interpretations gave the audience an insight into the transitional period of jazz when its roots were still tender and young.

Master of Ceremonies William Russell, a fine violinist, joined the fun on occasion; this New Orleans scholar swung gracefully with the rest of the musicians onstage, obviously enjoying himself tremendously.

After intermission the Trumpet Choir appeared—composed of Dizzy Gillespie, Bobby Hackett, Joe Newman, Jimmy Owens, with Wild Bill Davison and Ray Nance on cornet—and paid homage to Louis. "When It's Sleepy Time Down South" opened the second part of the evening, moving from soloist to soloist in a round robin. They swung back to melodies associated with Louis, and Dizzy thundered out a brilliant solo later on "I'm Confessin'." After his solo Diz told the audience, "I thank Mr. Armstrong for my livelihood." Each musician in turn paid tribute with a little speech. Davison: "I was raised on Louis. . . ." Hackett: "I'm his number-one fan." Joe Newman countered with "I'm his A-number-one fan. . . ." Each soloist continued the round robin

Roberta Flack caught in swirls of light. Onstage she projects a basic honesty and simplicity that puts her audience at ease.

with tune after tune associated with Louis, dusted off and resurrected with moving delight. Davison endowed "Them There Eyes" with a bouncy directness, punctuating each phrase with what sounded like a warm smile. Pianist Dave McKenna swung in behind him with a lively and melodic solo. Ray Nance simulated Louis's phrasing on "I'm in the Market for You," vocalizing with that rasp in all the right places and superimposing something of himself in the process. Jimmy Owens, on a somewhat battered antique flugelhorn, played a sensitive straight melody on "Nobody Knows the Trouble I've Seen," warmly relevant to the occasion. Backstage in the dressing rooms drummer Oliver Jackson watched Louis walking around in shorts and shirt before the program started, with a pacemaker sticking out of his pocket. "Not having a belt on, Louis had this aerial-looking wire dangling down. 'It's my short-wave radio,' Louis chuckled. 'Sometimes I pick up the news on it,' he said grinning."

Finally the evening's honored guest, looking healthy and fit, joined the crew onstage, receiving a standing ovation before he played a single note. He swung into his theme song, "Sleepy Time Down South" and then shifted into "Pennies from Heaven," with Bobby Hackett playing a lovely obligato. Louis played "Blueberry Hill" to close the set, obviously happy and pleased.

After a brief intermission the Preservation Hall Band appeared, with De De Pierce on trumpet replacing Punch Miller, who was unable to make the occasion because of illness. Their set included "Bourbon Street Parade" and some of the most-played Dixieland standards. Pianist Billie Pierce smashed out a lovely solo on "Tiger Rag," and the whole group, playing energetic ensembles, burst out with forceful blasts by Jim Robinson and Captain Handy. They had the audience leaping to their feet, cheering them on as they moved into "Panama" and filled the large stage with undiluted joy. A woman in the box-seat area shouted, "You make me feel alive!" and danced on her chair.

Above: Dave McKenna, a reticent pianist with an instinct for melodic invention.
Right: Ray Nance, a trumpet soloist who doubled on violin and on occasion could vocalize with the best of jazz singers.

Mahalia Jackson, in a long-sleeved aqua gown with sequins around her throat, stood center stage, bowed to the audience, and referring to Louis Armstrong, intoned, "If you don't love him, I don't think you know how to love." Mahalia burst out into the night with "Let There Be Peace" and moved on with a group of gospel songs expressing her faith, graceful and soaring, her magnetic quality reaching out again and again to the audience. Mahalia concluded her part of the evening with "Just a Closer Walk with Thee," and the Eureka Brass Band, Bobby Hackett, and the other participants of the evening joined Louis and Mahalia as the sky opened up with a brief downpour. Louis told the audience, "We don't want to keep you in the rain, folks." But the audience, oblivious to the showers, shouted for more, and Louis obliged with "Hello Dolly." Mahalia was oblivious to her hair tumbling down from the moisture, not even pausing to brush aside the locks over her brow, and she smilingly joining Louis for a few choruses. This obviously was a heartfelt tribute from the great singer who never until now had varied from her program of gospel music. The audience thundered out its appreciation. George Wein shouted out "Saints," an appropriate song for the close, with everyone singing out and joining the group onstage as Bobby Hackett wove his lyricism into the closing strains with a "Happy Birthday" obligato.

Saturday afternoon a series was presented, dubbed "workshops," which had some of the brightest moments of the year. At the trumpet workshop Dizzy Gillespie appeared with his horn and two cameras. He pranced around like a colt in his striped shorts, his feet encased in colorful boots from Lapland, and he opened with a jam session. Four trumpets, each distinctive in his own way, traded fours, their lusty power brightening up the gray skies overhead. When the group swung into "Sunny," Joe Newman took the first choruses before passing it on to Jimmy Owens on flugelhorn, who gave it a contemporary touch and played his closing choruses unaccompanied. Dizzy burst in, breathing fire,

181

with Jimmy clapping encouragement beside him. As Diz finished his solo, the sun poked out of the clouds as if summoned down for the occasion. It looked magical. They continued with Bird's "Now's the Time" with Ray Nance soloing. Light sparkled from the horns. The set closed with "Ode to Billie Joe," in which Joe Newman played a tasteful and inspired solo.

Jean Luc Ponty, whose jazz violin playing has been compared with the contemporary sounds of Ornette Coleman, was hampered by the sound system, but he overcame it in a duet with Mike White.

The drum workshop started late because of the time needed to set up four sets of drums. Chico Hamilton introduced Elvin Jones as "a man born in a drum." Elvin played a spirited set, with tenorist Frank Foster taking an emotion-filled solo on "Here's That Rainy Day." Chico Hamilton played with Steve Swallow on bass, Arnie Lawrence on electric sax, and Bob Mann on guitar. Garry Burton mixed his vibes with guest Keith Jarrett on electric and acoustic piano, first sending waves of blues- and gospel-rooted sounds sweeping over the field, then switching to a more complex cerebral approach. Tony Williams's Lifetime, with another barrage of electronic equipment, blaring speakers, and a set of yellow drums, moved from rock to jazz, adding nothing to the afternoon as the fog closed in on the few fans left on the field.

Guitarist Kenny Burrell opened Saturday evening while the crowds milled around the refreshment area, unmindful of the start of the concert, stood enjoying one of the treats of the refreshment stands this year, red beans and rice, prepared by New Orleans restaurant-owner Buster Holmes. Kenny's guitar work was too airy to compete with the noisy audience, just getting seated, but they started to quiet down when European expatriate Dexter Gordon strode out to join him. Dexter's six-and-a-half-foot frame and the stage lighting glinting off his tenor commanded attention. Burrell's guitar quickened with a

Left. Dizzy Gillespie is not only a great trumpeter but an enthusiastic chess player and, as pianist Ray Bryant put it, "He's a pool shark of the first order!" *Right.* Dexter Gordon has been an influence on many reedmen including John Coltrane. Unfortunately, his set was limited to two brief numbers.

new flow of chords in keeping pace with Dexter's brash and exciting power. It was Dexter's first appearance at the Festival, and he crowded a great deal of lusty power into "Boston Bernie" and remembered frustrations in a stunning solo on the lovely ballad "Darn That Dream." After these two brief numbers, Wein came out to rush the group off the stage. Dexter answered the producer with a prolonged chorus, bearing such emotional intensity that Wein faltered in his pushing exercise until Dexter had finished his solo.

The jazz violinists Jean Luc Ponty, Ray Nance, and Mike White returned, playing three widely divergent styles. White was the most innovative of the three, and he opened swinging and witty, but distortions in the amplification system marred his sound. Ponty played a long original with delicate modulations, creating a sonorous dipping and weaving quality soaring to the upper reaches but with a swinging vitality that always returned to equilibrium. Nance, playing in a less formalized manner, reached his audience with a touch. He started with a blues that had a warm expressive tension, endowing it with texture and beautiful richness of tone. Swinging into "Summertime," he gave it great emotional force, bursting into passionate statements, delicately modulating, then swelling out with a lusty swing. The rhythm accompaniment of George Duke on piano, Larry Ridley on bass, and Lennie McBrowne on drums provided just the right push and thrust.

The same rhythm section with guitarist Kenny Burrell backed the brass of Dizzy Gillespie, Ray Nance, Joe Newman, and Jimmy Owens as they contrasted interestingly together playing "Sunny," "Now's the Time," and "Ode to Billie Joe." Diz dazzled the audience with brilliant runs on a level few artists reach.

Don Byas, another master tenor player and expatriate, was making his first and only appearance at Newport this year. He joined Dizzy's new rhythm section in an

original, "Orgasm," and then stretched out on "Round About Midnight." The power he used to display with Count Basie's orchestra was still undiminished. His third number, "But Not for Me," took a frantic tempo, and Byas's fat sound tore asunder any romantic images, instead adding a depth of his own. Again the producer grabbed the microphone, breaking into the closing bars of the number.

Dizzy played brilliantly throughout his set. The contrast of his clowning image and the seriousness and intensity of his muted solo on an inspiring piece dedicated to the late Martin Luther King, entitled "The Brother King," left the audience transfixed in admiration.

Rain and an intermission broke off the music until Nina Simone appeared to play and sing a good set. "West Wind" was outstanding, and "To Be Young, Gifted and Black" was well received by the audience. She was followed by flutist Herbie Mann, who played one long number that made the audience fidget in their seats until George Wein relieved the situation by coming onstage.

The Ike and Tina Turner Revue had some highly entertaining moments. Sensuous and sexy Tina told the audience, "Tina's here to make you move, Tina's here to make you groove." And move she did, her aggressive energy projecting broad and deep, never stopping for an instant.

But all the entertainment up on that stage, as Ike and Tina Turner closed their set by disappearing into a cloud of smoke from dry ice, made one stop and wonder where jazz values must lie if the previous performers, jazz artists Dexter Gordon and Don Byas, could be pushed so unceremoniously off the stage by the producer so that they wouldn't take too much time.

The final Sunday afternoon program began with electronic rock groups, Nucleus from England and another similar-sounding group—the Fourth Way, led by a New Zealander.

The rest of the day was Roberta Flack's who highlighted her set by following "The Last Time" with "The First Time." She closed with a stunning version of "Let It Be." There were smiles all around for Badfoot Brown and his Bunion Bradford Marching Band, which had been created by its conductor, Bill Cosby, ostensibly to provide work for musicians. They were full of humor and provided a vehicle for Cosby to go into some of his routines.

The closing program on Sunday evening revealed little new. Later in the evening Cannonball Adderley's group appeared, but most people complained that there was too much talk and not enough music. Cannon played a brief two numbers, with acoustic and electric pianist Joe Zawinul making some potent statements and Cannon swinging fiercely with his alto, particularly on "Experience in E" and Zawinul's gospel-sounding "Country Preacher."

Drummer Buddy Rich followed with a crackling band set. Ella Fitzgerald closed out the night, looking trim in a green pants suit. She had beautiful backing from pianist Tommy Flanagan and Ed Thigpen on drums. Some of her material had been updated—"Girl from Ipanema" and "Spinning Wheel"—but she presented no surprises. She didn't really need any. Not after singing Duke's "Satin Doll" and "Crazy Rhythm," which included a short breathing-space solo by Tommy Flanagan.

Producer Wein then told the crowd of seventy-five hundred that there would be a Festival the following year. Backstage Wein criticized the Festival Field location. "I'd just as soon leave this place. It has outlived its usefulness."

The late Louis Armstrong onstage. *Left, bottom.* Trumpeter and close friend Bobby Hackett pays him tribute. Louis has had an all-pervasive influence on jazz and music in general.

1971

True to form, the 1971 swan song of the Newport Festival at Newport, Rhode Island, started twenty minutes earlier than scheduled, without any previous announcement.

Big bands heavily overloaded the programing on Friday evening. To open the evening, expatriate vibist Dave Pike, with a German rhythm section, played a four-number set. Pike played with a deft lightness, but his German guitarist leaned too heavily on his electronic equipment, muddying up the flow of ideas.

Stan Kenton's orchestra minus its leader, who was recuperating from an operation, suffered from his absence. The arrangements seemed heavy-handed and ponderous and showed little of the subtleties the band was capable of.

Buddy Rich and his orchestra came on with a swinging determination and much more clarity. Rich's drum solos were as spectacular as ever, and he closed with a much-shortened version of *West Side Story,* which got him a standing ovation.

There was quite a contrast when Duke Ellington's men settled down for their end of the evening. Breaking out with "Bravo, Togo," which featured some pugnacious tenor from Paul Gonsalves, they moved into an excerpt from *Afro-Eurasian Eclipse Suite,* featuring reedman Harold Ashby and dedicated to Marshall McLuhan. Norris Turney's flute work spiced up "The Bourbon Street Jingling Jollies" from Ellington's *New Orleans Suite*. Generally, though, the band lacked its usual fire, perhaps because the audience, unfamiliar with the many new pieces on the program, was unresponsive. Duke even injected a few "get in line" remarks from the side to his band, and he left the stage without a final bow, as was his custom.

The closing set was Roberta Flack's. Roberta had come up in the world since her performance the previous year. She played and sang with much feeling, but after thirty minutes there was a sameness about it all—tempo variations were absent. "Reverend Lee" had a certain eloquence, its clarity and vividness finally reached the audience, and they gave her a warm ovation.

The following afternoon's program had some delightful moments when the dignified Eubie Blake, who had played with Jim Europe's band during the First World War, took the stage. The eighty-eight-year-old pianist and composer explained to the crowd, "I used to play for millionaires at these mansions here and all over the civilized world." Relaxed and youthful, he romped through a group of rags and waltzes, moving into some of his compositions—"Memories of You" and, at the producer's request, his popular "I'm Just Wild About Harry." His program evoked an era of jazz prehistory that has few survivors. The audience was delighted and impressed, and as they gave him a standing ovation, he grabbed the microphone to say, "You don't know what this applause means to me. Thank you. Thank you very, very much."

Willie "The Lion" Smith followed; his two hands

The New York Bass Violin Choir onstage. This was the high point of the afternoon concert. Center stage is Bill Lee who served as bassist, singer and narrator. The choir played excerpts from Mr. Lee's "folk festival" called "One Mile East." Hearing six basses bowing in unison was a beautiful experience.

187

roamed the keyboard in a relaxed but disciplined manner while he chomped on his black cigar, derby tilted at an angle. He moved into a segment of delightful rags, shouting out at the end of each piece, "That's it!" or, "There it is!" He sprinkled a little Chopin in with some of his own compositions. "Echoes of Spring" was especially vivid. He then turned the piano over to one of his disciples, twenty-seven-year-old Mike Lipskin, who rendered James P. Johnson's "Snowy Morning," paying his dues to the great stride pianist.

Bassist Charlie Mingus roared like a lion that afternoon as he dusted off his great "Pithecanthropus Erectus." He displayed all the fire and originality he has long been noted for as his sextet swung wide and handsomely through some of his best originals. They did an irreverent and humor-filled takeoff of "Cocktails for Two," Mingus intermixing Spike Jones's intonations with Clyde McCoy's trumpet breaks. There was a rinky-tink broken-chorded piano solo by John Foster that had bits and pieces of the silent cinema strung through it, plus the added punch of Mingus grunting and goading them on as drummer Virgil Day played a *chunk-a-chunk* drum break with a cymbal crash exploding at the end. Mingus paid tribute to the great bassist Oscar Pettiford with a piece entitled "Oscar Pettiford Junior." Moving at breakneck tempo, it was curt and to the point with some sizzling tenor work and a chopping alto solo by Charlie McPherson, and it ended with an abrupt crunch.

Trumpeter Freddie Hubbard played two extended pieces, "Straight Life" and "Mr. Clean," both suggestive of the direction Miles Davis was taking. Tenorist Junior Cook and Hubbard played very long solos, backed with a good rhythm section.

The best of the afternoon came from the New York Bass Violin Choir, featuring seven of the finest bassists on the scene today. They played some astonishing music and showed what could be done at this level of sound without blasting or shattering eardrums in the process. Particularly impressive was the unison bowing,

188

Above. Trumpeter Freddie Hubbard, a former hard bopper, has paid his dues and moved on to more lush and lucrative musical settings.
Opposite. Ornette Coleman, whose act was cancelled during the riotous festival in 1960, finally made his appearance at Newport, dressed in a bright red suit. When I asked him why a red suit, he shrugged his shoulders and said, "Show Biz!"

Richard Davis and Lisle Atkinson providing a delicate melodic line behind them. Other bright and unusual features of the set were Bill Lee, who related stories of life in a small Alabama town, his points of interest emphasized with brilliant bass ensemble passages, and the impressive voices of Lee's two sisters, Consuela Lee Moorhead and A. Grace Lee Mims.

Ornette Coleman, wearing a brilliant red-orange suit, finally made it to Newport this year, after having been canceled in 1960 due to the riot. It was an auspicious occasion. His quartet provided some extra excitement as tenorist Dewey Redman took off on a rousing solo on "Airborne," Ed Blackwell giving firm support on drums. Dewey had his head precisely into Ornette's moods, making it seem like a complex conversational exchange. "Broken Shadows" took a milder tempo with subtle transitions, Ornette sinuously weaving his way through the solemn piece, echoing back and forth from tenor to alto. An expressive nervous energy emanated from "Skylife." Ornette played trumpet and electric violin with a gutty bass solo by Charlie Haden. The intensity increased as Ornette whined his violin with fierce determination and trumpeter Coleman took out the final choruses. They ended their set with another bristling and sharp-edged duel on "Science Fiction." It opened at a rocketing clip, the pace and pressure intensifying as Dewey came in with a upward-surging solo, almost frightening in its intensity, while bassist Haden bowed out savage barbs. The group took on an almost abrasive sound, rasping and sometimes incoherent in its energy. This was a potent afternoon. One of the best in memory.

The area looked ominous early in the evening, with fantastic congestion around the field for hundreds of yards. Teen-agers, freaked out on everything from wine to acid, clogged the gate area and all the streets leading to Festival Field. My family was with me, and I shuddered at the sight of children not much older than my two daughters openly guzzling wine and beer beside the security guards.

189

George Wein went out with a bullhorn to talk to a band of watchers on a hill overlooking the field. "We haven't got the money for the Festival," they shouted. "Why should we pay to get in?" It was useless. Finally in desperation he called the police command post to see if something could be done. His associate of many years, Gordon Sweeney, told me later, "They told George they could clear the hill for twelve hundred dollars. 'Do it,' he told them. Somehow they never got around to it, for reasons unknown."

The last concert at Newport opened with the Montreux Festival winners from Finland. Even as the music started, the tension was building up to an ugly mood outside and inside the Field.

Backstage, Chase, a recently organized nine-member jazz-rock group, was preparing to go on. Bill Chase described his group: "Most of us are ex-Vegas sidemen, and you've got to know what you're doing to play there. All of our numbers are written by us, all originals." The group went onstage and the audience liked them. When the band got off the stage, Gerry Mulligan and Dave Brubeck greeted them warmly.

Brubeck and Mulligan then played a brief set; Mulligan, fully bearded and long-haired, was restrained and lackluster and did not receive much support from Brubeck. The music of Burt Bacharach and Hal David dominated Dionne Warwicke's set, giving a sameness to the proceedings until she started to sing "What the World Needs Now Is Love." Shortly before nine thirty the chain-link fence surrounding the field was forced, and a thirty-foot section gave way with the older wooden fence cracking to the ground moments later. A horde of youths came sweeping into the park past the police and security forces toward the stage, smashing down the light snow fences along the way. I rushed over to my family sitting nearby to see what the hell was going on. The twenty thousand people in the park had been joined by an angry mob as George Wein came onstage joined by his wife, who edged over to Dionne Warwicke and whispered to her while she was still in the middle of a phrase. Dionne, in disbelief, went right on with her song.

When the fence gave way, MC Father Norman O'Connor came onstage with Wein to plead with the invaders. "We're trying to do a thing here. This is the only town that lets us in, and you can wipe us out," Wein pleaded. "You've got the whole thing in your hands!" Meanwhile, back at the gaping hole in the fence, the police quietly melted away in the crowd. The stage was soon overflowing with a mad band of freaks, who ripped the piano lid off and started to dance around wildly, breaking light fixtures and tearing and destroying anything they could get their hands on. The stage looked like a trash heap, littered with broken chairs and smashed music stands, while Father O'Connor grabbed a microphone and shouted, "This is the last Festival left on the East Coast. We can continue the Festival if you give us a chance." On Girard Avenue a hot-dog vender went blissfully on peddling his wares, unmindful of the confusion around him. The police started to lob tear-gas canisters at the north end of the field.

Bob Dick, a news editor from radio station WEAN, had been taping a broadcast on the stage when the action started. Much of what happened was taped. "Why don't you put some music up here and just let everybody camp and go home in a few days," a teen-ager shouted into the mike. Sounds of smashing wood, shouts, and screams came over the mike. Dick asked one of the youths, "What do you think you're accomplishing by this takeover?" "Nothing," was the reply.

Bill Chase (center) and his rock-oriented jazz group. During the appearance, a small private plane circled lazily overhead pulling a banner announcing his new record album. Bill Chase was to die in a private plane crash in 1974 with other members of his group.

Then Wein approached the mike and told the audience to remain calm and that the city of Newport had ordered the Festival closed down. The cancellation had been announced by Newport City Manager B. Cowles Mallory at the recommendation of Police Chief Frank H. Walsh. The action, Wein announced, was being taken for their safety.

Dick was forced offstage by the tear gas thrown by the police. Wein and his wife, Joyce, left the field about ten thirty saying, "There is simply nothing else we can do."

Around midnight a disheveled youth inquired at the field if there were any souvenir programs around.

Traffic was halted on all bridges by state troopers, who allowed only town residents or those with specific business in town to proceed in. As the people filed out of the field, some youths tossed Frisbees back and forth, completely oblivious to everything around them. On the stage a girl playfully lit pieces of paper, tossing them around; those below stamped them out as they floated down. A free-lance photographer who had been taking pictures of the proceedings was forced by a group on threat of bodily harm to remove and destroy his film. On the hillside at Miantonomi Park the bonfires burned brightly long after the audience had left.

At twelve thirty A.M. Senator and Mrs. Claiborne Pell, who had been at a party in Newport, decided to inspect the field. "I don't know what a U.S. senator can do, but let's walk down and see," he said. After his inspection tour of the wreckage he asked, "Why do they do it?" At seven in the morning about one hundred policemen moved into Miantonomi Park and, using a bullhorn, told the gathering, "You have fifteen minutes to put out your fires, take down your tents, and leave the area." An hour later the area had been cleared without any problems. Then, moving to the ticket-booth area around Connell

Highway, the police started clearing the parking lots. Some of the youths shouted obscenities at them, but they left without incident.

It was the end of the Newport Festival at Newport, Rhode Island. The security measures obviously had not taken into account the warning signals that had appeared. John F. Fitzgerald, a former city clerk for Newport, now town administrator for Middletown, Rhode Island, stated recently, "I don't think the last riot in particular could have been prevented. All precautions were taken . . . Wein had a sufficient number of security people patrolling the area, but it was impossible to control the crowds. [The crowd had congregated on a hill] for two or three days and apparently there never was any effort made to disperse them from that area. . . . it was one solid mass of people. . . . Whether it could have been prevented by not allowing them to get within fifty yards of the fence is the question. After they smashed through it was a question of numbers. . . . The mistake was made, I would assume, in allowing them to congregate there to begin with. I don't think all the police in the world could have prevented it then."

Amid recriminations hurled back and forth by the Festival office, the city council, and residents in the area, the town started to return to normal. Some of the councilmen blamed the action on outside agitators, others on narcotics. A few city councilmen who had obviously been foes of the Festival for many years reiterated that the city did not have the facilities to handle Festival crowds. Wein had also scheduled the rock opera, *Jesus*

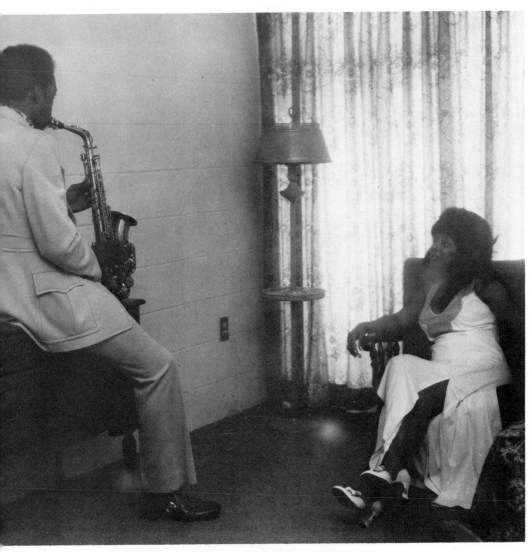

After the Festival had suddenly ended, Sonny Stitt made his way back to the Viking Hotel with his wife. He gets in a few final runs before packing his horns and leaving for his next engagement.

Christ, Superstar, but he canceled it. When questioned about his decision to fight for the jazz and folk festivals, he stated, "The opera is a one-nighter and a business proposition with me, but the folk and jazz festivals have meaning for me." Artists booked for presentation at the canceled Festival would probably not press for payment, it was announced. There was some sort of clause in their contract, Wein thought, that would take him off the hook, since the Festival had been canceled by the city.

The local newspapers reported a tearful Wein saying, "What happened out there is something only America can explain." Wandering back to Festival Field, I looked around at the scene of destruction—a jumble of smashed fences, splintered chairs, and music stands. I stood in the press pit, now littered with empty gallon wine bottles, crushed beer and soda-pop cans, and bits and pieces of wooden seats with their backs torn off. The lectern lay on its side in an unceremonious heap, having been thrown down from the stage. On the stage I looked at the scraped and torn piano, its nameplate ripped off, its ivory keys strewn on the floor beneath it, its guts hanging out.

At a press conference later Wein was questioned about the future. "This is not the end; it may be a beginning. The Newport Jazz Festival will continue," he said solemnly.

"Would the Festival, if resumed, ever be in this state?" he was asked.

"We know we'll find a community. Maybe it will have to be a metropolitan area," Wein said later.

The Festival office announced that refunds for tickets would be given for only Sunday's and Monday's performances. No money would be refunded for the interrupted Saturday night concert.

1972

On January 5, 1972, Wein announced plans for presenting the Festival in New York City in the coming summer. "We already have scheduled a dozen concerts in Carnegie Hall, a dozen concerts in Philharmonic Hall, and two large outdoor concerts in Yankee Stadium." The idea was to use parks, city streets, theaters, and churches so that a festival atmosphere would be created in the entire city. Vernon Jordan, the executive director of the National Urban League, stated that 55 percent of the profits would be donated to them, and "jazz devotee" former mayor Robert Wagner was selected to be chairman of the Newport Jazz Festival Committee of Concerned New York Citizens.

The Newport Festival–New York, as it was now officially named, was underwritten by a financial buffer zone of sponsors, and big names appeared on the advisory panel. (They promised, with apologies, to add more names the following year.) The sponsors included an old friend from Newport days, the Joseph Schlitz Brewing Company, who contributed twenty-five thousand dollars. American Airlines contributed seventeen thousand dollars, and Yamaha donated the official piano. Also there were forty or so organizations, ranging from the New York State Council on the Arts to St. Peter's Lutheran Church, who helped sponsor the Festival.

Wein said in his program that year: "As of this writing [June 8, 1972], I am not sure the Festival will make money. Our budget is very high, but all indications point to success. More important, however, is that we feel we made the correct move."

The logistical problems of the Festival were staggering. Concert sites varied from Carnegie Hall, the Staten Island ferry, and the streets of Brooklyn to that notable showcase for the arts, Yankee Stadium. With six months of planning, six hundred musicians, $604,000, and a six-man staff, somehow it all was put together. The newspapers reported a projected gate of one million dollars. The Teamsters Union insisted that their members accompany all musical instruments delivered to concert locations. The budget included fifty thousand dollars for advertising, eighty-seven thousand dollars for rental of Yankee Stadium, and twenty-two thousand dollars for rental of Radio City Music Hall with its six thousand seats. The Festival consisted of over thirty-five events, with ticket prices ranging from a top of $7 down to $4.50. It was also possible to purchase a series ticket for all events for $122 and save $28.50.

But these were not all Wein's problems. There was also the New York Jazz Musicians Festival. Young musicians were annoyed with the arrival of the Festival in New York. Archie Shepp, representing about five hundred musicians who had joined the organization, said, "We felt that if the festival was going to move from Newport to New York, then it should reflect that change from a rural to an urban setting where blacks want to control where and how their music is performed." They felt that the Festival was not including the talents of younger and more avant-garde musicians. The group presented nearly seventy-five concerts at such places around the city as the Harlem Music Center on St. Ni-

During the forties Sarah Vaughn sang with Billy Eckstine's star-studded orchestra. Howard McGhee remembers that whenever Sassy sang "I'll Be Seeing You," Bird would come swooping in on the second chorus. "Bird hated playing those stage shows, but he loved playing behind Sarah. But never on the first chorus."

cholas Avenue; Slug's, an East Side club; Sam Rivers's Studio Rivbea; Central Park; East River Park; and the New Federal Theater. Among the many participants were Frank Foster, Sam Rivers, Sun-Ra, Ken McIntyre, Clifford Jordan, Archie Shepp, and Noah Howard. Their concerts paralleled some of the larger Festival's output, starting on July third and ending on the tenth.

As it turned out, although some of Wein's events did not draw very well, there seemed to be enough jazz lovers in the city to provide audiences for both festivals without any serious hitches or trouble. And most of the logistical problems that the city of Newport had presented—lack of eating and sleeping facilities, transportation, and security—simply did not exist in New York City.

The press gave an enormous amount of space to the Festival with human interest stories, interviews, and coverage of the events themselves. Most of the city's newspapers were hard pressed to find competent reviewers for the job and ended up using writers from other entertainment fields. And, as some musicians complained later to me, much of the space was devoted to foreign, or newer, musicians or, more often, not to the music or musicians at all.

I scrambled around from one concert to another and finally decided to cover only things that I would be forced to listen to because of picture commitments or my own preferences. Some locations, because of union regulations, imposed limitations on photographing, making things difficult.

As for the music, there was an endless variety and enough to satisfy even the most demanding or eclectic listener. Sounds ranged from African drums and scholarly excursions into bootlegging records all the way to classical-sounding chamber music.

196

Dizzy Gillespie (left), holding a chess instruction book, pauses backstage at Carnegie Hall to laugh and reminisce with old friend Billy Eckstine. There was much to remember, the two having shared the bandstands of the Earl Hines Orchestra and of Eckstine's own star-studded band of the forties. When Billy broke up his band, he let Dizzy (who by then had his own band) help himself to the charts, music stands and microphones. *Opposite, top.* Pianist Norman Simmons stands between Billy and Diz.

Sunday evening, July 2, 1972

It was New York big-band night at Philharmonic Hall. Two of the bands came from television—Bobby Rosengarden from "The Dick Cavett Show" and Billy Taylor's defunct "David Frost Show" orchestra. Both bands had a chance to stretch out beyond the confines of their usual television roles, and both brought a tone of excitement to the stage. The Cavett band seemed more polished and swinging, Rosengarden's musicians etching some fine solos. The leader commented later, "It's nice to be able to play more than thirty seconds at a time."

Billy Taylor's twelve-member group, not as well rehearsed, had rougher edges. Sound problems further hampered them, with piano and reed sections sometimes overpowering the rest of the band.

The Thad Jones–Mel Lewis Band exploded with the mixture of pianist Roland Hanna, the precision strokes of bassist Richard Davis, the intensity of Joe Farrell's tenor solos, and Thad's pungent horn commentary. Trombonist Eddie Bert was subbing that evening for Quentin Jackson, and the only band-uniform jacket available belonged to Quentin, who weighed a hundred pounds more than Bert. "I felt pretty uncomfortable in it," he said wryly, "particularly when I had to come out center stage twice to solo. I felt like Groucho Marx." Mel Lewis remembered him looking as if he were wearing a tent that night.

One of the most innovative and important events at the Festival was the presentation of Ornette Coleman's composition "Skies of America." It was written for symphony orchestra and jazz quartet, a combination that had defied other composers' attempts. It is to producer George Wein's everlasting credit that he was able to present this performance by getting the necessary funding for it.

James Jordan, cousin of Ornette Coleman and producer of the Columbia Records release of "Skies of America," told me in a recent interview: "The funding of

197

Above. Maxine Sullivan sings with the World's Greatest Jazz Band.
Opposite. Sir Roland Hanna has on occasion taken his own tools to the job to tune the piano before going on.

the Newport Jazz Festival performance by the New York State Council on the Arts came in the form of monetary support of the American Symphony. George Wein also received money from the federal government for Ornette's appearance. The Newport Festival presentation differed from the British recording in that at the Festival he did it with the quartet. But the group did not qualify to perform with the English orchestra, according to English regulations. We knew it before we left, so we didn't run into any problems over there. Ornette and I spent almost a whole day with the conductor of the American Symphony Orchestra, Leon Thompson, getting him briefed on what we wanted from the performance. After coming back from England we had the music transcribed the way it was performed on the recording. We gave him the recording to listen to, went over the score with him, and spent considerable time together. We only spent six hours rehearsing the score, that's all. They performed it that same evening. The most important factor was the time we spent with the conductor."

Soloing was the domain of Ornette Coleman and the rest of his quartet—Dewey Redman on tenor, Charlie Haden on bass, and Ed Blackwell on drums. The improvisation brought an interchange of values and ideas that balanced and complemented with a lovely contrast of ideas each written section the symphony orchestra played. Ornette's alto interplayed against the textures and color of the full orchestra. Most importantly, the concert performance became a whole piece, not a grouping of two disparate elements. The concert was also a critical success.

Tuesday evening, July 4, 1972

The Carnegie concert billed Miles Davis, Sonny Rollins, and McCoy Tyner, but on the evening of the performance a sign in the main lobby stated tersely that Miles would not be playing at the two concerts, scheduled for five and nine P.M. No explanation was given.

Miles maintained later that he had never agreed to perform, and he accused George Wein of exploiting musicians. George said he had sent Miles a deposit. Others said that Miles was undergoing changes in his life and didn't feel in any shape to play.

Pianist McCoy Tyner remembered his own appearance that evening: "It was an enjoyable night. At least I didn't remember walkin' away feeling bad about it." The Tyner set had been buried under a horrendous barrage of drums by Al Mouzon. McCoy, laughing over it later, said, "I asked Mouzon about that when it was over, and he told me that it was his debut at Newport, and that he wanted to make an impression."

Miles's replacement, trumpeter Freddie Hubbard, played with utmost ease and spontaneity. He delighted the predominantly young audience and was brilliant toward the close of his set, thundering out lustily, pithy, and impudent.

Sonny Rollins seemed to be playing hide-and-seek with the audience, giving bits and snatches of tunes from the sides of the stage, leaning on his pianist Albert Dailey, giving him giant chunks of solo space. Dailey used these to good advantage, bristling with a steady rolling gait, then shifting into some lyrical romantic chords on "There Is No Greater Love." Rollins closed the set with a joyously attuned solo on "Sentimental Mood," playing with a sparkling melodic imagination; then he suddenly shifted gears and with a full-blown, cool detachment displayed his virtuosity on tenor.

Wednesday, July 5, 1972

The American Airlines-sponsored tribute to Lionel Hampton was a joyous romp for the audience, but the long rehearsal earlier in the day seemed to bear little relationship to what was finally presented onstage.

Moving around rapidly, Hamp mixed drums, voice, and vibes, tearing through bits of old arrangements and then suddenly slipping into a completely different mood,

swirling around with limitless energy or lilting and semi-serious as he saluted his confreres from his Goodman days.

Highlights were—Roy Eldridge with a stunning trumpet solo on "The Man I Love," crackling out later with "I've Got Rhythm"—but with the stage overloaded with talent, nothing was explored in depth. Organist Milt Buckner tried to pump some life into "Robbins Nest," with Illinois Jacquet taking his famous tenor solo. It was all nostalgia filled and interesting, but there were no surprises. Hamp brought out Gene Krupa, despite his vociferous protests, for an unannounced "Sing, Sing, Sing," and later trumpeter Cat Anderson stretched out with a tasty blues chorus or two. With Hamp we were prepared to pay our respect not to what he was saying at that moment, but to what he had said before throughout his long career.

Friday, July 7, 1972

In a Carnegie Hall program entitled "Interesting Directions," drummer Roy Haynes's group was outstanding. In a later interview Roy commented on the program: "George Wein told me before the start of the concert that Tony Williams had confided to him that he didn't want to follow my group. I mentioned it to Tony the day of the concert, and we kidded about it. Of course, we were very close, both being from Boston. Even George was surprised at Tony saying this. Here we were, Roy Haynes Hip Ensemble, with no publicity or record company pushing us or getting us publicity. We went out and played our fucking ass off. I was so proud of my group." His group consisted of tenor-basoonist George Adams, trumpeter Marvin Peterson, pianist Cedric Lawson, and bassist Don Pate. Their playing was tightly knit, fiercely determined, hotly concentrated. Roy had it all that afternoon, whether in ensemble or soloing. At the end of the set he put on a tense, brilliant display of rhythmic intricacies, his foot pedal sounding like a

Left. Lionel Hampton (front) and Milt Buckner have a romp at the keyboard. Hampton has always been ready to jam at a moment's notice. Buckner developed the playing of block chords in jazz. One of the people he influenced was pianist George Shearing. *Right.* Roy Haynes is the complete drummer.

hopped-up jackhammer. He had most of the youth-packed house out of their seats by the end of his solo.

Weather Report played also with a fierce intensity, but with amplified electronic music dominating. Wayne Shorter's soprano melded beautifully with the shrill sounds created by bassist Miroslav Vitous. Sounding both humorous and forceful, the instrumentalists seemed closely attuned to each other, as did the group as a whole. Electric-pianist Joe Zawinul created a world of sound of his own, although distortions ultimately resulted from faulty speaker placement and what sounded like some badly tuned equipment. He had to make constant adjustments while he played.

Archie Shepp, one of the organizers of the counter-festival, took time out to play with his competition, but his group seemed a little disheveled and disorganized. Despite a good solo by bassist Jimmy Garrison and some fine piano by Billy Green, the set as a whole pulled apart.

Duke Ellington stepped out on the stage of Carnegie Hall to present an afternoon of jazz with some of his illustrious alumni. They played the *Toga Brava Suite* in its entirety, the band swelling with that lusty quality they have when they're really into the mood and pace. The standard fare included "A Train," and Paul Gonsalves lashed out with a roaring tenor solo on "Rockin' in Rhythm." Later the band swung into less familiar but harmonious ground on "La Plus Belle Africaine."

The first of the alumni, drummer Sonny Greer, slight and rumpled but still with that swagger in his step, nervously approached the bandstand as Ellington gave him an effusive introduction. Sonny perched himself behind Rufus Jones's drums, still with his warm smile; he had barely settled into his seat when Duke called for "East St. Louis Toodle-oo." The band played a few bars, Ellington plunking out some ragtime chords. Then Duke stepped out from behind the piano and invited Sonny to

step down from the bandstand. Sonny hesitated for a brief moment, looking quizzically at his former boss; then he shuffled out from behind the set of drums as Duke said something about not wanting him to cut Rufus Jones, his drummer. Hopping down the last step in resignation, Sonny headed toward the wings.

Ray Nance, who had rehearsed with the band that afternoon, received even less complimentary treatment. Duke left him sitting backstage cooling his heels. These instances of Duke's sometimes contradictory nature were never fully explained.

Quentin Jackson said, "Duke didn't care what you did off the bandstand, but if he thought you were juiced, sometimes he would call one of the hardest numbers you did. He used to do that with Ben Webster. And not only Ben. If he caught anybody like that. He'd call 'Cottontail' for Ben, stomp it off real fast, and then sit at the piano and look at him. But he never could catch Paul Gonsalves off guard. Paul would sit there and nod, but when it came time to play, Paul would pick up his horn . . . and he would scare you to death! . . . and nobody would know how he did it."

Somehow Duke's music overcame these seeming rudenesses, leaving one wondering yet concentrating on the more positive sides of his performance.

Duke and company did an inspired "Harlem," which had originally been commissioned by conductor Arturo Toscanini. Duke ended up writing it in two versions, one for his orchestra and one for symphony and jazz orchestras combined.

Bobby Short paid his dues to former Ellington-band vocalist Ivie Anderson. He recalled his appearance at that Festival: "The band was on the road somewhere, and I was in town rehearsing for a little straw-hat music revue. I thought I wouldn't be able to do the concert because I couldn't reach Duke. I'd almost written George Wein a note saying I couldn't do it, but I received a phone call from Duke. He had a piano in his room so he gave me the keys over the telephone. We got the songs together, and I took off for the Cape to do my off-Broadway show. I took a dawn flight from Falmouth on Cape Cod to get to New York on time for what they told me was going to be a noon rehearsal. The concert was scheduled for one P.M. There I was onstage in my jeans rehearsing as the audience started to fill the seats. It was madness! I had my back to the audience, thank God! I rushed upstairs to my apartment over Carnegie Hall, changed my clothes, and dashed downstairs to do the concert. The concert was well received with good arrangements by Mercer Ellington. The most touching thing about the concert was when Duke came over and, leaning on the piano, stood there for most of my performance."

Bobby's tribute was followed by one of the most provocative segments of the afternoon: Duke's interpretation of his standard, "Mood Indigo." The lights went down low as old alumnus Tyree Glenn placed his plunger over the bell of his trombone and started to murmur softly, melding with the muted sounds of clarinets. As the notes started to fade away at the close of his solo, the melody line was picked up on perfect pitch by a voice in the background that soared with a natural brilliance, delicately modulating with an uncanny intensity of feeling that startled the audience into whispered conjectures as to where the sound was emanating from and who was doing the singing. When the arrangement drew to a close, Duke blithely stepped onstage to introduce a stunningly beautiful Rumanian singer, Aura Ruly. The audience gave her a standing ovation.

The concert ended with baskets of flowers inundating the stage as Duke told the audience how madly he loved them.

Saturday, July 8, 1972

Saturday evening the "Giants of Jazz" program began in an atmosphere familiar to Newport devotees. Shortly before the program began, a heavy rain started to ease

203

The late Jimmy Garrison's solo work was warm and lovely at times, at others intense and savage.

off. But the problems were enlarged at Yankee Stadium. The thirty thousand seats available for the concertgoers were only half-filled during the evening. Late arrivals being seated during the performance disrupted the music again and again. The planes flying overhead, the rumble of subway trains, and the general cacophony of city traffic noises did nothing to enhance the music.

The small stage set in the middle of the huge field with the vast stretches of seating, grass, and police barriers around its perimeter was not an effective arrangement.

Warming up the audience with a jam session only increased the confusion. The musicians were trying to establish rapport with the audience. But in the opening set it made little difference who was on that stage; trumpeter Clark Terry, trumpeter Joe Newman, guitarist Kenny Burrell, and many others tried to reach out, but the distance was too great. Nevertheless, some of the musicians sounded good. Tenorist Zoot Sims shone brightly on "What's New," tenorist Illinois Jacquet paced a double-time "Man I Love," and Joe Newman came through well despite bad acoustics and the echoes of his own solo on "Ode to Billie Joe." Brubeck and company, with Gerry Mulligan on baritone and altoist Paul Desmond, tried very hard, but the competition was too much. One of the musicians standing near the dugout listening said, "I feel like getting a subway token and going home."

When B.B. King finally appeared, he and his nine-piece band held onto the audience only a short while. After much shifting around of sound and stage equipment for Ray Charles, both for better sound and protection from the intermittently falling rain, the audience finally settled down. Obviously, this was what they had come to hear. As each number was greeted with shrieks of recognition and delight, he miraculously held them in his grip throughout the rest of the evening. Charles brought a tone of vast excitement that night, and his showmanship sparkled as he moved through "Georgia," "Eleanor Rigby," and a smashing production of Rudolf Friml's "Indian Love Call." The closer, "What'd I Say," had the audience on their feet screaming for more.

Wein later blamed the rain for poor attendance. "Next year we'll have twice as many people at Yankee Stadium," he told the press.

Sunday, July 9, 1972

One of the final concerts of this Festival was a program of gospel music presented at the cavernous Radio City Music Hall. The audience of two thousand barely filled the front section of the hall. Producer Tony Heilbut made the best of the seven groups, plus some soloists, that he had to work with. Willie Mae Ford Smith, the almost legendary performer who had inspired so many other singers along the way, still stirred up the audience. Dorothy Love Coates sang sacred songs, many of them her own compositions, and building slowly, digging in with cries of admonishment and praise, she had the crowd shouting back to her, "Help yourself, Dot."

The Dixie Hummingbirds, an all-male quintet on the gospel road since 1939, gave a rich variety of music, punctuated by the fine soloists within the group, Ira Tucker and James Walker, who swooped and moaned

with breathtaking facility. Other groups have used them as a model through the years, but the original still excited the audience thirty-three years later. But time limits were too tight to build up the kind of message this performance requires. An eleven A.M. closing was necessary to allow for preparation of the regular noon stage-and-film presentation; the gospel program could give one only a brief taste of what this jazz-root music has to offer.

There were many other bright moments and concerts, plus some free events around the city that were a heartening touch, but as a whole, the Festival presented too heavy a concentration of good music in too short a period of time. A listener had to evaluate and to be as selective as possible. As one associate of the producer put it, "It was enough to drive a jazz buff out of his head." One of the members of the press stated, "The Festival's emphasis on making their entrance into New York City a glorious experience made it rather like someone whose eyes are too big for his stomach."

At the close of the nine-day Festival Wein told the press, "I have no plans for going back to Rhode Island again. The Newport Jazz Festival–New York is now a permanent event."

Only ten of the fifty-six events were sold out. Wein had announced originally that there would be a small margin of profit, between $10,000 and $40,000, but later he said that he had lost $100,000. "We tried to do too much, and many of the events were in competition with each other," he said.

Wein received a commendation from Mayor John Lindsay for his decision to remain in New York City.

Maynard Ferguson (in white jump suit) onstage at Carnegie Hall.

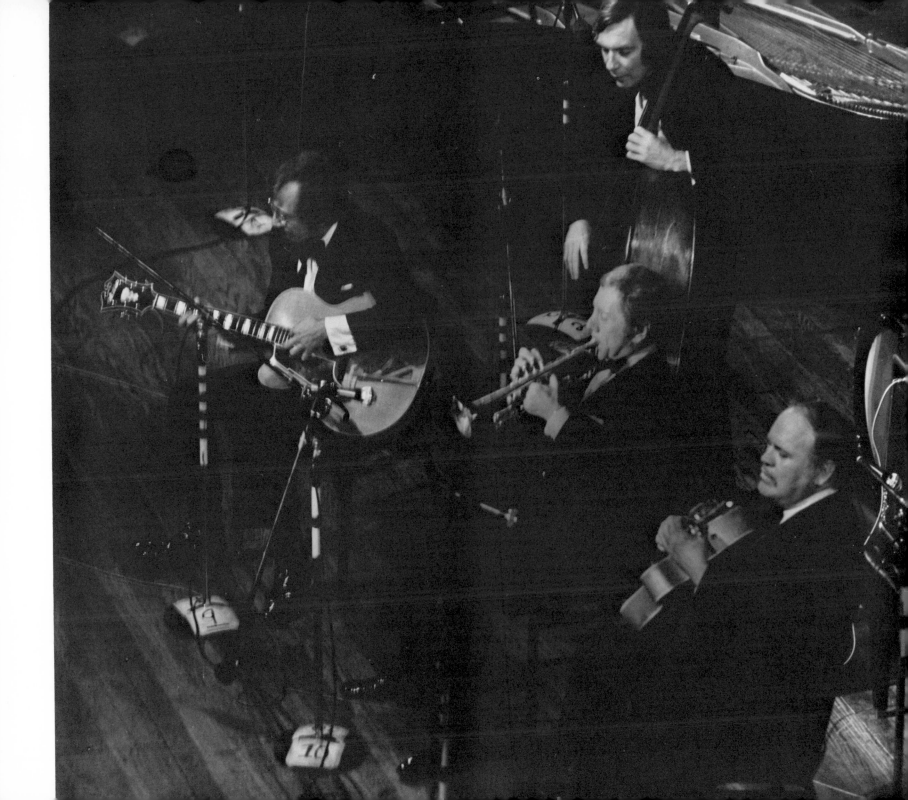

1973

At a plush Festival press party atop Rockefeller Center's Rainbow Grill George Wein announced, "The spirit of this year's Festival is unity." The producer stated further, "It took a lot of courage for the musicians to do what they did." When Juma Sultan, spokesman for the counterfestival, was presented, he repeated last year's fiery pre-Festival statement, which lashed out at the reigning powers-that-be who use black musicians without giving them the recognition that they deserve.

The producer solved the dissent by incorporating the countergroup into the Festival structure. It was implemented with a twenty-thousand-dollar allocation that subsidized a program of two performances a day for five days at a two-dollar admission charge at Harlem's Apollo Theater. The subsidy also provided for a series performed by the New York Musicians Organization at Lincoln Center's Alice Tully Hall. There was still a considerable amount of grumbling from some of the musicians but no open musical warfare. It was more a case of détente than a clasping of hands.

The internal organizational structure of the new Festival and the long-range planning involved raised problems in addition to the day-by-day crises that presented themselves. Concert arrangements, for example, had been made for Yankee Stadium until one of the staff members was chagrined to discover that the ball park had previously been booked for a Jehovah's Witnesses convention. Despite advertising presented for them, some of the major artists did not know until one month before the concert whether or not they would be able to make an appearance. There was a constant nightmarish reshuffling of both programing and artists. Then there were the commitments to be made for lighting and, in particular, sound equipment, a constant problem throughout the history of the Festival. But the staff of twenty or so, aided by an influx of thirty youths at Festival time to handle ticket requests, plus the obvious organizational ability of the producer made it all work.

Outside financial support from organizations and corporations also expanded. Atlantic and Columbia records made contributions. Atlantic took over two entire concerts at Carnegie Hall and featured a number of their artists. The Joseph Schlitz Brewing Company provided funds for two more concerts. Pan-Am supplied transportation from Europe for James Baldwin, one of the participating artists. The National Tea Council of the U.S. had conducted a talent search and supported two more concerts, the winner of which would appear at Carnegie Hall. Gretch Drums, Buddah-Cobblestone Records, and Yamaha also contributed.

As promised the previous year, there were more names on the advisory committee. But with a previously announced budget of $1,000,000, and with $400,000 in the till Wein announced that he must take in $50,000 a day for the next ten days just to break even.

Friday, June 29, 1973

It was almost like being back at Newport, Rhode Island. Rainy mist enveloped Wollman Amphitheater for

The Ruby Braff-George Barnes Quartet includes (left to right) Wayne Wright, guitar, Ruby Braff, trumpet, George Barnes, guitar, and bassist Mike Moore. With warmth and eloquence, they played a program of music associated with Fred Astaire.

207

the opening affair of the 1973 Festival. Onstage Gerry Mulligan had assembled a seventeen-piece band, the Age of Steam, with some really outstanding sidemen, including lanky and dour-faced trombonist Bobby Brookmeyer; trumpeters Jimmy Owens, Joe Newman, and Jon Faddis; and saxaphonist Tom Scott. In intermittent rain and gusty winds the 250 hardy fans in the audience were rewarded with one of the finest presentations that year. The eight-thousand-seat amphitheater reverberated early with swinging brass and reeds. Mulligan at one point dedicated a number to the President of the United States, ''A Weed in Disneyland.'' The music was full of sharp exchanges, exciting rapport, and an exuberant display of virtuosity. Tom Scott, a lesser-known virtuoso in the band, demonstrated fierce runs on both tenor and soprano that had an acrid quality, inflaming the other soloists. Mulligan played with lusty power and forcefulness, whether soloing or trading choruses with Brookmeyer or the rest of the band.

Gato Barbieri, from Rosario, Argentina, created some fiery moments of his own. Gato had first played alto in brilliant pianist-arranger Lalo Schiffrin's band in Buenos Aires. Switching to tenor sax later with some of his own groups, he had been very much affected by the playing of John Coltrane. His program combined the infectious rhythms of Latin America with a beautiful contrast in textures and melody that was undeniably distinct and original. The audience got caught up in his octet the way they had with Mulligan earlier.

Monday, July 2, 1973

When the preparations for the Count Basie reunion of the 1950 band at Carnegie Hall were first in progress, Thad Jones, who had starred in the trumpet section, was approached by the Festival office to join the other alumni for the two concerts. Says Thad, ''Either George or his office called me about it. When I spoke to George, I mentioned the fee, and he hit the roof. O.K., no dice.

208

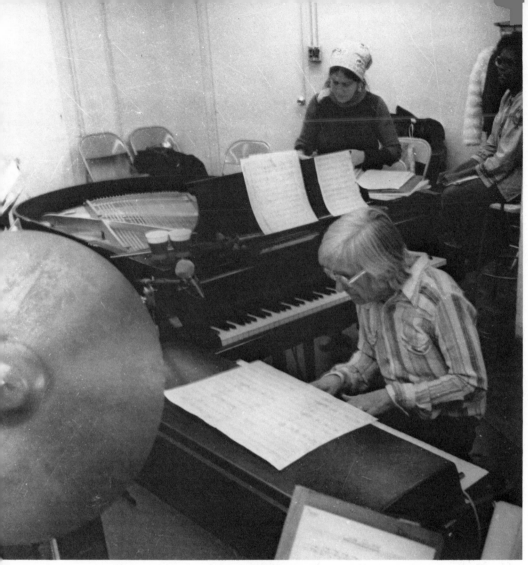

Above. Composer-arranger Gil Evans sits at his keyboards rehearsing some new arrangements. "Living spirit is the thing I look for most in music," he once said. "If I want to hear music that was alive once but is now more or less like a museum piece and I know I'm listening to it, that's something else. But I don't really listen to that kind of music very often anymore. I've already been thrilled with the wonder of it and I feel like going on and developing . . ." *Opposite.* Keith Jarrett is an oddity in the age of electronic instruments, sticking to the acoustic piano while most of his contemporaries use electronic keyboards exclusively. Jarrett's solos often last over an hour and encompass every musical form from the blues to classical.

This went on for about three weeks until finally Joe Newman, another alumnus, called and asked for a meeting with me. I found out the project had been Joe's idea. I finally said, 'O.K., Joe, I'll tell you what. I'll do it for you, but I'll only do one show, and I won't make any rehearsals, and I don't want any money for it. You can take the money George is supposed to give me and throw it out on the street. I don't care.' And that's why I did it, for Joe Newman and for the thrill of playing with Mr. Basie and the guys I came through that particular decade with.

"At the concert that evening I found myself getting into the music and remembering parts of the music that I used to play . . . and all of a sudden for several moments I didn't have to look at the music. It all flashed back to me, just like that! It was the spirit of the section. Snooky Young wasn't able to be there, unfortunately. Jon Faddis made it instead, but had Snooky been there, I think my happiness would have been complete. It was a very special thrill for me to see Marshall Royal again. I hadn't seen him in a great number of years."

The Count Basie reunion band presented an opportunity for Helen Humes to come out of retirement. Helen described how her appearance there came about: "Stanley Dance, the British jazz critic, came to my house in Louisville, telling me all night long about the Basie reunion. But I hadn't sung since my mother passed in 1967. I had sold my piano for ten dollars. I could have knocked myself in the head. All my records and my record player, just everything. I had told myself I wasn't going to sing anymore. But Stanley talked to me about the reunion, saying, 'It's going to be at Carnegie Hall and all the Basie people are going to be there.' I finally agreed if I could get someone to stay with Poppa. I found a lovely lady to take care of him. Poppa was happy that I was going when I told him that Count Basie wanted me to sing with him. My poppa said, 'That's fine, cause my baby sure can sing!'

209

Left. Reedman Grover Washington has had considerable success reaching younger audiences with jazz-tinged soul music. *Above.* Bassist Milt Hinton may very well go into the Guinness Book of World Records for playing at more Newport Jazz Festivals than any other musician.

"At the concert I was scared to death. Nellie Lutcher [pop singer of the late 40's and 50's] stood by my side until I went on. I told Nellie, 'I've got something wrong with my throat.' Nellie told me, 'Helen, now you're just nervous. Now don't worry.' Nellie went out to the drugstore and came back with chloroacetic and gargle and stuff which I took while Nellie stayed with me until I went on."

The concert was one of the Festival's highlights, with trumpeter Joe Newman displaying some of his formidable power and singer Joe Williams, who had joined the band in 1954, wailing his standards and some feeling blues. There was a beautiful and emotional response from both band members and audience. The Count's oldest working sideman, guitarist Freddie Green, still played unamplified guitar as he had through the years with that steadying hand and solidity of rhythm. Helen's reprise of her older material had a warm reception from the audience, who seemed to realize the importance of the occasion and cheered her wildly. When she had finished, Nellie Lutcher greeted her in the wings with a hug and kiss saying, "Now you see, you didn't have nothing to be scared of. You knew Basie was behind you!" Helen said, "I wasn't scared of Basie, I was scared of me! I hadn't looked at the lyrics, and I figured I would get out there and look at all the people and forget the lyrics and everything. All those things were running through my mind. I was glad that it happened all right."

That appearance was the start of a new career for Helen Humes. Shortly after, she toured Europe and started to record once again.

Friday, July 6, 1973

The second of two jam sessions at Radio City Music Hall started backstage when the musicians were going through the ritual of greetings, handclasps, and shouts of recognition. As the time drew near for their concert appearance, the talk grew more serious, but not subdued.

Pianist Earl Hines finally said, "Well, who's going to be the leader?" Everybody almost as one person shouted, "Not me! I don't want to be leader!" Louis Jordan (altoist and popular combo leader of late thirties and forties) said, "I've been leading most of my life. All I want to do is do this thing, get it over with, and go home." They all concurred. Nothing was resolved, and the conversation swung to what they were going to play. Then they started in on the subject of lengths of solos. Feelings ran high. All seemed to agree that everybody played too long these days. Altoist Sonny Stitt volunteered, "I only want a couple of choruses, and I'll be finished!" "Two for me, too," Louis Jordan put in. "I'll take two also," Earl Hines told them. "But it all turned out to be dressing-room talk," Oliver Jackson said later. Tenorist Sonny Rollins ended up taking fifteen or twenty choruses.

When they were finally assembled behind the huge curtain, the MC announced Earl Hines, who pushed through the curtain, seated himself at the piano, and started to play. He was soon joined by the rest of the group crowding onstage. Tiny Grimes, guitar-amplifier jack in hand, plugged into the first female plug he could find. It turned out to be in Milt Hinton's amplifier for his acoustic bass. There was a little wrangling about that, with Milt complaining, "Turn that thing down!" The jack stayed in as the musicians started to jam.

There was one more problem to be surmounted. No one knew what Earl was playing, including Earl. And most importantly, no one remembered what they had decided to play. They ended up with "I Only Have Eyes for You," and, fortunately, everyone knew it, but it wasn't the best selection for a jam session.

When everyone had had their fill of choruses, the team onstage couldn't seem to find the coda and didn't know how to end it. Earl finally got up off his piano stool and jumped out in front of the group. Toscanini couldn't have conducted them with more verve than Hines as he found the right switch and turned them off with a flair to everyone's sighs of relief.

At the close of their set vocalist Anita O'Day joined drummer Oliver Jackson and Milt Hinton with Jimmy Rowles on piano. It was a short, tight set. Oliver said later, "We hadn't had time for a rehearsal, and while we were playing 'Sweet Georgia Brown'—you know how she gives 'fours' to everybody—we played a chorus of fours. And as we were taking the tune out, I started playing it in six-eight, thinking she wanted us to split it in half, but everything was so confusing out there that it sounded like she was singing half time. I knew something was going on, and I looked over to Milt, but Milt sort of shrugged his shoulders as if to say, 'I don't know where it is.' We started to laugh nervously, looking at each other for directions. We ended up taking it out in three-four instead of the half time Anita wanted. She sounded better than I'd heard her sing in a long while, with Jimmy taking a beautiful chorus when she sang 'I Can't Get Started.' It was quite a jam session."

Earlier that evening Carnegie Hall had been host to a program called "Jazz Cabaret," which had featured a reunion of some of the great Cab Calloway orchestras. Trombonist Quentin Jackson was an alumnus of those days, and he commented, "I enjoyed doing it, but it wasn't what I thought it should be. There were some people out there that just didn't belong." Esther Phillips was one person he put in that category. "She just didn't belong in that type of thing. She wasn't around at the time, and she didn't fit into the mood that Calloway should have had. You see, it should have been more show business than music, because Calloway was show business," Quentin continued. "It should have been more Cotton Clubbish . . . there should have been more dancing and things. . . . We were using some of the original charts I had played when I was with the band. I must say I enjoyed the nostalgia part of it. I enjoyed being with him because he was a great leader. Running down those charts, I recalled the way it used to be, and certain guys that I wish had been there from the original band."

The concert received mixed reviews. Honi Coles had danced with Calloway's group, the Copasetics, but his performance that night was uninspired. Quentin explained what had gone wrong with the presentation: "If Honi could have had one of the old arrangements he used to dance by. . . . You know these things are done in such a rush that they don't have time. He used to have such beautiful music behind him when we played the theaters with him. Honi was one of the great unsung dancers. He was so clean and had so much class! We used to enjoy playing behind him because he always had such good music to play."

Two fine trombonists: *Right, top.* The late Quentin "Butter" Jackson. *Bottom.* Tyree Glenn who doubled on vibes.

After another mammoth presentation of jazz, the longest and costliest Festival in Newport Festival history, the press commented, "Jazz critics and historians could think of no event to match it in scope since jazz was born." The total cost exceeded $1,000,000, with musicians' fees exceeding $600,000. Producer George Wein commented for the umpteenth time, "We did too much," and he resolved to do some trimming of presentations and concerts. The group of concerts presented in the Wollman Amphitheater had lost the most money for the Festival. A Festival staff member commented that the idea behind the presentation of jazz in the outdoor amphitheater was to get back some of the flavor of the concerts at Newport, where practically all events had been held outdoors. Because of the enormity of the Festival, ideas that looked good in the planning stage couldn't be carried out on the concert stage.

As always, there were bright, swinging moments that paid off, and there were dismal failures, too, like the collaboration between Ray Charles and James Baldwin. The producer was just not able to stay on top of the mélange of presentations. "A Schlitz Salute to Jazz and the American Song" had been a notable success. The Wollman concerts were a failure, it was suggested, because of the five-dollar-a-head charge. But those outdoor concerts had some of the best music presented that year.

Wein said that he was going to examine scheduling very closely. "I think we will set up the Festival next year so that a person will be able to see all the Festival events if he so desires. Then maybe we won't be competing with ourselves."

213

1974

Since the previous year's Festival reportedly lost $150,000, there was a shift in strategy and concert locations in 1974. The bulk of the music presented was confined to the midtown area of the city, primarily at Carnegie Hall, Avery Fisher Hall at Lincoln Center, and the Pope Auditorium at Fordham University. The Festival retained the ten-day spread of jazz but lowered the budget to $600,000. Sponsors included the Jose Cuervo Tequilla Company, which sponsored a big-band ball at Roseland Dance City. Some of the best features continued, such as the rides up the Hudson River on the Staten Island ferry. Seminars were still being conducted at a couple of locations around the city, and there still were free concerts at Fordham University. Shea Stadium and Wollman Amphitheater, where the festival had suffered losses of $100,000, as well as smaller locations—the Apollo Theater, Alice Tully Hall at Lincoln Center, Carnegie Recital Hall, and St. Peter's Lutheran Church, where some of the more avant-garde groups had been presented—were slashed from the budget.

Producer George Wein summed up the uniqueness of New York City as a location for the Festival: "New York is the only place where you can do a program of eight piano soloists and sell every seat in the house." The producer had resigned himself to the fact that his Festival would never be a big money maker in the city. For some time Wein had taken an abbreviated version of the Festival to various places around the country and sold out; he commented that he could take the same show he had presented at Shea Stadium, primarily jazz and soul, to such places as Atlanta, New Orleans, or Detroit and get thirty thousand people attending the concert in one night. Somehow it all balanced out, and any losses suffered in the city presentations could be made up around the country.

Friday afternoon one of the Festival's free concerts was presented at Pope Auditorium at Fordham University. Alto saxophonist Lee Konitz was making one of his infrequent appearances at the Festival. The music presented was some of the most inspired heard that year. Dick Katz, the group's pianist, remembered the concert vividly: "The concert was a last-minute thing, and Lee deliberately did not want any preparation. Lee wanted to gamble entirely and see what would happen without any preparation at all. He wanted to throw us out in the water. . . . I kept pressing him. 'When I get to the auditorium,' I said, 'what are we going to do?' 'I'm not going to tell you,' Lee said. 'The only thing I'm going to tell you is to come on one at a time. We're going to stagger in. I'm going to play by myself for a while, Wilbur will join you, and then Beaver. Sort of a pyramid thing.' I remember waiting and wondering what I was supposed to do, or when to come on. The music sort of told me that. Lee kind of nodded in the middle of 'Body and Soul' for me to start. Later I was surprised to find myself alone on the stage. Everybody else had cut out, leaving me there by myself. I had to play solo for a while. It was a very exciting feeling, but I wouldn't want to make a career out of it. It would be a little too hard on the nerves. Lee is a musical extremist sometimes. Either he gets

Dwarfed by the monstrous stage of Radio City Music Hall, a group of jamming musicians is bathed in a battery of spotlights. Moments before they went onstage the producer had suggested that they play Duke Ellington's "Take the A Train." After everyone had taken twenty-three choruses, it became apparent that even an Ellington tune has its limitations.

215

into a very structured thing or goes the other way—all the way."

In their version of "Body and Soul" Lee played with a controlled urgency, bursting out with volatile clusters of notes. Rearranging the melody, he understated with his dry, uncluttered tonality and then assembled it whole. He caught the audience with a commanding solo that galvanized his rhythm section. Lee mixed the program up with ballads and faster tempos that displayed his wide range of talent—aurally graceful, pithy, and brilliant, yet with a warm depth.

At the rehearsal for a program entitled "The Musical Life of Charlie Parker" baritonist Cecil Payne remembered some of his own contacts with the brilliant and influential altoist through the years: "Shortly before going into the army in 1943 I remember Max Roach telling about the new sounds and how great Bird was. I was playing at the Seventy-eighth Street Taproom. Bird used to come down and jam, playing Lester Young's solos note for note too." Tenorist Bud Johnson was the man who shaped the Charlie Parker program for the New York Jazz Repertory Company's concert. He related some of the problems he encountered while preparing the music for presentation: "The biggest difficulty was getting the band members in shape. A lot of the guys, like Sonny Stitt, hadn't been reading music in years. They play what they feel and what they know and the way they know it, which is what is correct, but when you take the music off the record—plus Jay McShann, who brought in four arrangements from his old book, which we opened up the program with—it was hard to get those guys to play it like the music was . . . you know what I mean.

"When the guys go out and jam and play just from memory, well, it becomes difficult if you haven't been keeping up with your reading. Transcribing the original records is not a very difficult job. I did the original arrangements for 'Stormy Monday Blues' for Billy Eckstine, and I did the arrangement for 'Jelly, Jelly' also.

216

Left, top. Dizzy Gillespie shows Producer Wein a miniature tape recorder he has recently purchased. Jay McShann, seated at the piano, puffs on a cigarette and looks on as a rehearsal conducted by Budd Johnson continues. *Left, bottom.* That's baritonist Cecil Taylor in the foreground. *Opposite.* The weathered gentle face of Jay McShann.

"The most difficult part of the concert was the Jay McShann opening for the big band. It was very difficult to follow because they hear combos all the time. To play those old big swing arrangements, in which they were really swinging and the guys were really blowing, plus the solos in those arrangements too. I opened them up and stretched them out for them to play solos. Well, it was very hard to follow. We were trying to tell a chronological story of Charlie Parker."

The concert broke Parker's career into five segments. It started with his band days with the Jay McShann Orchestra from Kansas City and moved on to his association with Billy Eckstine's star-studded band, which included Dizzy Gillespie, Miles Davis, Dexter Gordon, Gene Ammons, Fats Navarro, Art Blakey, and Sarah Vaughan. The program then covered the Earl Hines Band, which Parker had joined to replace Budd Johnson; then there were the Dizzy Gillespie small groups; and finally the string ensemble he recorded and played with at the close of his career.

McShann was relaxed and enjoyed himself tremendously. A gentle man, he had mentioned during the rehearsal that the music was a particularly pleasurable part of his life. "Bird always seemed original to me, even then. But whatever he played said the blues. He knew them so well, and from the heart."

The McShann pieces were highlighted by stunning but brief solos by altoists Charlie McPherson and Phil Woods. Budd had done a fine job with the arrangements, and the musicians realized the importance of what they were doing and responded accordingly. Earl Hines played brilliantly, dwelling first on one of the arrangements from his pre-Parker days, then moving into "Piano Man," orchestrally rich and filled with delicately modulated changes played with utmost ease and spontaneity, swinging finally into a solo on "Close to Me." Billy Eckstine sang a medley that was well received by an audience steeped in the nostalgia of his older hits. Then altoist Sonny Stitt joined Dizzy in a round robin

217

that recalled the sides Diz had recorded with Parker, from "Be-Bop" and "Salt Peanuts," segueing into his own tasty version of "Can't Get Started," to his distinct individualizing of Monk's "Round About Midnight." Stitt played in that clipped, pugnacious style of his, whipping out savage phrases, while Dizzy projected a sensitivity that seemed to display what he felt for his friend and the music that he had created. When Dizzy's last note faded, the expression on his face brought to mind the look I had seen a few years before when he had been introduced to Bird's son, Baird. Diz had gently cupped his hand over the boy's head and said, "Bird's son . . ."

On Sunday night there were two blues concerts. Both early and late shows were entitled "The King's Road, Highway 61," denoting the long road taken by blues from the delta regions of the South to big-city Chicago. B.B. King was an apt MC for the program.

The program presented a broad perspective of the roots of so much of the blues- and rock-oriented music recently shipped back from England. Most of the rock-oriented kids of today had learned about the blues from Eric Clapton, Mick Jagger, and groups like Cream, but tonight's program was the real thing.

B.B. King's entrance was very quiet, and his program had a coolness born of the multitudinous pains and heartaches he had suffered from childhood. He didn't confine himself to ballads as he scrunched down over his guitar, "Lucille," and plucked out a series of nerve-tingling chords that were humorous, irreverent, and not without a quiet fury. After the concert he said, "I'm singing about things I've actually experienced." That seemed to be the key. B.B. King had a way of bending notes. It wasn't original, but he had taken it and spread it out a little more. Plucking a string, he would press his strong hand across the frets of his guitar, tightening up the string and raising the pitch, and just leave it there to peak. After he dove down to the lower part of the scale, he would shoot up fresh and vigorous once again,

Above. Pianists Jess Stacy (seated) and Eddie Heywood relaxing at the piano backstage before their performance.

218

Above. Behind the curtains at Fordham University, an intense Sonny Stitt holds the keys on Frank Foster's tenor to direct his playing of runs. For thirty minutes master reedman Sonny pointed out the effects Frank could produce by practicing blowing technique and knowing the scales as well as Stitt himself does.

Opposite, left. Looking through the curtain at the vast, airplane hangar-sized Radio City Music Hall as a group jams onstage. *Opposite, right.* Backstage Teddy Wilson's children wait for their father to finish his performance, dozing on a stairway that is part of the set for the regular stage shows. *Above.* Tom Whaley, former copyist for Duke Ellington, now blind, sits backstage and listens quietly.

always taking one by surprise. B.B. King had some fine backing in the guitar of Buddy Guy, who also came from delta country near Baton Rouge, Louisiana, and had been extremely impressed by the music of King and Bobby Bland whenever he had heard them play together. The harmonica player with the group was an early associate of Guy's, Junior Wells, from Memphis, Tennessee. He developed a playing style on his own, seeming to apply the harmonics of the guitar to the harmonica. His playing fused the trio and brought depth to the early part of the program.

King joined Bobby "Blue" Bland at the end of the program. This was a complete shift in sound from the looseness of the Chicago style to the brash brassiness of Bland's group, which had more of a show-biz orientation. Intermixed with them was the dusty-road sounds of an earlier period of the blues, produced by Hammie Nixon and Sleepy John Estes, as they played with an earthy quality that sometimes had the flick and glitter of sunshine. Johnny Shines, another Memphis man, had grown through the years until he had lost that early crude quality I used to hear on his records and instead seemed to be part of the brash and sexy tradition of bluesy soul today. Toward the end of the program Linda Hopkins with a great deal of aggressive, flamboyant energy gripped the audience with a collection of Bessie Smith and gospel numbers.

Among the bits and pieces I observed along the way was the stageload of drummers roaring and rebounding through the vast areas crowded with teen-agers who had turned out to see Diana Ross sing anything but jazz at Radio City Music Hall. It was heartening to see the lines swinging around for blocks to attend both shows, and as I stood in the wings photographing, I noticed the expression of surprise on Elvin Jones's face in my telephoto-mounted camera. Elvin described the action to me later. "During my solo my foot broke right through my drum. The pedal wasn't working right or something.

221

The "Thank You Concert" presented by the Festival at Lincoln Center Fountain Plaza. The Kid Thomas Preservation Hall Band is onstage. *Opposite*. A relaxed and casually dressed group of fans enjoy the sounds of New Orleans music. Some shield themselves from the blazing sun with umbrellas.

Funny thing. Nobody seemed to notice it. I glanced over to Buddy Rich, and he knew it. I thought of changing over to Max's drums but changed my mind and just concentrated on my snare and sock cymbal. We laughed about it afterward."

During the evening of the "Salute to Jazz and the American Song" at Avery Fisher Hall a young lady asked vocalist Bobby Short, "How many times have you been married?" "I've never been married at all," he replied. "That's very strange," she said, "because the MC, Dave Garroway, remarked onstage about your marvelous taste, and that you had marvelous taste in wives as well." "I thought to myself," he told me later, "that was interesting. . . . That night after the last show was over, I was waiting outside for my car to arrive. Garroway was leaving at that moment, and I turned to him saying, 'Thanks for a job well done.' He said, 'Oh, and give my best to Julie.' I thought for a minute, he thinks I'm Harry Belafonte, whose wife's name is Julie. Then a friend said, 'He thinks you're Bobby Troup, who's married to Julie London!' Can you believe that?"

As the Festival drew to a close, there was another free concert presented at the plaza of Lincoln Center. Traditional jazz echoed throughout the complex. Kid Thomas blared out a crisp solo on trumpet, and the rest of the group stomped merrily as the longest and most profitable Festival drew to a melodious close. Smiling couples hovered around the fringes of the concert area while women opened umbrellas to protect themselves from the glaring sun.

The Festival had made a profit of between $100,000 and $150,000, erasing the losses of the previous year. Little of the music presented opened up new avenues to more adventurous listening, but the conservativeness had paid off. George Wein summed up his feelings when he said, "We might even be more conservative next year. People feel more secure about a successful Festival. Why endanger that?"

They were rehearsing for the first concert of the 1975 Jazz Festival. It was to be a repeat of a program the New York Jazz Repertory Company had presented earlier that year.

Some of the sidemen who had originally performed had left on a State Department tour of the Soviet Union, performing the music of Louis Armstrong. Strangely enough, the Soviets had requested a fifteen-city tour of the earlier concert, which had been recorded by the Voice of America and beamed to Eastern Europe. Détente takes odd directions.

Dave Hutson, the music director, short and slightly plump, stood in the center of the room, alto sax swaying slightly on his neck strap. "Some of you were here before, but in case you didn't know, we're playing the music of Bix," he said wryly. "These arrangements we're playing are from the Jean Goldkette Orchestra and the Wolverines." Reaching over his music stand, he held up the chart of the first tune. " 'Clementine' just plays itself. There's a trumpet solo at D. The solo was written out the way Bix played it, but you don't have to play it that way. We're rehearsing this music in two three-hour sessions. That's a lot less than we gave it the first time 'round."

The sidemen were some of the best jazz musicians in the country. They ranged from a twenty-four-year-old cornetist, Warren Vache, who interpreted Bix Beiderbecke's solos with just the right tonality and feeling, to some of Bix's contemporaries who had sat alongside him in the original Goldkette Orchestra.

After a few false starts they ran down the most difficult parts of the arrangement; everything started to fall into place. Near the rear of the long rehearsal studio sat part of the rhythm section. Taciturn and blustery, with a violin propped under his chin, Joe Venuti, the seventy-one-year-old legendary jazz violinist, sat in a folding chair, his round stomach bulging out against the music stand. Beside him sat the equally brilliant guitarist, Bucky Pizzarelli, playing a Gretch seven-string guitar made especially for him. They complemented each other beautifully. The deep respect the two men had for each other transcended the nearly thirty-year difference in their ages. One could almost slice the empathy between them with a knife. Occasionally the sounds of Joe's gravelly voice mixed with outbursts of laughter from Bucky and the other musicians around them.

As Dave Hutson explained one particularly difficult section, he was interrupted by Venuti, who shouted, "Anything you don't understand, ask Jimmy McPartland!" Sounds of laughter. Jimmy had not arrived yet, but it was a gentle dig at the musician who had replaced Bix Beiderbecke in the Jean Goldkette Orchestra.

During the morning rehearsal there was foot tapping and a pervasive happy feeling on the part of the crowd, from families of some of the musicians and from jazz buffs that filled the studio. It was a feeling you could not get from an actual concert, since it resulted from the proximity of musicians to the listeners.

The music evoked an era many of those present were

There were sparks flying everywhere when tenor-man Zoot Sims (left) joined Joe Venuti's Blue Four. Behind Zoot is former Jean Goldkette trombonist Spiegle Wilcox with jazz violinist Joe Venuti (center) and behind him young enthusiast on bass baritone, Vince Giordano. The guitarist is Bucky Pizzarelli.

225

not old enough to remember, but the participation of some of the original members of the Goldkette Orchestra lent an authenticity to the music. Chauncy Moorhouse, the orchestra's original drummer, thin, white-haired, his clothes hanging from his frail body, sat on one side, taking the weight off his remaining leg (the other had been removed some years earlier). He knocked his cane against his artificial leg, smiling as he did it, having accepted his infirmity long ago and gotten on with his life.

Balancing himself on his two canes, he spoke to Vince Giordano, the young bass saxophonist and tuba player with the orchestra. Vince was a student of the Beiderbecke era of music, collecting sheet music, recordings, and other material from the period. The unusually strong feeling and quality of his performance showed that he had thoroughly immersed himself in the music.

Chauncy wanted to impart bits of Bixiana to whoever would listen, and Vince was a willing subject. He listened quietly as Chauncy spoke. "No one has equaled Bix's musical ability to write for the piano. Bix was aware of his lack of musical training and always considered himself at the bottom of the bush." Chauncy smoothed his hair as he said it. The break over, he gingerly edged his way back to his cymbal stand. Vince sat for a moment thinking over what he had just heard; then, rising, he lifted his tuba, blew a few notes, smiled, and settled down, turning to the arrangement that had just been announced.

As they ran down the opening sections of "Way Down Yonder in New Orleans," Marian McPartland, the orchestra's pianist, had to play six notes on the celeste as well as her piano solo. "I've been thinking of sending George [referring to producer George Wein] a note asking him if I get paid for doubling," she said, facetiously.

As they put the finishing touches on "Clarinet Marmalade," Dave Hutson discussed their onstage appearance: "The first note will be played in the dark, and as

Above. Jimmy McPartland (center) plays the cornet given to him by legendary jazz figure Bix Beiderbecke for an appreciative audience of fellow musicians including trumpeter Doc Cheetham (left). *Right.* Trombonist Bill Rank who played in the Jean Goldkette Orchestra was brought to New York for the New York Jazz Repertory concert that was part of the Festival program.

Left. Altoist and conductor of the program, Dave Hutson.
Above. Chauncy Morehouse (left), drummer with Jean Goldkette's Orchestra and sideman on a number of classic jazz recordings with Bix Beiderbecke, Frankie Trumbauer, and the Dorsey Brothers, also participated in The N.Y. Jazz Repertory Beiderbecke program. Here he converses with a drummer from another generation, Bobby Rosengarden.

soon as you play it, the house lights will come up, so *remember* your first note." Frank Williams in the trumpet section quipped, "If they don't, there'll be a catastrophe!" Laughter ran through the group.

As the orchestra moved from one arrangement to another, there were occasional grunts of pleasure from the bassist, Major Holley, known to his friends as Mule. "Like Heckle and Jeckle," he said, laughing, glancing toward Joe Venuti and Bucky Pizzarelli as they traded fours. Bucky's archly raised brow brought a quick smile to Joe's face repeatedly. They had complete rapport. "They'll never break that marriage up," Major said, laughing again. Joe's solos were greeted by knowing smiles from the rest of the musicians. It was a deep tribute to an artist. The very hunching of Joe Farrell's shoulder as he lifted it in time to the music, smile on his face, was a tribute. It was lovely to watch.

Spiegel Wilcox, cup of coffee in hand, edged past his fellow trombonist from the Goldkette Orchestra, Bill Rank. "Spiegel," Bill exclaimed, "you play as good as you ever did." His eyes shone as he said it. Spiegel smiled. "Ain't he nice?" he said. Later on, Joe Venuti took a beautiful solo, and in unison, from opposite sides of the room, Marian and late-arrival Jimmy McPartland rose and started to applaud. The rest of the orchestra joined in. It came from the heart.

They finished running down "Clementine" for a second time, and as they rose to take a break, Joe Venuti reached over with his violin bow pointing to the arrangement, and with a poker face remarked, "It's really an Italian song." I glanced at Bucky sitting beside him, and as he glanced back at me, we both broke up completely. My sides ached. In the narrow quarters I came close to knocking over Joe Farrell's sax stand, I was laughing so hard.

228

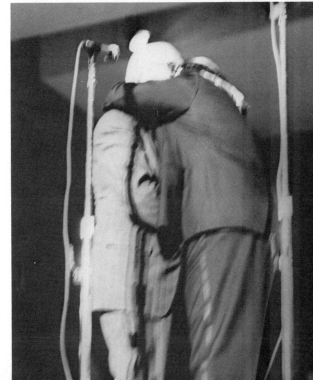

Opposite. Barney Josephson (left) accepts the applause of the audience and receives an emotional and unexpected embrace from Newport Jazz Festival producer George Wein. *Above.* Thelma Carpenter accepts a bouquet of flowers from an usher after her performance. *Left.* Comedian Timmie Rogers acted as both m.c. and entertainer.

Johnny Mince in the reed section had brought along an original song sheet of "Three Blind Mice," a tune that had been composed by Chauncy Moorhouse and Frankie Trumbauer. He busied himself gathering autographs on the sheet music from the original members of the Goldkette Orchestra.

As the rehearsal continued into the morning, they stopped for an occasional break. Tenor man Zoot Sims, a fine, swinging musician, noted for his pithy comments and dry humor, sat in front of his music stand hardly speaking all morning. He examined the chart in front of him as Hutson commented on a particular section of the arrangement.

"That section," he said, "will probably sound funny to you but—"

He was interrupted by Zoot, who interjected, "If you want to hear something funny, let me play my part all alone." Loud laughter. Later, during a break, Zoot and a couple of other musicians discussed the tempo of the arrangement they had been playing. Zoot remarked, "Yeah! I've got all these arrangements and this." He pointed to his protruding lip, wincing in pain as he said it.

"I want the people from Venuti's Blue Four to run their things down," Dave Hutson said. "The rest of you guys can go."

"And don't forget about the stage sound check," one of George Wein's staff interjected. "We've got to get a balance and check on the volume for the hall, so let's be onstage at five P.M."

Joe Venuti turned to Dave Hutson and said, "I'd like Zoot to do the 'blue' things with us." Johnny Mince had played them in the previous concert, but Joe had taken

229

Above. Aboard the ferry John F. Kennedy with the World's Greatest Jazz Band including (left to right) bassist Bobby Haggart, pianist Dick Welstood, and a front line of Bob Wilbur on alto, tenorman Bud Freeman, trumpeter Yank Lawson and trombonist Benny Morton. *Opposite.* The overflowing crowd jams the deck to hear the Kid Thomas Preservation Hall Band.

a liking to Zoot's tenor sound and wanted him to play instead. Zoot turned and remarked, "I don't mind if I know the tunes." The reenactment of the Joe Venuti–Eddie Lang Blue Four got underway with "China Boy." They ran it down slowly at first, but moving into the choppy-sounding bridge, they started to swing. From Joe's loud glissando they surged into a driving, raucous climax that seemed to catch everyone by the throat. Not confined to the transcribed sounds they had been rehearsing before, the music, goaded on by Joe on violin, caught fire. Between the broken chords and repeated phrases it was a wild, jamming free-for-all. White-haired Spiegel Wilcox leaned on the piano listening, his face all smiles and wonder. At the closing bars Chauncy Moorhouse pressed his two canes together, making a percussive sound; then he added another touch by pressing them down on the step of his sock cymbal to make a *cha-cha-chach* sound. The smile on his face said it all. This is jazz!

Thursday, June 26, 1975

"What's on top?" inquired drummer Panama Francis. "Fidgety Feet," a few musicians called out. The small ensemble swung into the first tune for Friday's concert. They ran it down briefly and moved onto "Tijuana." "Occasionally peace breaks out in 'Tijuana,'" piped in the tuba player. Later, during a break, he spoke with Bill Rank, who had been one of the original members of the Jean Goldkette Orchestra. Although the tuba player was the youngest, he seemed to be the most well informed about the music they were playing. "They're playing all this four-beat; when it was written, it was played two-beat." Rank answered the tuba player's query about what had happened to the original arrangements of the Goldkette Orchestra. "The Casa Loma Orchestra supposedly took them over when they took over the band.

Right. Benny Carter on alto sax. *Opposite.* Roseland Ballroom is the setting for those who like to dance as well as listen to jazz. For one evening each year, the crowds at the Ballroom become part of the Festival.

232

But I don't remember them ever playing them," he said tersely.

Dave Hutson made a sour face. " 'Tijuana.' Is this the one with that terrible tenor solo?" His question was directed at himself as he looked over the chart. He muttered, "I don't know all the changes yet, but no one has to be that accurate."

During one of the longer breaks Panama reminisced with the group. "The man handed me that paper, and I split from Miami, this fast." He gestured into the air with a whoosh. "Miami! I couldn't wait to get out of that town." He grimaced as if he had a bad taste in his mouth. "I was working all over Florida when I was fourteen, came to New York at eighteen. New York has been good to me. Six months after I came here I was playing with Roy Eldridge, at the Arcadia Ballroom, Why I've been playing professionally for forty-four years. They sent a lot of cats out of this town in pine boxes. They were all trying to turn the lights out! Why those jam sessions used to last all night! Work? I couldn't wait to get on that bandstand when I was at the Savoy." He underlined his remarks with a drum roll.

The rehearsal continued: They ran the changes down of "Big Boy," and as they came to the final chords, Johnny Mince crooked his elbow in a mock Charleston pose and chortled, "I love that tune!"

After the rehearsal ended, Bill Rank mused about Bix: "I used to get so involved in his solos that I would forget to come in on the chorus." The few survivors of the Goldkette Orchestra, who seldom got a chance in their daily lives now to reminisce, began to drag out the old stories of how it was in "those days," how it was to have known Bix, the man and the musician. Bill Rank smiled quietly into space as he continued to remember.

233

Friday, June 27, 1975

About six-thirty I wandered into the stage entrance, greeted Stewart, the stage manager of Carnegie Hall, and chatted with him for a while. We were interrupted by producer George Wein, dressed in a tuxedo, and three well-dressed men who entered the office with him. The tallest of the three looked at the stage manager and in a condescending tone said, "We're from NBC Television. We're doing a profile on George Wein. All we need is a shot of him, say in the wings, and a long-distance shot from the back of the hall. No sound." Stewart looked up at him from his desk, said nothing. It was a look that seemed to say he would take care of it. The foursome disappeared around the corner.

An hour or so into the first program of the Festival the back of the stage was suddenly lit garishly with powerful beams of floodlight, first stage left, then stage right. The beams were the camera lights of the NBC camera crew, photographing Mr. Wein "in the wings." Since Carnegie Hall no longer has wings per se, but rather only a screen that runs at an angle to the curtain, the bursts of light totally disrupted the ongoing music. The incident typified something Nat Hentoff had identified in a piece entitled "Bringing Dignity to Jazz," about the riots at the Newport Festival in 1960. Twenty-one years after the first Newport Jazz Festival concert, after all the improvements in technology, the Festival was still burdened by these instances of carelessness. They occur year after year partly because those who are occasionally critical of these and other Festival problems are sooner or later trapped into shutting up. Most of those who write about jazz end up one way or another as part of the programing of the next Festival year. They are called upon to write, program, announce, or edit programs. In short, financial considerations make the critics cater to the producer.

Tuesday, July 1, 1975

New York stank that night. Garbage was piling up all over the city because of a wildcat strike over the loss of jobs in the sanitation department. For part of the time at Avery Fisher Hall it seemed as if some of that garbage had spilled all over the stage and was being dumped on the audience.

Phyllis Diller was mistress of ceremonies at "The Schlitz Salute to Jazz and the American Song." A member of George Wein's staff confided that Ms. Diller had mentioned her love of jazz music to Wein and had offered her services as MC. Her offer had unfortunately been accepted. Although she stated between her introductions of the artists that she was there because she loved jazz, she spewed forth a torrent of pointless dirty jokes. It was alternately embarrassing and disgusting. A member of the audience new to jazz was heard asking, "Is this type of introduction done very often?" John S. Wilson of the *New York Times,* commenting on Ms. Diller's costume, said, "She looked like a technicolor ostrich." Then he mentioned her "nightclub one-liners." Patricia O'Hare in the *New York Daily News* had a much stronger opinion: "And whoever had the idea to bring someone named Phyllis Diller in to be part of the show ought to have his ideas blown out of his mind. She was vulgar, tasteless, foolish. A complete waste of time on everyone's part."

The same thing had occured in 1968, when Flip Wilson had been brought in to MC a program: He resorted to the same dirty-joke approach with which he had been so unsuccessful at Birdland during the sixties. The evening I saw him there, the audience was hip enough to

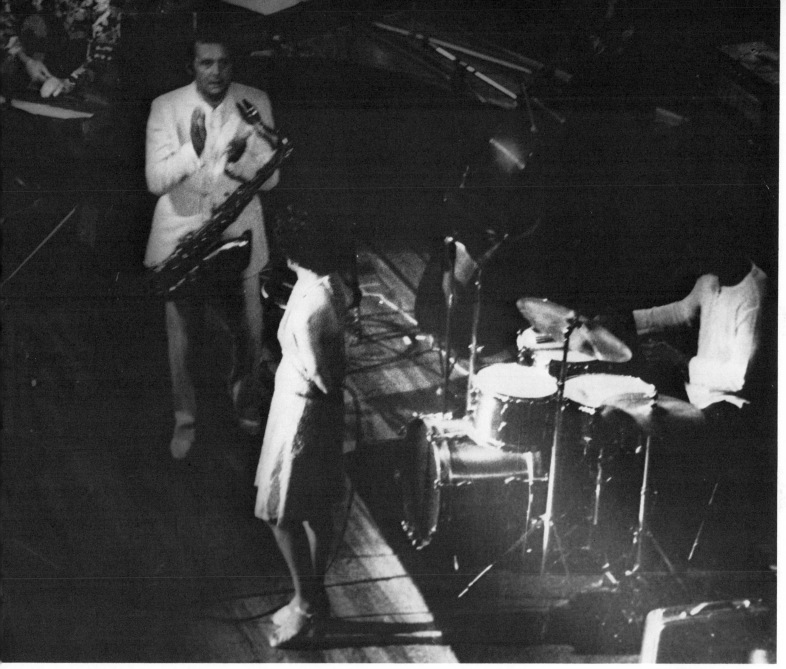

Heloisa Gilberto, a last-minute replacement for her ailing composer husband João, is accompanied by Stan Getz who applauds her after her performance.

Opposite. Jazz violinist Joe Venuti demonstrates his ideas on the piano for an appreciative audience consisting of jazz pianists Dill Jones (behind him) and (far left) Marian McPartland. Venuti's ancient alligator violin case rests on the piano in front of him.
Above. Vocalist Cleo Lane rehearses with bandleader husband Johnny Dankworth.

snicker him off the stage. Wilson's style had been bad taste then; Diller's was worse in 1975.

The program itself (Diller aside) moved from the skillful and concentrated power of guitarist Jim Hall to the forceful swinging of Zoot Sims on tenor in a Gershwin program. They made a simple, passionate statement of "Embraceable You," then brought a swinging fusion to the lovely "The Man I Love." Jim Hall was eloquent in his unaccompanied solo, "Someone to Watch Over Me."

Cy Coleman (pop composer-pianist) followed with an overlong group of songs he had composed through the years. At best on the far outskirts of jazz, he played pleasantly, and some fire was provided by his rhythm section—Larry Ridley on bass and Benny Thomas on drums. They moved from "Witchcraft" to "Hey, Look Me Over."

The program was saved in part by vocalist Helen Humes, who, completely relaxed, took over the stage and glistened in a delightful program of Fats Waller tunes. She delighted the audience with the same naturalness and infectious humor that Fats himself used to project. She sang "Keepin' Out of Mischief Now," followed by his "Honeysuckle Rose," then moving into one of his more serious compositions, "Black and Blue." The lyrics were as meaningful in 1975 as they had been when it was first written. The audience wanted more. "I just ran out of Waller tunes," she said apologetically, but she obliged them with a rollicking, "If He Flags My Train, I'm Sure Gonna Let Him Ride."

Chet Baker's sextet followed, playing a group of Rodgers and Hart songs. Chet's limited vocal ability, coupled with the fact that he obviously did not know the lyrics very well and also had misplaced his glasses, combined to produce little of value, aside from an expressive solo played by his vibist, Warren Chaisson, on "What Can I Say, Dear, After I Say I'm Sorry." It was not one of jazz's finest hours.

238

Above. Legendary tenor man Eddie "Lockjaw" Davis.
Opposite. Art Blakey has been called "The Rock of Ages." He's fifty-eight years old, but as one of his sidemen told me recently, "When you play with Art, there's no slacking off. He has more drive and energy than anyone else I might name." Art doesn't lean toward electronic music. "You turn off the switches," he says, "and there's no more music."

Thursday, July 3, 1975

Slinging my camera bag over my shoulder, I emerged from the darkened, confining atmosphere of the photographer's booth overlooking the stage at Avery Fisher Hall. It had been a long night: two concerts in one evening. The brightly lit corridor made me blink. The long narrow hallway was paved with light-colored tile, and slitlike windows on one side gave the only view of the outside world.

The long corridor turned a corner and wended its way past the dressing rooms. Hurrying to avoid the crowd of well-wishers pushing toward the dressing rooms, I moved quickly to the elevators.

The door opened, and I joined a packed crowd of departing musicians. "Hi Lock," I greeted tenorist Eddie "Lockjaw" Davis. He squeezed my shoulder and smilingly said, "Long time, Burt!" "You sure sounded good," I said. Lock and I had known each other for many years, but our paths did not cross very often these days. "Beautiful!" I said, turning to trumpeter Jimmy Nottingham, beside him. He smiled and touching my hand said quietly, "We had a good thing going." He said it without a trace of ego. Moments before he had torn up a crowded audience with a growly, gutsy solo. Now he shyly backed off from a compliment.

We walked down the short flight of steps, past the security guards, and out into the warm night air. At the curb stood a gray Cadillac with a liveried chauffeur standing by. "Is it ready?" asked Lockjaw, kidding. The chauffeur turned and in reply nodded his head and smiled. Jimmy Nottingham gave the car an appraising glance and shouted, "That's one of those l-o-o-o-o-ng-short ones!" Everybody laughed as we reached Broadway and turned north. It had been a fine evening.

239

1976

Amid all the bicentennial hoopla this year radio spots first presented a brief biography of the Newport Jazz Festival's producer and later touted the coming Festival. The "tall ships" and other bicentennial events, however, overwhelmed these efforts. It was unfortunate that jazz couldn't have been integrated into the regular programing of the bicentennial celebration. Jazz, after all, is one of this country's greatest contributions to the culture of the world, and Louis Armstrong's birthday on July fourth is symbolic of that.

George Wein's festival program, ignoring the fact that there had been no festival in 1961, persisted in calling this festival the 23rd. The festival had been extended to 11 days this year plus some other non-jazz events sponsored by Wein's booking organization, Festival Productions Inc. The press announced on June 9 the cancellation of a one-day Festival stand of Count Basie-Sarah Vaughan which was to have taken place at the World Trade Center Plaza. Other bicentennial events had been canceled along with them. The Port Authority had promised to foot the $40,000 security costs if a sponsor could be found for the concert. The question became academic when Count Basie accepted a booking at Aqueduct Racetrack for the concert date.

Others problems beset the producer when Parks Commissioner Martin Lang canceled three soul music concerts at Shea Stadium, citing a possible repetition of the disorders that had erupted there at another soul music concert two weeks earlier. Two of the canceled concerts on July 9 and 10 were being produced by

George Wein. Wein told the press that $35,000 worth of tickets had been sold for the two concerts and that $40,000 to $50,000 would be lost that had been spent on advertising, labor, and press parties for the events. "I can fight City Hall," Wein told the press, "but I can't win." Later he quipped, "I feel like the little boy who gets his face smashed by his mother and then is told, 'That's for what you might do.' "

The Festival opened at the overflowing gardens at Rockfeller Center. Wein made the usual statement about how New York had welcomed the Festival with open arms when they had arrived from Newport, Rhode Island. Dressed in a light gray suit, side vents blowing in a light breeze, the producer buzzed around with a back-slap here and a wave to a few friendly faces in the crowd of bystanders and tourists in the small, cramped, concert area.

Joe Newman and his Jazz Interactions Quintet played a brief set. Newman, in a natty, sky-blue shirt, golden horn flashing in the hide-and-seek sunlight, introduced vocalist Stella Marrs, who charmed the audience with a couple of numbers, well backed by the group. Wein came forward at the close of the concert, announcing, ". . . since the Festival is always full of surprises, here's another one," and Tony Bennett and pianist Bill Evans took a brief bow onstage, acknowledging the ovation, ending the afternoon.

Nineteen seventy-six brought a tightly knit festival to New York. The opening evening concert at Carnegie

Trumpeter Cootie Williams, trombonist Eddie Bert, and reedman Kenny Davern play a segment of Duke Ellington's "Mood Indigo" for a camera crew from ABC. The drummer in the background is Panama Frances. The television publicity was helpful, but the brief rehearsal time given to this Ellington material allowed no interruptions.

Hall featured a pop singer, Tony Bennett. Pianist Bill Evans accompanied Tony on "My Foolish Heart." Then, surrounding himself with a thirty-two piece orchestra that included everything from strings to a harp and tympanist, Bennett belted out over a dozen standards with some medleys that included Cole Porter's "What is This Thing Called Love?" through "Love For Sale," closing with an array of Ellington—"Don't Get Around Much Anymore" and "Sophisticated Lady."

It upset someone in the center of the orchestra seats, who stood up shouting, "This is supposed to be a jazz festival; bring back Bill Evans!" Evans, slumped over the keyboard, head buried in his chest, played well, but seemed quite out of place in the role of accompanist on that large stage.

This was a year of Festival tributes. There were four concerts honoring Duke Ellington, three for Count Basie, one for the late altoist Cannonball Adderley, a retrospective for pianist Herbie Hancock, one for John Coltrane, one for the Reverend John Gensel, pastor to the jazz community, and finally a salute to guitarist Tal Farlow.

If one could cope with the incessant street noises, the shriek of brakes and the general cacophony of traffic inching its way past the outdoor locations on Long Island and New York City, there was a feast of excellent music free for the listening. The concerts were sponsored by the Greenwich Savings Bank at a number of locations around the city. The performance at 51st Street and Avenue of the Americas provided the most excitement. The huge crowds were greeted each afternoon by a number of fine soloists and big bands that gave an excellent cross section of some of the contemporary currents in jazz. The audience overflowed into the street, blocking crosstown traffic, while cabbies and truckdrivers good humoredly paused to catch some of the fine sounds, one truckdriver loudly singing along on one occasion as Sy Oliver broke into some of his nostalgia-soaked arrangements from his days as a musi-

cian, singer and arranger with the Jimmy Lunceford and Tommy Dorsey orchestras. The Oliver Band was well disciplined and swinging, fresh from their current extended appearance at the Rainbow Grill atop Rockefeller Center. "We're going on a European tour in a few days," Sy told the enthusiastic crowd. "I'd like to take this audience with me."

Oliver, a thoroughly disciplined musician-conductor, and his band had some fine solo work from Candy Ross on trombone, pianist Clifford Smalls, and an effective rhythm section propelled by drummer Oliver Jackson with some excellent bass work by Leonard Gaskin. Sy worked on trumpet and vibes to good effect and the audience was very appreciative, cheering all the soloists. It was heartwarming to see altoist Haywood Henry getting his dues both on alto and soprano, and that smile on his face when he finished soloing seemed to say it all. Vocalist Buddy Smith sang well and delighted the crowd when he formed a singing trio with Candy Finch and Sy Oliver. Moving from the romantic "Don't Blame Me," or bouncing "Ain't She Sweet," to more uptempo numbers, "Well Get It," "For Dancers Only," through some more contemporary and rock-oriented tunes like "Feelings," the band combined eloquence with enthusiasm and a zest that reached out to everyone that afternoon. Other afternoons were filled with the sounds of the orchestras of Count Basie, Mercer Ellington, Earl Hines, and Buddy Rich, as photographers perched in nearby plane trees whose branches looked as if they would not support a sparrow. On one occasion I was instructed to warn the musicians about the narrow stage, which was constructed of steel supports and masonite panels, lest the trumpet section fall off the rear, which did not have the customary wooden stop for chairs.

Standing in the narrow space at the rear of the stage I watched friends drop by to pay court to Count Basie, who looked fit and relaxed, his blue yachting cap at a jaunty angle, rubbing his gray sideburns, wry smile on his round face as his sidemen started to fill the seats

The Count relaxes backstage before going on. A continual stream of musicians, friends and fans dropped by to say hello while the bandstand was being set up. Someone mentioned one of the first outdoor jazz concerts ever held, and Basie remembered it vividly. It had taken place on Randall's Island in New York City in 1938 and featured the Basie Band with singer Jimmy Rushing.

Right. The offspring of two famous jazz artists, Beverly Getz (rear mike), daughter of Stan Getz, and Cathy Rich, daughter of Buddy Rich, appear with Buddy's Killer Force at the Equitable Life Assurance Plaza for an outdoor concert. *Opposite.* Sy Oliver and his orchestra play a series of nostalgia tunes that harkened back to the Swing era.

THE
GREENWICH
SAVINGS
BANK

around him. After a few numbers his vocalist Bill Caffee climbed off the stage in his white dress band outfit and recreated the Benson and Hedges ads as a woman bystander, long cigarette bent askew, burned a neat, half-dollar-size hole on the front of his jacket while Caffee shrugged it off very coolly. At the final street fair on Monday I mounted a step stool that brought me up to stage level amid the swarm of people, to find as I clicked off my pictures that Sonny Stitt onstage was waving to me wildly. Tenorist Zoot Sims, head covered by a yachting cap, strode around the stage applauding along with the people, obviously feeling good.

It was a pleasant surprise to find Duke Ellington's former trumpet star Cootie Williams sitting near the door as I entered studio B of Bill's Music Rental studio. I hadn't spoken to Cootie in a number of years. After the social amenities, I watched the orchestra members trickling in, pausing to pay their respects to one another with hugs and warm greetings and handshakes as they entered the studio.

Cootie was making a guest appearance at two concerts recreating the music of Duke Ellington in the twenties and thirties. He sat, leaning slightly forward in the folding chair, dark skinned, hair slightly graying, dressed comfortably in a short-sleeved shirt and light gray slacks, stomach protruding over his belt, hunched with years of road trips, sleazy joints, nightclub and stage show appearances, skin taut and unwrinkled on his immobile features except for a slight discoloration and indentation on his upper lip that told of chops pressed tightly against a mouthpiece for over a dozen years with Duke's band and his own groups and orchestra.

Cootie's trumpet case was closed nearby and he sat chain smoking cigarettes as he talked about the way he now spends his time at the nearby racetrack. His cousin Melvin Edward Williams mused, ''That's about all Cootie does today—go to the track near his home in St. Albans to play and watch the horses. Since he got out of the

Above. During a N.Y. Jazz Repertory rehearsal of Ellington's music, television commentator Joel Segal (in doorway) arrived with his Channel 7 camera crew to photograph a segment for a newscast. Cootie Williams warms up on trumpet.
Opposite. Cootie mutes his horn as the rest of the trumpet section, Warren Vaché (left) and Joe Newman, relaxes.

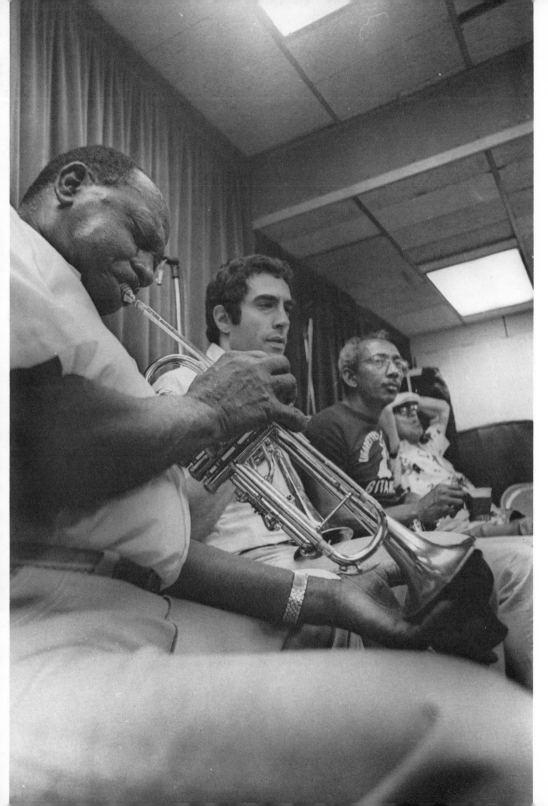

hospital a few months back he doesn't have any interest in playing much anymore. In many ways he's just like Duke. He don't like to look back. He doesn't have a single record at home of what he's done. Quite a contrast with Harry Carney's [Duke's longtime baritonist] widow. Why, she has everything Harry ever recorded. No, Cootie don't like to look back."

Cootie's appearance there gave a credence to the music. Conductor-pianist Dick Hyman was putting this tribute to Ellington together. Leaning over the music stand in front of him, leafing through the long yellow charts before him, he grimaced as he tried to figure out where the transcriber had gone wrong in his notations. His thin frame hunched over, pencil in hand, he went over the score bar by bar. At that moment, reedman Kenny Davern rushed in apologetically, whipping off his dark jacket as he settled into his seat in the sax section, muttering something to Hyman about having to do two television appearances during the day. Hyman excused him with a wave of the hand, glad that he could show up as a replacement for Bob Wilbur. "Hold it! Hold it! I cannot hear what's going on." The orchestra quieted down as the conductor switched on the portable casette recorder, holding it at arm's length as he listened to the original recording of the chart in front of him. His pencil skimmed the pages, trying to find the error.

Cootie clicked open his trumpet case, carefully removing his silver horn, and slowly fitted his mouthpiece to the instrument. He rose and walked the short distance to the piano gazing at the chart in front of him. Fingering each bar of music he mentally checked each note as the orchestra ran it down. Then, satisfied, he eased into his chair, pausing to light another cigarette.

"At bar sixty-six let it be a solo," Hyman said. "It will be a whole chorus of sax solos—" Hyman stopped abruptly. "You know what? Strangely enough, there's a bar missing." Dick Sudhalter walked over to the conductor and explained what he thought was wrong with

247

Opposite. At Bill's Music Rental Studio the New York Jazz Repertory Company rehearses the music of Duke Ellington. *Above.* Conductor Dick Hyman holds up a cassette recorder so that the musicians can hear what the original recording sounded like. *Left.* Al Cobbs keeps the charts and sets it all up so that rehearsals move smoothly.

the chart. "I have to admit it's perfectly right, only it's ass-backwards," Hyman said. "I'll cue you when to come in."

The orchestra ran "Cotton Club Stomp" down with a series of starts and stops. The 83-odd arrangements for the concert series of Duke's music had come from all over the country—California to New York—and some had been transcribed in England, where the older recordings were more easily accessible. They had been carefully transcribed and notated, arranger-copyist Al Cobbs' giving them more coherence for this orchestra. The band was under a great deal of pressure, having only four three-hour rehearsals spread over four days to get the presentation in shape. As one of the musicians said later, "You really have to be able to play and understand what is going on to make this gig." Somehow, all the New York Jazz Repertory concerts seemed to perform miracles. They always sounded good at their concert appearances.

At that moment the door swung open and Joel Segal, accompanied by a sound and camera man and trailed by a lighting technician, swept in, explaining that they were from television's Channel 7 and wanted to make a segment for the news show. It was an interruption that was not needed at this moment. But it was needed publicity for the Festival, and free, so the festival P.R. department had sent them down. "I'm feeling very uptight today," Hyman muttered as he thumbed through the pile of charts on the piano, trying to decide which arrangement the band had down. Hyman looked over to Al Cobbs, saying, "Black and Tan Fantasy." Cobbs dug through the stack and distributed the charts to the band. Cootie, horn in hand, slowly moved over to the trumpet section and seated himself beside cornetist Dick Sudhalter, glancing over at the arrangement. The band swung gracefully through the moody changes of the music. The cameraman stepped closer to the trumpet section, focusing on Cootie as the lighting was placed to best advantage. The sound technician followed,

unreeling wire as he walked, leaning over at one point to give a gentle shove at his connection to the camera. After they had run the music down a few times drummer Panama Francis and trombonist Eddie Bert exchanged admiring glances. "Now that's the way it should sound," Panama chortled. As the television crew huddled near Cootie Williams, the sixty-eight-year-old trumpeter cupped his plunger mute in his hand, tilted his horn down near his knees and started to solo. His horn spoke with a warmth that pervaded the room, and the growls emanated from his horn, first nearly then fully cupped, his fingers moving imperceptibly, the music sounding like laughter, seemingly fired with a youthful zeal. As he finished his solo the band members applauded him loudly. Cootie looked up and said, tongue in cheek, "I guess I get the gig." Laughter all around. As the camera crew swung around to photograph other soloists and sections, Cootie's cousin turned and said softly, "It took over two months to get Cootie to accept this gig. He just didn't want to do it. To put it bluntly, they made him an offer he couldn't refuse." I was glad that I had been there that afternoon.

Some of the press did not receive the four-part Ellington saga with much enthusiasm. The reviewers seemed to be waiting with bated breath for Duke himself to mount the bandstand. Unfortunately this was impossible. The total rehearsal time of most sections of each tribute concert was a mere twelve hours. And this rehearsal time was cut into considerably by a CBS camera crew that interrupted one rehearsal for over an hour and a half while they put some film in the can for a newscast. The same crew photographed part of Tony Bennett's performance, at one point turning on bright floodlights to get some footage, disrupting part of the early concert. But the musicians at the Ellington Saga from the New York Jazz Repertory Company were all of high caliber and performed well—brilliantly, considering the problems involved in translating 1920s or 1930s music and getting their heads back to that period of time in the

Right. Andrew White conducts a rehearsal of the music of John Coltrane. *Left.* White's own tenor and alto punctuated the sessions.

process. It was nothing short of miraculous that they were able to bring the concert off at all. One of the Company's members, a former Duke Ellington sideman, told me later, "This music should be played by cats in their twenties. The same age as Duke's band was when they made those records." Cecil Payne, baritonist on both the Ellington salute and the Coltrane tribute, said later, "I was able to play the more complicated Coltrane music more easily than the Ellington things." Of course Cecil had lived and grown up in the Bird and Coltrane idiom and was thus able to translate the arrangements more easily.

In all probability, and despite the limited funds available for the Ellington presentation, a more logical step would have been to have taken only two periods in his life, concentrated on perfecting those and worked on others at another time or festival. The National Endowment of the Arts had contributed $25,000 for the presentation, with the festival contributing another $25,000 to bring it to fruition.

Highlighting the whole Festival this year, Charlie Mingus brought the audience of Carnegie Hall roaring to their feet in a standing ovation with an exhilarating concert based primarily on a piece that he had first recorded in 1957, although the album was not released until five years later.

The concert, entitled "Mingus Flamenco," revolved around an extended piece, "Y'sabal's Table Dance," which Mingus had composed shortly after coming back from a blues-shaking jag in Mexico after splitting with his wife. Mingus described the experience very succinctly when he stated in the album's liner notes, "All the music in this album was written during a very blue period in my life. I was minus a wife, and in flight to forget her with an expected dream in Tijuana. . . . . . after finding myself with the sting of tequila, salt and lime in my mouth and burning in my nostrils, I decided to benefit musically from this experience and set out to compose and recreate what I felt and saw around me.

. . . . Y'sabel's Table Dance sums up all we could buy in Tijuana. It includes the far out strip tease—spots in the music played by the piano represent the scantily clad woman spinning from table to table, reaching her hand out for tips, bills, or what-have-you. This composition, I believe, contains the fire, the pulse, and all that I felt as I heard the tune in my head with the movement of her body. . . . ."

The concert was all of this and much more. In the fall of 1975, Mingus visited Barcelona, Spain, and became very impressed with the flamenco dancing that he saw there. Arriving back in New York City, he contacted various flamenco groups to see if he could put a program together in combination with his music. Mingus found the Azucana Y Edo Flamenco Dance group. It turned out to be an incendiary combination. After an extended set of Mingus's compositions, with his group cooking under the sinuous and sustained prodding of the bassist, who always was right there with shouts of encouragement, seeming to gouge large chunks of sweeping phrases filled with his own unique vision, unpretentious, insistent, provocative with his own personal intensity of feeling that never seemed to falter for a moment. That stage at Carnegie Hall was vibrantly alive. The Azucana Edo dance company moved onto the stage from both sides when the set ended. Each dancer illuminated the others, seeming to dance by sheer compulsion and passion but with elegance and grace. The stage was a whirlpool of movement echoing with the staccato sounds of castanets and leather heels, jolting the audience into shouts of delight and encouragement. When they joined Mingus's group with their two guitarists and vocalist it seemed to be the final catalyst for spontaneous combustion. The rhythms even propelled the giant proportions of Mingus to contribute a few choice movements at the close of the program, while his pianist Danny Mixon and drummer Danny Richmond swung out with a few steps of their own, encouraged by members of the flamenco group.

One of the brightest elements of this year's Festival were the picnic concerts presented mostly out-of-doors in northern New Jersey at Stanhope, where a privately owned enclave of restored colonial buildings proved an effective backdrop for jazz. A short hour's ride from New York City this year provided a chance to see the countryside without fumes amid some rolling acres of grass and trees. The music was spread out from a billowing green and white tent with 3,000 seats to a restored and fully functioning 1820 tavern, where guitarist Bucky Pizzarelli held sway in a crowd that jammed the building to the eaves. At a newly built gazebo vocalist-vamp Natalie Lamb provided some pleasant sounds accompanied by New Jersey's Red Onion Jazz Band while people lay on the grass under trees eating picnic lunches and listening with obvious pleasure. There was a delightful air of non-commercialism about the place, with handmade signs, and hardly a policeman in sight for the well-behaved crowds. The only complaints heard concerned the small number of toilet facilities in the area, something that used to be a common complaint at Newport. This location brought back memories of Newport and had much of the same ambience.

Their friend and sponsor from their Newport days, the Joseph Schlitz Brewing Company, which had been very generous through the years, this year provided $125,000 to defray the costs of four concerts and three jazz boat rides on the Staten Island Ferry. Although the Greenwich Savings Bank picked up the tab for most of the outdoor concerts, the Festival could not find a sponsor for their July 5 Bicentennial street festival and had to contribute $18,000 to cover its expenses.

Roy Haynes Hip Ensemble has finished its gig, musicians are being paid inside the car, and instruments are packed and waiting atop the hood. One of the group keeps a sharp eye on them so that they don't walk.

253

The Festival generously contributed the profits from one concert to aid Jazz Interactions, for which Benny Goodman contributed his services. Another concert, a Midnight Jazz Party and Jam Session, was held at Radio City Music Hall as a salute to the Reverend John Gensel, pastor to the jazz community, and the $20,000 raised was to go to the Duke Ellington Center and to defray some of jazzman Rahsaan Roland Kirk's medical expenses. Kirk had recently suffered a partial paralysis from a stroke, but it didn't prevent him from playing beautifully at the concert with only one arm. The Festival announced later in the year that Kirk had been presented with a check for $6000.

The festival grossed $370,000 this year and announced that it barely made it into the black. Without the subsidies it would have lost money. The subsidies and whatever profit was made from program sales was it, as far as profits were concerned.

The Newport Jazz Festival-New York remains a viable and productive part of jazz. Whether showcasing mainstream or new talent or in renewing interest in the older and less familiar areas and musicians of jazz it will only lose value when it stops breaking new ground.

The fact that it provides work for about 700 musicians each year is not enough reason to make its contributions important. There is evidence to support the criticism prevalent since it moved to New York City that it has deteriorated into a loosely organized and strung-together series of concerts under the banner of "festival." Many fans feel that much of the music provided during its tenure can be seen and heard throughout the year at concerts and in the profusion of nightclubs that abound in the New York City area and its outlying sub-

254

Above. A local resident of Stanhope, N.J. enjoys himself and fascinates some young visitors to the area by dressing in period clothes and riding around the village on an ancient bicycle. *Opposite.* Singer Natalie Lamb belts out a song accompanied by The Red Onion Jazz Band in the Gazebo at Waterloo Village. The friendly, relaxed, picknicking crowd, the fresh air, the rolling acres of countryside brought back some of the ambience of Newport.

urbs. This seems to be correct to a point, but the Festival has an opportunity to provide a melding of old and new, and to provide an outlet for the purely experimental that was not in evidence in 1976.

Signs seem to be appearing that the producer may have become disenchanted with New York's welcome mat. The Newport, Rhode Island, and Boston newspapers reported as far back as February of this year that he had examined Fort Adams State Park at Newport as a possible site for some concerts, and one of the Long Island papers quoted Wein recently that he had given up on the Nassau Coliseum site of some previous concerts because the 16,000 seater is just too big to handle. "I want to see how the New Jersey concerts work out. If they're succesful, I may want to go further out on Long Island in the future—perhaps to Suffolk County. I'd like to find a nice outdoor location out there. My idea is to make the Festival festive again, part of the community."

George Wein and the Newport Jazz Festival are indivisible—the ambience of the Festival is a reflection of his taste and judgment as they have developed over the years. The repeated appearances of the same artists year after year after year may or may not have made possible the presentation of other more creative and experimental artists. In response to a query in the press in this regard Wein replied this year, ". . . We could eliminate the obvious money losers if we just wanted to make money. But if we did, it wouldn't be a Festival anymore."

Summing up his career as a Festival producer, Wein once said, "Putting on a Festival takes a person with tremendous strength to hold a tremendous number of slightly crazy people together. They're all individualists. It drives me up the wall, but it's the life I chose."

The Newport Jazz Festival and jazz festivals in general are a particularly American phenomenon. The Newport Jazz Festival in its twenty-two-year history has been many things. It has produced important art and provided pure entertainment, not surprisingly sometimes at the same moment.

Jazz has surmounted riots and the inroads of commercialism, always renewing itself and moving on. The Festival is obviously here to stay. Some of the lessons came hard. Some never seemed to have been learned. Most of all the Festival presents an opportunity for the novice as well as the initiate to listen to, appreciate, and participate in, over a comparatively brief span of time, a surging and still developing art form. It is still the only one native to this country.

Jazz festivals have become not only big business, but extremely expensive to maintain at a high caliber. The Newport Jazz Festival will remain valid only as long as its producer commissions new works and employs some of the older and mainstream artists, thus providing a sense of history. There should always be a generous mixture of nostalgia, contemporary, and the avante and purely experimental. Only then will the Festival move from entertainment and contribute its full potential to the development of jazz.

The Newport Jazz Festival has brought jazz to worldwide attention in a way that no other vehicle could have done.

The feeling of camaraderie in the early years, the excitement of the large crowds, and the diversity of the music presented has opened up new areas in presentation with other festivals springing up around the country and the world. The Festival has provided new job opportunities for older as well as contemporary musicians and provided a much-needed outlet for older and newer works.

Most of all it has brought jazz to the attention of millions of people from completely divergent backgrounds, who now accept it as a true art form in a way it had never been accepted previously.

In the huge tent at Waterloo Village, New Jersey. Onstage is jazz buff Attorney-General William Hyland of N.J.

DISCOGRAPHY

Mono Number	Date and Title	Stereo Number	Date Recorded	Mono Number	Date and Title	Stereo Number	Date Recorded
1956					Rushing, Illinois Jacquet, Lester Young, Roy Eldridge and Jo Jones.		
Columbia CL 931	*Louis Armstrong & Eddie Condon at Newport*	None	July 5 & 6, 1956				
Columbia CL 932	*Dave Brubeck & J.J. Johnson-Kai Winding at Newport.*	None	July 6, 1956	Verve MG V-8244	(A-side) *Dizzy Gillespie at Newport*, with Mary Lou Williams; (B-side) *Count Basie at Newport*, with Joe Williams		July 6 & 7, 1957
Columbia CL 933	*Duke Ellington & the Buck Clayton All-Stars at Newport*	None	July 6 & 7, 1956	Verve MG V-8245	(A-side) *Gospel Singing at Newport*, the Drinkard Singers; (B-side) *The Back Home Choir*		July 7, 1957
Columbia CL 934	*Ellington at Newport featuring John Hodges*	CS 8648 (See 1958)	July 7–9, 1956		*Note: many of the Verve sides have been re-released and re-packaged and arranged differently under the title* The Newport Years.		
1957				**1958**			
Verve MG V-8232	(A-side) *George Lewis Band at Newport*; (B-side) *George Lewis and Turk Murphy at Newport*		July 4 & 6, 1957	Columbia CL 1244	*Newport 1958 featuring Mahalia Jackson*	CS 8071	July 7, 1958 & August 11, 1958
Verve MG V-8233	(A-side) *Red Allen at Newport*; (B-side) *Red Allen at Newport*, with Jack Teagarden and Kid Ory		July 4, 1957				
Verve MG V-8234	(A-side) *Ella Fitzgerald at Newport*; (B-side) *Billie Holiday at Newport*		July 4 & 6, 1957	Columbia CL 1245	*Newport 1958 featuring Duke Ellington with Gerry Mulligan*	CS 8072	July 3, 1958 & July 21, 1958
Verve MG V-8235	(A-side) *Teddy Wilson at Newport*; (B-side) *Teddy Wilson with Gerry Mulligan at Newport*		July 6, 1957	Columbia CL 1246	*Newport 1958 featuring the International Youth Band*	CS 8073	July 4 & 5, 1958
Verve MG V-8236	(A-side) *Toshiko at Newport* (B-side) *Leon Sash at Newport*		July 5, 1957	Columbia CL 1249	*Newport 1958 featuring the Dave Brubeck Quartet, with Paul Desmond*	CS 8082	July 3, 1958 & July 28, 1958
Verve MG V-8237	(A-side) *Eddie Costa Trio at Newport*, with Rolf Kuhn and Dick Johnson; (B-side) *Mat Matthews and Don Elliott at Newport*		July 5 & 6, 1957				
Verve MG V-8238	(A-side) *The Cecil Taylor Quartet at Newport*; (B-side) *The Gigi Gryce-Donald Byrd Jazz Laboratory at Newport*		July 5 & 6, 1957	Columbia CL 934	*Ellington at Newport*	CS 8648 (rechanneled stereo)	July 4, 1958
Verve MG V-8239	(A-side) *The Oscar Peterson Trio at Newport*; (B-side) *Sonny Stitt, Roy Eldridge and Jo Jones at Newport*		July 7, 1957	Atlantic 1289	*Ray Charles at Newport* Ray Charles, vocals, piano & alto sax; Bennie Ross Crawford Jr., baritone sax; David Newman, tenor sax; Lee Zedric Harper, first trumpet; Marcus Batisto Belgrave, second trumpet; Edgar L. Wills, bass viol; Richard Goldberg, drums.		July 6, 1958
Verve MG V-8240	*Coleman Hawkins, Roy Eldridge, Pete Brown, Jo Jones All-Stars at Newport*		July 5, 1957				
Verve MG V-8241	(A-side) *The Ruby Braff Octet with Peewee Russell at Newport*; (B-side) *Bobby Henderson at Newport*		July 5, 1957		On "Hot Rod," Ray Charles plays alto sax only. On "The Right Time" & "Talkin' 'Bout You," Ray Charles is joined on the vocal by the Raylettes. The solo girl vocal on "The Right Time" is by Marjorie Hendricks.		
Verve MG V-8242	*Dizzy Gillespie at Newport*		July 6, 1957				
Verve MG V-8243	(A-side) *Count Basie at Newport*, with Lester Young and Jo Jones; (B-side) *Count Basie at Newport*, with Jimmy		July 7, 1957				

The Basie bandstand at Equitable Life Assurance Plaza. Charts are laid out, instruments standing and ready, and fans crowd around the bandstand waiting for the musicians to appear.

1959

Mono Number	Date and Title	Stereo Number	Date Recorded
Top Rank RM-314	*Bundle from Britain:* Johnny Dankworth and His Orchestra at Newport		July 3, 1959
Metrojazz E 1005	*New Faces at Newport:* The Randy Weston Trio; The Lem Winchester Quartet		

1960

Mono Number	Date and Title	Stereo Number	Date Recorded
Chess 1449	*Muddy Waters and Otis Spann* James Cotton, harmonica; Otis Spann, piano; Muddy Waters, guitar, vocal; Tat Harris, guitar; Andrew Stevens, bass; Francis Clay, drums		July 3, 1960

1962

Mono Number	Date and Title	Stereo Number	Date Recorded
Impulse AS 31	*Newport All-Stars*		July 8, 1962

1963

Mono Number	Date and Title	Stereo Number	Date Recorded
R.C.A.	*Newport House Band and Newport All-Stars*		July 4, 1963
R.C.A. LPM 2763	*The Joe Daley Trio*	LSP 2763	July 5, 1963
R.C.A. 2762	*Joe Williams at Newport*		
R.C.A. Mono LP M2747	*Lambert, Hendricks and Bavan at Newport*	LSP 2747	July 5, 1963
Impulse AO 48	*McCoy Tyner Live at Newport*		July 5, 1963
	(Some of these sides were re-released under the title *Reevaluation: The Impulse Years,* AS 9235.)		
United Artists	*Dakota Staton, Live and Swinging*	VAS 6312	July 7, 1963
Atlantic 1413	*Herbie Mann Live at Newport* On "Desafinado" and "Garota de Ipanema," the personnel are: Herbie Mann, flute; Dave Pike, vibraharp; Don Friedman, piano; Attila Zoller, guitar; Ben Tucker, bass; Bob Thomas, drums. On the other 3 tunes, percussionists Willie Bobo & Carlos "Patato" Valdez are added.		July 7, 1963
Columbia CL 2178	*Miles & Monk at Newport*	8978	July 4, 1958 & July 4, 1963

Mono Number	Date and Title	Stereo Number	Date Recorded
Columbia CL 2179	*That Newport Jazz 1963 Festival "House" Band and Newport All-Stars* (Clark Terry, Zoot Sims, Coleman Hawkins, Bud Freeman)	CS 8979	July 4, 1963
Odyssey 31 16 0296	*Newport Jazz Festival All-Stars.*	(Reissue of CS 8979 no more release on Odyssey)	

Old Catalog #	Available for purchase through Columbia Special Products "Collectors Series":	Collectors Series #	
CS 8082	*Newport 1958 featuring the Dave Brubeck Quartet, with Paul Desmond*	JCS 8082	
CS 8979	*That Newport Jazz 1963*	JCS 8979	July 4 & 6, 1963
R.C.A. LPM 2777	*Martial Solal at Newport '63*	LSP 2777	July 7, 1963
R.C.A. LPM 2747	*Lambert, Hendricks and Bavan at Newport '63*	LSP 2747	July 5, 1963

1964

Mono Number	Date and Title	Stereo Number	Date Recorded
R.C.A. LPM 3369x	*Great Moments in Jazz, re-created at The Newport Jazz Festival,* featuring Edmond Hall, Max Kaminsky, Lou McGarity, Bud Freeman, Wingy Manone, Muggsy Spanier, George Brunis, Joe Thomas, Bobby Haggart, Peanuts Hucko	LSP 3369	July 1, 1964
R.C.A. LPM 3783	*From the Newport Jazz Festival—Tribute to Charlie Parker* (Howard McGhee, J.J. Johnson, Sonny Stitt)	LSP 3783	July 4, 1964

1965

Mono Number	Date and Title	Stereo Number	Date Recorded
Impulse 94	*Newthing at Newport,* John Coltrane	S 94	July 2, 1965
Atlantic 1445	*Herbie Mann—Standing Ovation at Newport* (The personnel on "Patato," "Stolen Moments" and "Mushi Mushi" are: Herbie Mann, flutes; Dave Pike, vibes; John Hitchcock & Mark Weinstein, trombones; Chick Corea, piano; Earl May, bass; Bruno Carr, drums; Carlos		July 3, 1965

Mono Number	Date and Title	Stereo Number	Date Recorded	Mono Number	Date and Title	Stereo Number	Date Recorded

"Patato" Valdes, conga drums.
    The same personnel are heard on "Comin' Home Baby," except that Ben Tucker, bass, replaces Earl May.)
    ("Comin' Home Baby" not recorded at Newport.)

1966

Atlantic 1471   *New Mann at Newport*   July 4, 1966
    On "Project S," "Scratch," "She's A Carioca" and "Summertime," the personnel are: Herbie Mann, flutes; Jimmy Owens, trumpet & flugelhorn; Joe Orange & Jack Hitchcock, trombones; Reggie Workman, bass; Carlos "Patato" Valdes, percussion; Bruno Carr, drums.
    On "All Blues," the personnel is the same except that Jimmy Knepper, trombone, replaces Jack Hitchcock, and Attila Zoller, guitar, is added.

Pacific Jazz PJ-10115   *The Jazz Crusaders—Recorded Live at the Newport and Pacific Jazz Festivals—1966*   July 2, 1966

1967

Victor LPM 3891   *Newport Uproar! Lionel Hampton and His All-Star Alumni Big Band*   LSP 3891   July 3, 1967

1971

Last Set at Newport   Atlantic SD-1607   July 3, 1971
The Dave Brubeck Quartet—featuring Gerry Mulligan, baritone; Jack Six, bass; Alan Dawson, drums

1972

Newport in New York '72 Jam Session, Vols 1 & 2 (2-record set)   Buddah CST 9025-2   July 3, 6 & 7, 1972

Newport in New York '72 Jam Session, Vols 3 & 4 (2-record set)   CST 9026-2

Newport in New York '72 Jimmy Smith Jam, Vol 5   CST 9027

Newport in New York '72 Soul Sessions, Vol 6   CST 9028

1973

Newport All-Stars—Tribute to Duke   BASF 20717   July 5, 1973

Ella Fitzgerald—Newport Jazz Festival Live at Carnegie Hall (2-record set)   Columbia KG 32557

PROGRAMS

Note: Full listings of performers are not available for all concerts because of last-minute substitutions and unannounced program changes

Saturday evening, July 17, 1954

John McClellan introduces Stan Kenton, MC, reading Prologue.

Eddie Condon: Traditional Jazz   Eddie Condon, guitar; with Wild Bill Davison, trumpet; Lou McGarity, trombone; Peanuts Hucko, clarinet; Ralph Sutton, piano; Jack Lesberg, bass; Cliff Leeman, drums

Bobby Hackett, trumpet; Peewee Russell, clarinet; Vic Dickenson, trombone; Buzzy Drootin, drums; Milt Hinton, bass

Lee Wiley, vocals   Accompanied by previous group

Jam Session   Many of the musicians who have appeared in program previously

Modern Jazz Quartet   Milt Jackson, vibes; Percy Heath, bass; Kenny Clarke, drums; Horace Silver, piano

Dizzy Gillespie Quintet   Dizzy Gillespie, trumpet; Hank Mobley, tenor; Wade Legge, piano; Charlie Persip, drums; Lew Hackney, bass

Lee Konitz Quartet   Lee Konitz, alto; Billy Bauer, guitar; Peter Ind, bass; Jeff Morton, drums

Oscar Peterson Trío   Oscar Peterson, piano; Ray Brown, bass; Herb Ellis, guitar

Gerry Mulligan Quartet   Gerry Mulligan, baritone; Tony Fruscella, trumpet; Red Mitchell, bass; Frank Isola, drums

Ella Fitzgerald, vocals   Accompanied by John Lewis, piano; Jimmy Woode, bass; Shadow Wilson, drums

Jam Session   All musicians who have previously appeared

Jam Session   Eddie Condon conducting; Dizzy Gillespie, Bobby Hackett, trumpets; Wild Bill Davison, cornet; Lee Konitz, alto; Gerry Mulligan, baritone; Vic Dickenson, trombone; Milt Jackson, vibes; Milt Hinton, bass; Jo Jones, drums

Sunday afternoon, July 18, 1954

The Place of Jazz in American Culture   Father Norman O'Connor, moderator; Henry Cowell, professor of music, Peabody Institute; Marshall Stearns, professor of English, Hunter College; Willis Janis, professor of music, Spelman College

Sunday night, July 18, 1954

Stan Kenton, MC

Tribute to Count Basie   Lester Young, tenor; Buck Clayton, trumpet; Vic Dickenson, trombone; Jo Jones, drums; Ray Brown, bass; Oscar Peterson, piano; Herb Ellis, guitar

Oscar Peterson Trio   Oscar Peterson, piano; Ray Brown, bass; Herb Ellis, guitar.

Johnny Smith, guitar   Accompanied by the Oscar Peterson Trio

George Shearing Quintet   George Shearing, piano; Jean "Toots" Thielemans, guitar; George Devens, vibes; Bill Clark, drums

Gil Melle Quartet   Gil Melle, tenor, baritone; Bill Phillips, bass; Lou Mecca, guitar; Vinnie Tuminelli, drums

Teddy Wilson, piano; Ruby Braff, trumpet; Gerry Mulligan, baritone; Bill Harris, trombone; Milt Hinton, bass; Jo Jones, drum

Lennie Tristano-Lee Konitz   Lennie Tristano, piano; Lee Konitz, alto; Billy Bauer, guitar; Peter Ind, bass; Jeff Morton, drums

Billie Holiday, vocals   Buck Clayton, trumpet; Lester Young, tenor; Vic Dickenson, trombone; Teddy Wilson, piano; Milt Hinton, bass; Jo Jones, drums

Gene Krupa Trio   Gene Krupa, drums; Teddy Napoleon, piano; Eddie Shu, tenor

Friday evening, July 15, 1955

Stan Rubin and His Tigertown Rive

Teddi King, vocals   Accompanied by Nat Pierce, piano, and other members of the Woody Herman Orchestra

Erroll Garner Trio   Erroll Garner, piano; Wyatt Ruther, bass; Fats Heard, drums

Woody Herman Orchestra   Woody Herman, clarinet, alto; Art Pirie, Richie Kamuca, Dick Hafer, tenor sax; Jack Nimitz, baritone sax; Charlie Walp, Jerry Kail, Cam Mullins, Ruben LaFall, Dick Collins, trumpet; Cy Touff, bass, trumpet; Dick Kenney, Keith Moon, trombone; Nat Pierce, piano; John Beal, bass; Chuck Flores, drums

Woody Herman, vocals   Erroll Garner, piano

Woody Herman Orchestra   Guest for one number, Erroll Garner

Roy Eldridge-Coleman Hawkins   Roy Eldridge, trumpet; Coleman Hawkins, tenor sax; Nat Pierce, piano; John Beal, bass; Jo Jones, drums   Vocals by Joe Turner

Louis Armstrong All-Stars   Louis Armstrong, trumpet & vocals; Barney Bigard, clarinet; Trummy Young, trombone; Billy Kyle, piano; Arvell Shaw, bass; Barrett Deems, drums   Velma Middleton, vocals

Saturday afternoon, July 16, 1955

Panel discussion

"Jazz from the Outside In"   Henry Cowell, composer and musicologist; Willis L. James, folklorist and musician; Eric Larrabee, editor of *Harper's;* Dr. Norman Margolis, psychiatrist; Marshall W. Stearns, jazz historian; Richard A. Waterman, anthropologist   Moderator: Father Norman O'Connor, C.S.P.

The Six   Bob Wilber, clarinet; Johnny Glasel, trumpet; Sonny Truitt, trombone; Bob Hammer, piano; Bill Britto, bass; Eddie Phyfe, drums

Saturday evening, July 16, 1955

Max Roch-Clifford Brown Quintet   Harold Land, tenor; Richard Powell, piano; George Morrow, bass

Lee Konitz Quartet   Lee Konitz, alto; Warne Marsh, tenor; Russ Freeman, piano; Bob Carter, bass; Buzzy Drootin, drums

Dinah Washington, vocals   Accompanied by the Max Roach-Clifford Brown Quintet

Chet Baker Quartet   Chet Baker, trumpet and vocals; Russ Freeman, piano; Jack Lawler, bass; Peter Lipman, drums (unscheduled appearance of Gerry Mulligan)

Bob Brookmeyer, valve trombone; Al Cohn, tenor; Ruby Braff, trumpet; Russ Freeman, piano; Jack Lawler, bass; Peter Lipman, drums

Marian McPartland Trio   Bill Crow, bass; Joe Morello, drums; joined later by Jimmy McPartland, cornet

Wild Bill Davison, trumpet; Bud Freeman, tenor; Peewee Russell, clarinet; Vic Dickenson, trombone; George Wein, piano; Milt Hinton, bass; Buzzy Drootin, drums

Teddi King and rhythm section

Dave Brubeck Quartet   Dave Brubeck, piano; Paul Desmond, alto sax; Bob Bates, bass; Joe Doge, drums

Finale   Brubeck's Quartet joined by Gerry Mulligan, baritone; Chet Baker, trumpet; Clifford Brown, trumpet; Max Roach, drums

Sunday afternoon, July 17, 1955

Panel discussion

"Jazz from the Inside Out"   Ernest Borneman, author and director; Dave Brubeck, musician; Nat Hentoff, editor of *Down Beat;* Wilder Hobson, author and journalist; Gerry Mulligan, musician; Father Norman O'Connor, C.S.P.; Gunther Schuller, musician; Billy Taylor, musician   Moderator: Marshall W. Stearns, Hunter College

Art Farmer, trumpet; Teo Macero, tenor; John La Porta, alto, clarinet; Eddie Bert, Britt Woodman, trombones; Mal Waldron, piano; Charlie Mingus, bass; Elvin Jones, drums

Sunday evening, July 17, 1955

Duke Ellington, narrator

The Modern Jazz Quartet   John Lewis, piano; Percy Heath, bass; Milt Jackson, vibraphone; Connie Kay, drums

The photographers in the press pit and the fans enjoy a big moment during the Festival of 1966.

Count Basie, piano; Lester Young, tenor; Ruby Braff, trumpet; Ed Jones, bass; Jo Jones, drums Jimmy Rushing, vocals

Miles Davis, trumpet; Zoot Sims, tenor; Gerry Mulligan, baritone; Thelonious Monk, piano; Percy Heath, bass; Connie Kay, drums

Dave Brubeck Quartet   Kai Winding, trombone; Bobby Hackett, trumpet; Ben Webster, tenor; Peanuts Hucko, clarinet; Billy Taylor, piano; Bill Reuther, bass; Jo Jones, drums

Kai Winding, J.J. Johnson, trombones; Dick Katz, piano; Bill Reuther, bass; Jo Jones, drums

Ben Webster, tenor; Bud Shank, alto; Bobby Hackett, trumpet; Bill Reuther, bass; Jo Jones, drums

Billy Taylor, piano; Bill Reuther, bass; Jo Jones, drums

Count Basie and His Orchestra   Count Basie, piano; Marshall Royal, Billy Graham, Frank Wess, Frank Foster, Charlie Fowlkes, saxophones; Joe Newman, Thad Jones, Reunald Jones, Wendell Culley, trumpets; Henry Coker, Benny Powell, Bill Hughes, trombones; Ed Jones, bass; Freddie Green, guitar; Sonny Payne, drums Joe Williams, vocalist

Thursday evening, July 5, 1956

Count Basie and His Orchestra

MC: Willis Conover

Modern Jazz Quartet

Toshiko   Toshiko Akiyoshi, piano; Percy Heath, bass; Ed Thigpen, drums

Sara Vaughan   Jimmy Jones, piano; Joe Benjamin, bass; Roy Haynes, drums

Eddie Condon   Eddie Condon, guitar; Wild Bill Davison, trumpet; Bud Freeman, tenor sax; Peanuts Hucko, clarinet; Lou McGarity, trombone; Gene Schroeder, piano; Jack Lesberg, bass; Cliff Leeman, drums

Charlie Mingus' Jazz Workshop   Ernie Henry, alto; Bill Hardman, trumpet; Mal Waldron, piano; Al Dreares, drums

Jutta Hipp   Jutta Hipp, piano; Ed Jones, bass; Ed Thigpen, drums

Count Basie and His Orchestra

Friday afternoon, July 6, 1956

Panel Discussion Casino Theater

"Jazz As Communication"   Marshall Stearns, moderator, Langston Hughes, George Wein, Bruce Cameron, Gene Hall

Friday evening, July 6, 1956

Buck Clayton, trumpet; Coleman Hawkins, tenor; J.J. Johnson, trombone; Dick Katz, piano; Benny Moten, bass; Gus Johnson, drums

J.J. Johnson and Kai Winding   Dick Katz, piano; Bill Crow, bass; Rudy Collins, drums

Dave Brubeck Quartet   Paul Desmond, alto; Norman Bates, bass; Joe Dodge, drums

Ella Fitzgerald, vocals   Tommy Flanagan, piano; Benny Moten, bass; Gus Johnson, drums

Louis Armstrong All-Stars   Trummy Young, trombone; Edmond Hall, clarinet; Billy Kyle, piano; Dale Jones, bass; Barrett Deems, drums

Saturday afternoon, July 7, 1956

Phineas Newborn Quartet   Phineas Newborn, piano; Calvin Newborn, guitar; George Joyner, bass; George Ritchie, drums

Teddy Charles Tentet   Jon Eardley, trumpet; Hal Stein, tenor; Gigi Gryce, alto; George Barrow, baritone; Hall Overton, piano; Don Butterfield, tuba; Addison Farmer, bass; Barry Galbraith, guitar; Ed Shaughnessy, drums

Saturday evening, July 7, 1956

Duke Ellington Orchestra

Bud Shank Quartet   Bud Shank, alto; Claude Williamson, piano; Don Prell, bass; Chuck Flores, drums

Teddy Wilson Trio   Teddy Wilson, piano; Al Lucas, bass; Jo Jones, drums

Jimmy Giuffre Quartet   Jimmy Giuffre, tenor, clarinet, baritone, with Bud Shank's rhythm section

Anita O'Day, vocals   Al Lucas, bass; Don Ritter, piano; John Poole, drums

Friedrich Gulda   Seldon Powell, tenor; Idrees Sulieman, trumpet; Jimmy Cleveland, trombone; Phil Woods, alto; Teddy Kotick, bass; Nick Stabulas, drums

Chico Hamilton Quintet   Chico Hamilton, drums; Jim Hall, guitar; Buddy Collette, clarinet; Carson Smith, bass; Fred Katz, cello

Duke Ellington Orchestra   Cat Anderson, Willie Cook, Clark Terry, trumpets; Ray Nance, trumpet, violin and vocal; Britt Woodman, John Sanders, Quentin Jackson, trombones; Jimmy Hamilton, clarinet and tenor; Russell Procope, alto and clarinet; Johnny Hodges, alto; Paul Gonsalves, tenor; Jimmy Woode, bass; Sam Woodyard, drums Jimmy Grissom, vocal on one number

Sunday, July 8, 1956

Panel Discussion

"The Future of Jazz"   Co-moderators: Nat Hentoff and Bill Coss Panelists: Friedrich Gulda, pianist; David Breckman, composer-conductor, director of Wide Wide World Tony Scott, clarinet; Lennie Tristano, pianist; Hall Overton, composer, pianist; Jimmy Giuffre, reedman; Quincy Jones, conductor, composer

Mario Patron Trio   Mario Patron, piano; George Joyner, bass; Ed Shaughnessy, drums

Thursday evening, July 4, 1957

MC: Willis Conover

The George Lewis Band   George Lewis, clarinet; Jack Willis, trumpet; Bob Thomas, trombone; Alcide Pavageau, bass; Joe Watkins, drums

Bobby Henderson, solo piano

The Henry Red Allen Band   Henry Red Allen, piano; Buster Bailey, clarinet; J.C. Higginbotham, trombone; Claude Hopkins, piano; Arvell Shaw, bass; Cozy Cole, drums

Jack Teagarden, trombone, vocals, joins Henry Red Allen band with guest, Kid Ory, trombone, replacing Teagarden for one number.

Don Abney, piano; Wendell Marshall, bass; Jo Jones, drums

Ella Fitzgerald, vocals   plus the aforementioned rhythm section

The Louis Armstrong All-Stars   Louis Armstrong, trumpet, vocals; Trummy Young, trombone; Edmond Hall, clarinet; Billy Kyle, piano; Squire Gersh, bass; Barrett Deems, drums Velma Middleton, vocals

Friday afternoon, July 5, 1957

The Ruby Braff Octet, with Peewee Russell   Ruby Braff, trumpet; Peewee Russell, clarinet; Sammy Margolis, tenor; Jimmy Welsh, valve trombone; Walter Paige, bass; Nat Pierce, piano; Steve Jordan, guitar; Buzzy Drootin, drums

The Toshiko Akiyoshi Trio   Toshiko Akiyoshi, piano; Gene Cherico, bass; Jake Hanna, drums

The Kai Winding Septet   Kai Winding, Carl Fontana, Wayne Andre, Dick Leib, trombone; Roy Frazee, piano; Barney Mallon, bass; Lou Mariner, drums

The Gigi Gryce-Donald Byrd Jazz Laboratory   Gigi Gryce, alto; Donald Byrd, trumpet; Hank Jones, piano; Wendell Marshall, piano; Osie Johnson, drums

Mat Mathews   Mat Mathews, accordion; Hank Jones, piano; Ernie Furtado, bass; Johnny Cressi, drums

The Bernard Peiffer Trio   Same rhythm section as on above group

The **Leon Sash Quartet** Leon Sash, accordion; Ted Robinson, tenor, clarinet, flute; Lee Morgan, bass; Roger Price, drums

The **Cannonball Adderley Quintet** Cannonball Adderley, alto; Nat Adderley, cornet; Junior Mance, piano; Sam Jones, bass; Jimmy Cobb, drums

Friday evening, July 5, 1957

The **Bobby Hackett Sextet** Bobby Hackett, cornet; Dick Cary, piano; Ernie Caceres, clarinet, vibes; Tom Givaltney, clarinet, vibes; Johnny Dengler, tuba; Buzzy Drootin, drums

Carmen McRae, vocals Ray Bryant, piano; Ike Isaacs, bass; Specs Wright, drums; Junior Mance, piano, and Jimmy Cobb, drums subbed a few numbers

The **George Shearing Quintet** George Shearing, piano; Jean Thielemans, guitar; Armando Peraza, congas and bongos; Al McKibbon, bass; Percy Brice, drums
Guest artists: Cannonball Adderley, alto; Nat Adderley, cornet, on one number

The **All Stars** Roy Eldridge, trumpet; Coleman Hawkins, tenor; Pete Brown, alto; Al McKibbon, bass; Ray Bryant, piano; Jo Jones, drums

The **Erroll Garner Trio** Erroll Garner, piano; Eddie Calhoun, bass; Kelly Martin, drums

The **Stan Kenton Orchestra** Stan Kenton, piano; Phil Gilbert, Sam Noto, Ed Leddy, Bill Catalano, Lee Katzman, trumpets; Archie LeCoque, Jim Amlotte, Kent Larsen, Don Reed, Kenny Shroyer, trombones; Bill Perkins, Lennie Neihaus, Wayne Dunst, Steve Purlo, reeds; Red Kelly, bass; Jerry McKenzie, drums

Saturday afternoon, July 6, 1957

The **Cecil Taylor Quartet** Cecil Taylor, piano; Steve Lacy, soprano; Buell Neidlinger, bass; Dennis Charles, drums

The **Jimmy Smith Trio** Jimmy Smith, organ; Ed McFadden, guitar; Don Bailey, drums

Eddie Costa Eddie Costa, piano; Ernie Furtado, bass; Al Beldini, drums
Guest artists, Rolf Kuhn, clarinet; Dick Johnson, alto

The **Don Elliott Quartet** Don Elliott, vibes, mellophone; Bill Evans, piano; Ernie Furtado, bass; Al Beldini, drums

Jackie Paris Joe Masters, piano; Joe Benjamin, bass; Jo Jones, drums

Joe Castro, piano

The **Horace Silver Quintet** Horace Silver, piano; Art Farmer, trumpet; Clifford Jordan, tenor; Teddy Kotick, bass; Louis Hayes, drums

The **Farmingdale High School Band, the Dalers** Directed by Marshall Brown (Band members listed with their ages.) Andrew Marsala (14), Barbara Stern (15), Harriette De Groff (17), Nina Rosalia (14), Lyman Van Nostrand (15), saxes; Dorene Romero (13), Leslie Pyenson (14), Marcia Lewis (15), flutes; James Schmidt (17), Edmund Green (13), Larry Sexauer (15), trombones; Michael Abene (14), John Calabrese (15), Larry Ramsden (17), William Burkett (15), drums

Saturday evening, July 6, 1957

The **Turk Murphy Band** Turk Murphy, trombone; Larry Conger, trumpet; Bill Napier, clarinet; Pete Clute, piano; Dick Lammi, banjo; Al Conger, bass; Thad Vanden, drums

Chris Connor, vocals Accompanied by Stan Free, piano

The **Dave Brubeck Quartet** Dave Brubeck, piano; Paul Desmond, alto; Norman Bates, bass; Joe Morello, drums

Teddy Wilson, piano; Milt Hinton, bass; Specs Powell, drums. Surprise guest: Gerry Mulligan, baritone

The **Gerry Mulligan Quartet** Gerry Mulligan, baritone; Bob Brookmeyer, valve trombone; Joe Benjamin, bass; Dave Bailey, drums

Billie Holiday, vocals Mal Waldron, piano; Joe Benjamin, bass; Jo Jones, drums; introductions by Johnny Mercer

The **Dizzy Gillespie Orchestra** Dizzy Gillespie, Lee Morgan, Carl Warwick, Ermet V. Perry, Talid Dawud, trumpets; Al Grey, Melba Liston, Rod Levitt, trombones; Benny Golson, Ernie Henry, Billy Mitchell, Jimmy Powell, Pee Wee Moore, reeds; Wynton Kelly, piano; Paul West, bass; Charlie Persip, drums
Austin Cromer, Melba Liston, Dizzy Gillespie, vocals

The **Eartha Kitt Dance Group** Themes: Primitive, The Blues, Modern Jazz
Arthur Mitchell, Claude Thompson, Harold Gordon assisting Miss Kitt in the dances
Accompanied by The Dizzy Gillespie Orchestra

Mary Lou Williams, piano Accompanied by the Dizzy Gillespie Orchestra

Sunday afternoon, July 7, 1957

Gospel Singing The Ward Singers, The Drinkard Singers, The Back Home Choir, directed by Jeff Hanks

John Hammond introduces MC Joe Bostic

The **Ward Singers** Mrs. Gertrude Ward, Mrs. Willis Ward Moultrie, Marion Williams, Kathleen Parham, Frances Steadman
Professor Herman Stevens, organ; Clara Ward and Sylvester Dean, piano

The **Back Home Choir** Fifty-voice choir directed by Jeff Hanks
Soloists: Carrie Smith and Charles Banks

Mahalia Jackson Accompanied by Mildred Fall, piano, and Dickie Mitchell, organ

Sunday evening, July 7, 1957

Jimmy Giuffre Trio Jimmy Giuffre, clarinet, tenor, baritone; Jim Hall, guitar; Ralph Pena, bass

The **Oscar Peterson Trio** Oscar Peterson, piano; Ray Brown, bass; Herb Ellis, guitar
Joined by Sonny Stitt, alto, tenor; Roy Eldridge, trumpet; Jo Jones, drums

Sarah Vaughan, vocals Accompanied by Jimmy Jones, piano; Richard Davis, bass; Roy Haynes, drums

The **Count Basie Orchestra** Count Basie, piano; Reunald Jones, Wendell Culley, Thad Jones, Joe Newman, trumpets; Henry Coker, Benny Powell,

Bill Hughes, trombones; Frank Wess, Bill Graham, Marshall Royal, Frank Foster, Charlie Fowlkes, reeds; Freddie Green, guitar; Ed Jones, bass; Sonny Payne, drums
Joe Williams, vocals

Lester Young, tenor, joins the band along with Roy Eldridge, trumpet; drummer Jo Jones and singer Jimmy Rushing

Joe Williams, vocals, joined by Sarah Vaughan for one number with the Basie Band.

Illinois Jacquet, Lester Young, tenors; Roy Eldridge, trumpet; Jo Jones, drums, along with the Basie Band

Wednesday, July 3, 1958

The **Editors' point of View** Hotel Viking, Newport, R.I.
Harold Hayes, *Esquire;* Leo Lerman, *Mademoiselle;* Maurice Zolotow, freelance writer; Sheldon Meyer, *Oxford Press;* Evelyn Harvey, *Glamour;* Louis Lorillard, president of the Newport Jazz Festival, moderator

Wednesday evening, July 3, 1958

Screening of six kinescopes of television programs dealing with jazz. Award to be given later.

Thursday evening, July 4, 1958

Willis Conover, MC

Rex Stuart and the Ellington Alumni All Stars Rex Stuart, cornet; Tyree Glenn, trombone; Cootie Williams, trumpet; Ben Webster, tenor; Oscar Pettiford, bass; Hilton Jefferson, alto; Sonny Greer, drums; Billy Strayhorn, piano

Marian McPartland Trio Marian McPartland, piano; Milt Hinton, bass; Ed Shaughnessy, drums
Gerry Mulligan, baritone, accompanies trio

Miles Davis Quintet Miles Davis, trumpet; John Coltrane, tenor; Julian "Cannonball" Adderley, alto; Bill Evans, piano; Jimmy Cobb, drums

Dave Brubeck Quartet Dave Brubeck, piano; Paul Desmond, alto; Joe Benjamin, bass; Joe Morello, drums

Duke Ellington and His Orchestra Duke Ellington, piano; Clark Terry, Ray Nance, Shorty Baker,

Cat Anderson, Francis Williams, trumpets; Quentin Jackson, Britt Woodman, John Sanders, trombones; Johnny Hodges, Harry Carney, Russell Procope, Jimmy Hamilton, Paul Gonsalves, reeds; Jimmy Woode, bass; Sam Woodyard, drums Guests: Gerry Mulligan, baritone; Lil Greenwood, Ozzie Bailey, vocals

Mahalia Jackson   Introduced by Frankie Laine Accompanied by the Duke Ellington Orchestra

Friday morning, July 5, 1958

Masonic Hall, Newport, R. I.
The Origin and Nature of the Blues, lecture by S.I. Hayakawa, illustrated by Eli's Chosen 7 and Jimmy Rushing, vocals

Friday afternoon, July 5, 1958

John La Porta Quartet   John La Porta, alto sax and clarinet; Jack Reilly, piano; Dick Carter, bass; Charlie Perry, drums

Jimmy Giuffre Three   Jimmy Giuffre, clarinet, tenor sax, baritone sax; Bob Brookmeyer, valve trombone; Jim Hall, guitar

Newport International Jazz Band   Palle Bolvic (Denmark), Roger Guerin (France), Dusko Gojkovic (Yugoslavia), Jose Manuel Magalhais (Portugal), trumpets; Christian Kellens (Belgium), Albert Mangelsdorff (Germany), Kurt Jarnsberg (Sweden), Erich Kleinschuster (Austria), trombones; Hans Salomon (Austria), Wladimiro Bas Fabache (Spain), Bernt Rosengren (Sweden), Jan Wroblewski (Poland), tenors; Ronnie Ross (England), baritone; Gilberto Cuppini (Italy), drums; Rudolf Jacogs (Holland), bass; George Gruntz (Switzerland), piano; Gabor Szabo (Hungary), guitar; guest soloist, Andy Marsala (U.S.A.), alto sax and clarinet
Marhsall Brown, director

Friday evening, July 5, 1958

Teddy Wilson Trio   Teddy Wilson, piano; Johnny Williams, bass; Bert Dahlander, drums

Benny Goodman and His Orchestra   Benny Goodman, clarinet; Billy Butterfield, Bernie Glow, Doc Severinsen, Taft Jordan, trumpets; Frank Rehak, Eddie Bert, Vernon Brown, trombones; Buddy Tate, Skippy Collucio, Ernie Morrow, Rudy Rutherford, Gene Allen, reeds; Henry Grimes, bass; Roy Burnes, drums; Kenny Burrell, guitar

Vocalists: Jimmy Rushing and Martha Tilton

Saturday morning, July 6, 1958

The Jazz Dance   Lecture by Dr. Marshall Stearns Musical illustrations by Leon James and Al Minns Masonic Hall, Newport, R.I.

Saturday afternoon, July 6, 1958

Critics Choice—Angelo Di Pippo Quartet   Angelo Di Pippo, accordion; Sam Most, flute; Tommy Potter, bass; Teddy Sommer, drums

Randy Weston Trio   Randy Weston, piano; George Joyner, bass; G.T. Hogan, drums Introduced by Allan Morrison, New York editor, *Ebony*

Don Butterfield Sextet   Introduced by Bill Coss, editor, *Metronome*
Don Butterfield, tuba; Lou Mucci, trumpet; Seldon Powell, clarinet, bass clarinet; Barry Galbraith, guitar; Bob Swan, percussion; vibes; Joe Venuto, drums, vibes

Willie "The Lion" Smith   Introduced by Leonard Feather, author, critic
Willie "The Lion" Smith, piano; Jimmy Zitano, drums

Beulah Bryant, singer, introduced by George Frazier, writer, columnist   Accompanied by Julian "Cannonball" Adderley, alto; John Mehegan, piano; John Neves, bass; Jimmy Zitano, bass

Bernard Peiffer Trio   Introduced by Leonard Feather
Bernard Peiffer, piano; Ernie Furtado, bass; Jimmy Campbell, drums

Lem Winchester Quartet   Presented by Leonard Feather
Lem Winchester, vibes; Jim Neves, bass; Ray Santisi, piano; Jimmy Zitano, drums

The Herb Pomeroy Band   Introduced by Dom Cerulli, Associate Editor, *Down Beat*
Herb Pomeroy, Bill Berry, Nick Capezuto, Lennie Johnson, Augie Ferretti, trumpets; Joe Ciarvadone, Bill Ligan, Gene DiStasio, trombones; Jimmy Mosher, Varty Haroutunian, Joe Caruso, Dave Chapman, Bobby Freedman, reeds; Ray Santisi, piano; Jim Neves, bass; Jimmy Zitano, drums

Saturday night, July 6, 1958

Pete Johnson   Pete Johnson, piano; Tom Bryant, bass; Jo Jones, drums

Joe Turner   Accompanied by the Newport Blues Band
Jack Teagarden, trombone; Lennie Johnson, Buck Clayton, trumpets; Georgie Auld, Buddy Tate, Rudy Rutherford, reeds; Kenny Burrell, guitar; Tom Bryant, bass; Jo Jones, drums; Pete Johnson, piano

Ray Charles   Ray Charles, vocals, piano & alto; Bennie Ross Crawford, Jr., baritone; David Newman, tenor; Lee Zedric Harper, first trumpet; Marcus Batisto Belgrave, second trumpet; Edgar L. Wills, bass; Richard Goldberg, drums. Plus the Raelettes, vocals

Big Maybelle   Big Maybelle, vocals; backed by the Newport Blues Band, Ray Bryant, piano, for one number

Gerry Mulligan Quartet   Gerry Mulligan, baritone; Art Farmer, trumpet; Bill Crow, bass; Dave Bailey, drums

Chuck Berry   Chuck Berry, vocals and guitar; accompanied by The Newport Blues Band

Maynard Ferguson and His Orchestra   Maynard Ferguson, Tom Slaney, Bill Chase, Clyde Reasinger, trumpets; Slide Hampton, Don Sebesky, trombones; Jim Ford, Carmen Leggio, Willie Maiden, Jay Cameron, reeds; John Bunch, piano; Jimmy Rowser, bass; Frank Dunlop, drums

Dakota Staton, vocals; accompanied by The Maynard Ferguson Orchestra

Mahalia Jackson   Gospel Songs   Mahalia Jackson accompanied by organ, piano

Sunday afternoon, July 7, 1958

Tony Scott Quartet   Tony Scott, clarinet; Jimmy Knepper, trombone; Henry Grimes, bass; Ed Levinson, drums

Les Jazz Modes   Julius Watkins, French horn; Charlie Rouse, tenor; Gildo Mahones, piano; Martin Rivera, bass; Ron Jefferson, drums

Anita O'Day, vocals
Accompanied by Jimmy Jones, piano; Whitey Mitchell, bass; John Poole, drums

Lee Konitz   Lee Konitz, alto; Henry Grimes, bass; Ed Levinson, drums

Billy Taylor Trio   Billy Taylor, piano; Earl May, bass; Ed Levinson, drums

Sonny Rollins Trio   Sonny Rollins, tenor; Henry Grimes, bass; Roy Haynes, drums

Thelonious Monk Trio   Thelonious Monk, piano; Henry Grimes, bass; Roy Haynes, drums

Sal Salvador-Sonny Stitt   Sal Salvador, guitar; Sonny Stitt, alto; Gildo Mahones, piano; Martin Rivera, bass; Louis Hayes, drums

Horace Silver Quintet   Horace Silver, piano; Louis Smith, trumpet

Sunday evening, July 7, 1958

Newport International Jazz Band

Jack Teagarden-Bobby Hackett   Jack Teagarden, trombone; Bobby Hackett, trumpet; Jerry Fuller, clarinet; Don Ewell, piano

Chris Connor, vocals; George Duvivier, bass; Chuck Wayne, guitar; Stan Free, piano; Ed Shaughnessy, drums

George Shearing Quintet   George Shearing, piano; Jean "Toots" Thielemans, guitar; Emil Richards, vibes; Armando Peraza, conga and bongo drums

Max Roach Quintet   Max Roach, drums; George Coleman, tenor; Booker Little, trumpet; Ray Draper, tuba; Art Davis, bass

Dinah Washington, vocals; Blue Mitchell, trumpet; Sahib Shihab, baritone; Melba Liston, trombone; Wynton Kelly, piano; Paul West, bass; Max Roach, drums

Don Elliott, Terry Gibbs, vibes; Urbie Green, trombone; Wynton Kelly, piano; Paul West, bass; Max Roach, drums; Dinah Washington, vocal for one number

Chico Hamilton Quintet Chico Hamilton, drums; Nat Gershman, cello; Eric Dolphy, alto; Hal Gaylord, bass; Johnny Pisano, guitar

Newport International Jazz Band Joined for one number by Louis Armstrong

Louis Armstrong All-Stars Trummy Young, trombone; Peanuts Hucko, clarinet; Billy Kyle, piano; Mort Herbert, bass; Danny Barcelona, drums Vocals by Velma Middleton
Joined for one number by Bobby Hackett, cornet, and Jack Teagarden, trombone

Thursday evening, July 2, 1959

Newport Jazz Festival All-Stars Buck Clayton, Ruby Braff, trumpets; Peewee Russell, clarinet; Bud Freeman, tenor saxophone; Vic Dickenson, trombone; Ray Bryant, piano; Champ Jones, bass; Buzzy Drootin, drums
Jimmy Rushing, vocals

The Four Freshmen Don Barbour, Ross Barbour, Bob Flanigan, Ken Albers, vocals

George Shearing with his new fifteen-piece orchestra

The Gene Krupa Quartet

The Ahmad Jamal Trio Vernel Fournier, drums; Israel Crosby, bass; Ahmad Jamal, piano

Count Basie and His Orchestra Joe Williams, vocals, and Dave Lambert-Jon Hendricks-Annie Ross singing group, accompanied by the Basie rhythm section

Count Basie and His Orchestra
Count Basie, piano; Billy Mitchell, Charlie Fowlkes, M. Royal, Frank Wess, Frank Foster, reeds; Joe Newman, Thad Jones, Wendell Culley, Snookie Young, trumpets; Al Grey, Benny Powell, Henry Coker, trombones; Freddie Green, Ed Jones, Sonny Payne, drums

Friday afternoon, July 3, 1959

The Mastersounds Buddy Montgomery, vibes; Monk Montgomery, Fender electric bass; Benny Barth, drums; Richie Crabtree, piano

The Kenny Burrell Trio Kenny Burrell, guitar; Ray Bryant, piano; guest Johnny Griffin, tenor. Roy Eldridge and Coleman Hawkins Quintet and Helen Humes, vocal

The Horace Silver Quintet

The Maynard Ferguson Orchestra

Friday evening, July 3, 1959

Johnny Dankworth and His Orchestra from London, England Dick Handon, Derrick Abbott, Stan Palmer, Ken Wheeler, Bob Carson, trumpets; Laurie Monk, Tony Russell, Danny Elwood, Garry Brown, trombones; Ron Snyder, trombone, tuba; Johnny Dankworth, alto, clarinet; Alex Leslie, baritone, clarinet, flute; David Lee, piano; Eric Dawson, bass; Kenny Clare, drums

Miss Dakota Staton, vocals

Thelonious Monk Quartet Thelonious Monk, piano; Charlie Rouse, tenor; Art Taylor, drums; Sam Jones, bass

Phil Napoleon and His Original Memphis Five Featuring Tony Spargo, drums

The Oscar Peterson Trio Oscar Peterson, piano; Ray Brown, bass; Ed Thigpen, drums

The Modern Jazz Quartet John Lewis, piano; Milt Jackson, vibes; Connie Kay, drums; Percy Heath, bass

Dizzy Gillespie Quintet

Saturday afternoon, July 4, 1959

New Rogers High School
Premiere performance of Jazz Ballet No. 1, featuring dancers Willy Sandberg, Jacqueline Walcott, Leon James, and Al Minns. (They will dance to the music of the Modern Jazz Quartet on tape.)

The Jimmy Smith Trio

The Charlie Mingus Quintet

The Jazz Messengers, with Art Blakey, drums

Toshiko Akiyoshi Trio With guest Barney Wilen, tenor

The Herbie Mann Quintet

Marshall Brown and the Newport Youth Band

Newport is a Lark Fashion Show Martha Holiday, commentator and producer.

Saturday evening, July 4, 1959

Erroll Garner Trio Erroll Garner, piano; Edward Calhoun, bass; Kelly Martin, drums

Duke Ellington and His Orchestra Guest: Jimmy Rushing, vocals

Sunday afternoon, July 5, 1959

Gospel John Hammond, MC
Julia Doyle, The Silvertone Singers, Professor Herman Stevens and the Stevens Singers, The Bradford Specials

Sunday evening, July 5, 1959

Stan Kenton and His Orchestra Guest artist: Charlie Mariano, alto

Dave Brubeck Quartet, featuring Paul Desmond Dave Brubeck, piano; Paul Desmond, alto; Eugene Wright, bass; Joe Morello, drums

Jack Teagarden, trombone; Bobby Hackett, cornet; joined by Don Goldie, trumpet

Miss Pat Suzuki, vocals, 6-piece orchestra led by Doc Severinsen, trumpet

The Kingston Trio Dave Guard, Bob Shane, Nick Reynolds, vocals, with David Wheat, bass

Buster Bailey, clarinet; Red Allen, trumpet; Jack Teagarden, trombone; J.C. Higginbotham, Kenny Burrell, guitar

Thursday evening, June 30, 1960

Marshall Brown and the Newport Youth Band Joined by Cannonball Adderley for one number with altoist Andy Marsala

The Cannonball Adderley Quintet

Nina Simone, vocals

The Art Farmer-Benny Golson Jazztet Art Farmer, flugelhorn; Benny Golson, tenor; Bernard McKinney, euphonium; Lex Humphries, drums; bass

The Dave Brubeck Quartet Dave Brubeck, piano; Paul Desmond, alto; Eugene Wright, bass; Joe Morello, drums

Maynard Ferguson Orchestra Gene Quill, alto; Rufus Jones, drums

Friday afternoon, July 1, 1960

Rudy Blesh Narrating the Stride Piano Eubie Blake, Willie "The Lion" Smith, Don Lambert, piano; with the Danny Barker Trio: Danny Barker, guitar; Bernard Addison, mandolin; Al Hall, bass

Friday evening, July 1, 1960

The Dizzy Gillespie Quintet Dizzy Gillespie, trumpet; Leo Wright, alto; Junior Mance, piano; Art Davis, bass; Al Dreares, drums

The Gerry Mulligan Big Band Bob Brookmeyer, trombone

The Louis Armstrong All-Stars Louis Armstrong, trumpet; Trummy Young, trombone; Barney Bigard, clarinet; Billy Kyle, piano; Mort Herbert, drums; Arvell Shaw, bass

Saturday afternoon, July 2, 1960

Ruby Braff, trumpet; Peewee Russell, clarinet; George Wein, piano; Don Kenny, bass; Buzzy Drootin, drums

Newport Youth Band Conducted by Marshall Brown
Narrated by Dom Cerulli

Herbie Mann Sextet With Michael Olatunji, percussion

Saturday evening, July 2, 1960

The Newport Youth Band Directed by Marshall Brown
(Same personnel as at other appearances)

Tyree Glenn, trombone; Tommy Flanagan, piano; Eddie Locke, drums; Tommy Potter, bass

Tyree Glenn and His Rhythm Section joined by Georgie Auld, tenor; and Harry Edison, trumpet

Dakota Staton, vocals with trio

Lambert, Hendricks, and Ross

Horace Silver Quintet

Ray Charles The Raelettes and Marjorie Hendricks

Oscar Peterson Trio Oscar Peterson, piano; Ray Brown, bass; Herb Ellis, guitar

Sunday afternoon, July 3, 1960

Langston Hughes narrating "The Blues" Muddy Waters, guitar, vocals; Otis Spann, piano; Tat Harris, guitar; Andrew Stevens, bass; James Cotton, harmonica; Francis Clay, drums

John Lee Hooker, guitar and vocals solo
Accompanied by the Muddy Waters Orchestra

Sammy Price, piano; Betty Jeannette, Lafayette Thomas, vocals; Dave Pochonet, drums

Butch Cage, violin; Willie Thomas, guitar; Doctor Harry Oster, commentary
All participants with Jimmy Rushing, vocals; and final selection sung by Otis Spann

Friday evening, July 6, 1962 (All events held at Freebody Park)

Tony Tomasso and the Jewels of Dixieland

Welcoming Address—U.S. Senator Claiborne Pell (D–R.I.)

Roy Eldridge, trumpet; with Bill Rubenstein, piano; Jim Neves, bass; Jo Jones, drums

The Dave Brubeck Quartet Paul Desmond, alto sax; Eugene Wright, bass; Joe Morello, drums
Guest artists: Carmen McRae, vocals, and Gerry Mulligan, baritone

Carmen McRae, vocals Accompanied by Norman Simmons, piano; Victor Sproles, bass; Walter Perkins, drums

The Gerry Mulligan Quartet featuring Bobby Brookmeyer (Quartet joined by Coleman Hawkins.)

Miss Carmen McRae Joe Williams, with the Harry Edison Quintet, will be joined by Miss Carmen McRae. The Harry Edison Quintet featured guest artists Roy Eldridge, trumpet; Coleman Hawkins, Jimmy Forrest, sax

Saturday afternoon, July 7, 1962

Panel Discussion—"The Economics of the Jazz Community" John Hammond, Columbia Records; Art d'Lugoff, Village Gate; Joe Williams; George T. Simon, N.Y. *Herald Tribune*, Sid Bernstein, producer; Charles Mingus. Moderator, George Wein

Marshall Stearns presents "A History of the Tap Dance and Its Relationship to Jazz" Bunny Briggs, Baby Laurence, Pete Nugent, Honi Coles, tap dancers; Jo Jones, drums
Roy Eldridge Quartet
Toshiko Mariano Trio

Saturday evening, July 7, 1962

The Gene Hull Orchestra, "The Jazz Giants"

Miss Carol Sloane, accompanied by Bill Rubenstein, piano; Coleman Hawkins, tenor sax

The Charles Mingus Sextet Booker Irvin, tenor sax; Richard Williams, trumpet; Charles McPherson, alto sax; Danny Richman, drums; featuring Toshiko Mariano, piano

Duke Ellington Orchestra With Bunny Briggs, Baby Laurence, dancers

The Max Roach Quartet, plus a choir of sixteen voices

Louis Armstrong All-Stars Trummy Young, trombone; Joe Darensbourg, clarinet; Billy Kyle, piano;

William Cronk, bass; Danny Barcelona, drums
Plus guest stars: Yank Lawson, trumpet; J.C. Higginbotham, trombone

Sunday afternoon, July 8, 1962

Panel Discussion: "Religion and the Concern for Jazz" Maurice Zolotow, writer; Rev. John Gensel, pastor, Advent Lutheran Church, Broadway at 63rd Street, N.Y.C.; Father Norman O'Connor, Catholic chaplain, Boston University; Rev. Eugene Callender, pastor, Church of the Master, N.Y.C.; Sonny Rollins, musician; Clara Ward, gospel singer. Moderator, Maxwell Cohen, attorney, N.Y.C.

MC: Duke Ellington

Joe Bucci Organ Trio Joe Bucci, organ; Eddie Stack, tenor sax; Jo Jones, drums

Clara Ward Gospel Singers

The Oscar Peterson Trio Oscar Peterson, piano; featuring Ray Brown, bass; Ed Thigpen, drums

Sonny Rollins & Co. Featuring Jim Hall, guitar; Miss Abbey Lincoln, vocals

Count Basie Orchestra Guest artists: Jimmy Rushing, Joe Williams, vocals

Sunday evening, July 8, 1962

Narrator: Willis Conover

Iron Curtain Jazz The "Wreckers" from Warsaw, Poland

The Newport Jazz Festival All-Stars Peewee Russell, clarinet; Ruby Braff, trumpet; Marshall Brown, trombone; Jo Jones, drums; John Neves, bass; George Wein, piano; Guest artist: Bud Freeman, tenor sax

Duke Ellington and His Orchestra Guest artist: Thelonious Monk

Aretha Franklin, vocals Accompanied by a rhythm section

The Thelonious Monk Quartet Featuring Charlie Rouse, tenor sax

Lambert, Hendricks and Yolande

The Newport '62 Discovery of the Year The Roland Kirk Quartet

Thursday evening, July 4, 1963

Freebody Park

The Meaning of Jazz

The Newport Jazz Festival House Band Howard McGhee, trumpet; Clark Terry, trumpet and flügelhorn; Coleman Hawkins, Zoot Sims, tenor sax; Joe Zawinul, piano; Wendell Marshall, bass; Roy Haynes, drums

The Thelonious Monk Quartet Charlie Rouse, tenor sax; Butch Warren, bass; Frankie Dunlop, drums: Guest Artist: Peewee Russell, clarinet

The Cannonball Adderley Sextet Cannonball Adderley, alto; Nat Adderley, cornet; Yusef Lateef, tenor sax, flute, oboe; Joe Zawinul, piano; Sam Jones, bass; Louis Hayes, drums

Nina Simone, vocals Accompanied by her trio.

Thelonious Monk Quartet Thelonious Monk, piano; Charlie Rouse, tenor; Butch Warren, bass; Frank Dunlop, drums. Guest artist: Peewee Russell, clarinet

Stan Kenton and His Orchestra Gary Slavo, Ronnie Ossa, Ron I. Keller, Bob Behrendt, Buzzy Mills, trumpets; Jigs Wigam, Chris Swanson, Bob Curnow, Jim Amlote, Dave Wheeler, trombones; Gabe Baltazar, Steve Marcus, Ray Florian, Archie Wheeler, Joel Kaye, saxophones; Tony Scodwekk, Bob Faust, Dave Horton, Bob Crull, mellophoniums; John Worstov, bass; Dee Barton, drums; Jean Turner, vocals
Guest artists: Zoot Sims, tenor sax; Charlie Mariano, Cannonball Adderley, altos

Friday afternoon, July 5, 1963

Freebody Park

New Faces in Jazz The Pennsbury High School Stage Band of Fallsington, Pennsylvania Don Smith, director

The McCoy Tyner Trio McCoy Tyner, piano; Bob Cranshaw, bass; Mickey Roker, drums Guest artists: Clark Terry, trumpet, flugelhorn; Charlie Mariano, alto

Miss Ada Lee: New Voice in Jazz, '63 Accompanied by the Howard McGhee Trio Howard McGhee, trumpet; Wendell Marshall, bass; Candy Finch, drums

Howard McGhee Trio Howard McGhee, trumpet; Phil Porter, organ; Candy Finch, drums

The Angelo Di Pippo Trio Angelo Di Pippo, accordion; Joe Benjamin, bass; Bob Rosengarden, drums

The Joe Daley Trio Joe Daley, tenor sax and flute; Russell Thorne, bass; Hall Russell, drums

The Paul Winter Sextet Paul Winter, alto sax; Dick Whitsell, trumpet; Jay Cameron, baritone sax; Warren Bernhardt, piano; Bob Cranshaw, bass; Harold Jones, drums

Friday evening, July 5, 1963

Paul Winter Sextet

The Maynard Ferguson Orchestra Maynard Ferguson, Nat Pavone, Bob Zattola, Dusko Gojkovic, trumpets; Don Doane, Ken Rupp, trombones; Lannie Morgan, alto sax; Willie Maiden, Frank Vicari, tenor saxes; Ronnie Cuber, baritone sax; Mike Abene, piano; Linc Milliman, bass; Rufus "Speedy" Jones, drums Guest artist: Sonny Stitt

The Gerry Mulligan Sextet Gerry Mulligan, baritone, piano on one number; Art Farmer, flugelhorn; Bob Brookmeyer, valve trombone; Jim Hall, guitar; Bill Crow, bass; Dave Bailey, drums

The Junior Mance Trio Junior Mance, piano; Bob Cranshaw, bass; Mickey Roker, drums

Joe Williams Accompanied by The Junior Mance Trio; joined later by Coleman Hawkins, Zoot Sims, tenor; Clark Terry, Howard McGhee, trumpets

Lambert, Hendricks and Bavan Accompanied by the Gildo Mahones Trio: Gildo Mahones, piano;

George Tucker, bass; Jimmie Smith, drums; guest artists: Coleman Hawkins, tenor; Clark Terry, trumpet and flugelhorn

The Dizzy Gillespie Sextet Dizzy Gillespie, trumpet; James Moody, alto, tenor, flute; Kenny Baron, piano; Chris White, bass; Rudy Collins, drums Guest: Milt Jackson, vibes

Saturday afternoon, July 6, 1963

"An Afternoon at the Hoofer's Club" Baby Laurence, Bunny Briggs, Pete Nugent, Charlie Atkins, Honi Coles, Charles Cook, Chuck Green, and Ernest Brown, tap dancers; accompanied by Howard McGhee and Clark Terry, trumpets; Gildo Mahones, piano; Wendell Marshall, bass; and Sam Woodyard, drums

Saturday evening, July 6, 1963
Presented by Marshall Stearns

Narrator: Father Norman O'Connor

The Newport Jazz Festival All-Stars Ruby Braff, cornet; Bud Freeman, tenor sax; George Wein, piano; Wendell Marshall, bass; Roy Haynes, drums

Ken McIntyre, alto sax, oboe, bass clarinet; Gildo Mahones, piano; Wendell Marshall, bass: Roy Haynes, drums

Newport Jazz Festival All-Stars George Wein, piano; Bud Freeman, tenor; Ruby Braff, trumpet; Wendall Marshall, bass; Roy Haynes, drums

The Ramsey Lewis Trio Ramsey Lewis, piano; El Dee Young, bass; Isaac "Red" Holt, drums

Miss Nancy Wilson, vocals Accompanied by The Ramsey Lewis Trio

The Sonny Rollins Quartet Paul Bley, piano; Henry Grimes, bass; Roy McCurdy, drums Guest artist: Coleman Hawkins, tenor

Duke Ellington and the Orchestra Cootie Williams, Ray Nance, Rolf Ericson, Eddie Preston, trumpets; Johnny Hodges, Russell Procope, Paul Gonsalves, Jimmy Hamilton, Harry Carney, saxophones; Lawrence Brown, Chuck Connors, Buster Cooper, trombones; Ernie Shephard, bass; Sam Woodyard, drums; Milt Grayson, vocalist Guest artists: Dancers Baby Laurence and Bunny Briggs

Sunday afternoon, July 7, 1963

Panel Discussion—Jazz on Records George Avakian, RCA Victor; Nesuhi Ertegun, Atlantic Records; Teo Macero, Columbia Records; Bob Thiele, Impulse Records; Don DeMichael, editor, *Down Beat;* Willis Conover, Sid McCoy Moderator: George T. Simon, NARAS

Sunday evening, July 7, 1963

The Westwood (Mass.) High School Dance Band; Paul H. Monaghan, director

The Martial Solal Trio Martial Solal, piano; Teddy Kotick, bass; Paul Motian, drums

Miss Dakota Staton, vocals Accompanied by: Billy Mitchell, Billy Root, tenor; Rudy Powell, alto; Snookie Young, trumpet; Al Grey, euphonium and trombone; Don Butterfield, tuba; Wendell Marshall, bass; Gildo Mahones, piano; Kalil Madhi, drums; Talib Daoud, conductor; Howard McGhee, rehearsal director and arranger except for two arrangements by Melba Liston.

The Herbie Mann Sextet Herbie Mann, flutes; Dave Pike, vibraphone; Don Friedman, piano; Ben Tucker, bass; Attila Zoller, guitar; Bobby Thomas, drums; Carlos "Patato" Valdez, conga; Willie Bobo, timbales

The Dave Brubeck Quartet Paul Desmond, alto sax; Eugene Wright, bass; Joe Morello, drums

The Jimmy Smith Trio Jimmy Smith, organ; Quentin Warren, guitar; Donald Bailey, drums

The John Coltrane Quartet John Coltrane, sax; McCoy Tyner, piano; Jimmy Garrison, bass; Roy Haynes, drums

Thursday evening, July 2, 1964

Great Moments in Jazz Narrator: Willis Conover

Joe Thomas, trumpet; J.C. Higginbotham, trombone; Ed Hall, clarinet; Billy Taylor, piano; Slam Stewart, bass; Jo Jones, drums

Louis Armstrong and His All-Stars Eddie Shu, clarinet, harmonica; Jewel Brown, vocalist; Big Chief Russell Moore, trombone; Billy Kyle, piano; Danny Barcelona, drums

Max Kaminsky, trumpet; Lou McGarity, trombone; Bud Freeman, tenor; Peanuts Hucko, clarinet; George Wein, piano; Bobby Haggart, bass; Buzzy Drootin, drums

Muggsy Spanier, cornet; Wingy Manone, trumpet; George Brunis, trombone; George Wettling, drums; Louise Tobin, vocal on one number Final number features many musicians on the evening program

Friday afternoon, July 3, 1964

New Faces in Jazz

The Dick Meldonian Quartet Dick Meldonian, soprano; Ken Ayden, valve trombone; Bucky Calabrese, bass; Lenny Seed, drums

Lou Bennett, organist

Rod Levitt Octet Rod Levitt, trombone; Bobby Zottola, trumpet; Gene Allen, George Marge, Buzz Renn, reeds; Sy Johnson, piano; John Beal, bass; Ronnie Bedford, drums

Miss Ethel Ennis With Billy Taylor, piano; Slam Stewart, bass; Jo Jones, drums; Walt Namuth, guitar

The George Russell Sextet: featuring Thad Jones George Russell, piano; Thad Jones, cornet; Brian Trentham, trombone; John Gilmore, tenor; Steve Swallow, bass; Albert Heath, drums; Sheila Jordan, vocal

Freddy Hubbard Quintet

Friday evening, July 3, 1964

Narrator: Mort Fega—WEVD

Mose Allison, piano, vocals

Sister Rosetta Tharpe, vocals

Thelonious Monk Quartet Thelonious Monk, piano; Bob Cranshaw, bass; Charlie Rouse, tenor; Ben Riley, drums

Stan Getz Quartet Stan Getz, tenor; Gene Cherico, bass; Joe Hunt, drums; Garry Burton, vibes Guest artists: Astrud Gilberto, vocals; Chet Baker, flugelhorn

Joe Williams, vocals   With Milt Hinton, bass; Grady Tate, drums
Ethel Ennis, vocal, joins Joe Williams in duets

Count Basie Orchestra   With Joe Williams, vocals

Saturday afternoon, July 4, 1964

Piano Workshop: Billy Taylor, narrator   Thelonious Monk, Dave Brubeck, Toshiko Mariano, Billy Taylor, Willie "The Lion" Smith, Joe Sullivan, George Wein
With Slam Stewart, bass; Jo Jones, drums

Saturday evening, July 4, 1964

Narrator: Father Norman O'Connor (Guest MCs: Jim Mendes and Fred Grady)

Dave Brubeck Quartet   featuring Paul Desmond, alto; Eugene Wright, bass; Joe Morello, drums

J.J. Johnson Quartet   J.J. Johnson, trombone; Harold Mabern, piano; Arthur Harper, bass; Louis Hayes, drums

Oscar Peterson Trio   Oscar Peterson, piano; Ray Brown, bass; Ed Thigpen, drums

Max Roach Quartet with Miss Abbey Lincoln present   The Freedom Suite

Tribute to Charlie Parker   Howard McGhee, trumpet; Sonny Stitt, alto, tenor; J.J. Johnson, trombone; Max Roach, drums; Harold Mabern, piano; Arthur Harper, bass

Gloria Lynne, vocals, with rhythm section

Sunday afternoon, July 5, 1964

Panel Discussion: "The Jazz Audience"   Arnold Shaw, E.B. Marks Co.; John Wilson, New York Times; Billy Taylor, WNEW; Mort Fega, WEVD; George Wein, Newport Jazz Festival

Sunday evening, July 5, 1964

Billy Barnwell Quintet

Jimmy Smith Trio   Jimmy Smith, organ; Quentin Warren, guitar; William Hart, drums

---

Oscar Brown, Jr.   Accompnied by Slam Stewart, bass; George Wein, piano; Ben Riley, drums

Ruby Braff, cornet; Ben Webster, tenor; Buck Clayton, trumpet; Slam Stewart, bass; Al Grey, trombone; Sir Charles Thompson, piano; Ben Riley, drums

Dizzy Gillespie Quintet   Featuring James Moody, alto

Jackie "Moms" Mabley, comedienne

Miss Sarah Vaughan, vocals, accompanied by the Bob James Trio

Thursday evening, July 1, 1965

MC: Father Norman O'Connor

Muddy Waters Blues Band   Otis Spann, piano; James Cotton, harmonica; Jimmy Lee Morris, electric bass; Billie Stepney, drums
Guest artists: Dizzy Gillespie, trumpet; James Moody, alto

Memphis Slim, piano; Willie Dixon, bass
Guest artist: Pete Seeger, vocal, banjo

Pete Seeger joins Max Kaminsky, trumpet; Bud Freeman, tenor; Morey Feld, drums; George Wein, piano

Dizzy Gillespie Quintet   Featuring James Moody, alto; Chris White, bass; Rudy Collins, drums; Kenny Baron, piano; Big Black, conga drums

The Les McCann Trio   Les McCann, piano; Paul Humphrey, drums; Richard Gaskin, bass

Modern Jazz Quartet   Connie Kay, drums; Percy Heath, bass; Milt Jackson, vibraharp; John Lewis, piano and musical director

Joe Williams, vocals   Accompanied by Dizzy Gillespie, trumpet, and the Les McCann Trio

Friday afternoon, July 2, 1965

The New Thing in Jazz: A Study of the Avant-garde   MC: Leonard Feather

---

The Jazz Composers Orchestra   Under the direction of Mike Mantler and Carla Bley with Milford Graves
Mike Mantler, trumpet; Roswell Rudd, trombone; John Tchicai, alto; Charles Davis, baritone; Carla Bley, piano; Milford Graves, drums; Ken McIntyre, Steve Swallow, bass

Archie Shepp Quartet   Archie Shepp, tenor; Bobby Hutcherson, vibes; Barre Phillips, bass; Joe Chambers, drums

Paul Bley Trio   Paul Bley, piano; Steve Swallow, bass; Barry Altschul, drums

Cecil Taylor Quintet   Cecil Taylor, piano; Bill Barron, tenor; Jimmy Lyons, alto; Andrew Cyrille, drums; Henry Grimes, bass

Friday evening, July 2, 1965

MC: Billy Taylor

Thelonious Monk Quartet   Thelonious Monk, piano; Charlie Rouse, tenor; Larry Sales, bass; Ben Riley, drums

Carmen McRae, vocals   With Norman Simmons, piano

Dizzy Gillespie Quintet

Art Blakey Sextet   Art Blakey, drums; Gary Bartz, alto; John Gilmore, tenor; Lee Morgan, trumpet; John Hicks, piano; Victor Sproles, Jr., bass

John Coltrane Quartet   John Coltrane, tenor, soprano; Elvin Jones, drums; Jimmy Garrison, bass; McCoy Tyner, piano

Saturday afternoon, July 3, 1965

Drum Workshop
Narrator, Billy Taylor
Featuring Louis Bellson, Art Blakey, Roy Haynes, Elvin Jones, Jo Jones, Buddy Rich, drums; George Coleman, tenor; Johnny Coles, trumpet; Billy Taylor, piano; Ben Tucker, bass

Saturday evening, July 3, 1965

MC: Mort Fega

Indiana University Sextet

Jam Session   Featuring Howard McGhee, trumpet; Sonny Stitt, alto; Tony Scott, clarinet; Illinois Jacquet, tenor; Toshiko Mariano, piano; Buddy Rich, drums; Ben Tucker, bass

Mieko Hirota from Tokyo, Japan, vocals   Accompanied by the Billy Taylor Trio
Billy Taylor, piano; Grady Tate, drums; Ben Tucker, bass

Dave Brubeck Quartet   Featuring Paul Desmond, alto; Eugene Wright, bass; Joe Morello, drums

Herbie Mann Octet   Herbie Mann, flutes; Dave Pike, vibes; John Hitchcock, Mark Weinstein, trombones; Chick Corea, piano; Earl May, bass; Bruno Carr, drums; Carlos "Patato" Valdez, conga drums; plus Ben Tucker, bass

Earl "Fatha" Hines   Earl "Fatha" Hines, piano; Earl May, bass; Louis Bellson, drums

The Duke Ellington Orchestra   Guest vocalist: Bea Benjamin

Sunday afternoon, July 4, 1965

MC: Fred Grady

Johnny Coles Quintet   Johnny Coles, trumpet; George Coleman, tenor; plus rhythm

Denny Zeitlin Trio   Featuring Denny Zeitlin, piano; Charlie Haden, bass; Jerry Granelli, drums

Wynton Kelly Trio   Wynton Kelly, piano; Paul Chambers, bass; Jimmy Cobb, drums

Wes Montgomery with the Wynton Kelly Trio   Featuring Wes Montgomery, guitar

Stan Getz Quartet   Stan Getz, tenor; Gary Burton, vibraharp; Steve Swallow, bass; Joe Hunt, drums; Carlos Lyra, guitar, vocal

The Dollar Brand Trio   Dollar Brand, piano; plus rhythm section

Attila Zoller Quartet Attila Zoller, guitar; Don Friedman, piano; Larry Ridley, bass; Joe Chambers, drums; Albert Mangelsdorff, trombone

Lee Konitz, alto, unaccompanied

Sunday evening, July 4, 1965

The Oscar Peterson Trio Oscar Peterson, piano; Ray Brown, bass; Louis Hayes, drums

Count Basie Orchestra

Frank Sinatra with the Count Basie Orchestra, conducted by Quincy Jones
Guests: trumpeter Harry Sweets Edison, and Sonny Payne, drums

Friday evening, July 1, 1966

MC: Father Norman O'Connor
Opening address: Senator Claiborne Pell

The Florida Jazz Quintet Robert Mack, tenor sax; Al Hall, trombone; Steve Davidoskie, piano; Rudy Ailles, bass; Elbert Hatchett, drums

Newport Jazz Festival All-Stars Ruby Braff, cornet; Bud Freeman, tenor sax; George Wein, piano; Jack Lesberg, bass; Buddy Rich, drums
Guest artist: Gerry Mulligan, baritone, alto

The Dave Brubeck Quartet Dave Brubeck, piano; Paul Desmond, alto sax; Eugene Wright, bass; Joe Morello, drums

The Jimmy Smith Trio Jimmy Smith, organ; James Clinton, bass; William Hart, drums

Miss Esther Phillips, vocals With rhythm accompaniment

The Archie Shepp Quintet Archie Shepp, tenor sax; Roswell Rudd, trombone; Charles Haden, bass; William "Beaver" Harris, drums; Howard Johnson, tuba

Saturday afternoon, July 2, 1966

The Jazz Crusaders Wayne Henderson, trombone and euphonium; Wilton Felder, tenor sax; Joe Sample, piano; Herbie Lewis, bass; Sticks Hooper, drums

The Bill Dixon Quartet with dancer Judith Dunn Bill Dixon, trumpet, flugelhorn; Sam Rivers, tenor sax, bass clarinet; Sunny Marray, percussion; Alan Silva, double bass
Judith Dunn, dancer, choreographer

The Charles Lloyd Quartet Charles Lloyd, tenor sax, flute; Keith Jarrett, piano; Cecil McBee, bass; Jack De Johnette, drums

The Horace Silver Quintet Horace Silver, piano; Woody Shaw, trumpet; Tyrone Washington, tenor sax; Larry Ridley, bass; Roger Humphries, drums

The John Coltrane Quintet John Coltrane, tenor sax; Pharoah Saunders, tenor sax; Alice McLeod, piano; Jimmy Garrison, bass; Rashied Ali, drums

Saturday evening, July 2, 1966

The Charlie Byrd Trio Charlie Byrd, guitar; Gene Byrd, bass; Bill Reichenback, drums

Miss Nina Simone, vocals Lyle Atkinson, bass; Bobby Hamilton, drums; Ruby Stevenson, guitar, flute

The Stan Getz Quartet Stan Getz, tenor sax; Garry Burton, vibes; Roy Haynes, drums; Steve Swallow, bass

The Mel Lewis-Thad Jones Orchestra Bill Berry, Thad Jones, Jimmy Nottingham, Danny Styles, Richard Williams, trumpets; Bobby Brookmeyer, Cliff Heather, Tommy McIntoch, Jack Rains, trombones; Pepper Adams, baritone sax, clarinet; Eddie Daniels, tenor sax, clarinet, flute; Jerome Richardson, alto sax, flute; Richard Davis, bass; Sam Herman, guitar; Hank Jones, piano; Mel Lewis, drums

Joe Williams, vocals Accompanied by the orchestra

The Thelonious Monk Quartet Thelonious Monk, piano; Larry Gales, bass; Ben Riley, drums; Charlie Rouse, tenor sax

Sunday morning, July 3, 1966

Rev. Malcolm Boyd, narrator; Rev. John G. Gensel; Charlie Byrd, guitar; with his Jazz Ministry Band
Music by Howard and Sandy McGhee. Clifford Jordan, tenor; Wallace Walston, Howard McGhee, trumpet; Andy Bey, vocals

Sunday afternoon, July 3, 1966

The Al Cohn-Zoot Sims Quintet Al Cohn, Zoot Sims, tenors; Jack Lesberg, bass; Gene Taylor, piano; Buddy Rich, drums

The Herman Herds: The Woody Herman Orchestra Guest artists: Stan Getz, Al Cohn, Zoot Sims, tenors; Gerry Mulligan, baritone; Buddy Rich, drums

Tony Bennett and Woody Herman's Orchestra

Sunday evening, July 3, 1966

MC: Billy Taylor

Rhode Island Youth Stage Band

Misja Mengleberg Quartet, from The Netherlands Hans Bennink, drums; Misja Mengleberg, piano

Teddy Wilson, piano
Guests: Clark Terry, trumpet and vocals; Gene Taylor, bass; Buddy Rich, drums

The Duke Ellington Orchestra Duke Ellington, piano; Cat Anderson, Mercer Ellington, Herbie Jones, Cootie Williams, trumpets; Lawrence Brown, Chuck Connors, Buster Cooper, trombones; Harry Carney, baritone sax, clarinet, and bass clarinet; Paul Gonsalves, tenor sax; Jimmy Hamilton, tenor sax, clarinet; Johnny Hodges, alto sax; Russell Procope, alto sax, clarinet; John Lamb, bass; Sam Woodyard, drums

Miss Ella Fitzgerald with the Jimmy Jones Trio Jimmy Jones, piano; Sam Woodyard, drums; and the Duke Ellington Orchestra Ed Thigpen subs for Woodyard with Ella

Monday afternoon, July 4, 1966

Guitar Workshop Charlie Byrd, Kenny Burrell, Grant Green, Attila Zoller, George Benson, and Connie Smith, guitar; Ross Tompkins, Billy Taylor, George Wein, piano; Gene Taylor, bass; Billy Kay, Mike Deluca, drums; Lonnie Liston Smith, organ; baritone Taylor, bass

Trumpet Workshop Dizzie Gillespie, Bobby Hackett, Ruby Braff, Red Allen, Clark Terry, Carl Warwick, Thad Jones, Howard McGhee, Kenny

Dorham, trumpets; Russ Tompkins, piano; Jimmie Owens, flugelhorn; Red Allen, trumpet, vocals; Teddi King, vocals

Monday evening, July 4, 1966

MC: Leonard Feather

Florida Jazz Quintet

Father Tom Vaughn Trio Father Tom Vaughn, piano; Ben Jordan, bass; Dick Riordan, drums

The Miles Davis Quintet Miles Davis, trumpet; Wayne Shorter, tenor sax; Herbie Hancock, piano; Ron Carter, bass; Tony Williams, drums

The Herbie Mann Septet Herbie Mann, flute; Jimmy Owens, trumpet, flugelhorn; Joe Orange, trombone; Jack Hitchcock, vibes, trombone; Reggie Workman, bass; Bruno Carr, drums; Carlos Valdez, conga

The Dizzy Gillespie Quintet Dizzy Gillespie, trumpet; James Moody, tenor sax; Kenny Baron, piano; Frank Schifano, bass; Otis "Candy" Finch, drums

Count Basie and the Orchestra with Guest Jimmy Rushing, vocals Bill Henderson, vocals

The Count Basie Orchestra Count Basie, piano; Al Aarons, George Cohn, Wallace Davenport, Phil Gilbeau, Roy Eldridge, trumpets; Henderson Chambers, Al Grey, William Hughes, Grover Mitchell, trombones; Eddie Davis, Eric Dixon, Charles Fowlkes, Robert Plater, Marshall Royal, saxophones; Fred Green, guitar; Sonny Payne, drums; Norman Keenan, bass; Bill Henderson, vocalist

Friday evening, June 30, 1967

Olatunji and Company Twelve-piece orchestra

Earl "Fatha" Hines, piano, joined later by Ruby Braff, cornet

Newport Jazz Festival All-Stars Bud Freeman, tenor sax; Ruby Braff, cornet; Peewee Russell, clarinet; Don Lamond, drums; Jack Lesberg, bass; George Wein, piano
Guest artist: Bud Johnson, tenor, soprano

Willie "The Lion" Smith with Don Ewell, piano. Solo and duets

Buck Clayton and Buddy Tate with the Count Basie Rhythm Section Count Basie, piano; Buck Clayton, trumpet; Buddy Tate, tenor; Freddie Green, guitar; Norman Keenan, bass; Rufus Jones, drums

Count Basie and his Orchestra Harry Sweets Edison, Gene Goe, Sonny Cohn, Al Aarons, trumpets; Grover Mitchell, Harlan Floyd, Richard Boone, Bill Hughes, trombones; Bobby Plater, Sal Nistico, Eric Dixon, Charlie Fowlkes, reeds; Freddie Green, guitar; Sonny Payne, drums Joe Williams, vocals

The Birth of Bop Thelonious Monk, piano; Dizzy Gillespie, trumpet; James Moody, alto; Percy Heath, bass; Max Roach, drums

Modern Jazz Quartet John Lewis, piano; Milt Jackson, vibes; Percy Heath, bass; Connie Kay, drums

Albert Ayler Quintet Albert Ayler, tenor, alto, soprano; Don Ayler, trumpet; Michel Sampson, violin; Bill Folwell, bass; Milford Graves, drums

Saturday afternoon, July 1, 1967

Five Faces of Jazz

The Living Jazz Trio Bill Lalli, piano; Jimmy Johnson, bass; Ed Cotter, drums

Herbie Mann Quintet Herbie Mann, flutes; Roy Ayers, vibes; Chick Ganemian, oud; Bruno Carr, drums; Michael Olatunji, congas, gourd

Gabor Szabo Trio Gabor Szabo, guitar; Hal Gordon, congas; Bill Goodwin, drums

Herbie Mann Quintet Guest artists: Albert Mangelsdorf, trombone; Michael Olatunji, congas, gourd; Dizzy Gillespie, trumpet

Saturday evening, July 1, 1967

Newport Concert Band

Olatunji Group

Gary Burton Quartet Gary Burton, vibes; Larry Coryell, guitar; Steve Swallow, bass; Steve Martin, drums

Nina Simone and Trio

Earl "Fatha" Hines Quartet with Bud Johnson, tenor

Herbie Mann Quintet

Dizzy Gillespie Quintet

John Handy Quintet

Buddy Rich and His Orchestra plus Dizzy Gillespie, trumpet

Sunday morning, July 2, 1967

Jazz Mass Interdenominational choir and The Billy Taylor Trio

Sunday afternoon, July 2, 1967

The Sharps and Flats Orchestra from Tokyo, Japan, under the direction of Nobuo Hara, Tsukahara/Nobuo, leader and tenor saxophone; Tanigu-chi/Kazunori, tenor saxophone; Maekawa/Hajime, alto saxophone; Suzjki/Khoji, alto saxophone; Maekawa/Nobuyuki, baritone saxophone; Taniyama/Tadao, trombone; Suzuki/Hiroshi, trombone; Munekiyo/Hiroshi, trombone; Ochi/Haruo, bass trombone; Morikawa/Shuzo, trumpet; Fukushima/Teruyuki, trumpet; Shinohara/Kunitoshi, trumpet; Sanami/Hiroshi, trumpet; Makamura/Yoshio, drums; Ogawa/Takeuchi/Hiroshi, bass; Noguchi/Takeyoshi, guitar; Yamamoto/Housan, Shakuhachi (Japanese wood instrument)

Booker Ervin Quartet

Vibes Workshop Bobby Hutcherson, vibes; Billy Taylor Trio; Gary Burton, vibes; later aided by Steve Swallow, bass; Roy Haynes, drums; Red Norvo, vibes, xylophone; Milt Jackson, vibes; Lionel Hampton, vibes

Sunday evening, July 2, 1967

The Blues Project Andy Colberg, alto

Marilyn Maye, vocals

Bill Evans Trio Bill Evans, piano; Eddie Gomez, bass; Philly Joe Jones, drums

Max Roach Quintet

Woody Herman and His Orchestra

Miles Davis Quintet Miles Davis, trumpet; Wayne Shorter, tenor; Herbie Hancock, piano; Tony Williams, drums

Monday afternoon, July 3, 1967

Don Ellis and His Orchestra Twenty-piece orchestra

Rolf Kuhn Quartet Rolf Kuhn, clarinet; Joachim Kuhn, piano; Jimmy Garrison, bass; Aldo Romano, drums

Milford, Massachusetts, Youth Band under direction of Boots Mussulli—a 54-piece orchestra

Monday evening, July 3, 1967

Milford, Massachusetts, Youth Band with guests Illinois Jacquet, tenor, bassoon; with Milt Buckner, organ; Alan Dawson, drums; joined later by George Duvivler, bass

Red Norvo All-Stars Red Norvo, vibes, xylophone; with Don Lamond, drums; Ruby Braff, cornet; Jack Lesberg, bass; George Wein, piano

Dave Brubeck Quartet With Dave Brubeck, piano; Paul Desmond, alto; Alan Dawson, drums

Sarah Vaughan, accompanied by her Trio

Wes Montgomery Trio

Lionel Hampton and His Alumni Orchestra Snookie Young, James Nottingham, Joe Newman, Herb Pomeroy, Wally Davenport, trumpets; Al Grey, Garnett Brown, Britt Woodman, Benny Powell, trombones; Jerome Richardson, George Dorsey, Frank Foster, Dave Young, Eddie Pazant, saxophones; Steve Little, drums; George Duvivier, bass; William Mackel, guitar; John Spruill, piano. Joined later by Milt Buckner, organ, piano; Illinois Jacquet, tenor; Alan Dawson, drums

Thursday evening, July 4, 1968

Newport Concert Band Conducted by J. Rice Moody

New York College of Music Jazz Ensemble

Mongo Santamaria Octet, featuring Hubert Laws, flute; Jim Hall, guitar; Victor Gaskin, bass; Roy McCurdy, drums Hall joined by guitarist Barney Kessell

Garry Burton Quartet Garry Burton, vibes; Larry Coryell, guitar; Steve Swallow, bass; Roy Haynes, drums

Cannonball Adderley Quintet Cannonball Adderley, alto; Nat Adderley, flugelhorn; Joe Zawinul, piano; Victory Gaskin, bass; Roy McCurdy, drums

Nina Simone, vocals and piano Henry Lemming, guitar; Samuel Lemon, guitar, vocals; Eugene Taylor, bass; Red Clark, drums

Friday afternoon, July 5, 1968

Rufus Harley, bagpipes, tenor, soprano

The Archie Shepp Sextet Archie Shepp, tenor; Howard Johnson, tuba; Grachan Moncur, trombone; Mohammed Ali, percussion; Wilbur Ware, bass; Leroy Anderson, drums; Leroy Bib, vocals

Elvin Jones Trio Elvin Jones, drums; Joe Farrell, tenor, soprano, flute; Jimmy Garrison, bass

Dizzy Gilespie Quintet Dizzy Gillespie, trumpet, vocals; James Moody, alto; Mike Longo, piano; Paul West, bass; Candy Finch, drums Guest artist; Vi Redd, alto, vocals

The Clark Terry Orchestra Randy Brecker, Clark Terry, Jimmy Owens, Ziggy Harrel, Lloyd Michaels, trumpets; Frank Wess, flute, alto; Joe Farrell, Bobby Donovan, Lou Tabachin, saxophones; Jimmy Cleveland, Julian Priester, Wayne Andre, Jack Jeffers, trombones; Don Friedman, piano; Joe Benjamin, bass; Grady Tate, drums

Friday evening, July 5, 1968

Schlitz Salute to Big Bands

Count Basie Orchestra Al Aarons, Sonny Cohn, Gene Goe, Oscar Brashaer, trumpets; Marshal Royal, Charles Fowlkes, Bobby Plater, Eddie "Lockjaw" Davis, saxophones; Harlen Floyd, Grover Mitchell, Bill Hughes, Richard Boone, trombones; Count Basie, piano; Freddie Greene, guitar; Norman Keenan, bass; Harold Jones, drums
Quinin Williams, Richard Boone, vocals
Guest artist: Joe Thomas, tenor

MC: Andre Baruch

The Woody Herman Orchestra Woody Herman, clarinet, alto, soprano; Frank Vicari, Sal Nistico, Jules Rowell, Ronnie Cuber, Joe Alexander, saxophones; Robert Yance, trumpet, flute; Bill Hunt, Thomas Nygaard, Bill Byrne, David Luell, trumpets; Bobby Burgess, Joe Marguez, Melvin Wanzo, trombones; Nat Pierce, piano; Carl Pruitt, bass; Ed Soph, drums
Guest artists: Jack Leonard, vocals; Erskine Hawkins, trumpet; Bob Eberle, vocals

Charlie Barnett, alto, soprano Conducting The Duke Ellington Orchestra, with the following substitutions: Clark Terry, trumpet; Nat Pierce, piano; Steve Little, drums

The Duke Ellington Orchestra Duke Ellington, piano, arranger; Cat Anderson, Herbie Jones, Cootie Williams, Mercer Ellington, trumpets; Laurence Brown, George "Buster" Cooper, Chuck Connors, Jimmy Cleveland, Money Johnson, trombones; Harry Carney, baritone; Harold Ashby, sax, clarinet; Johnny Hodges, alto; Paul Gonsalves, tenor; Jeff Castleman, bass; Rufus Jones, drums; Dick Wilson, second drummer
Tony Watkins, Trish Turner, dancers, joined by Woody Herman

The Dizzy Gillespie Orchestra Dizzy Gillespie, Martin Banks, Steve Furtado, Al Bryant, trumpets; Al Gibbons, Chris Woods, Buddy Terry, Harold Vick, Bill Phipps, James Moody, saxophones; Kiane Zawabi, Ashley Fernall, Jack Jeffers, trombones; "Patato" Valdez, congas; Mike Longo, piano; Paul West, bass; Candy Finch, drums; Art Blakey, second drummer
Directed by Gil Fuller
Guest artist: Benny Carter, alto sax

Saturday afternoon, July 6, 1968

University of Illinois Jazzmen Directed by John Garvey

Montego Joe Septet Eddie Preston, trumpet; Bobby Brown, tenor; Eddie Diehl, guitar; Sonny Morgan, bongos; Montego Joe, congas; Herb Bushler, electric bass; Ralph Dorsey, drums

Tal Farlow Quartet Tal Farlow, guitar; Johnny Knapp, piano; Junie Booth, bass; Mousie Alexander, drums

Sonny Chris Quartet Sonny Chris, alto; Billy Taylor, piano; Junie Booth, bass; Mousie Alexander, drums

Duke Ellington, piano; Johnny Hodges, Benny Carter, altos; Jeff Castleman, bass; Speedy Jones, drums

Sadao Watanabe, alto; Jeff Castleman, bass; Billy Taylor, piano; Speedy Jones, drums

Saturday evening, July 6, 1968

Alex Welsh Band Alex Welsh, cornet; Roy Williams, trombone; Johnny Barnes, clarinet, baritone; Fred Hunt, piano; Jim Douglas, guitar; Tony Bayless, bass; Lennie Hastings, drums
Guest artists: Bud Freeman, tenor; Peewee Russell, clarinet; Ruby Braff, cornet; Joe Venuti, violin; George Wein, piano

MC Joan Crawford, introducing Duke Ellington
Duke Ellington and His Orchestra

Hugh Masakela Quintet Hugh Masakela, trumpet, vocals; Al Abreu, tenor; William Anderson, piano; Henry Franklin, bass; Chick Carter, drums

Dionne Warwick, vocals with orchestra

Sunday afternoon, July 7, 1968

An Afternoon with Ray Charles Ray Charles, piano, vocals; Virgil Jones, Phil Gibeaux, Wallace Davenport, trumpets; Curtis Amy, Clifford Scott, tenor; Claude Miller, Clifford Scott, alto; Henry Coker, trombone, two other trombones; Billy Preston, piano, dancing, electric organ; unknown bass; Roger Humphries, drums
The Raelettes, vocals; Andy Baxter, vocals

Sunday evening, July 7, 1968

MC: Flip Wilson

Montreux Festival Winners

The Palle Mikkelborg Quintet, Denmark Palle Mikkelborg, trumpet; Bernt Rosengren, tenor; Alex Riel, drums

Ramsey Lewis Trio

The Sound of Feeling The Andrece Twins (Alyce and Rhae), vocals; Garry David, piano, marxophone; Joe Roccisano, soprano; McReed Lewis, piano; Cleveland Eaton, bass; Maurice White, drums

Horace Silver Quintet Randy Brecker, trumpet; Benny Maupin, tenor; Horace Silver, piano; John Williams, bass; Billy Cobham, drums

Roland Kirk Roland Kirk, tenor, Stritch, flute, nose flute, manzello, clarinet; Ron Burton, piano; Vernon Martin, bass; Joe Texidor, percussion; Jimmy Hobbs, drums

Don Ellis Orchestra Don Ellis, electric trumpet; and a seventeen-piece orchestra

Thursday evening, July 3, 1969

Joshua Light Show

Newport Concert Band J. Rice Moody

George Benson George Benson, guitar; organ, drums, reeds

Sunny Murray Sextet Sunny Murray, drums; Dave Burrell, piano; Teddy Daniels, trumpet; Carlos Ward, alto; Luqman Lateef, tenor; Alan Silva, bass

Freddie Hubbard Quintet Freddie Hubbard, trumpet; Junior Cook, tenor; Harold Mabern, piano; Wayne Dockery, bass; Louis Hayes, drums

Anita O'Day, vocals Accompanied by rhythm section

Phil Woods and His European Rhythm Machine Phil Woods, alto; George Gruntz, piano; Henri Texier, bass; Daniel Humair, drums

Sun Ra and His Space Arkestra Sun Ra, piano; Pat Patrick, baritone; John Gilmore, Marshal Allen, reeds

Young-Holt Limited Unnamed trumpet; Harold Mabern, piano; El Dee Young, electric bass; Isaac Red Holt, drums
Guest artist: Jeremy Steig, flute

Bill Evans Trio Bill Evans, piano; Eddie Gomez, bass; Marty Morell, drums
Guest artist: Jeremy Steig, flute

Kenny Burrell, guitar

Friday afternoon, July 4, 1969

Lighthouse Skip Prokof, drums; Paul Hoffert, organ; trombone; two trumpets, one alto; two electric guitars; two electric cellos; one electric violin; cello; conga; cowbell

Jam session Howard McGhee, conductor, trumpet; Kenny Dorham, Jimmy Owens, trumpets; Benny Green, Albert Mangelsdorf, trombones; Charlie McPherson, alto; Paul Jeffrey, Brew Moore, Buddy Tate, tenors; Cecil Payne, baritone; Ray Nance, violin; Hamp Hawes, piano; Slam Stewart, Larry Ridley, bass; Art Blakey, drums; Jimmy Smith, organ; for part of last number, Eddie Jefferson, vocals

Hamp Hawes, piano; Larry Ridley, bass; Art Blakey, drums

Friday evening, July 4, 1969

Count's Rock Band Steve Marcus, soprano; tenor

Jeff Beck, electric guitar

Ten Years After Alvin Lee, guitar, vocals; Leo Lyons, bass; Ric Lee, drums; Chick Churchill, organ

Blood, Sweat and Tears David Clayton-Thomas, vocals; Bobby Colomby, drums; Jim Fielder, bass; Dick Halligan, keyboard; Jerry Hyman, trombone, recorder; Steve Katz, guitar; Fred Lipsius, alto, piano; Chuck Winfield, Louis Soloff, trumpets, flugelhorn

Jethro Tull Ian Anderson, flute, mouth organ

Roland Kirk Roland Kirk, reeds; Glen Cornick, bass; Clive Bunker, drums; Nick Abrahams, guitar

Saturday afternoon, July 5, 1969

Newport All-Stars Ruby Braff, cornet; Red Norvo, vibes; Tal Farlow, guitar; Larry Ridley, bass; Jack De Johnette, drums; Mavis Rivers, vocals

Miles Davis Quartet Miles Davis, trumpet; Chick Corea, electric piano; Dave Holland, bass; Jack De Johnette, drums

John Mayall John Mayall, harmonica, vocals; Johnny Almond, reeds, flute; John Mark, acoustic guitar; Steve Thompson, electric bass

Mothers of Invention with Frank Zappa

Saturday evening, July 5, 1969

Illinois State Band

Eero kovistoninen Quartet

Winners of the Montreux Jazz Festival Eero Kovistoninen, tenor, alto

Dave Brubeck Quartet Dave Brubeck, piano; Gerry Mulligan, baritone; Jack Six, bass; Alan Dawson, drums

Art Blakey's Jazz Messengers Woody Shaw, trumpet; Carlos Garnett, tenor; George Cables, piano; Jan Arnet, bass; Art Blakey, drums

Garry Burton Quartet Garry Burton, vibes; Jerry Hahn, guitar; Larry Ridley, bass; Bill Goodwin, drums

Sly and the Family Stone

The World's Greatest Jazz Band Bob Wilber, soprano; Bud Freeman, tenor; Lou McGarrity, Carl Fontana, trombones; Ralph Sutton, piano; Bob Haggart, bass; Gus Johnson, drums Maxine Sullivan, vocals

Stephane Grappelli, electric violin; Tal Farlow, guitar; George Wein, piano; Larry Ridley, bass; Gus Johnson, drums

O.C. Smith, vocals

Sunday afternoon, July 6, 1969

MC: Maceo Parker, organ, tenor

Dee Felice Trio Dee Felice, piano, plus rhythm

James Brown, vocals

Marva Whitney, vocals

Nipsey Russell, comedian

Sunday evening, July 6, 1969

The Joshua Light Show (throughout)

Illinois State Band

B.B. King B.B. King, guitar

Johnny Winter, guitar, vocals Joined later by B.B. King

Herbie Hancock Sextet Herbie Hancock, piano; Johnny Coles, trumpet; Garnett Brown, trombone; Joe Henderson, tenor; Buster Williams, bass; Albert Heath, drums

Willie Bobo Sextet

Buddy Rich Orchestra Guest artist: Gerry Mulligan, baritone

Led Zeppelin

Friday evening, July 10, 1970

The Schlitz Salute to Louis, a New Orleans Tribute to Louis Armstrong

---

The Eureka Brass Band Percy Humphrey, trumpet, leader; DeDe Pierce, Lionel Ferbos, trumpets; Paul Crawford, Jim Robinson, trombones; Orange Kellin, clarinet; Capt. John Handy, alto sax; Allan Jaffe, bass horn; Cie Frazier, drums; Booker T. Glass, bass drum; Willie Humphrey, Grand Marshall

Bobby Hackett Quintet Hackett, cornet; Benny Morton, trombone; Dave McKenna, piano; Jack Lesberg, bass; Oliver Jackson, drums

The New Orleans Classic Ragtime Band Lionel Ferbos, trumpet; Paul Crawford, trombone; Orange Kellin, clarinet; Bill Russell, violin; Lars Edergran, piano, director; James Prevost, bass; Cie Frazier, drums

Trumpet Tributes to Louis Armstrong Dizzy Gillespie, Bobby Hackett, Joe Newman, Ray Nance, Wild Bill Davison, Jimmy Owens, trumpets, cornets, flugelhorn; Morton, Tyree Glenn, trombones; Dave McKenna, piano; Larry Ridley, bass; Oliver Jackson, drums

Louis Armstrong vocal, with Hackett, Glenn, McKenna, Lesberg, and Jackson

The Preservation Hall Jazz Band DeDe Pierce, trumpet; Jim Robinson, trombone; Willie Humphrey, clarinet; Capt. John Handy, alto sax; Billie Pierce, piano, vocal; Allan Jaffe, bass horn; Cie Frazier, drums; George Wein, guest pianist

Mahalia Jackson accompanied by Gwen Lightner, piano; Cleveland Clency, organ

Finale Armstrong, Miss Jackson, Hackett, the Eureka Brass Band, and others.

Saturday afternoon, July 11, 1970

Drum Workshop Jo Jones, Philly Joe Jones, Elvin Jones, Chico Hamilton

Violin Workshop Jean-Luc Ponty, Mike White, violins; Kenny Burrell, guitar; Larry Ridley, bass; Lennie McBrowne, drums

Trumpet Workshop Dizzy Gillespie, Joe Newman, trumpets; Ray Nance, cornet; Jimmy Owens, trumpet, flugelhorn; rhythm section as above

---

Sadao Watanabe Quartet Watanabe, soprano saxophone; Yoshio Suzuki, electric piano; Yoshiaki Masuo, guitar; Hirotami Tsunoda, drums

Elvin Jones Quintet Frank Foster, George Coleman, tenor sax; Ky Fuchi, piano; Wilbur Little, bass; Jo Jones, drums

Chico Hamilton Quartet Arnie Lawrence, amplified alto sax; Bob Mann, guitar; Steve Swallow, bass; Hamilton, drums

The Gerry Mulligan Sextet Gerry Mulligan, baritone, piano on one number; Art Farmer, flügelhorn; Bob Brookmeyer, valve trombone; Jim Hall, guitar; Bill Crow, bass; Dave Bailey, drums

Tony Williams Lifetime Larry Young, organ; John McLaughlin, guitar; Jack Bruce, bass, vocal; Williams, drums, vocal

Saturday evening, July 11, 1970

Kenny Burrell Trio Burrell, guitar; Larry Ridley, bass; Lennie McBrowne, drums; Dexter Gordon, tenor sax, with the Burrell Trio

The Fiddlers Jean-Luc Ponty, Ray Nance, Mike White, violins, with George Duke, piano; Ridley, bass; Bill Goodwin, drums

Dizzy Gillespie Quintet Gillespie, trumpet, vocal; Mike Longo, piano; George Davis, guitar; Larry Rockwell, bass; David Lee, drums

Don Byas tenor sax, with Gillespie rhythm section

Nina Simone Show

Herbie Mann Quintet Steve Marcus, soprano sax; Mann, flute; Sonny Sharrok, guitar; Miroslav Vitous, bass; Billy Cobham, drums

Ike and Tina Turner Revue Ike Turner, guitar, leader; Tina Turner, vocal; The Ikettes, dancers and singers, and backup band of trumpet, trombone, tenor and baritone sax, organ, guitar, bass, drums

Sunday afternoon, July 12, 1970

Montreux Festival Winner Nucleus (Great Britain) Ian Carr, flugelhorn, Brian Smith, tenor and soprano sax; Carl Jenken, piano, oboe; Chris Speddings, guitar; Jeff Clyne, bass; John Marshall, drums

The Fourth Way Mike White, violin; Mike Nock, piano; Ron McClure, bass; Eddie Marshall, drums

Roberta Flack vocal, piano; with David Williams, bass; Bernard Sweetney, drums

Shuggie Otis guitar, with members of Bill Cosby Band

Bill Cosby and Badfoot Brown and the Bunions Bradford Marching and Funeral Band George Bohannon, amplified trombone; Rudolph Johnson, tenor sax; Arthur Adams, Ted Dunbar, Al Vescovo, guitars; Stu Gardner, organ, vocal; Kenny Barron, Gildo Mahones, electric pianos; Monk Montgomery, Ron Johnson, electric bass; Jimmy Smith, Freddie Waits, drums; Cosby, conductor

Albert King guitar, vocals, with his quartet.

Sunday evening, July 12, 1970

Eddie Harris Quartet Harris, amplified tenor sax, trumpet; Jodie Christian, piano; Louis Peers, bass; Bob Crowder, drums

Les McCann Limited McCann, piano, vocal; Jimmy Rowser, bass; Donald Dean, drums; Buck Clarke, congas

Leon Thomas vocal, with his group: James Spaulding, flute, alto sax; Arthur Sterling, piano; Joe Kearny, bass; Sherman Ferguson, drums; Sonny Morgan, Richard Landrum, Gene Golden, congas

Cannonball Adderley Quintet Nat Adderley, trumpet, vocal; Cannonball, alto and soprano sax; Joe Zawinul, piano, electric piano; Walter Booker, bass; Roy McCurdy, drums

Buddy Rich Orchestra Mike Price, John Madrid, Ernie Jones, George Zonze, trumpets; Rick Stepton, Tony Lada, Sherman King, trombones; Richie Cole, Bob Martin, Pat LaBarbera, Don Englert,

Bob Suchoski, reeds; Dave McRae, piano; Walt Namuth, guitar; Rick Laird, bass; Rich, drums

Ella Fitzgerald with the Tommy Flanagan Trio Flanagan, piano; Frank DeLa Rosa, bass; Ed Thigpen, drums

Friday evening, July 2, 1971

Dave Pike Set Dave Pike, vibes; Volker Kriegel, guitar; Hans Rettenbach, bass; Peter Baumeister, drums

Stan Kenton Orchestra Co-leaders: Mike Vax and Dick Shearer; Claude Sifferlin, piano; Mike Vax, trumpet; Dennis Noday, trumpet; Gary Pack, trumpet; Paul Adamson, trumpet; Joe Marcinkiewitz, trumpet; Dick Shearer, trombone; Mike Jamieson, trombone; Fred Carter, trombone; Mike Wallace, trombone; Graham Ellis, trombone; Quin Davis, sax; Richard Torres, sax; Kim Frizell, sax; Willie Maiden, sax; Chuck Carter, sax; John Von Ohlen, drums; Gary Todd, bass; Ramon Lopez, Latin

Buddy Rich Orchestra Buddy Rich, drums; Richard Cole, Pat La Barbera, sax; Don Englert, sax, flute; Joe Calo, Jim Mosher, sax; Tony Di Maggio, Bruce Paulsen, John Leyes, Tony Lada, trombone; Jeff Stout, Lin Bivano, John De Flon, Joe Giorgiana, trumpet

Duke Ellington Orchestra Duke Ellington, piano; Harold Ashby, sax, clarinet; Norris Turney, Paul Gonsalves, Harry Carney, sax; Malcolm Taylor, Chuck Connors, Mitchell "Booty" Wood, trombone; Charles "Cootie" Williams, Harold "Money" Johnson, Mercer Ellington, Cat Anderson, Eddie Preston, trumpet; Joe Benjamin, bass; Rufus Jones, drums; Wild Bill Davis, organ; Tony Watkins, vocalist; Bobbie Gordon, vocalist

Roberta Flack, vocals Roberta Flack, piano; David William, bass; Bernard P. Sweetney, drums; Nathan Page, guitar

Saturday afternoon, July 3, 1971

Eubie Blake, piano; Willie "The Lion" Smith, piano; Mike Lipskin, piano

Charles Mingus Sextet Charlie Mingus, bass; Lonnie Hilyer, trumpet; Charles McPherson, alto

sax; Bobbie Jones, tenor sax; John Foster, piano; Virgil Day, drum

Donny Hathaway

Freddie Hubbard Freddie Hubbard, trumpet; Louis Hayes, drums; Junior Cook, tenor sax; Mickey Bass, bass; Joe Bonner, piano; plus unknown, electric guitar.

New York Bass Violin Choir Bill Lee, bass; Richard Davis, bass; Ron Carter, bass; Milt Hinton, bass; Lisle Atkinson, bass; Sam Jones, bass; Michael Fleming, bass; Sonny Brown, percussion; Consuela Lee Moorehead, piano; A. Grace Lee Mims, vocal

Ornette Coleman Quartet Ornette Coleman, alto; Dewey Redman, tenor; Charlie Haden, bass; Ed Blackwell, drums

Saturday evening, July 3, 1971

Montreux Jazz Festival Award Winners from Finland

Chase Bill Chase, trumpet; Dennis Johnson, bass; Ted Piercefield, trumpet; Phil Porter, organ; Terry Richards, vocal; Jay Burrd, drums; Angel South, guitar; Jerry Van Blair, trumpet; Alan Ware, trumpet

Dave Brubeck Quartet Dave Brubeck, piano; Jack Six, bass; Alan Dawson, drums Guest artist: Gerry Mulligan, baritone

Dionne Warwicke, vocals Joe Mele, piano, conductor; Lee Valentine, guitar; Ralf Rost, bass; Ray Lucas, drums

Newport Jazz Festival—New York (now located in New York City) Saturday, July 1, 1972

Schlitz Salute to Jazz I
Philharmonic Hall, two Performances—5:00 P.M. and 9:00 P.M.

Giants of Jazz Dizzy Gillespie, trumpet; Sonny Stitt, alto, tenor; Kai Winding, trombone; Thelonious Monk, piano; Al McKibbon, bass; Max Roach, Art Blakey, drums; Big Black, conga; Billy Eckstine, Sarah Vaughan, vocals

Sarah Vaughan Accompanied by Carl Schroeder, piano; Jimmy Cobb, drums

Billy Eckstine Accompanied by Bobby Tucker, piano; Charlie Persip, drums

Schiltz Salute to Jazz II
Carnegie Hall, two Performances—5:00 P.M. and 9:00 P.M.

The Modern Jazz Quartet

Stan Getz Quartet Stan Getz, tenor; Hank Jones, piano; Stanley Clarke, bass; Airto Moreiro, drums Guest artist: Gary Burton, vibes

Pharoah Saunders Quintet Pharoah Saunders, tenor, soprano; Joe Bonner, piano; Cecil McBee, bass; Jimmy Hopps, drums; assorted percussion Dee Dee Bridgewater, vocals

Carnegie Recital Hall, 7:45 P.M.
Miss Truth Glory Van Scott; Louis Johnson Dance Theatre, including Dolores Vanison, Jimmy Thurston, Freda Vanderpool, C and the Shells; Danny Mixon, piano; Wayne Dockery, bass; Cliff Barbaro, drums; Noel Pointer, violin; Danny Holgate, musical director; Shirley Prendergast, lighting director; Alice E. Carter, costumes; Horacena Taylor, production stage manager
Miss Truth was written in honor of Miss Van Scott's grandmother, Matilda Brown Demyers.
Miss Truth will also be performed on Sunday, July 2, Monday, July 3, Tuesday, July 4, Wednesday, July 5, at 7:45 P.M., and on Sunday, July 9 at 3:30 P.M.

Sunday afternoon, July 2, 1972, 1:00 P.M.

Connoisseur Concert A
Carnegie Hall

J.P.J. Quartet Budd Johnson, tenor; Dill Jones, piano; Bill Pemberton, bass; Oliver Jackson, drums

The Mary Lou Williams Trio Mary Lou Williams, piano; Milton Suggs, bass; Mickey Roker, drums

Cecil Taylor solo piano

Roland Kirk Quartet

Sunday evening, July 2, 1972, 5:00 P.M. and 9:00 P.M.

Jones-Lewis & TV-Jazz Philharmonic Hall Bobby Rosengarden and The Dick Cavett Show Orchestra; Billy Taylor and The David Frost Show Orchestra; Thad Jones-Mel Lewis Orchestra

Carnegie Hall, two performances, 5:00 P.M. and 9:00 P.M.
Swing Lives

Benny Carter with the Swing Masters   Harry Edison, Taft Jordan, Carl Warwick, Joe Thomas, trumpets; Tyree Glenn, Quentin Jackson, Benny Morton, Dickie Wells, trombones; Barry Carter, Earle Warren, Howard Johnson, Buddy Tate, Budd Johnson, Haywood Henry, saxophones; Teddy Wilson, piano; Bernard Addison, guitar; Milt Hinton, bass; Jo Jones, drums

Maxine Sullivan, vocals
Accompanied by Teddy Wilson, piano; Milt Hinton, bass; Jo Jones, drums

Count Basie and His Orchestra   With guests Joe Williams and Al Hibbler, vocals; Al Grey, trombone MC: Joe Franklin

Midnight Dance
The Commodore Hotel
Count Basie and His Orchestra, Sy Oliver and His Orchestra, playing the music of Jimmie Lunceford

Buddy Smith, vocals

Rock Band from Texas

Monday morning, July 3, 1972

Seminar
Lincoln Center Library and Museum of the Performing Arts Auditorium
Panel 1. Bootlegging and the Recording Industry
Chairman: Walter C. Allen, Rutgetrs University
Panelists: Arnold S. Caplin, Biograph Records; Bob Porter, producer, writer, discographer; Howard N. Beldock, attorney
Panel Coordinators: Richard Seidel, Mary Prioli

Monday afternoon, July 3, 1972

Connoisseur Concert B
Carnegie Hall, 1:00 P.M.

Don Burrows Quintet

Lee Konitz Quartet   Lee Konitz, alto, soprano; Marshall Brown, valve trombone; Mike Moore, bass; Dick Katz, piano; Barry Altschul, drums

Ruth Brisbane, vocals
And the Legend of Bessie Smith
Accompanied by Roland Hanna, piano; Victor Sproles, bass; Charlie Persip, drums

Benny Green, trombone; Roland Hanna, piano; Victor Sproles, bass; Charlie Persip, drums

Monday evening, July 3, 1972

Stan & Woody
Philharmonic Hall, two performances, 5:00 P.M. and 9:00 P.M.
Woody Herman and His Orchestra and Alumni, Al Cohn, Stan Getz, Flip Phillips and Zoot Sims, tenors; Chubby Jackson, bass; Red Norvo, vibes, xylophone

Stan Kenton and His Orchestra   with guest vocalist June Christy

Chase, Bill & Elvin
Carnegie Hall, Two Performances, 5:00 P.M. and 9:00 P.M.

Elvin Jones Quartet   Elvin Jones, drums; Steve Grossman, Dave Leibman, reeds; Gene Perla, bass

Bill Evans Trio   Bill Evans, piano; Eddie Gomez, bass; Marty Morel, drums

Chase

Schlitz Midnight Jam Session I
Radio City Music Hall

Group 1   Bud Freeman, tenor; Benny Carter, alto; Bobby Hackett, Roy Eldridge, trumpets; Vic Dickenson, trombone; Jim Hall, guitar; Larry Ridley, bass; Bobby Rosengarden, Gene Krupa, drums

Group 2   Stan Getz, tenor; Dizzy Gillespie, trumpet; Benny Green, trombone; Milt Jackson, vibes;

Kenny Burrell, guitar; Mary Lou Williams, piano; John Blair, violin; Percy Heath, bass; Big Black, congas; Max Roach, drums

Group 3   Flip Phillips, Zoot Sims, Dexter Gordon, Rahsaan Roland Kirk, tenors; James Moody, alto; Harry Edison, trumpet; Kai Winding, trombone; Mary Lou Williams, Herbie Hancock, pianos; Chuck Wayne, guitar; Larry Ridley, bass; Tony Williams, drums

Tuesday afternoon, July 4, 1972

Hudson River Boatride
Staten Island Ferry: 10:30 A.M.; 1:00 P.M.; 3:30 P.M. Kid Thomas Preservation Hall Band from New Orleans, Papa French and the Original Tuxedo Jazz Band from New Orleans, Papa Bue's Viking Jazz Band from Copenhagen

Tuesday evening, July 4, 1972

Ornette & Mingus
Philharmonic Hall, two performances, 5:00 P.M. and 9:00 P.M.

Ornette Coleman Quartet, Skies of America   Ornette Coleman, alto; Dewey Redman, tenor; Charlie Haden, bass; Ed Blackwell, drums
American Symphony Orchestra conducted by Leon Thompson

Charles Mingus and a twenty-four piece orchestra

Freddie, Sonny, and McCoy
Carnegie Hall, two performances, 5:00 P.M. and 9:00 P.M.

Freddie Hubbard Sextet   Freddie Hubbard, trumpet; Junior Cook, tenor; George Cables, piano; Alex Blake, bass; Lennie White, drums

Sonny Rollins Quartet   Sonny Rollins, tenor; Al Dailey, piano; Larry Ridley, bass; David Lee, drums

McCoy Tyner Quintet   McCoy Tyner, piano; Sonny Fortune, alto, flute; Calvin Hill, bass; Al Mouzon, drums

Wednesday morning, July 5, 1972

Seminar
Lincoln Center
Panel II: Greats of the Swing Era—An Oral History Panel
Chairman: Walter C. Allen, Rutgers University

Wednesday afternoon, July 5, 1972

Connoisseur Concert C
Carnegie Hall, 1:00 P.M.

Gato Barbieri Quintet   Gato Barbieri, tenor; Lonnie Liston Smith, piano; Stanley Clarke, bass; Ed Watkins, congas; Airto Moreiro, drums

Eubie Blake, solo piano

Kenny Burrell Trio   Kenny Burrell, guitar; Richard Wyands, piano; Larry Ridley, bass; Freddie Waits, drums

Herbie Hancock Sextet   Eddie Henderson, flugelhorn, trumpet; Benny Maupin, reeds; Julian Priester, trombone; Herbie Hancock, keyboards; Stanley Clarke, bass; Billy Hart, drums

Wednesday evening, July 5, 1972

American Airlines Tribute to Lionel
Philharmonic Hall, two performances, 5:00 P.M. and 9:00 P.M.

Charlie Byrd Trio

Lionel Hampton and His Orchestra   Bernard Purdie, drums; Richard Williams, trumpet; Bue Pleasant, organ; Richard Davis, bass; Curtis Fuller, trombone
Guest artists: Cat Anderson, Roy Eldridge, Joe Newman, trumpets; Dexter Gordon, Illinois Jacquet, tenor; Garnett Brown, trombone; Milt Buckner, organ, piano; Teddy Wilson, piano; Gene Krupa, drums

Carnegie Hall, two performances, 5:00 P.M. and 9:00 P.M.

Lee Wiley   Eddie and the Gang

The World's Greatest Jazz Band of Yank Lawson and Bob Haggart
Artists appearing: Bobby Hackett, Wild Bill Davison, Max Kaminsky, cornets; Joe Thomas, trum-

276

pet; J.C. Higginbotham, Benny Morton, George Brunis, trombones; Barney Bigard, clarinet; Willie "The Lion" Smith, Dick Hyman, pianos; Bucky Pizzarelli, guitar; George Duvivier, Larry Ridley, basses; Buzzy Drootin, Don Lamond, drums

Lee Wiley, vocals Accompanied by Bobby Hackett, cornet; Bucky Pizzarelli, guitar; Teddy Wilson, piano; George Duvivier, bass; Don Lamond, drums

World's Greatest Jazz Band Yank Lawson, trumpet; Bob Haggart, bass; Billy Butterfield, trumpet, flugelhorn; Vic Dickenson, Eddie Hubble, trombones; Bob Wilber, clarinet, soprano saxophone; Bud Freeman, tenor saxophone; Ralph Sutton, piano; Gus Johnson, drums

Thursday morning, July 6, 1972

Lincoln Center
Panel III: Social Science Research and Jazz—Past, Present, Future
Chairman: Charles Nanry, Rutgers University
Panelists: Gideon Vidgerhaus, Phillip S. Hughes, Sociology Department, Carlton College, Ottawa, Ontario, Canada; James Patrick, professor of music, Princeton University; David Cayer, Rutgers University

Thursday afternoon, July 6, 1972

Sacred Concert
Carnegie Hall

Dizzy Gillespie and John Motley and the New York All-City Choir

Dizzy Gillespie Sextet Dizzy Gillespie, trumpet; Al Gafa, guitar; Mike Longo, piano; Garry King, bass; Big Black, congas; Mickey Roker, drums

John Motley conducting the New York All-City Choir

Thursday evening, July 6, 1972

An Evening of New Orleans Jazz
Philharmonic Hall, two performances, 5:00 P.M. and 9:00 P.M.

Kid Thomas's Preservation Hall Band

De Jon's Olympia Brass Band

Papa French's Original Tuxedo Jazz Band
Including: Dave Bartholomew, Kid Thomas, Milton Batiste, Kid Sheik Cola, trumpets; Albert Burbank, Louis Nelson, Raymond Burke, clarinets; Emanuel Paul, tenor; Harold De Jon, alto; Bob Greene, piano; Andrew Jefferson, drums; Sweet Emma Barrett, the Bell Gal, piano and vocals; Ellyna Tatum, vocals and dancing
Anderson Miner, Fats Houston, grand marshals
Robert Pete Williams, guitar, vocals
Roosevelt Sykes, guitar, vocals

Carnegie Hall, two performances, 5:00 P.M. and 9:00 P.M.

Oscar, Cannonball and Mahavishnu Cannonball Adderley, alto; Nat Adderley, cornet; George Duke, keyboards; Walter Booker, bass; Roy McCurdy, drums

Oscar Peterson, solo piano

Mahavishnu Orchestra with John McLaughlin John McLaughlin, guitar; Jerry Goodman, violin; Jan Hammer, piano; Rick Laird, bass; Billy Cobham, drums

Midnight Jam Session II
Radio City Music Hall, July 6, 1972

Group 1 Cat Anderson, Jimmy Owens, trumpets; Buddy Tate, tenor; Charles McPherson, alto; Milt Buckner, organ; Roland Hanna, piano; Charlie Mingus, bass; Alan Dawson, drums

Group 2 Joe Newman, trumpet; Nat Adderley, flugelhorn; Illinois Jacquet, Budd Johnson, tenors; Gerry Mulligan, baritone; Tyree Glenn, trombone; Jaki Byard, piano; Chubby Jackson, bass; Elvin Jones, drums

Group 3 Clark Terry, Howard McGhee, trumpets; Sonny Stitt, Dexter Gordon, Zoot Sims, Rahsaan Roland Kirk, tenor, Stritch, Manzello and whistle; Kai Winding, trombone; Chuck Wayne, guitar; Herbie Hancock, piano; Larry Ridley, bass; Tony Williams, drums

Group 4 Curtis Mayfield, vocal, lead guitar; Master Henry Gibson, bongos, congas; Craig McMullen, guitar; Lucky Scott, bass; Scott Harris, drums

Friday morning, July 7, 1972

Lincoln Center 10:30 A.M.
Panel IV: Jazz As Recorded Art—1972
Chairman: William M. Weinberg, Rutgers University
Panelists: Don Schlitten, independent producer, Buddah/Cobblestone, MPS/BASF, RCA; George Butler, director, Blue Note Records; Orrin S. Keepnews, artists & repertoire director, Milestone Records; Dan Morgenstern, editor, Down Beat; Billy Taylor, musical director, co-owner radio station WSOK; Freddie Hubbard, musician

Friday afternoon, July 7, 1972

Interesting Directions
Carnegie Hall
Weather Report Wayne Shorter, soprano; Joe Zawinul, keyboards; Miroslav Vitous, bass; Eric Gravett, Don Um Romao, percussion, drums

Tony Williams Lifetime Tony Williams, drums; Khalid Yasin, organ; Tad Dunbar, percussion; Don Allas, percussion
Tepuilla, vocals, dancing

Roy Haynes Hip Ensemble Roy Haynes, drums; Marvin Peterson, trumpet; George Adams, tenor, bassoon; Cedric Lawson, Don Pate

Archie Shepp Quintet Clarence Sharpe, alto; Archie Shepp, reeds; Billy Green, Jan Hammer, piano; Charles Greenlee, trombone; Cal Massey, flugelhorn; Jimmy Garrison, bass; Beaver Harris, drums; Juma Sutan, Nene De Fänse, percussion; unknown added bass
China Lin, Waheeda, vocals

Friday evening, July 7, 1972

Yankee Stadium
Joe Newman, Clark Terry, trumpets; Illinois Jacquet, Zoot Sims, tenor; Jimmy Smith, organ; Kenny Burrell, B.B. King, guitar; Roy Haynes, drums

Ed Rowe, trumpet; Bobby Forte, tenor; Earle Turbinton, alto; Louis Hubert, baritone; Joseph Burton, trombone; B.B. King, vocals, guitar; Milton Hopkins, guitar; Ron Levy, piano; Wilbert Freeman, bass; Sonny Freeman, drums

Dave Brubeck Trio Dave Brubeck, piano; Jack Six, bass; Alan Dawson, drums
Guest artists: Paul Desmond, alto; Gerry Mulligan, baritone

Ray Charles and His Orchestra and the Raelettes, vocals

Saturday morning, July 8, 1972

Seminar
Lincoln Center
Panel V: Current Trends in Jazz Education
Chairman: Larry Ridley, chairman, music department, Livingston College, and jazz artist
Panelists: William Fowler, University of Utah; Alan Dawson, Berklee School of Music and jazz artist; Clem De Rosa, secondary school academician

Saturday afternoon, July 8, 1972

Connoisseur Concert D
Carnegie Hall

Duke Ellington and His Orchestra with Alumni Barney Bigard, clarinet; Sonny Greer, drums
Bobby Short, vocals, in a Tribute to Ivie Anderson
Accompanied by Beverly Peer, bass; Dick Sheridan, drums
Aura Rully, Betty Plummer, Anita Moore, vocals

Teremasa Hino Quintet from Japan Teremasa Hino, trumpet; Takao Uematsu, tenor; Kiyoshi Sugimoto, guitar; Miko Masuda, piano; Yoshio Ikeda, bass; Motohike Hino, drums

Saturday evening, July 8, 1972

Yankee Stadium

Herbie Mann, flute; David "Fathead" Newman, tenor; Paul Rebillot, electric piano; Sonny Sharrock, guitar; Andy Musson, bass; Reggie Ferguson, drums

Les McCann, vocals, piano; David Spinnoza, guitar; Jimmy Rouser, bass; Buck Clarke, congas; Donald Dean, drums

Dizzy Gillespie, trumpet; Sonny Stitt, tenor; Thelonious Monk, piano; Kai Winding, trombone; Al McKibbon, bass; Art Blakey, drums

Roberta Flack, vocals, piano; Eric Gayle, guitar; Richard Tee, electric piano; Tony Plumeri, bass;

Jerry Jemmott, fender bass; Ralph McDonald, percussion; Grady Tate, drums

Lou Rawls, vocals, with Orchestra

Sunday morning, July 9, 1972

Gospel Concert
Radio City Music Hall
Dorothy Love Coates, The Consolers, Jessy Dixon and The Dixon Singers, R.H. Harris and The Gospel Paraders, The Dixie Hummingbirds, Willie Mae Ford Smith, Marion Williams

Sunday afternoon, July 9, 1972

Brooklyn Museum, Brooklyn, N.Y.
Papa French and His Tuxedo New Orleans Jazz Band; Harold Dejan's Olympia Brass Band; Afri-Asian Jas Musiq; Ethno Media Ensemble; The Funky Latin Ensemble; The Muse Combo; Malumbo; The Reverend Kirkpatrick; The Brooklyn Heights Youth Center Steel Band; The Children of God; Robert Pete Williams and Ron Williams; Glory Van Scott; The Shells S Singers

Sunday evening, July 9, 1972

St. Peter's Luthern Church

Spiritual Concert

Max Roach and the J.C. White Singers With Billy Harper, tenor; Stanley Cowell, piano; Cecil Bridgewater, trumpet; Reggie Workman, bass

Friday afternoon, June 29, 1973

Woolman Amphitheater, Central Park

Gerry Mulligan's Age of Steam Gerry Mulligan, baritone sax; Art Farmer, Jimmy Owens, flugelhorns; Joe Newman, Jon Faddis, trumpets; Bob Brookmeyer, Wayne Andre, trombones; Pete Phillips, bass trombone; Jim Buffington, French horn; Tony Price, tuba; Frank Wess, Tom Scott, Al Klink, Wally Kane, saxes; Sam Brown, guitar; Joe Venuto, vibes and percussion; Hank Jones, electric piano; Chuck Israels, bass; Bill Goodwin, drums

Margie Joseph, vocals, accompanied by Willie Tee and the Gators

The Newport Ensemble George Wein, piano; Roland Price, guitar; James Spaulding, reeds and flute; Larry Ridley, bass; Al Harewood, drums

Charles Lloyd Quintet Charles Lloyd, tenor, flute; Steve McKnight, guitar; Sherman McKinney, bass; Woody Theus, percussion

Gato Barbieri, Latin America Gato Barbieri, tenor; Domingo Cura, bomba, indio; Kuelo Palacio, guitar and charango; Raul Mercado, quena; Amadeo Monks, guarani harp; Adleberto Cebasco, bass

Friday evening, June 29, 1973

Carnegie Hall

The Benny Goodman Quartet Benny Goodman, clarinet; Lionel Hampton, vibes; Teddy Wilson, piano; Gene Krupa, drums
Guest artist: Slam Stewart, bass

The Ruby Braff-George Barnes Quartet Ruby Braff, cornet; George Barnes, guitar; John Giuffrida, bass; Wayne Wright, guitar

Philharmonic Hall, Lincoln Center, 6:00 P.M. and 10:00 P.M.

B.B. King Blues Barn Clarence "Gatemouth" Brown, vocals; Arthur "Big Boy" Crudup, guitar, vocals; Lloyd Glenn, B.B. King, guitar, vocals; Jay McShann Trio, Big Mama Willie Mae Thornton, vocals; Joe Turner, vocals; Eddie "Cleanhead" Vinson, alto; Muddy Waters Blues Band, Lloyd Glenn, piano

Saturday Morning, June 30, 1973

Frontiers in Jazz Research and Disco 73
Library and Museum of Performing Arts: How Goes The Blues? Robert F. Green, Phyl Garland, Dr. Leonard Goines, Atente (Frederick Roach), B.B. King.

Saturday afternoon, June 30, 1976

Wollman Amphitheater, Central Park

Guitar Explosion George Barnes, Chuck Wayne—Joe Puma Duo, George Benson and rhythm section, Jim Hall–Tal Farlow with Jay Leonhart, fender bass; Tiny Grimes and rhythm section, Alhaje Bai Konte, Kora; Pat Marino, Larry Coryell and Foreplay Quartet, Roy Buchanan

Saturday evening, June 30, 1973

Atlantic Records presents two concerts
Carnegie Hall, 6:00 P.M. and 10:00 P.M.

Donny Hathaway Donny Hathaway, piano, electric piano, vocals plus rhythm section

Herbie Mann Quintet Herbie Mann, flutes; David "Fathead" Newman, tenor, flute; Gerry Friedman, Bob Mann, guitar; Pat Rebillot, piano; Willie Weeks, bass; Carlos "Patato" Valdez, conga; Andrew Smith, drums

Carnegie Hall, 10:00 P.M.

Donny Hathaway

Black Heat Leon Rodney Edwards, trumpet; Raymond Lee Thompson, tenor; Bradley Owens, guitar; Johnell Gray, piano; Naamon Jones, bass; Esco Cromer, drums; Raymond Green, percussion, with David Newman, saxes & flute

Philharmonic Hall, Lincoln Center, 7:30 P.M.

Sonny Rollins Quintet Sonny Rollins, tenor; Walter Davis, Jr., piano; Masuo, guitar; James Leary, bass; David Lee, drums

Mary Lou Williams Trio Mary Lou Williams, piano; with bass and drums

Keith Jarrett, solo piano

New York Musicians Jazz Festival
Alice Tully Hall, 1 Performance
Roy Brooks Artist Truth, Ray Nance Quintet, Charlie Rouse Quartet, Stars of Afrika, We Music House

Carnegie Recital Hall, 1 Performance
Carnegie Corporation Presents

Jazz—The New Generation Valerie Capers Conducting the Manhattan Contemporary Jazz Ensemble Workshop—15 musicians, 11 singers from the Manhattan School of Music
Valerie Capers, piano, with guests Lysle Atkinson, bass; Al Harewood, drums

Midnight Jam Session Radio City Music Hall Roy Ayers, Gato Barbieri, Ed Blackwell, Bobby Brookmeyer, Garnett Brown, Marion Brown, Don Cherry, Jimmy Garrison, Stan Getz, Milford Graves, Charles Haden, Roy Haynes, Joe Henderson, Freddie Hubbard, Howard Johnson, Elvin Jones, Rahsaan Roland Kirk, Herbie Mann, Cecil McBee, Gerry Mulligan, David Newman, Jimmy Owens, Marvin Peterson, Sam Rivers, Zoot Sims, Archie Shepp, Clark Terry, Cedar Walton. Reggie Workman, bass; Tom Scott, tenor; Roland Hanna, piano; Dizzy Gillespie, trumpet; Anita O'Day, vocals, accompanied by Jimmy Rowles, piano; Earl "Fatha" Hines, piano; John Mayall, guitar, vocals; Louis Jordan, alto; Tiny Grimes, guitar; Jeremy Steig, flute; Ralph Townes, guitar; John Faddis, trumpet

Sunday, July 1, 1973

Staten Island Ferry, 10:30 A.M., 1:00 P.M., 3:30 P.M.

Hudson River Boatride

The Percy Humphrey Preservation Hall Band from New Orleans Percy Humphrey, trumpet; Albert Burbank, clarinet; Frank Demond, trombone; Narvin Kimball, banjo; James "Sing" Miller, piano; Chester Zardis, bass; Dave Oxley, drums

The Drootin Bros. Band Al Drootin, tenor sax & Clarinet, and Buzzy Drootin, drums

Sunday evening, July 1, 1973

Joseph Schlitz Brewing Company Salutes The Life and Times of Ray Charles
Carnegie Hall, two performances
Written and arranged by James Baldwin and featuring **Ray Charles and His Orchestra**
Special guest artists: Cicely Tyson, David Baldwin, David Moses

Philharmonic Hall, two concerts
Duke Ellington and His Orchestra Duke Ellington, piano; Cootie Williams, Harold "Money" Johnson, Johnny Coles, Mercer Ellington, trumpets; Murray McEachern, Vince Prudente, Chuck Connors, trombones; Harold "Geezil" Minerve, Russell

Procope, Paul Gonsalves, Harold Ashby, Harry Carney, reeds; Joe Benjamin, bass; Rufus Jones, drums; Nita Moore, Tony Watkins, Alice Babs, vocals

Mandrill   Ric "Doc" Wilson, tenor sax, percussion, vocals; Claude Cave, organ; Omar Mesa, guitar; Lou Wilson, congas, trumpet; Carlos Wilson, trombone, flute, alto sax, guitar, timbales; Fudgie Kae, bass; Neftali Santiago, drums

Alice Tully Hall
New York Musicians Five Boroughs Jazz Festival   Aboriginal Music Society, Ken McIntyre Quartet. Rene McLean Quartet. Marvin Peterson's Hannibal. Joe Lee Wilson plus four

St. Peter's Lutheran Church, 8:00 P.M.
Max Roach's Freedom Now Suite

Carnegie Recital Hall, 8:00 P.M.
The Carnegie Hall Corporation Presents Jazz— The New Generation

Steve Kuhn Quartet   Steve Kuhn, clarinet; Ron McClure, bass; Bruce Ditmas, drums; Sue Evans, percussion

Zane Massey Sextet

Monday morning, July 2, 1973

The Rutgers Institute of Jazz Studies at Newark in association with the Institute of Pan African Culture at the University of Massachusetts in Amherst present a series of concerts called **Frontiers in Jazz and Discon 73**
Library and Museum of Performing Arts
10 AM: Profile—Billie Holiday   Christopher White, Johnetta B. Cole, Nat Hentoff, Albert Murray, William Dufty

1 PM: A.B. Spellman, Milt Gabler, Ram Ramirez, Hazel Scott, Artie Shaw

3 PM: Motion Picture Images of Billie Holiday

Monday afternoon, July 2, 1973

Wollman Amphitheater, Central Park
An Afternoon of Jazz for Children and Adults

Fran Allison

Charles Mingus Quintet   Charles Mingus, bass; Ronald Hampton, trumpet; Bobby Mover, alto sax; George Adams, tenor sax; Don Pullen, piano; Roy Brooks, drums

Don Cherry and the Organic Music Theater   Don Cherry, pocket trumpet

Professor Longhair, piano, vocals

Snooks Eaglin

Milt Buckner–Jo Jones Duo, organ, drums, plus tap dancers Baby Laurence, Buster Brown, Chuck Green, John McPhee, L.D. Jackson

Monday evening, July 2, 1973

Carnegie Recital Hall, One Performance
Jazz—The New Generation
Music Workshop of Staten Island with Kenny Washington, drums

Apollo Theater, 7:00 P.M.
Herbie Mann

Horace Arnold

Howard McGhee Orchestra

Roseland Ballroom, 9:00 P.M.
A Thirties Ball

Duke Ellington and His Orchestra

Count Basie and his Orchestra   Count Basie, piano; Sonny Cohn, Waymon Reed, Pete Minger, Steve Furtado, trumpets; Mel Wanzo, Bill Hughes, Frank Hooks, Henry Coker, trombones; Bobby Plater, Eric Dixon, Curtis Peagler, John Williams, Eddie "Lockjaw" Davis, saxophones; Freddie Green, guitar; Norman Keenan, bass; Sonny Payne, drums; Jimmy Ricks, vocals

Woody Herman and The Young Thundering Herd   Woody Herman, clarinet, alto sax, vocals; Bill Byrne, William Blanton, Gil Rathel, Bill Stapleton, R. Kindred, trumpets; Jimmy Pugh, Harold Garrett, G. Sharp, trombones; Frank Tiberi, Greg Herbert, J. Lowther, L. Pyatt, saxophones; Andy Laverne, piano; Wayne Darling, bass; Ed Soph, drums

Fashion Show   sponsored by the Wool Bureau, *Harper's Bazaar* and the Arthur Murray Dance Studio. Choreographed by the Arthur Murray Dance Studio. Guest of honor: Andy Kirk

Tuesday afternoon, July 3, 1973

Wollman Amphitheater, Central Park, 1:00 P.M.

Mose Allison Trio

Stan Getz Quartet   Stan Getz, tenor sax; Richie Beirach, piano; Dave Holland, bass; Jack De Johnette, drums

Marian McPartland Trio

Modern Jazz Quartet   Milt Jackson, vibes; John Lewis, piano; Percy Heath, bass; Connie Kay, drums

Tuesday morning, July 3, 1973

Frontiers in Jazz and Discon 73—Library and Museum of Performing Arts

Jazz As Recorded Art Form   Richard Seidel, Teo Macero, Carla Bley, Vic Chirumbalo, Stanley Cowell, Mike Cuscuna, Joe Fields, J.R. Taylor

Symposium on the Sociological and Social Science Aspects of Jazz Research   Charles Nanry, Monroe Berger, Acklyn Lynch, Billy Taylor, Irving Louis Horowitz, Max Roach, James Turner, William Quinn

Tuesday evening, July 3, 1973

Carnegie Hall, 6:00 P.M. and 10:00 P.M.
American Airlines Salute to Count Basie—Now and in Retrospect

Count Basie and His Orchestra Today   Joe Williams, Helen Humes, vocals

Reunion of the Great 1950s Basie Band   Jon Faddis, Sonny Cohen, Thad Jones (on early concert only), trumpets; Al Grey, Henry Coker, Benny Powell, trombones; Marshall Royal, Ernie Wilkins, Frank Wess, Frank Foster, Charlie Fowlkes, reeds; Freddie Green, guitar; Eddie Jones, bass; Sonny Payne, drums

Apollo Theater, 6:00 P.M.
Irene Reid
Dizzy Gillespie Quintet
Kenny Burrell Trio

Apollo Theater, 10:00 P.M.
Charles Mingus
Rod Rodgers Dance Company
Junior Mance Trio

Philharmonic Hall, one Performance
A Jazz Salute to the American Song

Irving Berlin   Jimmy McPartland, cornet; Herbie Hall, clarinet; Vic Dickenson, trombone; Al Hall, bass; Art Hodes, piano; Al Harewood, drums

Fats Waller   Earl Hines, piano; Al Casey, guitar

Cole Porter   Teddi King, vocals; Ellis Larkins, piano

Duke Ellington—Billy Strayhorn   Rahsaan Roland Kirk, reeds; Marian McPartland, piano; Larry Ridley, bass; Al Harewood, drums

Harold Arlen   Barbara Carroll, piano; Sylvia Syms, vocals

Gershwin   Modern Jazz Quartet

Jimmy van Heusen   Dave Brubeck, piano

Rodgers and Hart   Mabel Mercer, vocals, accompanied by Stan Getz, tenor

Alec Wilder   Gerry Mulligan, baritone

Alice Tully Hall, 7:00 P.M.
New York Musicians Jazz Festival
Caravan, Ted Daniel Quintet, Clifford Jordan Quintet, Earl Cross Nonette, Danny Mixon

Shea Stadium, 8:00 P.M.
Soul Session at Newport
Stevie Wonder, Staple Singers, Ramsey Lewis Trio, Billy Paul, Grover Washington Quartet

Wednesday, July 4, 1973

Louis Armstrong Stadium, 1:00 P.M.
Jazz Jamboree, A Tribute to Louis Armstrong Count Basie, Darius Brubeck, Dave Brubeck, Cab Calloway, Barbara Carroll, Al Casey, Doc Cheatham, Cozy Cole, Eddie "Lockjaw" Davis, Wild Bill Davison, Vic Vic Dickenson, Drootin Bros., Roy Eldridge, Ella Fitzgerald, Stan Getz, Dizzy Gillespie, Tyree Glenn, Al Grey, Tiny Grimes, Herb Hall, Earl Hines, Art Hodes, Freddie Hubbard, Helen Humes, Elvin Jones, Max Kaminsky, Emme Kemp, Gene Krupa, Ellis Larkins, Yank Lawson, Howard McGhee, Dave McKenna, Marian McPartland, Jimmy McPartland, John Mayall, Turk Murphy, Ray Nance, Marty Napoleon, Joe Newman, Anita O'Day, Larry Ridley, Sam Rivers, Jimmy Rowles, Arvell Shaw, Archie Shepp, James Spaulding, Sun Ra, Billy Taylor, Clark Terry, Sarah Vaughan, Eddie Vinson, Grover Washington, Bob Wilber, Cootie Williams, Joe Williams, Reggie Workman, Al Cobetti, George Kirby, Eubie Blake.

Carnegie Hall, 6:00 P.M. and 10:00 P.M.
Michel Legrand and His Orchestra
Sarah Vaughan, vocals, with rhythm section
Guest artist: Stan Getz

Tom Scott's L.A. Express Scott, tenor sax; Larry Carlton; guitar, Joe Sample, piano; Max Bennett, bass; John Guerin, drums

Philharmonic Hall, 6:00 P.M. and 10:00 P.M.
New Orleans, Ragtime and Stride

Percy Humphrey Preservation Hall Band

Joe Turner, Wally Rose, pianos

Turk Murphy Septet Turk Murphy, trombone; Bob Helm, clarinet & soprano sax; Leon Oakley, cornet; Bill Carroll, tuba; Carl Lunsford, banjo; Peter Clute, piano; Jimmy Stanislaus, vocals

The Music of Jelly Roll Morton as played by the Bob Green Orchestra Bob Green, piano; Herb Hall, clarinet; Ephie Resnick, trombone; Ernie Carson, trumpet; Danny Barker, banjo; Milt Hinton, bass; Tommy Benford, drums

Apollo Theater, 7:00 P.M.
Dakota Staton

Two Generations of Brubeck

Art Blakey

Alice Tully Hall, 7:00 P.M.
New York Musicians Jazz Festival

Walter Bishop, Jr., Trio; Norman Connors and The Dance of Magic, featuring Jean Carn, vocals; Paul Bley Trio; Paul Jeffrey Quintet

Shea Stadium, 8:00 P.M.
Jazz at Shea

War, Roberta Flack, Freddie Hubbard Quintet, Rahsaan Roland Kirk & The Vibration Society, Jimmy Witherspoon with Robin Ford, guitar

Thursday, July 5, 1973

Library and Museum of Performing Arts
Frontiers in Jazz Research and Discon 73

The Drum Max Roach, Jo Jones, Archie Shepp, John Bracey, Bill Hasan, Dr. John Lovell Jr., Dan Morgenstern, Fred Tillis

The Dialectic of Sound—Charlie Parker, John Coltrane Acklyn Lynch, Maxine Roach, Bill Cole, Dizzy Gillespie, Archie Shepp

Wollman Amphitheater, Central Park, 1:00 P.M.

Art Ensemble of Chicago Lester Bowie, trumpet; Roscow Mitchell, Joseph Jarman, reeds; Malachi Favors, bass; Don Moye, drums

Sam Rivers Trio Sam Rivers, tenor sax, soprano sax, flute, piano; Richard Davis, bass; Norman Connors, drums, vibes, tympani & assorted percussion instruments

Ray Barretto and His Orchestra

Archie Shepp Tentet Archie Shepp, tenor & soprano saxes; Grachan Moncur, trombone; Dave Burrell, piano; Jimmy Garrison, bass; Beaver Harris, drums

Carnegie Hall, 7:30 P.M.
Salute to Ella Fitzgerald With Ella Fitzgerald, Ellis Larkins, Roy Eldridge, Eddie "Lockjaw"

Davis, Al Grey and the Chick Webb Orchestra under the direction of Eddie Barefield: Dick Vance, Taft Jordan, Francis Williams, Frank Lo Pinto, trumpets; George Matthews, Al Cobbs, Garnett Brown, Jack Jeffers, trombones; Chauncey Haughton, Pete Clark, Arthur Clark, Bob Ashton, Heywood Henry, reeds; Cliff Smalls, piano; Larry Lucie, Eldridge Davis, Al Grey, Tommy Flanagan, Joe Pass, guitar; Beverly Peer, Keter Betts, bass; Freddie Watts, Panama Francis, drums

Apollo Theater, 7:00 P.M.
Carmen McRae, Rahsaan Roland Kirk, Roy Haynes Hip Ensemble, Jazz Opera Ensemble, Louis Jordan

Philharmonic Hall, Two Performances, 6: P.M. and 10:00 P.M.
The Tea Council of the U.S. Presents
John Mayall Jazz and Blues Fusion John Mayall, harmonica, guitar, piano, vocals; Blue Mitchell, trumpet, flugelhorn; Red Holloway, tenor sax; Freddie Robinson, guitar; Victor Gaskin, bass; Keef Hartley, drums

Plus National Winners of the Tea Talent Search—The Lightmen Plus One, from Houston, Texas; Petrus, from Rochester, N.Y.; Electric Black, from Denver, Colorado

Chuck Mangione Chuck Mangione, flugelhorn; Gerry Niewood, sax and flute; Al Johnson, bass; Joe La Barbera, drums

John Blair John Blair, sitar; Bob Sardo, electric piano; John Miller, bass; Jerry Herskovitz, drums; Daniel Benzebulun, conga

Carnegie Recital Hall, 8:00 P.M.
The Carnegie Hall Corporation Presents
Jazz—The New Generation
Ken Smickle Quintet, The Brotherhood of Sound, The Nia Ensemble

Friday, July 6, 1973

Wollman Amphitheater, Central Park, 12 Noon

Two Generations of Brubeck with the Dave Brubeck Trio Dave Brubeck, piano; Jack Six, bass; Alan Dawson, drums
Guest artist: Paul Desmond

The Darius Brubeck Ensemble Darius Brubeck, keyboards; Chris Brubeck, trombone, electric bass; Perry Robinson, clarinet; Sam Bergonzi,

tenor sax; David Dutemple, electric bass; Mickey Roker, drums

Dizzy Gillespie Quintet Dizzy Gillespie, trumpet; Al Gafa, guitar; Mike Longo, piano; Earl May, bass; Mickey Roker, drums

Hubert Laws Septet

Carmen McRae

Alice Tully Hall, 1:00 P.M.
Youth and Jazz

Jazz Interactions Workshop Orchestra
Twenty-seven pieces directed by Joe Newman

The Jazzmobile Workshop Orchestra
Directed by bassist Paul West

All-City High School Jazz Orchestra
Directed by Clem De Rosa and Marian McPartland
Guest artist: Sonny Stitt, alto

The Brooklyn Boroughwide Chorus and Band
Conducted by Eddie Bonnemere

Carnegie Hall, 6:00 P.M. and 10:00 P.M.
6:00 P.M. Special Concert
Sun Ra and his Space Arkestra Sun Ra, space organ; John Gilmore, tenor sax; Pat Patrick, baritone sax; Danny Thompson, baritone sax, flute; Danny Davis, Marshall Allen, Larry Worthington, Leroy Taylor, reeds; Akh-tal-Ebah, trumpet, flugelhorn; Lamont McClamb, trumpet; Lex Humphries, Alzo Wright, drums; Stanley Morgan, Russell Branch, percussion; Robert Underwood, Harry Richards, space drums; June Tyson, Judith Holton, Cheryl Bank, Ruth Wright, vocals

10:00 P.M. Jazz Cabaret
Cab Calloway and the Reunion of the Cab Calloway Orchestra With Dizzy Gillespie, Doc Cheatham, Johnny Letman, Mario Bauza, trumpets; Tyree Glenn, Quentin "Butter" Jackson, George Matthews, trombones; Eddie Barfield, Pete Clark, Walter "Foots" Thomas, Illinois Jacquet, Sam "The Man" Taylor, Heywood Henry, reeds; Cliff Smalls, piano; Danny Barker, guitar; Milt Hinton, bass; Cozy Cole, drums
Nellie Lutcher
Louis Jordan and his Tympany Five

280

Esther Phillips
Honi Coles and the Copasetics
Tyree Glenn Quartet

Philharmonic Hall, 7:30 P.M.
Return to Forever Chick Corea, electric piano;
Bill Connors, electric guitar; Stanley Clarke, electric bass and acoustic bass; Lenny White, drums;
Mingo Lewis, percussion

Weather Report Wayne Shorter, saxes; Joe Zawinul, keyboards; Miroslav Vitous, bass; Eric Gravatt, drums; Dom Um Romao, percussion

Apollo Theater, 6:00 P.M.
Max Roach, Ruth Brown, Robin Kenyatta

Apollo Theater, 10:00 P.M.
Elvin Jones; Eleo Pomare Dance Company;
Charles Earland Trio; Stan Getz

Alice Tully Hall, 7:00 P.M.
New York Musicians Jazz Festival
Milford Graves, Byard Lancaster, Leon Thomas,
Melodic Artet
Dave Burrell Quintet

Radio City Music Hall, 12 Midnight
Midnight Jam Session II
Walter Bishop, Art Blakey, Larry Coryell, Eddie
Daniels, John Faddis, Art Farmer, Curtis Fuller,
Dizzy Gillespie, Eddie Gomez, Tiny Grimes, Barry
Harris, Jimmy Heath, Earl Hines, Milt Hinton, Louis
Jordan, Eric Kloss, Lee Konitz, Mel Lewis, John
Mayall, Blue Mitchell, Marty Morrell, George Mraz,
Cecil Payne, Larry Ridley, Red Rodney, Sonny
Stitt, Ralph Towner, Eddie "Cleanhead" Vinson,
Bill Watrous, and special guest Miss Anita O'Day

Saturday July 7, 1973

Library and Musum of the Performing Arts
Frontiers in Jazz Research and Discon 73

10 A.M.: jazz Education Larry Ridley, Charles
Suber, David Baker

1 P.M.: Educators Workshop David Baker, Larry
Ridley, Ted Dunbar; The Verona High School

Staten Island Ferry Slip No. 3, 10:30 A.M., 1:00 P.M.,
3:30 P.M.
Hudson River Boatride

Olympia Brass Band from New Orleans Harold
Dejan, alto sax; Emanuel Paul, tenor sax; Milton
Batiste, George "Kid Sheik" Cola, Edmond Foucher, trumpets; William Brown, tuba; Paul Crawford, Gerald Joseph, trombones; Nowell "Papa"
Glass, bass drum; Andrew Jefferson, snare drum;
Anderson Minor, grand marshal

Wild Bill Davison Sextet Wild Bill Davison, cornet; Jerry Fuller, clarinet; Eddie Hubble, trombone; Claude Hopkins, piano; George Duvivier,
bass; Cliff Leeman, drums

Wollman Ampitheater, Central Park, 12 Noon
Drum Shtick

Part I: Art Blakey and his Jazz Messengers Bill
Hardman, trumpet; Carter Jefferson, tenor sax;
Cedar Walton, piano; Mickey Bass, bass; with special guest Roy Haynes, drums; Sonny Stitt, alto,
tenor

Part II: Gretsch Greats Elvin Jones, Jo Jones,
Mel Lewis, Freddie Waits, Tony Williams, with
Tequila, vocals

Part III: M'Boom With Roy Brooks, Joe Chambers, Omar Clay, Max Roach, Warren Smith, Freddie Waits

**Part IV: Randy Weston's African
Rhythms** eighteen-piece orchestra

Saturday evening, July 7, 1973

Carnegie Hall

So-Lo Piano
Dedicated to Art Tatum With pianists Bill Evans,
Earl Hines, Art Hodes, Ellis Larkins, Brooks Kerr,
Dave McKenna, Jimmy Rowles, George Shearing,
Billy Taylor, and special guest Eubie Blake

Philharmonic Hall, 7:30 P.M.
Airto Airto Moreira, percussion; David Amaro,
guitar; Flora Purim, vocals and acoustic guitar;
Hugo Satorusso, organ; Hugo Thielmann, bass;
Jorge Satorusso, drums

Roy Ayers and Ubiquity

Doug Kershaw Country Jazz Doug Kershaw, violin; Vernon Pilder, electric steel guitar; Ty Corbett,
bass; Billy Tubb, drums

Alice Tully Hall, 7:00 P.M.
New York Musicians Five Boroughs Jazz Festival
Abdulla, Joe Rigby–Chris Capers, Hakim Jami Sextet, Frank Foster, Noah Howard's Black Ensemble

Carnegie Recital Hall, 8:00 P.M.
Carnegie Hall Corporation Presents
Jazz—The New Generation
Natural Essence, Safari East

Sunday evening, July 8, 1973

Nassau Coliseum, 8:00 P.M.

Jazz and Soul on the Island: Tito Puente and His
Orchestra; Duke Ellington and His Orchestra;
Ray Charles and His Orchestra; Donny Hathaway; Special Guest Star Aretha Franklin, vocals,
with orchestra, string section; The Prima Donnas,
vocals, dancing

Frontiers in Jazz Research and Discon 73
Sixth Annual Conference on Discographical Research. Hickman Hall, Douglass College, New
Brunswick, N.J.

Saturday, July 7

10: A.M.: Voice Print Techniques for Identification
of Jazz Soloists, Lawrence G. Kersta; Danceband
Orchestrations, Tony Hagert

1:30 P.M.: the Goldkette, Whiteman and Pollack
Bands Bill Challis, Chauncey Morehouse, Jimmy
McPartland

3:30 P.M.: Profile—Bessie Smith Chris Albertson,
Jack Gee, Jr., Alberta Hunter

7 P.M.: films from the collection of Ernie Smith

Friday, June 28, 1974

Pope Auditorium, Fordham University, 2:00 P.M.
A Tribute to Dizzy Gillespie
The C.B.A. Ensemble under the direction of Jimmy
Owens
Featured guest soloist: Sonny Stitt

Carnegie Hall, 7:30 P.M. and 11:30 P.M.
New York Jazz Repertory Company
The Musical Life of Charlie Parker: Kansas City,
The Roots: Jay McShann; The Emergence: Earl
Hines and Billy Eckstine; New York, the Bebop
Explosion: Dizzy Gillespie; The Culmination:

Parker with strings; The Disciples: Sonny Stitt,
Phil Woods and Charles McPerson with members
of the NYJRC. Willis Conover, compere.

Saturday afternoon, June 29, 1974

Music of The New Breed

Norman Connor's Dance of Magic Norman Connors, drums; "Hannibal" Marvin Peterson, trumpet; Carlos Garnett, tenor; Lawrence Kilian,
congas; Don Pate, bass; Elmer Gilyon, tilos,
sampa, percussion
Jean Carn, vocals

Roland Hanna's New York Jazz 4 Roland Hanna,
piano; Frank Wess, flute, reeds; Ron Carter, bass;
Ben Riley, drums

Dewey Redman 5

Michael Urbaniak Michael Urbaniak, violin; Urszula Dudziak, keyboards; Pawdl
Jarzebski, bass; Czeloaw Barikowski, drums

Carnegie Hall, 8:00 P.M.
Schlitz Salute to Cafe Society
Honorary Guest: Barney Josephson

Teddy Wilson Sextet Teddy Wilson, piano; Doc
Cheatham, trumpet; Vic Dickenson, trombone;
Milt Hinton, bass; Teddy Wilson, Jr., drums; Kenny
Davern, soprano

Sammy Price, solo piano Rose Murphy, piano,
vocals Dorothy Donegan, solo piano The Dixie
Hummingbirds Thelma Carpenter, vocals Timmie Rogers, MC, comedian

Avery Fisher Hall, 8:00 P.M.
Nina An evening with Nina Simone, vocals, piano

Saturday, June 29, 1974

Pope Auditorium, 2:00 P.M.

Babs Gonzales Expubidence Featuring Cecil
Payne, baritone; Harold Maybern, piano; Chris Fuller, trombone; Wilbur Little, bass; Sonny Brown,
drums

Radio City Music Hall, Midnight
Midnight Jam Session
Part 1: Jam for Duke Elek Bacsik, John Blair,

Garry Burton, Roy Eldridge, Art Farmer, Stan Getz, Dizzy Gillespie, Roy Haynes, Earl "Fatha" Hines, Budd Johnson, Gerry Mulligan, Larry Ridley, Jimmy Smith, Sonny Stitt, Freddie Waits, Bill Watrous, Teddy Wilson, Phil Woods, and others

Part 2: Blues at Two Mike Bloomfield, Paul Butterfield, Helen Humes, Danny Kalb, Jack McDuff, Jay McShann, David Bromberg, Patti Bowen and others

Sunday, June 30, 1974

Carnegie Hall, 7:30 P.M.
Solo Piano I
Eubie Blake, Bill Evans, Johnny Guarnieri, Eddie Heywood, Jess Stacy, Dick Wellstood, Teddy Wilson, and hostess Marian McPartland

Carnegie Hall, 11:30 P.M.
Solo Piano II
Herbie Hancock, Keith Jarrett, and McCoy Tyner

Avery Fisher Hall, 7:30 P.M. and 11:30 P.M.
The King's Road, Highway 61: An Evening of the Blues Buddy Guy and Junior Wells, Hammie Nixon and Sleepy John Estes, B.B. King, Johnny Shines
Linda Hopkins, vocals

Bobby Blues Band with Mel Jackson and The Mellow Fellows

Monday, July 1, 1974

Pope Auditorium, Fordham University, 2:00 P.M.

Teo Macero Teo Macero, Phil Woods, Lee Konitz, alto; George Young, Don Palmer, Stan Getz, tenor; Gerry Mulligan, baritone; Dick Katz, piano; Mike Moore, bass; Joe Beck, guitar; Teddi King, vocals

Milford Graves Trio Milford Graves, drums; Art Williams, trumpet; Hugh Glover, saxophone

Carnegie Hall, One Performance, 8:00 P.M.
Jazz on the Hammond Jimmy Smith, Wild Bill Davis, Charles Earland, Don Lewis, Jack McDuff, and Shirley Scott

Roseland Ballroom, 9:00 P.M.
Jose Cuervo Big Band Ball Dance to the music of Harry James and His Orchestra and Sy Oliver

and His Orchestra, plus Tito Puente and His Orchestra in a special salute to Latin Jazz.

Tuesday, July 2, 1974

Pope Auditorium, Fordham University 2:00 P.M.

The Vic Dickenson All-Stars Featuring Budd Johnson, soprano, tenor; Hank Jones, piano; Joe Newman, trumpet; Larry Ridley, bass; Jackie Williams, drums

The Wild Magnolias

Carnegie Hall, One Performance, 7:30 P.M.
Lionel Hampton Presents
Harry James and His Orchestra

Lionel Hampton Quartet Lionel Hampton, vibes; Teddy Wilson, piano; Milt Hinton, bass; Buddy Rich, drums

Carnegie Hall, One Performance, 11:30 P.M.
The Byrd and the Headhunter

Herbie Hancock 5 Herbie Hancock, piano; Bennie Maupin, reeds; Bill Summers, conga, percussion; Paul Jackson, bass; Michael Clark, drums

The Donald Byrd 7 Donald Byrd, trumpet; Allan Curtis Barnes, tenor and soprano saxophones, flute; Kevin Kraig Ioney, keyboards; Barney Perry, guitar; Pericles "Perk" Jacobs, Jr., percussion; Keith Killgo, drums; Joe Hall III, bass

Avery Fisher Hall, One Performance, 7:30 P.M.
Keith & Gary

Keith Jarrett Quintet Keith Jarrett, piano, wood flute, soprano saxophone, primitive xylophone; Dewey Redman, reeds; Charlie Haden, bass; Paul Motian, drums; Guilherme Franco, percussion

The Chamber Orchestra, directed by Arnold Eldus Keith Jarrett joins orchestra with Paul Motian, drums

Gary Burton 4 Gary Burton, vibes; Mike Goodrich, guitar; Ted Seibs, drums; Steve Swallow, bass
Guest artist: Ralph Towner, guitar

Avery Fisher Hall, 11:30 P.M.
A Schlitz Salute to the Divine Sarah
Sarah Vaughan, vocals

Wednesday, July 3, 1974

Pope Auditorium, Fordham University, 2:00 P.M.

The Jazz Professors Bill Baron, Ray Copeland, Bill Dixon, Ted Dunbar, Ken McIntyre, Jimmy Owens, Larry Ridley, and Freddie Waits

The Paul Jeffrey Octet

Carnegie Hall, 7:30 P.M.
Chick and Gato

Gato Barbieri Ensemble Gato Barbieri, tenor; Eddy Martinez, piano; Paul Metzke, electric guitar; Howard Johnson, bass, tuba; Portinho, drums; Ray Mantilla, conga, timbaleta; Ray Armando, conga, percussion

Chick Corea—Return to Forever Chick Corea, piano; Bill Connors, electric guitar; Stanley Clarke, bass; Lenny White, drums

Carnegie Hall, 11:30 P.M.
Mingus, Max, and The Messengers

Charlie Mingus Quintet Charlie Mingus, bass; George Adams, tenor; Hamiel Bluitt, baritone; Don Pullen, piano; Dannie Richmond, drums

Max Roach 4

Art Blakey and The Jazz Messengers Art Blakey, drums; Olu Dara, trumpet; Carter Jefferson, tenor saxophone; Cedric Lawson, piano; Stafford L. James, bass

Avery Fisher Hall, 7:30 P.M. and 11:30 P.M.
A Schlitz Salute to Jazz and The American Song
MC Dave Garroway
A Salute to Fred Astaire

Ruby Braff—George Barnes Quartet Ruby Braff, cornet; George Barnes, guitar; Wayne Wright, second guitar; Mike Moore, bass

Duke Ellington–Billy Strayhorn Music Bobby Short, vocals, with rhythm section

Alec Wilder Music Jackie Cain, Roy Kral, vocals; Roy Kral, piano

Kurt Weil Music Gerry Mulligan, baritone

Richard Rodgers Music Johnny Mathis, vocals, with quartet

Bart Howard Music

Mabel Mercer, vocals Accompanied by Jimmy Lyon, piano; joined by Johnny Mathis

Nassau Veterans Memorial Coliseum, One Performance, 8:00 P.M.
A Schlitz Salute to Jazz and Soul Gladys Knight and the Pips, the O'Jays, Billy Eckstine, Kool & the Gang, Tower of Power

Tower of Power Lenny Williams, lead vocals; Lenny Pickett, tenor sax, flute, vocals; Emilio Castillo, tenor sax, vocals; Steve Kupka, sax, vocals; Greg Adams, trumpet, flugelhorn, vocals; Mic Gillette, trumpet, trombone, vocals; Bruce Conte, guitar, vocals; Chester Thompson, organ, piano, vocals; Frank Prestia, bass; David Garibaldi, drums; Brent Byars, conga drums

Gladys Knight and the Pips Gladys Knight, Merald Knight, William Guest, Edward Patten

The O'Jays Eddie Levert, Walter Williams, William Powell

Kool and the Gang Robert "Kool" Bell, bass guitar; Ronald Bell, tenor saxophone; Dennis Thomas, tenor saxophone, flute; Claydes Smith, lead guitar; Robert "Spike" Mickens, trumpet; Ricky West, electric piano; George "Funky" Brown, drums

Thursday, July 4, 1974

Avery Fisher Hall, 7:30 P.M.

A Cool One

Stan Getz 4 Stan Getz, tenor; Albert Dailey, piano; Chin Suzuki, bass; Lamar Barker, drums

Gerry Mulligan 5   Gerry Mulligan, baritone; Joe Venuto, vibes and percussion; Hank Jones, piano; Jack Six, bass; Bill Goodwin, drums

Bill Evans 3   Bill Evans, piano; Eddie Gomez, bass; Marty Morell, drums

Avery Fisher Hall, 11:30 P.M.
Crusaders and Elvin

Crusaders   Wilton Felder, tenor, bass; Wayne Henderson, trombone; Joe Sample, piano; Stix Hooper, drums

Elvin Jones   Elvin Jones, drums; Frank Foster, Steve Grossman, reeds; Roland Prince, guitar; Milton Suggs, bass

The Platina Jazz Group   Roman Kinsman, flute, alto; Nachum Pereferkovitch, Alonatural, Fender, piano; Lev Zarzinsky, bass; Aaron Kaminsky, drums, percussion

Friday, July 5, 1974

Pope Auditorium, Fordham University 2:00 P.M.

The Lee Konitz Quartet   Lee Konitz, alto; Wilbur Little, bass; Dick Katz, piano; Beaver Harris, drums

Carnegie Hall, 7:30 P.M.
Friends of Eddie Condon and Ben Webster   Barney Bigard, clarinet; Eddie ''Lockjaw'' Davis, Bud Freeman, Buddy Tate, tenor; Budd Johnson, Zoot Sims, tenor, soprano; Illinois Jacquet, tenor, bassoon; Wild Bill Davison, Bobby Hackett, cornet; Joe Venuti, violin; Milt Hinton, bass; Jo Jones, Cliff Leeman, drums; Milt Buckner, piano; Vic Dickenson, trombone
Maxine Sullivan, vocals

Clark Terry Sextet   Clark Terry, trumpet, flugelhorn; Arnie Lawrence, alto; Jimmy Heath, tenor; Ronnie Mathews, piano; Wilbur Little, bass; Ed Soph, drums

Carnegie Hall, 11:30 P.M.
A Hot One

Freddie Hubbard 5   Freddie Hubbard, trumpet; Junior Cook, tenor; George Cables, piano; Kent Binkley, bass; Ralph Penland, drums

McCoy Tyner 5

Saturday, July 6, 1974

Carnegie Hall, 1:00 P.M.

The Music of Tommy Dorsey and **McKinney's Cotton Pickers:**
A New York Jazz Repertory Company concert

The Music of Tommy Dorsey
Directed by Sy Oliver

The New McKinney's Cotton Pickers
Musical director, Dave Hutson
Louis Barnett, tenor, clarinet; Tate Houston, baritone, tenor, clarinet; Ernie Rodgers, baritone; John Trudell, trumpet; Tom Saunders, Paul Klinger, cornets; Al Winters, trombone; Orrin Foslien Jr., banjo; J.R. Smith, tuba; Mill Vine, piano; Chet Forest, Mel Fudge, drums
Dave Wilborn, vocals

Carnegie Hall, 7:30 P.M.
Stan and Maynard

Stan Kenton and His Orchestra

Maynard Ferguson and His Orchestra

Avery Fisher Hall, 7:30 P.M. and 11:30 P.M.
Guitar Impressions   Laurindo Almeida, Charlie Byrd, The Eleventh House featuring Larry Coryell, Tiny Grimes, and Oregon with Ralph Towner, Roy Buchanan

Charlie Byrd Trio   Charlie Byrd, guitar; Joe Byrd, bass; Michael Stephans, drums

Oregon   Ralph Towner, guitar; Glen Moore, bass, piano; Paul McCandless, oboe, English horn; Collin Walcott, sitar, tabla, winds

Larry Coryell—The Eleventh House   Larry Coryell, guitar; Mike Mandel, electric keyboards, synthesizers; Mike Lawrence, electric trumpet; Danny Trifan, bass; Alphonse Mouzon, percussion

Carnegie Hall, 11:30 P.M.
Late Night Party With Basie

Count Basie and His Orchestra, with Joe Williams, vocals

Sunday, July 7, 1974

Staten Island Ferry, 10:30 A.M., 1:00 P.M., 3:30 P.M.

A Schlitz Salute to Jazz on the Hudson River Boat Ride

Kid Thomas Preservation Hall Band

World's Greatest Jazz Band of Yank Lawson and Bob Haggart   Yank Lawson, trumpet; Bob Haggart, bass; Bob Wilber, soprano, clarinet; Bud Freeman, tenor; Benny Morton, trombone; Ralph Sutton, piano; Gus Johnson, drums

Carnegie Hall, 7:30 P.M. and 11:30 P.M.
A Schlitz Salute to Latin Roots

El Gran Combo,   Willie Colon, Eddie Palmieri, La Sonora Matancera   (produced in association with Felipe Luciano)

Mightnight Jam Session
Radio City Music Hall, Midnight
Jam Session for Diana, featuring Diana Ross   Clark Terry, trumpet, flugelhorn; Joe Newman, trumpet; Urbie Green, trombone; Eddie ''Lockjaw'' Davis, Charlie Rouse, tenors; Hank Jones, piano; Milt Hinton, bass; Freddie Waits, drums
Diana Ross, with her own group, plus nine jazz musicians
Elvin Jones, Max Roach, Art Blakey, Buddy Rich, drums; Charlie Mingus, bass; Joe Farrell, tenor; Howard McGhee, trumpet; Roland Hanna, piano; Milt Buckner, organ, piano; Jimmy Garrison, bass; Michael Urbaniak, violin; plus others.

July 8, 1974, Noon

Thank you concert
Lincoln Center Fountain Plaza

Kid Thomas's Preservation Hall Jazz Band

Roosevelt Field Mall 5, Hempstead, L. I., N.Y., Noon to 2:00 P.M.
Sy Oliver Orchestra

Equitable Life Assurance Plaza, Avenue of Americas at 51st Street, N.Y., N.Y.
Yank Lawson and Bobby Haggart Group

Friday evening, June 27, 1975

Carnegie Hall, One Performance 7:30 P.M.
The New York Jazz Repertory Company Plays the Music of Bix Beiderbecke   Dave Hutson, musical director
Francis Williams, Jimmy McPartland, Johnny Glasel, trumpets; Warren Vaché, cornet; Zoot Sims, Eddie Daniels, Johnny Mince, reeds; Bill Rank, Spiegle Willcox, Jack Jeffers, trombone; Vince Giordano, tuba; Joe Venuti, violin; Dill Jones, Marian McPartland, piano; Major Holley, Milt Hinton, bass; Bucky Pizzarelli, guitar; Panama Francis, drums

The Blue Four   Joe Venuti, violin; Zoot Sims, tenor; Bucky Pizzarelli, guitar; Vince Giordano, tuba

Carnegie Hall, One Performance
Jam Session with the New York Jazz Repertory Company   Chet Baker, Wayman Red, Charlie Sullivan, trumpets; Eddie Daniels, Zoot Sims, Cecil Payne, reeds; Garnett Brown, John Gordon, trombones; Patti Bown, Billy Taylor, piano; Chris White, Lisle Atkinson, bass; Al Mouzon, Freddie Waits, drums

Saturday evening, June 28, 1975

Carnegie Hall, One Performance
Tribute to Mahalia Jackson
Marion Williams, The Sensational Nightingales, J.C. White Singers, Dorothy Love Coates, Claude Jeter, Sallie Martin, Thomas A. Dorsey
Produced by Tony Heilbut

Radio City Music Hall, One Performance
Schlitz Presents Midnight at the Oasis:
Maria Muldaur, vocals, and Geoff Muldaur, The Original Jug Band

The Benny Carter Orchestra   Benny Carter, alto; Seldon Powell, tenor; Cecil Payne, baritone; Danny Stiles, Jimmy Nottingham, trumpet; Garnett Brown, trombone; Frank Wess, flute, reeds; Bucky Pizarelli, guitar; Milt Hinton, bass; Grady Tate, drums

Sunday, June 29, 1975

Staten Island Ferry, 10:30 A.M., 1:00 P.M., 3:30 P.M.
Jazz on the Hudson River Boat Ride
Bob Crosby and the Bobcats   Bob Haggart, bass; Eddie Miller, tenor; Yank Lawson, trumpet, from the original Bobcats, with Johnny Mince, clarinet;

George Masso, trombone; Chuck Foldes, piano; Ron Traxler, drums

Carnegie Hall, One Performance
The Trumpet and the Drum   Harry James and His Orchestra and Buddy Rich and His Big Band

Ruby Braff–George Barnes Quartet

Monday, June 30, 1975

Noon to 2:00 P.M.
Equitable Life Assurance Plaza Concert
Earl Hines Orchestra

The Hammond Organ Company Presents
Jazz on the Hammond   Jack McDuff, Rhoda Scott, Don Lewis, Larry Young

Roseland Ballroom
Big Band Ball   Count Basie and His Orchestra; Mercer Ellington and the Duke Ellington Orchestra; Miyami and the New Herd (an orchestra from Japan)

Tuesday, July 1, 1975

Equitable Life Assurance Plaza Concert
Bobby Hackett plus 5

Lionel Hampton Orchestra

Carnegie Hall, One Performance, 7:30 P.M.
Dizzy and Freddie   Dizzy Gillespie Quartet; Freddie Hubbard Quintet

Carnegie Hall, One Performance, 11:30 P.M.
Solo Piano   Eubie Blake, John Lewis, Dorothy Donegan, Cedar Walton, Dyck Hyman, Barry Harris, Roland Hanna, Harold Mabern, Bernard Peiffer, Marian McPartland

Avery Fisher Hall, One Performance
Schlitz Salute to Jazz and the American Song
MC: Phyllis Diller

Music of Gershwin   Zoot Sims, tenor; Jim Hall, guitar

Music of Cy Coleman   Played by Cy Coleman, piano, vocals

Music of Fats Waller   Helen Humes, vocals

Music of Ellington–Strayhorn   Johnny Hartman, vocals; Ellis Larkins, piano

Rodgers and Hart   Chet Baker, trumpet; vibes, bass, drums

Music of Harold Arlen   Margaret Whiting, vocals

Avery Fisher Hall, One Performance, 11:30 P.M.
The Midnight Miles   Miles Davis with Orchestra

Wednesday, July 2, 1975

Noon to 2:00 P.M.
Equitable Life Assurance Plaza
Bobby Hackett Plus 5

Carnegie Hall, One Performance, 7:30 P.M.
All in the Brubeck Family   Dave Brubeck and Two Generations of Brubeck
Dave Brubeck, piano, with guest Paul Desmond, alto; Darius Brubeck, keyboards; Chris Brubeck, bass, trombone; Danny Brubeck, drums

System Tandem from Czechoslovakia

Carnegie Hall, One Performance, 11:30 P.M.
Stanley Turrentine, Jon Klemmer, and Hampton Hawes

Avery Fisher Hall, One Performance, 7:30 P.M.
Gato and Chuck   The Gato Barbieri Ensemble and Chuck Mangione Quartet

Avery Fisher Hall, One Performance, 11:30 P.M.
An Evening with Stan Getz and His Friends

Charlie Byrd, guitar

Stan Getz Quartet   Stan Getz, tenor; Al Dailey, piano; Clint Houston, bass; Billy Hart, drums

Jimmy Rowles, solo piano

Stan Getz, tenor; Garry Burton, vibes

Stan Getz Quartet   Guest: Heloisa Gilberto, vocals

Stan Getz and Mabel Mercer, vocals

MCs: Marian McPartland, Alec Wilder

Thursday, July 3, 1975

Equitable Life Assurance Plaza
Zoot Sims Quintet   Zoot Sims, tenor; Marky Markowitz, trumpet; Jimmy Rowles, piano; Major Holley, bass; Mike De Pasqua, drums

Carnegie Hall, 1 Performance
Presenting Jon Lucien   Jon Lucien, vocals; George Benson Quintet; special guest Milt Jackson, vibes

Carnegie Hall, 1 Performance
The In Crowd   Ramsey Lewis Trio, Max Roach, and the J.C. White Singers

Avery Fisher Hall, 1 Performance
Monk and Keith   Thelonious Monk Quartet, Keith Jarrett Quartet, Oregon

Thelonious Monk Quartet   Thelonious Monk, piano; Paul Jeffrey, tenor; Larry Ridley, bass; Thelonious Monk Jr., drums

Keith Jarrett Quartet   Keith Jarrett, piano; Dewey Redman, tenor; Charlie Haden, bass; Paul Motian, drums

Oregon

Avery Fisher Hall, One Performance
Cleo & Johnny

Cleo Laine and John Dankworth   Johnny Dankworth and His Orchestra

Friday, July 4, 1975

Carnegie Hall, One Performance, 7:30 P.M.
McCoy & Mingus   McCoy Tyner Quintet; Charles Mingus Quintet

Carnegie Hall, One Performance, 11:30 P.M.
Lionel Hampton Presents Lionel Hampton and His Inner Jazz Circle   Lionel Hampton, Milt Buckner, Eddie "Lockjaw" Davis, Panama Francis, Sarah McLawlor, featuring Richard Otto
Special guests: Joe Newman, trumpet, and Sylvia Syms, vocals
Sylvia Syms accompanied by Mike Abene, piano; Randy Brecker, trumpet; Jay Leon Hart, bass; Panama Francis, drums

Avery Fisher Hall, One Performance
Schlitz Salute to the Jazz Hall of Fame
Barney Bigard, Bobby Hackett, Earl Hines, Jo Jones, Red Norvo, Joe Venuti, Teddy Wilson, Milt Hinton, Oliver Jackson, plus the legendary Jabbo Smith and John Hammond
MC: Vic Dickenson
Plus films of many of the jazz greats

Avery Fisher Hall, One Performance
Sonny & Bobbi   Sonny Rollins, tenor, and Bobbi Hmphrey, flute

Saturday, July 5, 1975

Carnegie Hall, One Performance, 7:30 P.M.
Stan & Woody   Stan Kenton and His Orchestra and Candido, Woody Herman and his Orchestra Candido, bongos

Carnegie Hall, One Performance, 11:30 P.M.
Maynard–Wildlife   Maynard Ferguson Orchestra, Bill Watrous and Manhattan Wildlife Refuge

Avery Fisher Hall, One Performance
Byrd and the Messengers   Donald Byrd and the Blackbyrds; Art Blakey and the Jazz Messengers Tania Maria, vocals, piano; Helio, bass; Boto, drums

Avery Fisher Hall, One Performance
The Divine Sarah   An Evening with Sarah Vaughan
Featuring Percy Heath, bass

Nassau Coliseum, One Performance, 8:00 P.M.
Schlitz Saturday Night Salute to Soul and Jazz   The O'Jays; Isley Brothers; Harold Melvin and the Blue Notes; Herbie Mann and the Family of Mann; Return to Forever with Chick Corea and Stanley Clarke
The winner of Soul Search '75—Oliver Canidy

Sunday, July 6, 1975

Sunday, July 6, 1975

Staten Island Ferry, 10:30 A.M., 1:00 P.M., 3:30 P.M.
A Schlitz Salute
Jazz on the Hudson River Boat Ride Papa
French and the Original Tuxedo Jazz Band from
New Orleans and Michael Attenoux, Nice, France,
Festival Winner

Carnegie Hall, One Performance, 8:00 P.M.
Schlitz Salute to Salsa Tito Puente and His Orchestra; Ray Barretto and His Orchestra; Tipica 73,
produced by Felipe Luciano

Nassau Coliseum, One Perfrmance, 8:00 P.M.
**Schlitz Sunday Night Salute to Soul and
Jazz** The Stylistics; Temptations; B.B. King; B.T.
Express; Cannonball Adderley

The Sylistics Russell Thompkins, Jr., lead singer;
Airrion Love, Herbert Murrell, James Smith, James
Dunn

New Birth
Conducted by Harvey Fuqua
Composed of The Nite-Liters, the Mint Juleps, The
New Sound, and Alan Frye

B.T. Express Rich Thomas, lead guitar; Bill Risbrook, tenor, flute; Louis Risbrook, electric bass;
Carlos Ward, flute, piccolo, alto, clarinet; Terrell
Woods, drums; Dennis Rowe, congas, vocals; Barbara Joyce Lomas, vocals

Cannonball Adderley Quintet Cannonball Adderley, alto; Nat Adderley, cornet; Mike Wolf,
piano; Walter Booker, bass; Roy McCurdy, drums

June 27, 1975

Roosevelt Field Mall 5, Hempstead, L. I., N.Y.,
Noon to 2:00 P.M.
Sy Oliver Orchestra

Equitable Life Assurance Plaza, Avenue of
Americas at 51st Street, N.Y., Noon
Yank Lawson and Bobby Haggart Group

Friday, June 25, 1976

Rockefeller Center, Channel Gardens, Noon

**The Joe Newman Jazz Interactions Orches-
tra** Joe Newman, trumpet; Ted Dunbar, guitar;
Frank Foster, tenor; Bob Cranshaw, bass; David
Lee, Jr., drums; Harold Mabern, piano; Stella
Marrs, vocals
Appearance only of Tony Bennett, Bill Evans

The Newport Jazz Festival, New York, and The
Greenwich Savings Bank present a series of con-
certs from 12 Noon to 2:00 P.M. at the Equitable
Life Assurance building, Avenue of the Americas
at 51st Street They are identified as Equitable
Life Assurance concert

Earl "Fatha" Hines

There were a group of concerts presented at Roosevelt Field Shopping Mall, Long Island, N.Y. at
2:00 P.M. They are identified by Roosevelt
Field Shopping Mall

The World's Greatest Jazz Band

Carnegie Hall, Two Performances
Schlitz Salutes an Evening with Tony Bennett
Tony Bennett plus the Bill Evans Trio

Bill Evans Trio Bill Evans, piano; Eddie Gomez,
bass; Elliot Zigmund, drums; thirty-two piece orchestra including jazz musicians Frank Wess,
flute, reeds; Joe Wilder, trumpet; Urbie Green,
trombone

Schlitz Salutes Blues at Midnight
Radio City Music Hall
Fats Domino, Bobby Blue Band; Muddy Waters;
Mike Bloomfield
Plus the winner of the Schiltz Soul Search
'76—Ben Mobley, piano, vocals

Saturday afternoon, June 26, 1976

A Secial Newport Jazz Festival Segment at Beautiful Waterloo Village, Stanhope, N.J.
Waterloo Village, 12 Noon to 5:00 P.M.

Gospel Picnic Gospel Music organized by Rev.
Wyatt T. Walker, Canaan Baptist Church, Harlem
Canaan Baptist Concert Choir; Expositions of In-
stitution Church of God in Christ (Brooklyn);

Greater Bible Way Radio Choir (Brooklyn); King's
Temple Gospel Choir (Hempstead, L.I.); Mass
Choir of First Baptist Church (Englewood, N.J.);
Mount Olive Baptist Mass Choir (Hackensack,
N.J.): Voices of Convent (NYC)
Allen's Arc; John Hason Singers; Michael Powell
Ensemble; Voices of the Temple
Soloists: Elaine Clark; Janet Coleman; Fred Grip-
per; Frances Jackson; Carl Murray; Houston
Owens; John Paxton
Special Guest: Carolyn Byrd, gospel star of *Bub-
bling Brown Sugar*
Clinton Utterbach, musical director; Eugene Coo-
per, talent coordinator
Presentation of first annual Newport Gospel
Awards

Saturday evening, June 26, 1976

Waterloo Village, Stanhope, N.J.
New Jersey Salutes a Native Son

Count Basie and His Orchestra in concert plus
guest Eubie Blake, piano Count Basie, piano;
Bob Mitchell, Lem Biviano, Peter Minger, Sonny
Cohn, trumpets; Bobby Plater, Jimmy Forrest,
Danny Turner, Eric Dixon, Charlie Fowlkes, reeds;
Mel Wanzo, Curtis Fuller, Al Grey, Bill Hughes,
trombones; Freddie Greene guitar; John Herd,
bass; Butch Miles, drums; Bill Caffey, vocals

Carnegie Hall, One Performance, 7:30 P.M.
Mingus Flamenco Charlie Mingus Sextet in a
special program of flamenco jazz with the Azu-
cena y Edo Flamenco Dance Group
Charles Mingus, bass; Ricky Ford, tenor; Jimmy
Knepper, trombone; Jack Walrath, trumpet; Danny
Mixon, piano; Dannie Richmond, drums
Dancers—Paco Alonso, Alicia Montes, Maria Arw-
shan, Sylvia Alvarado; Manuel Arena (guest artist)
Singers—Manolo Correa, Domingo Alvarado
(guest artist)
Guitarists—Guillermo Rios, Roberto Reyes

Carnegie Hall, One Performance, 11:30 P.M.
Cobham/Duke
**The Billy Cobham/George Duke Band, Spec-
trum** Billy Cobham, drums; George Duke, keyboards; John Scofield, guitar; Alphonso Johnson,
bass

Sunday afternoon, June 27, 1976

Waterloo Village, 12:00 Noon to 5:00 P.M.

The Red Onion Jazz Band with Natalie Lamb,
vocals

Bucky Pizzarelli, guitar, at The Towpath Tavern

Dick Welstood, piano, at The Grist Mill

Rio Clemente, piano, at The Homestead House

Main Tent Concerts—Earl Hines, solo piano

Pee Wee Erwin, trumpet; Teddy Wilson, piano;
Eddie Hubble, trombone; Victor Gaskin, bass;
Bobby Rosengarden, drums
Alternate with group: Warren Vaché, cornet;
Kenny Davern, soprano, clarinet; Cliff Leeman,
drums; Wayne Wright, guitar
Guest artist: Attorney General William Hyland of
N.J., clarinet

Sunday afternoon, June 27, 1976

Carnegie Hall, One Performance, 1:00 P.M.
Braxton/Curson/Coleman
Anthony Braxton, Ted Curson and Company,
George Coleman Septet

Anthony Braxton Orchestra Anthony Braxton,
reeds; George Lewis, trombone; Richard Abrams,
piano; Dave Holland, bass; Barry Altschul, drums
Plus assorted flutes, clarinets, and reeds

Ted Curson and Company Ted Curson, trumpet;
Chris Woods, alto; Nick Brignola, baritone, sax-
ello; Jim McNeely, piano; David Friesen, bass;
Steve McCall, drums; Sam Jacobs, percussion

George Coleman Septet

Sunday evening, June 24, 1976

Carnegie Hall, One Performance, 7:30 P.M.

Ellington Saga—Part I
"The 20's" performed by the New York Jazz Rep-
ertory Company
Guest artist: Cootie Williams

Carnegie Hall, One Performance, 11:30 P.M.
A New York Jazz Repertory Company Concert
Tribute to Trane
McCoy Tyner Quintet; Elvin Jones Quartet; An-
drew White and the New York Jazz Repertory
Company in a special tribute to John Coltrane

Elvin Jones Quartet Elvin Jones, drums; Pat La Barbera, reeds; Ryo Kawasaki, guitar; David Williams, bass

McCoy Tyner Sextet McCoy Tyner, piano; Joe Ford, alto; Ron Bridgewater, tenor; Charles Fambrough, bass; Eric Gravatte, drums; Guilherme Franco, percussion

New York Jazz Repertory Company Orchestra Andrew White, conductor, tenor, alto; arranger McCoy Tyner, piano; Steve Novosel, bass; Elvin Jones, drums; Cecil Payne, baritone, soprano

Monday June 28, 1976

Equitable Life Assurance concert

The World's Greatest Jazz Band Yank Lawson, trumpet; Bobby Haggart, bass; Joe Muranyi, clarinet, vocals; Marty Napoleon, piano; Cliff Leeman, drums; Sonny Russo, trombone; George Masson, valve trombone

Roosevelt Shopping Mall Concert

Sy Oliver and His Orchestra

Monday evening, June 28, 1976

Carnegie Hall, One Performance, 7:30 P.M.

Benny Goodman Salutes Jazz Interactions Benny Goodman, Teddy Wilson, and Jazz Interactions All-Stars: Joe Newman, Frank Foster, Bob Cranshaw, David Lee, Ted Dunbar MC: John Hammond

Carnegie Hall, One Performance, 11:30 P.M. Keith Jarrett Keith Jarrett Trio: Jan Garbarek, soprano, tenor, and Charlie Haden, bass; with twenty-nine-piece string orchestra conducted by Dennis Russell Davies

Tuesday, June 29, 1976

The Sy Oliver Orchestra Sy Oliver, trumpet, vibes, vocals: Candy Ross, trombone, vocals; Dickie Harris, trombone; Heywood Henry, alto; Joe Powell, alto; Leonard Gaskin, bass; Oliver Jackson, drums; Buddy Smith, vocals

Ellington Saga—Part II "The 30's" performed by the New York Jazz Repertory Company Guest soloist: Cootie Williams Pug Horton, vocals Vic Dickenson, trombone; Clifford Smalls, piano; Bobby Rosengarden, drums

Carnegie Hall, One Performance Schlitz Salutes Art, Horace, and Freddie **Art Blakey and The Jazz Messengers** Art Blakey, drums; Bill Hardman, trumpet; David Schnitter, tenor saxophone; Mickey Tucker, piano; Chris Amberger, bass

Horace Silver Quintet Horace Silver, piano; Tom Harrell, trumpet; Bob Berg, tenor; Steve Beskrone, bass; Eddie Gladden, drums Guest artist: Freddie Hubbard, trumpet

City Center, One Performance **Herbie Hancock Retrospect** Herbie Hancock, Tony Williams, Wayne Shorter, Freddie Hubbard, Ron Carter, Bill Hart, Eddie Henderson, Bennie Maupin, Julian Priester, Buster Williams

Wednesday, June 30, 1976

Roosevelt Shopping Mall Concert

Mercer Ellington Orchestra

Carnegie Hall, One Performance

Ellington Saga—Part III Mercer Ellington and His Orchestra plus New York Jazz Repertory Company

The Duke Ellington Orchestra Mercer Ellington, conductor Dave Young, Percy Marion, tenors; Alvin Batiste, clarinet; Harold Minerve, Vincent York, alto; Edward Ellington II, guitar; Barry Lee Hall, "Sweet Willie" Singleton, James Bolden, Ray Copeland, trumpets; Chuck Connors, Ray Harris, Malcolm Taylor; trombones; Rocky White, drums; Lester Jordan, J.J. Wiggins, Jr., bass

Carnegie Hall, One Performance **Monk and Dizzy** Thelonious Monk Quartet, Dizzy Gillespie Quartet, plus 100 Voices conducted by John Motley

Thelonious Monk Quartet Thelonious Monk, piano; Paul Jeffrey, tenor; Rodney Jones, Larry Ridley, bass; Thelonious Monk, Jr., drums

Dizzy Gillespie Quintet Dizzy Gillespie, trumpet; Rodney Jones; guitar; Benjamin Brown, bass; Mickey Roker, drums; Assedin Weston, congas

City Center, One Performance **Jazz Today and Tomorrow**

Weather Report and Brecker Brothers Band

Thursday, July 1, 1976

City Center, One Performance **Stan and Maynard**

Stan Kenton and His Orchestra

Maynard Ferguson and His Orchestra Maynard Ferguson, trumpet, flugelhorn, superbone (valve-slide trombone), firebird (valve-slide trumpet), baritone horn, French horn, pocket horn; Stan Mark, Ron Tooley, Dennis Nooday, trumpets; Randy Purcell, Church Bennett, trombones; Mark Colby, tenor, soprano; Mike Migliore, alto, soprano; Bobby Militello, baritone, flute; Biff Hannon, piano; Gordon Johnson, bass; Bob Wyatt, drums

Radio City Music Hall

Midnight Jazz Party and Jam Session Salute to Rev. John Gensel

Clark Terry, Harry Sweets Edison, trumpets; Zoot Sims, Illinois Jacquet, tenors; Kenny Burrell, guitar; Count Basie, piano; Milt Hinton, bass; Roy Haynes, drums

Bill Evans, piano; Eddie Gomez, bass; Elvin Jones, drums Joined by Lee Konitz, alto; Wayne March, tenor Sarah Vaughan, vocals; with her trio

New York Jazz Repertory Company Dizzy Gillespie, Jon Faddis, Freddie Hubbard, trumpets; Sonny Stitt, Eddie "Lockjaw" Davis, Anthony Braxton, reeds; Herbie Hancock, piano; Charlie

Mingus, George Duvivier, bass; Art Blakey, Tony Williams, drums Joined by Roland Kirk, reeds

Friday, July 2, 1976

Equitable Life Assurance Plaza Concert

Mercer Ellington and His Orchestra same personnel as Duke Ellington Orchestra

Friday afternoon, July 2, 1976

N.Y.U. Loeb Center

Children's Jazz Concert George Kleinsinger's "Tubby the Tuba Meets a Dixieland Band" and a New Orleans Jazz Parade, narrated by Clark Terry, Major Holly is Tubby on the tuba

Clark Terry, trumpet, flugelhorn; Pee Wee Erwin, trumpet; Vic Dickenson, trombone; Phil Bodner, clarinet; Dick Wellstood, piano; Major Holley, bass and tuba; Bucky Pizzarelli, guitar; Panama Francis, Danny Gottieb, drums

Friday evening, July 2, 1976

Carnegie Hall, One Performance, 7:30 P.M. Cannonball Special

A Newport Salute to the late Cannonball Adderly "Big Man—the Legend of John Henry" A jazz musical composed by Julian "Cannonball" Adderley Starring Joe Williams as John Henry; Nat Adderley's Black and Blues Band; Denis Delapenha as Carolina; Don Blakey as Jassawa; Paul Gleason as the Sheriff and Bull Maree; chorus; music by Julian and Nat Adderley; lyrics by Diane Lampert and Peter Farrow; concert version by Diane Lampert and George W. George, based on a book by Paul Avila Mayer, G.W. George, and Peter Farrow; produced by Nat Adderley, assisted by Olga Adderley; Executive Producer George Wein

Carnegie Hall, One Performance, 11:30 P.M. **Buddy Rich and His Killer Force** Plus Lee Konitz, alto, and Wayne Marsh, tenor Buddy Rich, drums; Dave Stahl, Dean Pratt, Ross Konikoff, trumpets; Rick Stepton, Clint Sharman, Dave Boyle, trombones; Charlie Legand, Alan Gaudin, Frank Basile, Steve Marcus, Bob

Mintzer, Turk Mauro, reeds; John Burr, bass; Barry Kener, piano
Beverly Getz and Cathy Rich, vocals

Saturday, July 3, 1976

Roosevelt Field Shopping Mall Concert

Maynard Ferguson and His Orchestra

Kid Thomas and the Preservation Hall Jazz Band plus The World's Greatest Jazz Band of Yank Lawson and Bob Haggart
Staten Island Ferry, 10:30 A.M., 1:00 P.M., 3:30 P.M.
Schlitz Salutes Jazz on the Hudson River Boat Ride

The World's Greatest Jazz Band   Yank Lawson, trumpet; Bobby Haggart, bass; George Masso, Sonny Russo, trombones; Johnny Mince, clarinet; Marty Napoleon, piano; Bobby Rosengarden, drums

Kid Thomas and The Preservation Hall Jazz Band   Kid Thomas, trumpet and leader; Homer Eugene, trombone; Paul Barnes, clarinet; Emanuel Paul, tenor; Joseph Butler, bass; Emanuel Sayles, banjo; Dave Williams, piano; Alonzo Stewart, drums

Saturday evening, July 3, 1976

Carnegie Hall, One Performance

Schlitz Salutes an Evening with Sarah Vaughan
Sarah Vaughan, vocals, with Earl Schroeder, piano; Bob Magnusson, bass; Jimmy Cobb, drums
Marty Paitch conducting a string orchestra

Carnegie Hall, One Performance
Schlitz Salutes Basie Today and Yesterday
Count Basie and His Orchestra—1976

Count Basie Reunion Band   Count Basie, piano; Sonny Cohn, Joe Newman, Paul Cohen, Jon Faddis, trumpets; Benny Powell, Bill Hughes, Al Grey, Wayne Andre, trombones; Ernie Wilkins, Frank Wess, Frank Foster, Billy Mitchell, Charlie Fowlkes, reeds; Eddie Jones, bass; Sonny Payne, drums; Joe Williams, vocals

Sunday, July 4, 1976

Carnegie Hall, One Performance

Ellington Saga—Part IV
"The 40's" performed by the New York Jazz Repertory Company with guests: Al Hibbler and Barney Bigard

Carnegie Hall, One Performance, 11:30 P.M.
Guitar Salute to Tal
Tal Farlow Quartet   Tal Farlow, guitar; Hank Jones, piano; Jack Six, bass; Roy Haynes, drums

Jim Hall Trio   Jim Hall, guitar; Don Thompson, bass; Terry Clarke, drums

Kenny Burrell Trio   Kenny Burrell, guitar; Lysle Atkinson, bass; Freddie Waits, drums

Monday afternoon, July 5, 1976

52nd Street Jazz Fair
52nd Street and 53rd Street between Avenue of Americas and Fifth Avenue

The U.S. Navy Band Commodores
Chief Musician Jeffrey A. Taylor, director
Chief Musicians Steve Griffith, Conrad "CJ" Landry, Jack Estlinbaum, and Musicians First Class Ron Diehl, Gary Buckley, reeds; Musicians First Class Gary Adams, Ron Belanger, Bob Pomerleau, and Chief Musician James W. Howard, trumpets; Chief Musician Bryce Concklin and Musicians First Class Robert Rannells, Leland Gause, Howard Lamb, trombones; Musician First Class Charles Wilson, piano; Musician First Class James Warren, guitar; Chief Musician Louis Hinds, bass; Chief Musician Leonard Cuddy, percussion; Musicians First Class Evangeline Bailey and Robert Drummond, vocalists

Roy Haynes Hip Ensemble   Roy Haynes, drums; Bill Saxton, reeds; Mecos Fiorillo, guitar; Dave Jackson, bass
Plus Sonny Stitt, reeds, with the Barry Harris Trio   Gary Bartz Quintet, Hannibal's "Sunrise," Beaver Harris' 360 Degrees Music, Machito's Band, Joe Newman Quintet, New Orleans Preservation Hall Jazz Band, The Original Traditional Jazz Band, Zoot Sims Quintet, Sam Rivers Trio, Charles Rouse and Company, Clark Terry, and from South Africa, The Jazz Ministers

Monday evening, July 5, 1976

Roseland Ballroom
Festival Farewell Dance

Count Basie and His Orchestra
Plus Salute to the Grande Parade Du Jazz Festival of Nice, France, with Milt Buckner, Eddie "Lockjaw" Davis, Vic Dickenson, George Duvivier, Sweets Edison, Panama Francis, Illinois Jacquet, Maxim Saury, Zoot Sims, Buddy Tate, Clark Terry, Cootie Williams

287